THE SOCIOLOGY OF THE FAMILY

'This is the first collection ... on family life since Anderson first published his reader some twenty-five years ago. It brings together ... key pieces that have been published within the last ten years and does ample justice to the richness and variety of the empirial work which has been done in this field. The merits of this work include a continuing sense of the importance of gender in the analysis of family processes and an awareness of the links between social research and social policy.'

Dr David Morgan, Department of Sociology, University of Manchester

For Chris

The
Sociology
of the Family

A READER

Edited by
Graham Allan

BLACKWELL
Publishers

Copyright in this edition © Blackwell Publishers Ltd 1999
Editorial matter and organization copyright © Graham Allan 1999

First published 1999

2 4 6 8 10 9 7 5 3 1

Blackwell Publishers Ltd
108 Cowley Road
Oxford OX4 1JF
UK

Blackwell Publishers Inc.
350 Main Street
Malden, Massachusetts 02148
USA

British Library Cataloguing in Publication Data

A CIP catalogue record for this book is available from the British Library.

Library of Congress Cataloging-in-Publication Data

The sociology of the family: a reader / edited by Graham Allan.
   p.   cm.
  Includes bibliographical references and index
  ISBN 0–631–20267–6 (hardcover: alk. paper). – ISBN 0–631–20268–4
(pbk.: alk. paper)
    1. Family. 2. Marriage. 3. Kinship. I. Allan, Graham A.
  HQ518.S655 1999
  306.8–dc21   98–34508
                                        CIP

Commissioning Editor: Jill Landeryou
Desk Editor: Jack Messenger

Typest in Sabon on 10.5/12pt
by PureTech India Ltd, Pondicherry
http://www.puretech.com
Printed in Great Britain by MPG Books Ltd, Bodmin,Cornwall

This book is printed on acid-free paper

Contents

Figures

Tables

Acknowledgements

I would like to thank Graham Crow, Stevi Jackson and Janet Walker for their advice on material to include in this Reader. As always, Graham Crow has been especially helpful in finding sources and lending me books. Thanks are also due to Chris Allan, Peter Allan, Sue Allan and Nicola Brown for help with the editing process.

I am very grateful to the following authors and publishers for permission to reproduce the chapters contained in this book:

Chapter 1:   Janet Finch and Penny Summerfield: 'Social reconstruction and the emergence of the companionate marriage, 1945–59' in David Clark (ed.), *Marriage, Domestic Life and Social Change*, © Routledge, 1991.

Chapter 2:   Gail Hawkes: 'Liberalizing heterosexuality', chapter 7 of *A Sociology of Sex and Sexuality*, © Open University Press, 1996.

Chapter 3:   David Cheal: 'The one and the many: modernity and postmodernity', chapter 5 of *Family and the State of Theory*, © Harvester Wheatsheaf, 1991.

Chapter 4:   Jean Duncombe and Dennis Marsden: 'Love and intimacy: the gender division of emotion and "emotion work": a neglected aspect of sociological discussion of heterosexual relationships', *Sociology*, 27: 221–41, 1993, Cambridge University Press, © British Sociological Association.

Chapter 5:   Jeffrey Weeks, Brian Heaphy and Catherine Donovan: 'Partners by choice: equality, power and commitment in non-heterosexual relationships', © Jeffrey Weeks, Brian Heaphy and Catherine Donovan.

Chapter 6:   Carolyn Vogler and Jan Pahl: 'Money, power and inequality in marriage', *Sociological Review*, 42: 263–88, 1994, Blackwell Publishers, © Editorial Board of Sociological Review.

Chapter 7:   James Nazroo: 'Uncovering gender differences in the use of marital violence: the effect of methodology', *Sociology*, 29: 475–95, 1995, Cambridge University Press, © British Sociological Association.

Chapter 8:   Susan McRae: 'Cohabitation or marriage? – cohabitation', chapter 4 of *Cohabiting Mothers: Changing Marriage and Motherhood?*, © Policy Studies Institute, 1993.

Chapter 9:   Nickie Charles and Marion Kerr: 'Women's work', chapter 3 of *Women, Food and Families*, Manchester University Press, 1988, © Nickie Charles and Marion Kerr.

Chapter 10:   Lydia Morris: 'The household and the labour market', in C. C. Harris (ed.), *Family, Economy and Community*, © University of Wales Press, 1990.

Chapter 11:   Graham Crow and Mike Hardey: 'Diversity and ambiguity among lone-parent households in modern Britain', in C. Marsh and S. Arber (eds), *Families and Households: Divisions and Change*, Macmillan, 1992, © British Sociological Association.

Chapter 12:   Jane Millar: 'State, family and personal responsibility: the changing balance for lone mothers in the United Kingdom', *Feminist Review*, 48: 24–39, 1994, © Jane Millar.

Chapter 13:   Martin Richards: 'The interests of children at divorce', in M. T. Meulders-Klein (ed.), *Familles et justice: justice civile et évolution du contentieux familial en droit comparé*, © 1997 Bruylant, Brussels/LGDJ, Paris.

Chapter 14:   Hilary Graham: 'The informal sector of welfare: a crisis in caring', *Social Science and Medicine*, 32: 507–15, 1991, © Elsevier Science.

Chapter 15:   Janet Finch and Jennifer Mason: 'Obligations of kinship in contemporary Britain: is there normative agreement?', *British Journal of Sociology*, 42: 345–67, 1991, Routledge. © British Journal of Sociology/Routledge.

Chapter 16:   Sara Arber and Jay Ginn: 'Gender differences in informal caring', *Health and Social Care in the Community*, 3: 19–31, 1995, © Blackwell Science.

Chapter 17:   Sally Baldwin and Jane Carlisle: 'Living with disability: the experiences of parents and children', chapter 5 of *Social Support for Disabled Children: A Review of the Literature*, Social Work Services Inspectorate, HMSO, Edinburgh. Crown copyright: reproduced by permission of the Controller of Her Majesty's Stationery Office.

Introduction

The main purpose of this book is to provide students with easy access to a range of the more important articles on aspects of contemporary British family life to have been published in recent years. At a time when the number of students in higher education is increasing disproportionately compared to increases in library resources, one of the most common problems students face is finding relevant reading material at the time when it is needed. By bringing together some of the best papers recently published on the sociology of the family, it is hoped that this volume will in some measure help students – whether they are taking degrees in sociology or social policy, or in other subjects like nursing, social work or medicine in which a knowledge of family organization and relationships is important – to access the key ideas and issues informing contemporary debates in the field.

In addition, the time seems ripe in other ways for a Reader such as this. It is now 25 years since Michael Anderson first published his well-received *Sociology of the Family*, and more than 15 years since its modified second edition appeared (Anderson, 1971a; 1980). Since then there have been no major British collections of already published articles in the area of family sociology. Significantly, Anderson's volume was originally published at a time when family and kinship matters were receiving a good deal of attention from sociologists of different persuasions. As well as various kinship and community studies which questioned the supposed decline of traditional family solidarity – for example, Young and Willmott (1957), Willmott and Young (1960), Rosser and Harris (1965), Bell (1968) and Firth, Hubert and Forge (1970) – historical demographers like Laslett (1965) and Anderson (1971b) himself were also undertaking novel investigations of past family arrangements. So too a critical literature on dominant models of family living emerged in Britain and America through the writings of, among others, Laing and Esterson (1964), Cooper (1971), Dreitzel (1972) and Zaretsky (1973).

For some while after this though, family sociology became quite unfashionable. Significant questions were raised about the methodologies used in some of the studies (see Bell and Newby, 1973), but more importantly the development of the women's movement altered the agenda of research into domestic life quite substantially. While there had been previous studies of inequalities within families, for example Blood and Wolfe (1960) in America and Gavron (1968) in Britain, the failure of much American family sociology – especially its failure to adopt a critical perspective about the structural divisions within domestic organization, and their links to wider social and economic inequalities – fostered a climate in which 'family research' became devalued. Although some influential studies in family sociology appeared (Voysey, 1975; Askham, 1984; Holme, 1985), in general, the 'action' lay elsewhere, for example in studies of gender and household inequalities, in debates about 'public' and 'private' boundaries, and in analyses of paid and unpaid work (Oakley, 1974, 1976; Barker and Allen, 1976a, 1976b; Finch and Groves, 1983; Siltanen and Stanworth, 1984). Of course, all these topics were pertinent to family sociology, but they were framed much more by feminist perspectives and understandings than they were informed by existing models from the sociology of the family.

Indeed, as Wilson and Pahl (1988) and Morgan (1996) among others have argued, in many ways feminist research set the parameters for the sociology of the family during much of the 1970s and 1980s. For all intents and purposes, a focus on family sociology became synonymous with an analysis of women's experiences, particularly within the domestic sphere. While in some regards this appeared detrimental to the field of family sociology as a consolidated area of research – at the very least it led to some aspects of family life being largely ignored within sociology – much more significantly it helped regenerate the field in ways which ultimately opened new and exciting lines of enquiry. Thus the 1990s has seen a blossoming of research into family issues, though the perspectives informing the study of family relationships and family organization are distinct from those dominant in earlier periods.

In addition, of course, the family remains an area of intense personal and social significance. Not only are family matters a central concern in many people's lives (Scott, 1997), but equally at a political level there has been much debate around the current state of 'the family'. Governments throughout the Western world have had to face a number of dilemmas which are a direct consequence of the fiscal implications of changing family demographics and ideologies. Of course, as with 'community' (Williams, 1975), social and political concern over the supposed decline of 'family values' is endemic; in every era comparisons are made with a 'golden' mythologized family of past time. At the root of this is the dynamic character of family life. 'The family' – and using such a static and universal terminology itself misrepresents the reality of people's household and kin relationships – inevitably alters with time. This is inherent to family life. At its simplest, relationships within individual families are modified as a result of time and ageing. The family created by a couple committing themselves to one another and setting up home is evidently different from that 'same' family when there are young children present; or when there are adolescent children; or when there are grandchildren. It is different when both partners are in full-time employment or when they are not, and different again when a parent is being cared for or when the couple are retired. Such life-course changes inevitably influence family organization and family relationships, even if there are no 'unexpected' changes through, for example, death or divorce.

More importantly though, dominant family patterns also change as a result of changes in other spheres of activity. As Medick (1976) has expressed it, families and households can only be understood properly when they are seen as component elements of wider systems of production, consumption and reproduction. Yet how families produce, consume and reproduce, what part they play within these processes, will inevitably depend on the modes of production, consumption and reproduction dominant in the society, or more accurately dominant within that part of the social and economic formation occupied by that individual family unit. Thus, for example, the demands made on families involved in peasant/subsistence farming differ from those made on families during early phases of industrialization and urban growth, and equally are different to those developing in late modernity.

The current concerns of governments – for example, with increases in divorce, the growing number of unmarried mothers and the rise in the number of infirm elderly people needing some level of support – are themselves a result of changing social and economic circumstances in the contemporary period; changes in the ways in which households and kin units produce, consume and reproduce. The problems are novel ones which reflect far more than a putative decline in family solidarity and family values. They are issues rooted in the broader patterns of freedom and constraint experienced by individuals, and cannot be resolved by appeals to past family behaviour. Certainly, governments can influence family life, in particular through their command of material resources – taxation and benefit policies, housing allocations, employment policies – but equally families need to be understood as an element within the wider economic and social formation of which they are part. Altering this is much more difficult, and of course, in an era of globalization, to a large degree outside the direct control of individual governments.

The changes occurring in contemporary family life should not be underestimated. In Britain, as in other Western societies, there have been very significant shifts, especially with regard to household and family formation and dissolution, generating patterns that were quite unimaginable forty or fifty years ago. The most obvious of these are the changes in divorce. In the late 1960s there were some 50,000 divorces per year, which represented a little over 4 for every thousand marriages. The Divorce Reform Act, 1969, which took effect in the early 1970s, led to an increase to 120,000 divorces per year in 1972 (9.5 per thousand marriages). Since that time the rate and number of divorces has steadily increased, so that in the mid-1990s there were almost 160,000 divorces, a rate of 13.7 per thousand marriages. Given a continuation of these trends, it is likely that roughly half of all the marriages taking place in the late 1990s will end in divorce.

More than 50 per cent of all divorces involve couples with dependent children. Thus, these trends alone would have led to an increase in the number of lone-parent households. In addition, however, the number of births to unmarried women has also increased dramatically. In 1976 9 per cent of all births were to unmarried mothers, with 29 per cent of all teenage mothers being unmarried. By 1995 34 per cent of all mothers were unmarried, including 86 per cent of teenage mothers, though it should be noted that currently some 50 per cent of all children born outside marriage are born to couples who are cohabiting. As a result of both these factors the number of lone-parent households in Britain has grown from under 600,000 in 1971, involving 1 million children, to 1.4 million (with 2.3 million children) by 1992. Thus at any time close to 20 per cent of dependent children are living in a lone-parent household.

There have been other significant changes too. People are less likely to marry now than a generation ago; those who do typically do so at a later age. There are more second marriages and more step-families. There are also far more people cohabiting outside marriage in the 1990s than there were in the 1970s or 1980s. Indeed, it is now normal for couples to cohabit for some period prior to marriage, though in the late 1960s only 5 per cent of people marrying for the first time did so (Haskey and Kiernan, 1989; Haskey, 1995). Overall, the result of these demographic shifts is that there is now far more diversity in the household and family patterns people construct than there was during the first three-quarters of the twentieth century. To some degree, the regularities there then were in most people's family experiences made it reasonable to conceptualize family life in terms of a family life cycle, i.e. a progressive series of ordered stages through which most individuals passed. Now such a notion makes far less sense; the diversity there is means that people's family 'careers' lack the consistent order of a generation and more ago.

These changes reflect not just a change in family and household demography, but also a change in what people want and expect from their family relationships. Culturally, there is a strong sense that marriage as a form of relationship has been altering; so too parents' ties with their dependent children are generally held to be based on different principles now than, say, two generations ago. The language used about family issues itself reflects these changes: spouses have become 'partners'; people 'cohabit' rather than 'live in sin'; the idea of a 'shot-gun wedding' has largely disappeared; even 'adultery' has been replaced by the less stigmatizing notion of 'affair'. This changing vocabulary is indicative of changing attitudes, and highlights the idea that family and household matters are never static. Precisely because household and family are so central within social life, the relationships involved inevitably alter with whatever changes are occurring in the wider social and economic formation.

But, in addition, there are other sources of diversity within contemporary Britain which have an impact on the patterning of family relationships and domestic life. For example, there has been a significant change in the acceptability of gay relationships, with the result that there are now far more gay couples openly sharing households than there were in the past (see chapter 5, this volume). Importantly too, British society has become far more ethnically diverse than it was. The migration of individuals and families from the Caribbean, South Asia, East Africa and other parts of the Commonwealth in the second half of the twentieth century has resulted in much more variation in the organization of family and kinship relations than existed previously. As with nearly all migrant groups, beliefs about the 'right' ways of ordering domestic and family matters are strongly rooted in their different cultures and play a significant part in the construction and maintenance of the moral orders they value. Unfortunately, there are still very few studies of the different patterns of family and kinship solidarities which are emerging as these migrant groups become more settled in Britain. However, as with the old community studies, research into other aspects of ethnic minorities' social and economic experiences often contain interesting material on domestic and family patterns; see, for example, Afshaw (1989), Ballard (1994), Bhachu (1985) and Westwood and Bhachu (1988).

The readings included in this book have been chosen both to reflect the different changes there have been, but also to locate them within their broader context and evaluate their impact. Family issues are of consequence socially and politically, so it is not surprising that politicians and other public figures, along with the media more generally, often pronounce on the inadequacies, or otherwise, of the ways that family relationships are currently patterned. This volume provides a means of assessing the validity of the arguments that are promulgated. As well as emphasizing the degree of change there has been, the readings also demonstrate the continuities which exist in issues of family solidarity. Change there has most certainly been, but this does not imply there is no stability. Nor does it indicate that family life is in 'decline'; in this regard, difference does not mean decay.

The book is divided into five broad topic areas. Part I focuses on change in family relationships. However, rather than concentrating on demographic shifts (see Allan and Crow, 1999, for a discussion of these), it explores how the nature of the personal and social relationships within families and households has altered with the development of what Giddens (1991) terms 'late modernity'. Part II is concerned with the character of contemporary marriage and other equivalent partnerships. Building on the material in Part I, it concentrates on the structure of marital ties and, in particular, the extent to which inequality and power differentials remain central to its organization. Part III looks at domestic organization. It is particularly concerned with the work that is done within households, work which is usually highly gendered, often unrecognized and nearly always unpaid. The chapters included here examine the impact of this division of labour on different household members and show that in this sphere at least change has been less radical than is sometimes assumed. Part IV is concerned with the impact of divorce and the growth of lone-parent families. As well as examining the different circumstances of such families, it also addresses the ways in which marital separation and divorce affect children. Part V is organized around aspects of care provision and kinship. As well as being concerned with gender differences in family roles, it explores the understandings people have of their obligations, the division of caring which emerges within (and between) households, and the ways in which health and other state policies and practices impinge on, and thereby help structure, family organization.

Many important readings have had to be left out for reasons of space, and, as noted, in certain areas appropriate papers are not available. However, the five parts of this volume are key areas within the sociology of the family, and the readings included within each one are among the most significant to be published in recent years. Between them, they provide a very good introduction to the contemporary character of British family life. It is hoped that by bringing them together in one volume, students will not only have easy access to them but will also be inspired to delve further into the sociological literature on family relationships and household organization. The social and demographic changes currently occurring, together with the quality of research now being conducted within this field, make for a very exciting and dynamic area of study.

REFERENCES

Afshaw, H. (1989), 'Gender roles and the "moral economy of kin" among Pakistani women in West Yorkshire', *New Community*, 15: 211–25.

Allan, G. and Crow, G. (1999), *Families, Households and Society*, London: Macmillan.

Anderson, M. (1971a), *The Sociology of the Family*, Harmondsworth: Penguin.

Anderson, M. (1971b), *Family Structure in Nineteenth Century Lancashire*, Cambridge: Cambridge University Press.

Anderson, M. (1980), *The Sociology of the Family* 2nd edn, Harmondsworth: Penguin.

Askham, J. (1984), *Identity and Stability in Marriage*, Cambridge: Cambridge University Press.

Ballard, R. (1994), *Desh Pardesh: The South Asian Experience in Britain*, London: Hurst.

Barker, D. and Allen, S. (1976a), *Sexual Divisions and Society*, London: Tavistock.

Barker, D. and Allen, S. (1976b), *Dependence and Exploitation in Work and Marriage*, London: Longman.

Bell, C. (1968), *Middle Class Families*, London: Routledge & Kegan Paul.

Bell, C. and Newby, H. (1973), *Community Studies*, St Albans: Allen & Unwin.

Bhachu, P. (1985), *Twice Migrants: East African Sikh Settlers in Britain*, London: Tavistock.

Blood, R. and Wolfe, D. (1960), *Husbands and Wives: The Dynamics of Married Living*, Glencoe: Free Press.

Cooper, D. (1971), *The Death of the Family*, Harmondsworth: Penguin.

Dreitzel, H. P. (1972), *Family, Marriage and the Struggle of the Sexes*, New York: Macmillan.

Finch, J. and Groves, D. (1983), *A Labour of Love: Women, Work and Caring*, London: Routledge & Kegan Paul.

Firth, R., Hubert, J. and Forge, A. (1970), *Families and Their Relatives*, London: Routledge & Kegan Paul.

Gavron, H. (1968), *The Captive Wife*, Harmondsworth: Penguin.

Giddens, A. (1991), *Modernity and Self-Identity*, Cambridge: Polity Press.

Haskey, J. (1995), 'Trends in marriage and cohabitation: the decline in marriage and the changing pattern of living in partnerships', *Population Trends*, 80: 5–15.

Haskey, J. and Kiernan, K. (1989), 'Cohabitation in Great Britain', *Population Trends*, 58: 23–32.

Holme, A. (1985), *Housing and Young Families in East London*, London: Routledge & Kegan Paul.

Laing, R. D. and Esterson, A. (1964), *Sanity, Madness, and the Family*, London: Tavistock.

Laslett, P. (1965), *The World We Have Lost*, London: Methuen.

Medick, H. (1976), 'The proto-industrial family economy', *Social History*, 1: 291–315.

Morgan, D. H. J. (1996), *Family Connections*, Cambridge: Polity Press.

Oakley, A. (1974), *The Sociology of Housework*, London: Martin Robertson.

Oakley, A. (1976), *Subject Housewife*, Harmondsworth: Penguin.

Rosser, C. and Harris, C. (1965), *The Family and Social Change*, London: Routledge & Kegan Paul.

Scott, J. (1997), 'Changing households in Britain: do families still matter?', *Sociological Review*, 45: 591–620.

Siltanen, J. and Stanworth, M. (1984), *Women and the Public Sphere*, London: Hutchinson.

Voysey, M. (1975), *A Constant Burden*, London: Routledge & Kegan Paul.

Westwood, S. and Bhachu, P. (1988), *Enterprising Women: Ethnicity, Economy, and Gender Relations*, London: Routledge.

Williams, R. (1975), *The Country and the City*, St Albans: Paladin.

Willmott, P. and Young, M. (1960), *Family and Class in a London Suburb*, London: Routledge & Kegan Paul.

Wilson, P. and Pahl, R. (1988), 'The changing sociological construct of the family', *Sociological Review*, 36: 233–66.

Young, M. and Willmott, P. (1957), *Family and Kinship in East London*, London: Routledge & Kegan Paul.

Zaretsky, E. (1973), *Capitalism, the Family and Personal Life*, New York: Harper Row.

Part I

Changing Families

As noted in the Introduction, family demography has changed radically since the 1970s. In particular, patterns of cohabitation, marriage, child-bearing and divorce have all altered to a degree that was not foreseen at that time. The character of people's family and household relationships has also been altering, though not in such a dramatic fashion. The first three chapters of this book are all concerned with examining and understanding these changes. Chapter 1, by Janet Finch and Penny Summerfield, focuses explicitly on the ways in which understandings of marriage altered in the mid-part of the twentieth century. Finch and Summerfield discuss the factors that fostered the growth of a companionate ideal within popular conceptions of marriage during this period. Moreover, they highlight the degree to which the notion of companionate marriage was implicitly premised on a marked division of labour generally seen as rooted in an apparently 'natural' gender order. While the developments in marriage entailed in the shift towards a 'companionate' form were seen at the time – and still are to some degree – as a significant departure from previous patterns, the reality was that they built upon these, sustaining marital inequalities, though in a modified guise. The volume from which this chapter is taken, David Clark's *Marriage, Domestic Life and Social Change* (1990), also contains other chapters concerned with the contemporary development of marital ideologies. Readers interested in this area should consult the chapters by Richards and Elliott and by Finch and Morgan in Clark (1990). Mansfield and Collard's *The Beginning of the Rest of Your Life?* (1988) can also be recommended as one of the best recent British empirical studies of marital ideologies and realities.

Gail Hawkes's 'Liberalizing Heterosexuality' (chapter 2, this volume), taken from her book *A Sociology of Sex and Sexuality* (1996), is also concerned with the changes there have been in heterosexual partnerships in recent years, as well as with the expression of sexuality more broadly. In particular, she addresses the ways in which sexual activity has increasingly become 'uncoupled' from marriage, yet how at the same time despite this relaxation of sexual mores a 'male-orientated heterosexuality' has remained dominant. As well as describing some of the significant shifts there have been in cultural attitudes towards sexuality, Hawkes demonstrates that these changes were elements within a much broader set of socio-economic transformations affecting Britain and other industrially developed societies in the second half of the twentieth century. With changes in economic production and consumption, an increased emphasis on citizenship, and the growth of 'consumerism', life-style issues come to the fore, with choice and reflexivity emphasized more strongly than in the past. Changes in sexual freedoms and sexual expression are aspects of this, especially with regard to what Giddens (1991) has termed 'the reflexive project of the self'. In turn these changes influence cultural understandings of marriage and partnership, helping to shape the satisfactions and rewards people expect from these ties and the character of their commitment to them. Readers wanting to explore these issues further will find Giddens's *The Transformation of Intimacy* (1992) of interest, even if they disagree with some of the claims made in it, as well as Beck and Beck-Gernsheim's *The Normal Chaos of Love* (1995). They should also consult the other chapters in Hawkes (1996).

Chapter 3 – taken from David Cheal's *Family and the State of Theory* (1991) – is more general than the other two. However, like the others, it is concerned with changes occurring in domestic life, but its focus is on how these changes have challenged traditional sociological approaches and theories about the family. In particular, it explores the difficulties in accounting for the increasing diversity occurring in family and household patterns. It raises important questions about our understanding of what 'the family' is. At an everyday level, this may seem straightforward. However, the variety of forms of domestic organization and familial solidarity which are now constructed by people over their life course make definitions of 'family' far more complex than in the early and mid parts of the twentieth century. The rise in long-term cohabitation, divorce, remarriage, step-families, and births to single mothers, for example, all render some of the previously dominant ideas about family development suspect. Yet what occurs in the family sphere never occurs in isolation; family organization is one element of a wider structural complex. Thus the changes we are currently witnessing in family patterns need to be understood in terms of wider structural shifts. At the end of his chapter, Cheal raises important questions about the nature of these wider changes, relating the apparent disorganization within the family realm to the possibility that Western society is entering a postmodern phase in which old certainties – and established patterns of behaviour – are increasingly called into question. Put simply, should the significant changes in family patterns occurring in the last part of the twentieth century be seen as developments of existing patterns or as a much more radical fragmentation signifying a breakdown in family solidarities as traditionally understood? The rest of Cheal's (1991) book is a useful starting point for those interested in theoretical developments in family sociology. Although very different in its approach, David Morgan's *Family Connections* (1996) can also be recommended.

REFERENCES

Beck, U. and Beck-Gernsheim, E. (1995), *The Normal Chaos of Love*, Cambridge: Polity Press.

Cheal, D. (1991), *Family and the State of Theory*, Hemel Hempstead: Harvester Wheatsheaf.

Clark, D. (1990), *Marriage, Domestic Life and Social Change*, London: Routledge.

Giddens, A. (1991), *Modernity and Self-Identity*, Cambridge: Polity Press.

Giddens, A. (1992), *The Transformation of Intimacy*, Cambridge: Polity Press.

Hawkes, G. (1996), *A Sociology of Sex and Sexuality*, Buckingham: Open University Press.

Mansfield, P. and Collard, J. (1988), *The Beginning of the Rest of Your Life? A Portrait of Newly-Wed Marriage*, London: Macmillan.

Morgan, D. H. J. (1996), *Family Connections*, Cambridge: Polity Press.

1

Social Reconstruction and the Emergence of Companionate Marriage, 1945–59

Janet Finch and Penny Summerfield

The purpose of this chapter is to explore the development of marriage and family life in the period of postwar social reconstruction and up to the end of the 1950s. We have chosen to focus principally on the emerging concept of *companionate marriage* which, in our view, is the most distinctive feature of domestic life during this period.

Central to the aims of the postwar social reconstruction was the desire to consolidate family life after the disruptive effects of war and to build a future in which marriage and the home would be the foundations of a better life. Partly this required the kind of economic and environmental reconstruction which would provide a physical and material environment conducive to stable family life – most obviously the rebuilding of houses destroyed by war and 'slum clearance' programmes which would reshape decaying urban areas. The prominence of this aspect of postwar reconstruction is evidenced by a Gallup Poll produced at the time of the 1945 election, which showed that 40 per cent of voters saw housing as the major issue of the election campaign (Thane, 1982, p. 260).

In much of the official and semi-official literature of the period, this physical reconstruction of living conditions was seen as providing the backdrop for the consolidation of stable family life, based upon the type of relationship between marriage partners which itself was suited to the postwar world. Although the phrase 'companionate marriage' had been employed as early as the 1920s, it is in the postwar period that it appears more widely, being used to summarize a set of ideas about marriage which ranged from the notion that there should be greater companionship between partners whose roles essentially were different, through the idea of marriage as 'teamwork', to the concept of marriages based on 'sharing', implying the breakdown of clearly demarcated roles. 'Partnership' and 'equality' in marriage clearly can mean very different things and both can be traced in the literature of this period. The prominence of these ideas about companionate marriage in the 1950s marks one of the key shifts from the idea of marriage as an institution to marriage as a relationship (Morgan, 1991).

In the first two sections of this chapter we discuss the advent of an ideology of companionate marriage, drawing on bodies of literature concerning the birth rate and motherhood, women's sexuality and girls' education and women's employment, in order to explore the different meanings contained within it and their inconsistencies and limitations. Such ideological constructions influenced perceptions of the lived reality of marriage in this period. Sociologists interested in the question of how marriage was developing were not free from them, and indeed contributed to them. In the third section of the chapter we therefore use contemporary empirical sociological studies not as an 'uncontaminated' account of reality, but as a source which gives some sense of the interplay between ideological constructions and lived experience. Further, sociological writing on marriage in the 1950s was very well known, and influenced thinking about British society and social policy well beyond the confines of academic scholarship.

In spite of the optimistic tone in which companionate marriage was discussed in both 'official' sources and sociological writing, there were underlying anxieties about whether it would in fact live up to the expectations of the optimists, or whether it might prove to be incompatible with marital stability. Such fears were voiced in particular in discussions of divorce and also of juvenile delinquency. The fourth section of the chapter reviews the warnings sounded in the period about the dangers of the companionate style for the future of marriage.

We finish by listening briefly to some dissenting voices among those thinking and writing about marriage in this period, from a minority which subscribed neither to the optimism of the protagonists of companionate marriage nor the pessimism of those who doubted its viability. This enables us to draw together our discussion by considering the question which no sociologist then posed: was the companionate marriage in a woman's interests, or did the benefits accrue mainly to the male?

The Birth Rate, Motherhood and Models of Marriage

We begin by considering an issue which was of prime importance to public discussions of family life at the end of the Second World War – the birth rate and the overall shape of the British population. Prewar and wartime anxiety about the falling birth rate of the 1930s which reached a record low in 1940, gave rise to intense discussion about the possibility that the population would fall below replacement level. This preoccupation peaked in the years 1945–7. Public discussion which surrounded it had obvious implications for ideas about motherhood in the immediate postwar period, but also contained a number of implications for models of marriage appropriate to a situation where women were to be encouraged officially to produce children.

The main clearing house for 'pronatalist' ideas concerning ways in which the birth rate might be raised was the Royal Commission on Population (RCP), which reported in 1949. Its policy recommendations embraced larger family allowances (introduced in 1945) starting with the first rather than the second child in a family; 'family services' for 'mothers of young children', including a glittering array of assistance from home helps and 'sitters in', to rest homes for mothers, nurseries, nursery schools and children's playgrounds; and health care based on the new National Health Service to provide the normally healthy married woman, rather than just those medically at risk, with advice on all aspects of reproduction, as well as treatment where necessary. Finally, the housing shortage was felt to be one of 'the main deterrents of parenthood' and a programme was urged of building more and larger houses and modernizing old ones in the context of a rent- and rate-rebate system linked to family size (Royal Commission on Population [RCP], 1949, paras 658–79). To summarize, postwar British pronatalism was concerned with improving the material conditions of motherhood in order to promote it as a function.

Motherhood, it was assumed, would take place within marriage. 'Unmarried mothers' were by the early 1950s depicted in psychosociological literature as 'pathologically disturbed' (Riley, 1983, p. 196). Yet in spite of the importance of marriage as a site for the developments advocated, it was given relatively scant attention in postwar pronatalism. In so far as marriage was discussed overtly there were contradictory elements in the way in which it was conceptualized. The recommendations of the RCP reflected the view that the cause of raising the birth rate had been impeded by 'the movement for equality of the sexes' originating in the nineteenth century, in two ways. First, as more women were drawn into paid work a potential conflict was created with the demands of motherhood. One might expect the Commission to have brought forward proposals to ease this situation but it did not. The second effect of greater equality between the sexes, in the Commission's view, was to weaken the traditional dominance of the husband and to give more emphasis to 'the wife's role as companion to her husband as well as a producer of children'. On one level it was difficult to disapprove of this tendency towards companionate marriage especially in so far as it had raised women's status. On the other hand, in the process of becoming 'more considerate' to their wives, husbands had shown themselves increasingly reluctant to put them through the hardship and danger of 'unrestricted childbearing', with the unfortunate effect – from the Commission's point of view – of contributing to the fall in family size to an average of just over two children (RCP, 1949, para. 103). In this sense, companionate marriage itself was potentially a threat to the birth rate, even if in other respects it was to be welcomed. Many of the RCP's policy recommendations were intended to reconcile what was seen as a 'modern' marital style based on a small number of children, with the three- or four-child family regarded by the Commission as essential to the national interest.

Evidence given to the RCP reflects similar contradictions, although some of it welcomes the advent of companionate marriage rather more enthusiastically than the official report. Particularly, groups on the left, such as the Fabian Society, put greater emphasis on the role of the wife as a companion to her husband, and also paid more attention to the issue of working wives. Though their views were not incorporated in the report, they are indicative of left-wing thinking which influenced the sociological approaches we shall be reviewing later in this chapter. The Fabians saw the 'new marriage' of the postwar world as 'teamwork' between husband and wife, in contrast to the separatism of marriages a generation earlier which was seen as leading to 'sex antagonism'. In 'comradely' marriages the individual interests of wives were to be subsumed within those of the family group, in an analogous way to that in which 'citizens' of either sex were expected to put the interests of the community before their own in the wider society. The Fabian prescription for motherhood endeavoured to reconcile the interests of the family and the community. For the sake of the family, mothers should not combine motherhood with paid work when their children were young, but in the interests of society, wives 'must realize they should give part-time service to the community when the children are older'. Part-time paid work generally was mentioned, and more specifically 'teaching and welfare work' (Fabian Society, quoted by Riley, 1983, p. 176).

All this was seen as belonging in the context of marriage as teamwork, but no thought was given in these sources to how the 'team' was to be constructed, in the sense of the roles of its members, their degree of equality, and the issue of leadership. In other words, no one questioned the sexual division of labour: power in the home and shifting its balance were not on the agenda. The implication of this ideology of marriage was that wives were to add to conventional subservience to an admittedly 'more considerate' but still breadwinning husband, a responsibility to be his 'companion', to produce and rear more children and to engage in paid work in response to social needs if and when they could do so without ill effects on either husband or children.

Only a minority of those involved in pronatalist debates voiced qualms about the possibilities of achieving genuinely companionate marriage in which wives would be persuaded to have more children, without doing something about income sharing between husbands and wives. They included the Labour MP Edith Summerskill, Edward Hulton, the editor of *Picture Post*, and two wartime feminist organizations – the Six Point Group and the Women's Publicity Planning Association – formed respectively in 1941 and 1943 to protest against the conscription of women without commitment to equal pay and to support a parliamentary bill removing all sex-based discrepancies from British legislation (Riley, 1983, pp. 174–5, 179). They advocated legislating to give wives a proportion of their husbands' incomes. It is in the writings of these groups that one finds some hints that companionate marriage might not be wholly in women's interests. But while social policy might intrude in all sorts of ways on the mother, intervention into the 'private' relations between husbands and wives was not considered appropriate in 'orthodox' circles.

Ironically, almost by the time the RCP report was available, fears about the declining birth rate had subsided in the postwar baby boom. At this point the specifically pronatalist political agenda receded, but concern with the conditions of motherhood consolidated in the 1950s around the issue of maternal deprivation. If anything, these ideas are even more difficult to reconcile with the concept of companionate marriage – or at the very least they imply a version in which there is a clear division of roles between husband and wife.

The view that maternal care in infancy was crucial for the physical development of the child had long roots stretching back to the late nineteenth century. The medical profession had easily grafted on to such views the idea that emotional development also depended upon it. The Ministry of Health used the authoritative pronouncements of its Medical Officers of Health about the physical and emotional harm day nurseries would do to children to limit the supply of wartime nurseries set up to free mothers for war work in the Second World War (Summerfield, 1984). In 1952 the publication of John Bowlby's *Maternal Care and Mental Health* gave further psychological credence to such views which were popularized in the 1940s and 1950s above all by D. W. Winnicott, through radio broadcasts and in the press. He depicted the marital home as a private, emotional world in which mother and child were bound to each other and in which the mother had control and found freedom to fulfil herself. In Winnicott's view it was natural and inevitable that she would want such an existence, to the exclusion of any alternatives (Winnicott, 1957).

Such a view of motherhood represents a narrowing of some aspects of pronatalism. No longer were women being told that they ought to have opportunities to pursue 'outside interests', even if only in order to do their social duty and preserve their marriages. Children were expected to be their consuming passion, and childrearing and paid work were seen as mutually exclusive. Bowlby argued that maternal deprivation caused by any sort of absence, including mothers working, led to delinquency and psychosis in their children. Winnicott also warned of the perils awaiting the 'latch key child'. The tendency to see successful childrearing in terms of constant mothering rendered the father relatively unimportant. Where did the emphasis on the mother leave marriage as a team? The 1950s fixation on the mother rather than the parent contributed to the construction of the companionate marriage as a form in which men and women had markedly different roles in spite of an appearance of greater togetherness than in earlier marital styles.

Images of Companionate Marriage in Other Literature of the Period

We have paid particular attention to the issue of childbearing, and especially to the Royal Commission on Population, because of the Report's official status and its key importance in distilling ideas about family life in the immediate postwar years. However, various other bodies of official and semi-official literature of the 1940s and 1950s can be used to trace the development of ideas about companionate marriage. We shall look briefly in this section at three of these: writing on women's sexuality, on girls' education and on married women's employment.

Women's sexuality

An emphasis on sexuality was an important dimension of marriage during this period and of course this fits with the emerging notion that marriage should be seen as a relationship, not simply as an institution. Marital stability was increasingly seen as dependent on both contraception and sexual pleasure in the 1940s and 1950s. Pronatalist literature acknowledged the widespread use of contraception, and though some of the contributors (e.g. Hubback, 1947; Mass Observation, 1945) would have liked to restrict access to it in order to encourage in people 'a more courageous and robust faith in life among those who do not want more children owing to a defeatist attitude' (Hubback quoted by Riley, 1983, p. 160), the Royal Commission on Population advocated its wider availability. It argued that it was necessary for the better spacing of children, but more fundamentally it was felt that birth control was now 'generally accepted' and the clock could not be turned back. Even the Anglican church had (after giving Marie Stopes hell for two decades) come round. 'Christians are generally agreed upon the need for responsible family planning' wrote the Church of England Moral Welfare Council in 1957 (quoted by Birmingham Feminist History Group, 1979, p. 58).

Such sources considered the use of birth control as a palliative for poor health or a way for couples to raise their standard of living, and not as a means by which, as of right, a woman could control her fertility, nor as the path to greater sexual freedom. However, the literature on sexuality was growing, bringing with it the message that married couples had a duty to give each other sexual pleasure, and that this was increasingly important for a successful marriage. Indeed it has been argued that in the United States the concept of 'companionate marriage' was based on 'a new domestic ideal of "mom" as sexy housewife' (Ferguson, 1989, p. 115). Kinsey et al., in *Sexual Behavior in the Human Female* published in Britain in 1953, asserted that women could and did enjoy sex. And during the 1950s numerous public bodies including the church and the Marriage Guidance Council agreed that pleasurable marital sex was important, increasing the burden on women to give, as well as receive and express, pleasure.

There was, however, anxiety in some quarters that pleasurable sex was not stopping at the marriage bed and that the emphasis on it would in fact undermine the stability of marriage. Rowntree and Lavers, authors of *English Life and Leisure* published in 1951, believed that the new emphasis on 'eroticism' in the media and the open availability of contraceptives were encouraging indulgence in 'illicit sexual relations'. Their analysis of what they saw as a rising (though unquantifiable) tide of immorality was based on the view that many aspects of postwar Britain were leading to the submergence of spiritual life in 'selfishness and hedonism'. As far as marriage and the family were concerned, such indulgence had a destabilizing effect both in so far as it led to illegitimate births, abortions and venereal disease, and through the deceit within the family which it encouraged. A strong streak of puritanism ran through their work.

Illicit (i.e. extramarital) sex was seen as an 'obsessional activity, the desire for which grows with indulgence...to the satisfaction of which are sacrificed energy, time, money and thought that should have been harnessed to constructive purposes' (Rowntree and Lavers, 1951, p. 214). Not only the viability of marriage but that of Britain as 'a great and vigorous nation' depended on the checking of 'sexual excesses' (ibid.: p. 215).

Such views put a further burden on companionate marriage, of which we are building a cumulative picture. Such marriage was to be between considerate, breadwinning husbands and comradely but thoroughly maternal wives surrounded by numerous children. The wives were told by some sources that they should maintain 'outside interests' and even that they had a duty to do paid work if they could fit it around their primary domestic role. But other sources frowned on anything lessening their ties to children, particularly paid work, warning that if they did such work they would irreparably damage the mental health of their 'latch key children'. At the same time husbands and wives were told that the stability of their marriages, the viability of marriage as an institution and even the future of the country, depended on regular marital sex which they should enjoy to the exclusion of sexual indulgence outside marriage.

The education of girls

To add a further level of complexity to the picture which we are building, when we look at literature of this period concerned with the education of girls, it appears that there is an almost complete withdrawal from the idea of companionate marriage, even in its most conservative versions. Indeed much educational prescription of the 1940s and 1950s contradicted the ideology of marriage as teamwork. None of the commentators thought it necessary for boys to learn about their responsibilities as future husbands and fathers, nor to develop any special skills they might require, beyond those associated with acquiring sufficient education to get a steady job of an appropriate sort given their individual mix of ability and social status. This would enable them to fulfil what was expected of them as men, and by implication becoming a breadwinner was an aspect of this (see Board of Education, 1943; Newsom, 1948; Central Advisory Council for Education, 1959). Educational prescription for girls, on the other hand, heavily emphasized their future roles as wives and mothers. Domestic science, argued the Norwood Report (Board of Education, 1943), was valuable because young girls were all 'potential makers of homes'. John Newsom in 1948 disagreed that girls should be taught domestic skills before they left school, as most would do by the age of 15, because they would forget them by the time they married. However, as adults they should attend continuation classes in domestic science in County Colleges, for the benefit of their husbands' digestions (Newsom, 1948, p. 127) and the stability of their marriages. But though domestic skills were not to be taught to schoolgirls, Newsom wanted to give their education a thoroughly domestic orientation, preparing them for what he saw as their true destination as wives and mothers and reflecting what he saw as the interests of all but a tiny minority of 'academic' girls. In his scheme all subjects would be linked together by their applicability to the home (ibid.: chapter 6).

Newsom's book *The Education of Girls* was not an official report, but its tone was echoed in the Crowther report (Central Advisory Council for Education, 1959), which emphasized the preoccupation of the majority of girls with domesticity and also personal relationships, and recommended that their schooling should reflect these alleged interests. Both Newsom and Crowther acknowledged the long-standing pattern of girls engaging in paid work between school and marriage, but dismissed such work as inherently less important than the sort of paid work done by boys and men. It was seen as inevitably un- or semi-skilled with a low training component, since it was widely recognized as a mere stopgap before a young woman commenced her true 'career', that of a wife and mother. Even informal education within, for example, the Youth Service and the Girl Guides, was designed to promote a girl's 'social maturity and technical competence at her job as home maker' (Ministry of Education, 1960). Girl Guides could acquire strings of badges indicating their proficiency as cooks, child carers, seamstresses, knitters and nurses, crowned, once they had enough, by the 'Little House' emblem of domestic proficiency.

The emphasis within prescriptive literature on the education of girls in and for domesticity inevitably produced a one-sided view of whom within marriage was primarily responsible for the home. At the same time, no one recommended that either girls or boys should think about the difficulties of meeting the demands that the new ideal of the companionate marriage might make, especially given the reality of a rising proportion of wives engaging in paid work during the 1950s. Such literature deepens one's scepticism about the concept of the companionate marriage used at this time. It increasingly appears to have given no more than a gloss to the conventional division of labour and distribution of economic power between husband and wife, while imposing new demands on women to be more comradely wives, more devoted mothers of more children, more satisfying and satisfied sexual partners and more professional homemakers.

Married women's employment

Logically one might expect that more equal marriages should mean that both women and men have similar opportunities to engage in all aspects of public and private life, including employment. However, this was not the dominant theme of the period. Reference has already been made to the ways in which the relationship between women's employment and marriage was depicted in pronatalist and educational literature. As we have seen, within orthodox opinion, as represented by the Royal Commission on Population, the paid employment of wives was not compatible with producing larger families. However, in the view of some commentators it might be necessary to permit some women to pursue careers alongside motherhood, lest they abandon the latter altogether, and according to others, wives of older children might be required to engage in paid employment for the general good of society. Psychological and educational literature, on the other hand, regarded paid work as something which would cease on marriage/motherhood as far as the majority of women were concerned.

However, simultaneously in the 1940s married women were being urged to return to paid work to fill gaps in the labour force created by the labour shortage in particular areas and types of work. Teaching was one of these. In 1949 the Ministry of Education issued a document urging married women to return to teaching, arguing that schools would gain from their maternal qualities although it said nothing about the impact of such a dual role on marriage (Ministry of Education, 1949, p. 5). In relation to manual work, the official literature similarly emphasized the benefits to production of the employment of married women (e.g. the application of 'household pride', the steadiness and sense of responsibility older married women brought to the work compared with flightier young single women).

As far as managing the double burden was concerned, part-time work, introduced on a large scale during the war to recruit women who were otherwise exempt from mobilization, was seen as the answer (Summerfield, 1984, chapter 6). Part-time work would enable married women to perform all their essential wifely and maternal tasks without threatening the stability of their marriages or detracting from their productivity at work. Employers might have to allow 'latitude...for the performance of home duties' mainly in terms of the arrangement of hours and leave (Smith, 1961, p. 22), but no change in the nature of marriage was required. The economic benefits of their work were small, so part-time women workers could be seen unthreateningly as supplementing a family income earned principally by the husband. A survey in 1948 showed that these were the values that women themselves espoused. Women workers were reported as saying that 'women should go out to work only if they could carry out their duties to their homes and families' (Thomas, 1948, p. 3). The repetition of such views in another survey undertaken in the late 1950s suggests that the higher postwar female participation rates had not altered the basic belief that home and family came first in a woman's life. In this survey, married women workers were presented as wanting to earn as much as possible 'to raise the standard of living of the family as a whole' rather than for themselves (Smith, 1961, p. 20). A wife's earnings would thus not significantly enlarge her own independence, though they would enable a couple to spend on the new 'family' consumables of the fifties, such as processed foods, synthetic clothing, vacuum cleaners, fridges and washing machines, to the production of which the new married women workers were themselves contributing.

The literature on women's employment did not prescribe the most appropriate marital style to go with it, yet it implied marriages in which husbands would tolerate wives working, and thus husbands who were not committed to the bourgeois ideology of the man as sole breadwinner (Thomas, 1948, p. 19). It was an implication which fitted comfortably with the concept of companionate marriage without upsetting the conventional distribution of economic and other power within marriage. At the same time it imposed another strain on women. In addition to the demands that a wife should be more comradely, more motherly, more sensuous and a better homemaker, was added the expectation that she should be a part-time wage earner.

Thus, in exploring the concept of companionate marriage which developed during the 1940s and 1950s, a rather contradictory picture emerges. The idea of companionate marriage was being officially encouraged whilst at the same time there were anxieties that – if pushed too far – it could undermine other features of family life which were seen as central to its stability: the position of the man as main breadwinner, the incentive to produce and rear children, the attachment to one lifelong sexual partner. We have highlighted particularly the implications of these ideas about companionate marriage for women. Superficially they appear to be in women's interests but we have argued that, by producing quite contradictory pressures, they actually placed strains upon women especially by pushing them towards a type of marriage which made extra demands without necessarily providing extra rewards.

We have constructed this argument on the basis of official and semi-official literature, but how far does our case match up to the social reality of what was happening in women's lives during the 1940s and 1950s? To pursue that question, we turn now to a different kind of literature from this period.

Marriage and Family in Sociological Writing

In the fifteen years following the end of the Second World War, the young but expanding discipline of sociology took marriage and family life as one of its key topics. We are fortunate in having a number of contemporary empirical studies for this period, and they form the basis of our discussion here. What do these studies tell us about domestic life in general and marriage in particular? Do they document a noticeable change towards the companionate model? If so, what were its implications for women and men?

The picture of marriage which emerges from these different sources is in some ways puzzlingly diverse. From the windows of the Institute of Community Studies, the modern husbands of working-class Bethnal Green could be seen pushing the pram or playing with their children in the park, activities which, according to the researchers, their fathers and grandfathers would have found shocking. In advanced middle-class Woodford, husbands would go so far as to make a commitment to wash the dishes every night and do the hoovering on Saturday mornings. Meanwhile, in the Yorkshire mining town of Ashton, they were still throwing their dinners on the back of the fire if the wife had failed to select the right menu (Dennis, Henriques and Slaughter, 1956; Young and Willmott, 1957; Willmott and Young, 1960). Some showed the signs of 'partnership' much more obviously than others. Were the researchers documenting differences in marriage customs in different localities, or different social classes, or different occupational groups? Were some people simply quicker than others to latch onto the idea of companionate marriage?

We shall explore these questions initially by drawing upon the 1950s' socio-logical literature and then, in the following section, consider different kinds of data which shed light on the image of postwar marriage which emerges from these studies. We have selected three prominent themes which emerge from this literature, which can be summarized in three words: optimism, cosiness, anxiety.

Optimism: the security of family life in a welfare state

We have already indicated that economic, social and environmental reconstruc-tion formed the essential backdrop to the more qualitative changes to family life upon which we are focusing. The building of decent houses, new towns and the establishment of a welfare state which took care of its citizens 'from cradle to grave' were the soil upon which, *inter alia*, family life could flourish.

The sociological studies of the period reflect a spirit of optimism about the beneficial consequences of the newly established welfare state: the basic eco-nomic pressures were being taken off an increasing number of people; living standards were rising, bringing with them the prospect of a more secure and more satisfying family life. This tone of optimism is clearly in evidence in the influential Bethnal Green studies of working-class family life (Young and Will-mott, 1957; Willmott and Young, 1960; and see discussion in Fletcher, 1962). The authors of these studies argued that the conditions of the household had changed dramatically by comparison with those described in earlier generations of studies on the working classes in London, done by Mayhew, Booth and Rowntree. Key changes were: improved housing conditions and less sharing of houses; shorter working hours and higher wages for men in a situation of full employment; smaller family size, easing the pressure on household budgets; increased life expectancy and improved medical care, making it less likely that one or more parent would die whilst their children were young (Young and Willmott, 1957, pp. 17–27).

The general tone of optimism is evident in the Bethnal Green studies and elsewhere, but it is not universal. For example, in a study done in London in 1949–51, Spinley compared the family life of young people in two contrasting social groups, one selected from 'one of the worst slums in London' and the other a group of public school boys (Spinley, 1953). The living conditions which he describes do not seem to show much sign of significant postwar improve-ments. Moving outside London, in another study done at around the same time as the Bethnal Green research, Dennis and colleagues were discussing the conditions of family life in a Yorkshire mining community which they named Ashton. Although certainly not subject to overcrowding and poor housing conditions of the type described by Spinley, the men and women of Ashton did not seem to have much money to spare and many of them still needed to worry about the male breadwinner missing even one day's work (Dennis, Henriques and Slaughter, 1956, pp. 185–6).

If we go beyond specific studies of family life, some other sociologists were not entirely convinced of the efficacy of the welfare state. Although in a political sense poverty was 'rediscovered' in the 1960s, this was possible in part because some sociologists, especially Peter Townsend, who was publishing on poverty in the 1950s, were not seduced by the benefits of the social reconstruction, and the more obvious signs of the 'affluent society', into believing that the noble aim of eradicating poverty had actually been achieved (Townsend, 1954; Coates and Silburn, 1971).

Although the message of optimism comes across strongly in some writing, the evidence of sociological studies is actually rather mixed on the issue of whether the material conditions of family life really had improved, or what proportions of the population benefited from this. It is difficult to discern how many people during this period really were enjoying the kind of material conditions which were thought to be conducive to a more companionate style of marriage.

Cosiness: the nuclear family and companionate marriage

A major theme in this literature is that the 'new' family life was much more home-centred in various senses. Houses had become more pleasant places and people now had more money with which to make them comfortable; relationships within the wider kin group were becoming less significant and the nuclear family household was of enhanced importance; men as well as women were more likely to centre their lives on the home in a significant way. The image of the new family life is therefore essentially one of cosiness, in which people live in tight little units, rather inward-looking, interacting very much more with each other than with others outside the household, harmonious for the most part. This picks up on a dominant theme in American sociology of this period (Parsons and Bales, 1956) although often the British studies do not refer to the American literature explicitly.

A more companionate style of marriage was seen as an integral part of this package. Many of the sociologists of this period seemed wholly convinced that they were indeed observing its rapid spread. There was a general sense that the creation of this type of family life was a natural consequence of the social and economic changes of the postwar world. This view is expressed most explicitly by Josephine Klein (1965) who, although her work was published after the period which we are considering, was writing sympathetically about studies published in the 1950s and trying to draw out their common themes. She attributes the development of companionate marriage, and the consequent reduced attachment to kin, explicitly to growing prosperity:

> In the traditional communities . . . when financial stress intensifies, the rift between husband and wife must deepen. The man will work more overtime, and so be in the house less than before. The woman will rely more on her kin, hence be involved with her spouse less than before. The poorer the family is, the more restricted their lives will become, and the less man and wife will have to share emotionally and socially. Conversely . . . where the stress is lifting, one tends to find more affectionate relations between members, or at least more interaction which

expresses and demonstrates such affection, more consultation between members and a less authoritarian structure. (Klein, 1965, p. 291)

Authors of the period saw the changing status of women as an integral part of the new family life, although whether a consequence or a cause is not always clear. For the most part, writers presented the changed position of women as a matter of uncontentious progress, both inside and outside the family. A particularly explicit example of this can be found at the end of the first chapter of *Family and Kinship in East London*, where Young and Willmott have no difficulty in concluding that 'man and wife are now partners':

There is a new kind of companionship, reflecting the rise in status of the young wife and children which is one of the great transformations of our time. There is now a new approach to equality between the sexes and, though each has its peculiar role, its boundaries are no longer so rigidly defined, nor performed without consultation...man and wife are partners. (Young and Willmott, 1957, p. 30)

This partnership model of marriage apparently reached its full flowering in places like middle-class Woodford where, despite the fact that many travelled into London to work, men as well as women had become strongly oriented to the home and the nuclear family:

Most Woodford men are emphatically not absentee husbands. They hurry back from their offices and factories, arriving between 6 and 7, to spend the evening at home, and they are there for two full days at weekends. It is their work, especially if rather tedious, which takes second place in their thoughts. They are as devoted as their wives to the house they share. (Willmott and Young, 1960, p. 21)

Meanwhile one wonders what the miners' wives of Ashton would have made of being told that the era of the companionate marriage, based on equality between the partners, had arrived. The picture of the marriage relationship which emerges from this study is very different: the man's centre of activity lay firmly outside the home; the house was the woman's domain; a clearly bounded division of labour, between the male breadwinner and the female homemaker, was evident at every turn. Dennis and colleagues are very clear on this point. Although men might grow vegetables in an allotment or do some household repairs, none of these activities are of the type which would 'demand co-operation or encourage the growth of companionship between husband and wife' (Dennis, Henriques and Slaughter, 1956, p. 183). Marriage in Ashton had a clearly understood contractual basis, expressed most concretely at the point where the husband handed over part of his wages to his wife:

The husband's duty to his family goes little further than delivering part of his wage each Friday. Here the duties and responsibilities of his partner begin. It is for him to earn the money and for her to administer it wisely. In actual fact this means that the wife takes virtually all the responsibility for the household and the family. (Dennis, Henriques and Slaughter, 1956, p. 196)

These arrangements are a particularly clear example of what feminists later were to argue about marriage: that essentially, from women's point of view, it is a labour contract (Delphy, 1984). This is very far removed from cosy companionship.

Varieties of experience in marriages

How do we account for this apparent variation in the experience of marriage in the 1950s? This was an issue which interested sociologists working in the period, and they came up with a range of possible answers, of which we will mention four. First, social-class differences: it was suggested that middle class marriages were inherently more companionate. This was an obvious possible explanation although it was difficult to get it to fit the empirical evidence, since the Bethnal Green research on working-class couples so confidently portrayed the younger ones as having already slotted into the companionate mode. Second, and as a variation on a similar theme, the authors of the Ashton study were inclined to explain the distinctiveness of the marriage relationship in their research in specific occupational terms. The distinctive features of the mining industry (long days in an all-male environment, physically demanding work, an occupationally homogeneous community) were conducive to a particular type of family organization, they argued.

A third line of argument was quite simply that contemporary studies were documenting social change, which took place at a variable rate in different localities. The implication was that everyone would catch up sooner or later. This view is implicit throughout Young and Willmott's work and of course it is very much in tune with the general tone of optimism about social reconstruction. They were to elaborate it most fully in a book published in 1973, where they suggested that this progressive form of family life had slowly percolated down the class structure from the middle class to different levels of the working class. The onward march of progress was inevitable.

Fourth, the work of Elizabeth Bott (1957) – in many ways the most interesting and sophisticated sociological study of family life in this period – suggested that different types of marriage relationship were the product of a wider set of relationships in which individuals are involved, rather than of their personal or social characteristics. Bott's carefully documented study of twenty couples shows that the nature of a couple's relationships with their wider kin network is closely linked to the type of relationship which they have with each other. Couples whose networks of relationships were close-knit needed to rely less on each other for practical and emotional support, and therefore were likely to develop a marriage in which each has their own sphere and tasks. Where the network of a couple was rather loose-knit, they needed to rely on each other more and therefore were likely to develop a more co-operative conjugal relationship. This line of argument represents a rather more subtle, complex and less deterministic way of explaining variations in the incidence of companionate marriage than do the others. It is also consistent with the findings of other studies, in that close-knit networks were more likely to be found in certain localities than in others.

But in the end, it seems difficult to judge on the basis of these studies just how far the fifteen years following the Second World War was a period in which the cosy nuclear family, with companionate marriage as its cornerstone, became a widespread reality. Looking at these studies from a distance of three or four decades, we have a niggling worry about the way in which all the authors take for granted the desirability of this family model. One is bound to wonder how far the fact that they were enthusiastically seeking this phenomenon influenced the evidence which they found.

These sociological studies are also somewhat restricted in scope, in the sense that there must have been other variations on domestic life which simply were not covered. An obvious example is that none of the sociological studies of the family published in this period sets out to encompass black as well as white families, yet this was a period in which migration from the New Commonwealth was firmly established. Sociologists of the family seem barely to have noticed its potential significance. The first British sociological study in a non-white area was actually conducted in the late 1950s, but it concentrates more on employment than on family relationships and in any case was not published until some years later (Patterson, 1963). When one adds this to the lack of attention paid to gender issues in these studies of family life, the evidence starts to look very partial. It was only after the impact of second-wave feminism that sociologists began to question what the cosy nuclear family might mean for women.

Anxieties about Companionate Marriage

The theme of optimism and cosiness has its counterpoint in the sociological literature. This is a sense of anxiety that perhaps things have gone too far, or not in the right direction, or that they are getting a bit out of hand. These anxieties also are reflected in some official literature of the period. In this section we will look at evidence from both types of source, as a way of exploring some key contradictions about the concept of companionate marriage and also highlighting some themes which were to become prominent in debates about marriages in the following three decades.

The sense of anxiety in sociological literature

In the sociological literature, a source where this sense of anxiety is made explicit is Fletcher's book on *Marriage and Family in Britain*, which was published in 1962 but which drew all its evidence from 1950s' sociological studies. This book was written explicitly to counter views, expressed in public debate, that the quality of family life was actually deteriorating rather than improving and that its decline was responsible for the growth of other social evils. Much of this anxiety was focused upon two issues: divorce and juvenile delinquency. In a way, each was seen as a consequence of greater postwar prosperity, of the easing of the conditions of family life, and of the trend towards a more isolated nuclear family. Fletcher sets out the parameters of these issues very clearly in his introduction:

> What effects have industrial and urban changes, the increase in material wealth, the increased provision of education, the new independence of women, the new affluence and freedom of teenagers, and other aspects of modern society had upon the nature and stability of the family? Are these changes such that we can welcome and encourage them? Or are they to be feared and opposed? Do they constitute a deterioration or an improvement of moral standards and family relationships? Is the family really to blame for all the ills modern society is said to suffer – crime, delinquency, irresponsibility, hooliganism – as many moralists would have us believe? Or are such changes false, unjustified and harmful? (Fletcher, 1962, p. 12)

Fletcher's own answer to this is essentially twofold: things are not as bad as they seem when the facts are examined and placed in historical perspective; the changes which people worry about are really signs of social and economic progress, and therefore basically to be welcomed. Whether or not his work was convincing as an intervention in public debate need not concern us here. But the very fact that he felt the need to write this kind of book picked up on the underlying anxiety in many of the sources which we are reviewing in the 1950s.

Concern with the stability of marriage as a lifelong relationship seems to have been quite widely shared. Bott, for example, felt the need to point out that – in her estimation – the different types of conjugal relationships which she had identified were an equally stable basis for marriage and that in principle people could be happy in either contrasting arrangement (Bott, 1957, pp. 217–18). Young and Willmott present the conditions of working-class life in the postwar period as inherently *more* stable as a basis for marriage than arrangements in earlier generations, but at the same time there is a clear concern that marriage breakdown be avoided wherever possible (Young and Willmott, 1957, p. 22).

Much of the apparent anxiety about juvenile delinquency was focused on the image of the slum and the social organization associated with it. In the slum, lawlessness of both minor and major kinds was encouraged by a family life which was impoverished in every sense. In the area which Spinley studied in the late 1940s, he linked high levels of delinquency explicitly with childrearing practices such as unplanned children, so-called broken homes, and mothers going out to work, as well as to material poverty (Spinley, 1953, pp. 131–2). The same kinds of anxieties were reflected, perhaps less overtly, in other studies of the period, even in the very different social setting of Ashton (Dennis, Henriques and Slaughter, 1956). The slum, as it had been known before the war, was supposed to be disappearing, and with it the undesirable patterns of behaviour which it promoted. But it looked as if increased prosperity was having the effect of increasing rather than decreasing a tendency to irresponsible and lawless behaviour among the young and 'the family' in general – women in particular – looked conveniently available to be blamed.

These issues are addressed explicitly in Fyvel's book *The Insecure Offenders*, given the subtitle 'Rebellious Youth in the Welfare State'. It was published in 1961 and reflects very much the concerns of the period which we are discussing, in particular the idea that affluence has created its own problems. Young people are seen here as the *victims* of the welfare state, expressed most graphically in Teddy Boy culture:

> For some years, each Saturday and Sunday towards dusk, I used to witness a curious procession. From my distant window I could see small, dark figures of boys and half-grown youths, all of them wearing the identical Teddy Boy suits at that time in fashion. All of them, as if drawn by a magnet, made off in the same direction towards the main streets beyond the big railway stations ... aesthetically a God-awful wilderness, but to the boys obviously representing life with a capital L. (Fyvel, 1961, p.10)

The most visible sign that something was changing was the rising rates of juvenile crime and Fyvel reflects a common theme when he argues that the weakening of family life must be seen as a major cause of this. Increased rates of women's employment certainly play a prominent part in his analysis, although he, in company with other writers, is keen not to condemn this out of hand. However, 'everything has its price' and this trend has contributed to a 'new social atmosphere ... whereby "home" for many boys and girls becomes less important in their lives and the rules of the irresponsible gang therefore become more important' (ibid.: p. 129). Men are part of the problem too. Changes in the types of jobs which men do, in the employment of women, and in the greater capacity of teenagers to earn good wages all have 'diminished the status of the working-class father as head of the family', thus reducing men's capacity to exercise authority over their teenage children (ibid.: p. 130). One cannot help noticing that men are seen as the unwitting parties to the weakening of family life, whereas women are treated – at least in part – as active initiators of these changes through their desire to be in the labour market. In reflecting a sense of anxiety about these features of family life, most of the sociological literature seemed inclined to put up a spirited defence of a postwar family as a success story. In that sense, optimism was the more dominant theme, but, at the same time, there was an underlying uncertainty about what had really been created, a sense perhaps that there was more to the 'new' family than was meeting the sociological eye.

Anxieties about companionate marriage: the Royal Commission on Marriage and Divorce

The subtext of anxiety about marriage in sociological writing was mirrored in the postwar discussion of divorce which led to the setting up in 1951 of the Royal Commission on Marriage and Divorce (RCMD) which reported in 1955. Indeed the public debate generated by its publication was one major reason why sociologists felt the need to defend contemporary marriage and family life. The concern of the Commission focused on 'the large number of marriages which each year are ending in the divorce court' (Royal Commission on Marriage and Divorce, 1956, p. 39). The proportion of marriages terminated by divorce had risen from 1.6 per cent in 1937 to 7.1 per cent in 1950. It had sunk slightly from this high point, to 6.7 per cent in 1954, but had not returned to the prewar level (RCMD, 1956, p. 369).

The Commission was concerned to discover the causes of the higher divorce rate. Two factors made divorce more widely available. Changes in the law in 1937 made cruelty, insanity and desertion grounds for divorce for the first time (in addition to adultery). And the Legal Aid and Advice Act of 1949 provided help with the costs of divorce for those who could not previously have afforded it. The Commission considered that to some extent the postwar pattern was entirely understandable. Wartime pressures on marriage, notably 'over hasty' marriages and wartime separations, had led to a natural increase after the war. And there had been a sharp rise in 1952 because a 'backlog' of cases could now be brought under legal aid. But it was felt that the effects of war should have worked themselves out by the 1950s and that 1952 should have been an exceptional year which would not be repeated. Instead, the higher rate of divorce seemed to have become a permanent phenomenon. The report stated: 'Weighing all the evidence before us, we are satisfied that marriages are now breaking up which in the past would have held together' (RCMD, 1956, para. 42).

Why was this so? The 'complexities of modern life', the housing shortage and the falling average age of marriage were cited. But the Commission was most concerned about the 'greater demands' now made of marriage. Like the Royal Commission on Population (RCP), it presented modern marriage based on greater equality between the sexes in a favourable light, as a natural outcome of historical changes, particularly the emancipation of women: 'Women are no longer content to endure the treatment which in past times their inferior position obliged them to suffer. They expect of marriage that it shall be an equal partnership; and rightly so' (RCMD, 1956, para. 45). But just as the RCP feared that this kind of marriage was in some ways dysfunctional, since it had inevitably led to smaller families, so the RCMD feared that it gave rise to all kinds of pressures which threatened the viability of marriage itself. Though desirable, the companionate marriage was, in short, a high-risk venture:

The working out of this ideal exposes marriage to new strains. Some husbands find it difficult to accept the changed position of women; some wives do not appreciate that their new rights do not release them from the obligations arising out of marriage itself and, indeed, bring in their train certain new responsibilities. (Ibid.)

Just what these rights and responsibilities were, the Commission did not spell out, but it sounds as if its members meant by 'responsibilities' the conventional 'duties' of wives and mothers, which still needed to be performed even if a woman had a right to greater freedom to pursue the 'outside interests' stressed by the RCP and the paid work for which she was in demand in the labour market. The report asserted that the contemporary emphasis on sexual satisfaction had weakened restraints on extramarital sex and that the 'community' was more inclined to 'acquiesce' in divorce, especially in view of the growing tendency for public figures to resort to it.

Taken together, all these factors were leading couples to 'take the duties and responsibilities of marriage less seriously than formerly' even though companionate marriage made greater demands, such that 'more not less should be put into it' (ibid.: para. 47). The paternalistic recommendations of the Commission suggest an underlying lack of confidence in companionate marriage. The proposed solution for the rising tide of marriage failures was 'education in the widest sense' which could be achieved 'by specific instruction before marriage, and by providing facilities for guidance after marriage and for conciliation if breakdown threatens' (ibid.: para. 51). In a statement confusingly cast in the male gender (but presumably intended to embrace women as well as men in the universal 'he'), the Commission recommended that moral and social sanctions should be re-implanted. The ultimate remedy lay 'in fostering in the individual the will to do his duty by the community; in strengthening his resolution to make marriage a union for life; in inculcating a proper sense of his responsibility towards his children' (ibid.). As to the question of the availability of divorce, the Commission was evidently not united. On the one hand it stated the belief that making divorce more difficult to obtain would not stop marriages breaking down. But on the other hand it ended the first section of the report with a dire warning. The tendency 'to resort too readily and too lightly to divorce' might lead to the abandonment of 'the conception of marriage as a life-long union of one man with one woman' (ibid.: para. 54). If that happened some of those on the Commission believed it would be better to abolish divorce altogether.

Dissenting Voices: Titmuss and Gorer

The tone of the Report of the Royal Commission on Marriage and Divorce was both moralistic and in places hysterical, implying that the general optimism about companionate marriage was fundamentally misplaced. Meanwhile, most sociologists were inclined to put up a spirited defence of postwar changes, whilst demonstrating similar anxieties. There are other writers, however, who enable us to get a different perspective upon the reality of marriage in the 1940s and 1950s by taking a longer view and by writing in a way which does not betray an obvious investment in demonstrating that contemporary marriage was 'good' or 'bad'. The two writers whom we find helpful in this respect are R. M. Titmuss and Geoffrey Gorer.

R. M. Titmuss struck a note which challenged many of the assumptions of the RCMD. He saw plenty of problems in postwar marriage, but no grounds for serious anxiety. His analysis is so valuable because it was based on an understanding of the demographic changes which had taken place over the previous fifty years. This enables him to contextualize contemporary changes in a longer view. He identified five important factors: the fall in family size, the concentration of childbearing in the early years of marriage, the increasing life expectancy of women, the rising proportion of married women in the female population and the falling average age of marriage. The RCMD stated that 'matrimony...is not so secure as it was a hundred or even fifty years ago' (RCMD, 1956, para. 70, xii), but Titmuss argued that there was evidence that marriage had never been so popular. More marriage at an earlier average age had been accompanied by an increase in the years of married life experienced by married couples, since declining death rates meant people were married for longer. Moreover, in 1955 three-quarters of those who divorced also remarried (Titmuss, 1958, p. 100). And smaller and more concentrated families meant that couples had more years of married life without children to care for.

Titmuss noted that the ideology of marriage had changed profoundly since Victorian times: 'the idea of companionship in marriage is being substituted for the more sharply defined roles and codes of behaviour set by the Victorian patriarchal system' (ibid.: p. 98). In common with others reviewed above, he did not look into the implications of such a style for marital relations. Nor did he present his view of what companionate marriage might mean in practice. But he did state that the ideal created higher expectations which might not always be met, particularly in view of the demographic changes which meant that more people were 'exposed to the hazards of married life and childrearing' for longer (ibid.: p. 100). He focused on the particular problems confronting married women as a result of these changes. By the age of 40, a 1950s wife had typically completed her mothering role, but had 35 to 40 years of life ahead of her, and more opportunities both for spending money and for leisure than ever before. The tendency for older married women to engage in paid work was one response, but it was accompanied by two sorts of problems, the difficulty for such women to gain training or enter pensionable occupations, and the conflicts they encountered about their roles as 'mothers, wives and wage-earners' (ibid.: p. 102).

Taking all the social changes together, Titmuss regarded a higher marital failure rate as unsurprising (ibid.: p. 98). But he felt that those companionate marriages which did survive represented a higher level of marital achievement than hitherto. Rather than fearing change and moralizing about re-education in marital responsibilities as the RCMD had done, he pointed to the need for social policies which would support women in their new roles.

The other writer who represents something of a dissenting voice – though in a very different way from Titmuss – is Geoffrey Gorer. We draw here upon his survey published as *Exploring English Character* in 1955, which attempts to document the lived reality of people's lives and which contains some revealing evidence about the marital aspirations and achievements of both sexes in Britain in the 1950s. It sheds interesting light on the gendered nature of companionate marriage.

The ideology of companionate marriage might lead one to expect that men would have valued wives sharing their interests, but this was referred to by only 8 per cent of Gorer's sample. Top of the male list of 'qualities admired in spouses' was 'good housekeeper' (29 per cent) (Gorer, 1955, pp. 125–6). The RCMD's opinions might lead one to expect wives to value husbands who gave them freedom. But wives seemed to hanker after a companionate style defined according to their own interests, based on more involvement on the part of husbands in their wives' 'responsibilities'. The qualities most commonly valued by wives were 'understanding' (33 per cent), 'thoughtfulness' (28 per cent) and 'sense of humour' (21 per cent). As far as spouses' failings were concerned, men mentioned 'nagging, scolding, fault finding' most frequently (29 per cent), and women mentioned 'selfishness' (56 per cent) (ibid.: pp. 128–9). What did they mean by that? It was the 'domestic deficiencies' of men that most annoyed women, 'laziness, untidiness and meanness with money' (ibid.: p. 129).

The volume of female complaints about men's domestic shortcomings, and male complaints about 'nagging' coupled with men's stress on wives' qualities as housekeepers, suggest two things. First, expectations were frequently not fulfilled. Second, while women were increasingly keen on marriage which might be defined as companionate from a wife's point of view, implying an understanding husband who involved himself in domestic tasks and shared his income with her, relatively few men were interested in such a marriage, and many resented the pressure their wives put them under to achieve it.

What one gets from both Gorer and Titmuss (though in very different ways) is a realism about the nature of the changes which actually were occurring in the 1950s and a sense of what it is sensible to expect of marriages, given prevailing social and economic conditions.

Conclusion

The ideology of marriage which has been drawn from the various bodies of literature examined in this chapter did not have at its core a concept of marriage as an 'equal partnership'. The literatures of pronatalism and motherhood, sexuality, education and employment did not in fact subscribe to such an ideal, even though the marital norm running through it was of companionate marriage, sometimes described as 'teamwork'. As we have seen, the cumulative picture that can be derived from such literature is of modern marriages which were far from symmetrical. Husbands were expected to be more considerate and might now tolerate their wives doing paid, part-time work outside the home, but they were still to be principal breadwinners. Otherwise very little was said about their role in marriage. The new expectations were heaped on wives, who were to be more comradely, and might be permitted to have outside interests, but were also to be better mothers of larger families, better sexual partners and better home-makers. They were only to take on paid work if they could do so without either making their children psychotic or neurotic, or detracting from their domestic duties. Sociological studies tended to reflect the same expectations, whilst giving very positive support to ideas about partnership in marriage and mostly portraying contemporary family life as a success story.

The reality of the lived experience of marriage in the 1940s and 1950s remains somewhat elusive although – as Titmuss pointed out – marriage had never been so popular in statistical terms as it was in the postwar period. The image of marriage as an equal partnership may well have been very attractive, but the evidence which we have discussed suggests quite strongly that, in reality, it imposed particular pressures upon women. Picking up on the limits in Gorer's research, we suggest that there was a profound dissonance between the postwar ideology of companionate marriage in which the benefits were all on the husband's side, and the lived experience in which wives were striving, evidently not successfully, for a companionate marriage which worked to their advantage.

ACKNOWLEDGEMENTS

We should like to thank Susan White for her enthusiastic typing and David Morgan and Oliver Fulton for their critical comments.

REFERENCES

Birmingham Feminist History Group (1979), 'Feminism as femininity in the 1950s?', *Feminist Review* 3.

Board of Education (1943), *Curriculum and Examinations in Secondary Schools* (Norwood Report), London: HMSO.

Bott, E. (1957), *Family and Social Network*, London: Tavistock.

Bowlby, J. (1952), *Maternal Care and Mental Health*, Geneva: World Health Organization.

Central Advisory Council for Education (1959), *15 to 18* (Crowther Report), London: HMSO.

Coates, K. and Silburn, R. (1971) *Poverty: The Forgotten Englishmen*, Harmondsworth: Penguin.

Delphy, C. (1984), *Close to Home*, London: Hutchinson.

Dennis, N., Henriques, F. and Slaughter, C. (1956), *Coal is our Life*, London: Tavistock.

Ferguson, A. (1989), *Blood at the Root: Motherhood, Sexuality and Male Dominance*, London: Pandora.

Fletcher, R. (1962), *Marriage and the Family in Britain*, Harmondsworth: Penguin.

Fyvel, T. (1961), *The Insecure Offenders*, London: Chatto & Windus (reprinted by Penguin in 1963).

Gorer, G. (1955), *Exploring English Character*, London: Cresset Press.

Hubback, E. (1947), *The Population of Britain*, London: Allen & Unwin.

Kinsey, A. C., Pomeroy, W. B., Martin, C. E. and Gebhard, P. H. (1953), *Sexual Behavior in the Human Female*, Philadelphia: Saunders.

Klein, J. (1965), *Samples from English Cultures*, vol. II, London: Routledge & Kegan Paul.

Mass Observation (1945), *Britain and Her Birthrate*, London: Advertising Services Guild.

Ministry of Education (1949), *Report of a Working Party on the Supply of Women Teachers*, London: HMSO.

Ministry of Education (1960), *The Youth Service in England and Wales* (Albermarle Report), London: HMSO.

Morgan, D. (1991), 'Ideologies of marriage and family life', in D. Clark (ed.), *Marriage, Domestic Life and Social Change*, London: Routledge.

Newsom, J. (1948), *The Education of Girls*, London: Faber & Faber.

Parsons, T. and Bales, R. (1956), *Family: Socialisation and Interaction Process*, London: Routledge & Kegan Paul.

Patterson, S. (1963), *Dark Strangers: A Sociological Study of the Absorption of a Recent West Indian Migrant Group in Brixton, South London*, Bloomington: Indiana University Press.

Riley, D. (1983), *War in the Nursery: Theories of the Child and Mother*, London: Virago.

Rowntree, B. S. and Lavers, G. R. (1951), *English Life and Leisure*, London: Longman.

Royal Commission on Marriage and Divorce (RCMD) (1956), *Report*, Cmd. 9678, London: HMSO.

Royal Commission on Population (RCP) (1949), *Report*, Cmd. 7695, London: HMSO.

Smith, J. H. (1961), 'Managers and married women workers', *British Journal of Sociology*, 12: 12–22.

Spinley, B. (1953), *The Deprived and the Privileged*, London: Routledge & Kegan Paul.

Summerfield, P. (1984), *Women Workers in the Second World War: Production and Patriarchy in Conflict*, London: Croom Helm.

Thomas, G. (1948), *Women and Industry: An Inquiry into the Problem of Recruiting Women to Industry Carried Out for the Ministry of Labour and National Service, the Social Survey*, London: Central Office of Information.

Thane, P. (1982), *The Foundations of the Welfare State*, London: Longman.

Titmuss, R. M. (1958), *Essays on the Welfare State*, London: Unwin.

Townsend, P. (1954), 'Measuring poverty', *British Journal of Sociology*, 5: 130–7.

Willmott, P. and Young, M. (1960), *Family and Class in a London Suburb*, London: Routledge & Kegan Paul.

Winnicott, D. W. (1957), *The Child and His Family: First Relationships*, London: Tavistock.

Young, M. and Willmott, P. (1957), *Family and Kinship in East London*, London: Routledge & Kegan Paul (reprinted by Penguin in 1962).

Young, M. and Willmott, P. (1973), *The Symmetrical Family*, London: Routledge & Kegan Paul.

2

Liberalizing Heterosexuality?

Gail Hawkes

From the mid-twentieth century onwards, distinctive features became evident in sexual mores and sexual behaviour, the essence of which is the now familiar epitaph, 'the swinging sixties'. In popular imagination, the decade of the 1960s in modern industrial societies is specifically associated with sexual liberation. The decade has its own iconography – the mini-skirt, flowers, long hair, public nudity, hallucinogenic drugs. All were the domain of the young and all directly or indirectly involved or entailed open confrontation of the sexual mores of the previous generation. Young people of this period adopted sex just as their own children were to adopt recreational drugs as a marker of the boundary between their world and that of their parents. There was both truth and oversimplifica tion in this popular understanding. The 'truth' was that there was something distinctively different in the construction of heterosexuality in the second half of the twentieth century; the oversimplification lay in the assumption that, quali- tatively, different equalled better.

The most obvious feature of the liberalization of heterosexuality in retrospect was the uncoupling of sex from marriage and reproduction. While the avail- ability of the contraceptive pill was one principal factor in this shift, it will be suggested that the disengaging of sex from marital monogamy entailed more complex processes, of which the development of the contraceptive pill was one crucial element. The second distinctive feature of the liberalization of heterosexuality was its relationship with the commodification of desire. It has already been suggested (Hawkes, 1996) that legitimate sexual acts and sexual pleasures were those which corresponded to the Fordist production process – repetitive and reproducible detailed tasks with a single endpoint in mind, mutual orgasm. In this sense, sex might be understood as a product, an outcome of a preordained labour process. Planned, pleasurable, ordered sex was thus the reflection of a wider socio-economic ethos of planning, and one which reflected the prevailing ideological organization of the work process.

This chapter suggests that the liberalization of heterosexuality reflected many of the features of 'flexible accumulation' – an organization of the work process that was dependent on rapidly manufactured and short-lived consumption patterns for its viability. In order to fan flagging demand in a market saturated with 'consumer durables', products and, increasingly, ideas were promoted not for their utilitarian characteristics, but for more esoteric and fleeting, even at first sight irrelevant, associations. The common feature in the promotion of the qualities of the products on offer was the emphasis placed on 'choice' and the implication that making such a choice was a vital element in shaping, even creating, the self. 'Choice' became the lifeblood of late capitalism, a motif that was as dynamic and all-pervasive as its predecessor – 'rationality'.

The third distinguishing feature of liberalizing heterosexuality was the some-times complex role played by women in challenging – both theoretically and in practice – the long-established and insidiously effective construction of sexual pleasure, which was, they argued, male-defined, male-centred and, quite simply, wrong. The final feature is the implication that heterosexuality has ceased to be a fixed terrain, interlocking gendered desire and institutions of lifetime marriage or long-standing monogamy. The work of Anthony Giddens will be reviewed and examined in this regard, particularly the potential of his reflexive selves and plastic sexuality to offer a truly liberalized heterosexuality.

Uncoupling Sex

The permissive era's object was to recruit women into active engagement in heterosexuality. (Campbell, 1982, p. 136)

The 1960s and 1970s put sex on the market as an element of human life, which was not necessarily, nor even desirably, to be spoken about in the same breath as marriage, reproduction and monogamy. Yet at the same time, this 'uncoup-ling' of sex entailed more conservative elements, which continued to bind women, and their sexuality, to revamped but recognizably male-orientated heterosexuality.

Uncoupled sex at first sight was the antithesis of the previously promoted marital sex. Marital sex implicitly supported the stereotype of the supportive yet passive sexual hygienist, the wife whose responsibility was the sexual house-keeping of her husband. Marital sex was at least potentially reproductive sex and, despite the enthusiastic promotion of suitably contained sexual pleasure, essentially *respectable* sex. The respectability lay largely in the fact that however much emphasis was placed on sexual pleasure, the pleasure was contained within the fixed framework of a monogamous partnership, and reinforced by the ideology of 'the family' as the only legitimate site of reproduc-tion.

But the security of this framework was beginning to fracture in the postwar years. The challenges came from a number of directions. First, there was a slow yet steady escalation of the economy, with an accompanying increased demand for labour to full employment. With the economic independence that this offered, women were less likely to see marriage as the only reliable source of economic security for the future as well as the present. Second, and relatedly, full employment offered the young unprecedented and early independence from their parents and the constraints of the parental home. The moral distance between parent and offspring made possible by both full employment and the 1947 Education Act's recruits to higher education, opened up a space in which an alternative teenage culture flourished.

In the 1960s, and in contrast to its former reluctance to involve itself in moral issues, the state enacted a series of statutes that were specifically moral in their subject matter if not their intent. Divorce, contraception, pornography, homosexuality and abortion were all the focus of legislation designed to confront uncomfortable yet unavoidable social issues. The unprecedented involvement of the state in the apparent promotion rather than restriction of sexual freedom was consistent with the postwar ethos of the benevolent pluralist state whose task was to balance and mediate between opposing factions in the interests of the 'greater good'. Christie Davies (1980) has argued that in regard to the Acts relating directly or indirectly to sexual morality, rather than actively promoting more relaxed sexual mores, the state was concerned to avoid the worst consequences of continued non-intervention on these issues: illegal abortions, unwanted pregnancies, fragmented families. The legislation was driven by pre-existing and increasingly evident problems relating to these aspects of sexual behaviour, rather than seeking actively to swing public actions or opinions. The 'negative utilitarianism' that Davies outlines sought to provide a limited legal framework in which the troubling consequences of illegality of abortion, contraception and homosexuality could be avoided.

Notwithstanding these changes, the central moral frameworks remained largely intact. Homosexuality continued to be marginalized as a sexual choice by the caveat of 'consenting adults in private'. Public displays of same-sex love were still illegal. Abortion and contraception were permissible in specific and straightened circumstances and remained under the jurisdiction of the medical profession.

Yet this legislation reflected and implicitly condoned the uncoupling of 'acceptable sex' from marriage and the heterosexual reproductive couple. In a context of full employment and the increasing economic and political profile of young people, attention shifted to a more serious scrutiny of their sexuality. Once denied or ignored, young people's sexuality had become a 'social problem'. In 1964, the British Medical Association published a report on the connection between venereal disease and sexual promiscuity among the young. This was the impetus for the commissioning of the first study of sexual behaviour in young people by Michael Schofield, published in 1965. Schofield found that at the age of eighteen, 34 per cent of boys and 17 per cent of girls were sexually experienced (Schofield, 1965, p. 223). His findings suggested that the changes in sexual behaviour reflected an autonomous teenage subculture whose basis was the cinema and a 'media-created image' of how young people ought to behave (ibid.: pp. 234–5).

Though the availability of contraception was initially restricted to married women, by 1975 the DHSS drafted a circular to local health authorities encouraging them to provide contraception advice and treatment to all women regardless of marital status or age. The impetus behind this quietly radical departure from traditional anxieties was not a commitment to sexual freedom, but concerns about escalating abortion and premarital pregnancy figures, particularly among young women. The circular was also a tacit acknowledgement of a slow but persistent trend in extramarital sexual experience that had been evident since the interwar years, but which had been fed by the flowering of a sub-culture of economically independent young people.

The state-sanctioned relaxation of sexual mores, and in particular the availability of reliable contraception that women themselves could choose, suggested a full frontal attack on the traditional parameters of the formerly impervious heterosexual hegemony. Wider sexual experience was at least condoned, at most positively encouraged. Even firmly mainstream sexologists like Alex Comfort and Helena Wright were, by the 1960s, extolling the advantages of premarital sex with more than one partner. In the wake of the work of Kinsey et al. (1948, 1953) and Masters and Johnson (1966, 1970), the 'scientific truth' of women's active sexuality could no longer be denied. The clitoris had been let out of the closet and would not be returned. The 'discovery' and then celebration of women's sexual prowess was, from the beginning, a double-edged sword. On the one hand, it finally dispelled the myth of sexual anaesthesia promoted so vigorously in the previous century. Women no longer had to deny their desires and feelings. On the other, this discovery of the scientists of sex (no doubt not so much of a discovery for many women) was immediately expropriated as the principal component of a new construction of women's sexuality by men.

The theme of this new discourse was, if women were blessed with this magical path to multiple orgasm it was their duty to use it. The attainment of sexual pleasure became the new marker of liberated femininity. What might have offered the key to sexual autonomy for women was subordinated in the service of promoting, even rejuvenating, the heterosexual coital imperative. The enthusiasm with which this discovery was received was fuelled by the incorporation of the pursuits of sexual pleasure into the radical programmes of what might be called the new Utopian socialists. The work of Reich and Marcuse promoted the central role of active engagement in sexual and orgasmic freedom in the confrontation of the disenchanted and dehumanized consequences of twentieth-century capitalism (Robinson, 1972; Weeks, 1985, pp. 157–77). This revolutionary potential of sexual pleasure became the popular motif of challenges to the Establishment, expressed through the media of theatre, novels, music and fashion.

As Lynne Segal (1987) has pointed out, this about-face in sexual mores was experienced as 'liberating' for those who came to adulthood in this period. Yet its siren call enticed many for too long to remain uncritical of the hidden agenda. But the enthusiastic promotion of women's sexual freedom within a male-defined paradigm had a number of unforeseen consequences; within less than a decade, women began to question the reality of the much vaunted 'freedom to fuck'. And they did so from a variety of political positions and experiences.

Perhaps the first consequence was that there was a specific separation of experiential spheres for women. The degree to which women could explore the possibilities of sexual autonomy was dependent on whether or not they were married and, in particular, whether they were mothers. In one sphere, there was 'the single girl', free, swinging, sexually uncomplicated and protected by the pill. This woman occupied a sphere of economic independence, though not one which equalled male counterparts. Her social independence was marked by living arrangements, by disposable income not drained by responsibility to parents or children – a world that was increasingly commodified, packaged and sold as desirable and a statement of personal freedom. The promoted figure in this sphere was a 'new woman' whose sexuality was not draped in the respectable garb of motherhood or modest femininity. This new woman was promoted as an unashamed and enthusiastic 'sexual consumer'.

In 1962 a book was published that was to become the bible for many women (much as they might want to forget it now!) who had embraced the lifestyle of the 'working girl'. *Sex and the Single Girl*, written by Helen Gurley Brown, later to become the American editor of *Cosmopolitan*, unashamedly offered sex as an essential element in the lifestyle choice of single women. For Gurley Brown (1962, p. 75), premarital chastity was 'a cultural blight', the suppression of women's 'natural predilection to be sexy'. 'Being sexy' was what this book and a generation of its progenitors was to sell women:

> Liking men is sexy. It is, by and large, the sexiest thing you can do. But I mean really liking, not pretending. And there is a lot more to it than simply wagging your tail every time a man pats you on the head. You must wag your tail, of course – his collie dog does *that* much – but there are about five thousand more aggressive ways to demonstrate liking, none of which is dashing along to the nearest motel. You must spend time plotting how to make him happier. Not just him ... *them!* (Gurley Brown, 1962, p. 90)

Being sexy often had little to do, directly, with 'having sex'. In the hiatus of the 1960s, between the dismantling of traditional constraints and the emergence of second-wave feminism, being sexy was, as Linda Grant (1993, p. 119) put it, 'smart, not sluttish'. Being sexy entailed fine-tuning and monitoring of make-up, dress, entertainment patterns, living arrangements, even what car one drove.

In retrospect, the logic of this promoting of independent sexiness for women was contradictory. Ostensibly aimed to confront Gurley Brown's suburban married 'mouseburger' with the single independent mistress of her own life, this bible of lifestyle imposed a new set of imperatives which sexualized *every* aspect of women's existence. The single working girl had become another figure in the landscape of a manufactured market, this time not for efficient domestic appliances but for an endless variety of accoutrements with which to ensure 'sexiness' – the signifiers of which were as traditional and male-orientated as those which accompanied the figure of the erotic housewife.

However, this upfront, dynamic, commercialized sphere had a more shadowy and more distressing counterpart, epitomized in the contexts of the newly built, out-of-town suburbs. The homogeneous and untroubled appearance of the neat house hid the unhappiness and frustration of the women for whom this was life. The figure in this sphere is one who received less attention unless it was ridicule and disbelief. For these women epitomized femininity, motherhood and the perpetuation of the traditional gendered roles. Why, then, would they not be happy? In the post-Freudian world, these were the winners in the biological and cultural race, those who were able to realize their full feminine potentials. These women were also targets for the image-makers, who romanticized the chintz-walled prison until the inhabitants began to believe that their lack of enthusiasm for this nirvana was an indication of physical or mental disorders (Friedan, 1965).

Mature Western capitalism drove the commodification of sex in this hard-sell of individual freedom, which was an integral part of the production not just of goods and services, but also of needs, wants and moralities. A central element in this production was the manipulation of women and their sexuality. As Juliet Mitchell (1971, p. 42) has argued, 'women were used, sexually and aesthetically to sell themselves to themselves'.

For what it promoted, as the Gurley Brown extracts show (which typify the tone of her book, and to a great extent the age), was that sexual freedom, defined simplistically as more sex, opened the door for women to enjoy equal participation in sexual citizenship. The structural obstacles that had been the pillars supporting patriarchal domination for centuries had been draped in new cloth, but their presence and to a large extent their function remained. While these were more easily disguised in the hard-sell of swinging sexiness directed towards the newly economically independent single girl, they remained in high profile in the experience of women who followed the still well-cleared path to marriage and maternity.

In many ways, the housewife and mother was redundant in late capitalism. Much of the traditional domestic labour was dismantled by technological advances, although this proceeded more rapidly in the USA than in Britain (Mitchell, 1971, p. 138). If the late capitalist family had left any role for women unrelieved by technology, it was motherhood. If one doubts that, still in the late twentieth century, a full-time mother is not encouraged to rank sexual desire high in her life profile, one should consult the monthly journals whose titles – *Good Housekeeping, Parent* – suggest their readers exemplify this category. The separation of spheres, evident in the ideological sell as much as in the experience, desexualized motherhood.

The dark side of this reconstruction of women's experience and context are graphically depicted in the work of Betty Friedan in the USA and Hannah Gavron in Britain (Friedan, 1965; Gavron, 1966). While there were some distinctions between the details of the lives lived by women who were 'captive wives and housebound mothers' (Gavron, 1966), there were striking and disturbing commonalities. Women were disproportionately suffering from depression, tranquillizer and alcohol dependency, as well as other less specified mental disorders. For the still male-dominated medical profession, this was evidence of women rejecting their biologically determined female roles. However, the unthinking acceptance of the rhetoric of sexual freedom blighted the lives of a significant proportion of a generation of women.

In the celebrations that accompanied the decline of traditional constraints, these women were forgotten, or viewed as objects of pity – even sometimes by their sisters. But the 'natural homemaker' and the 'sexual hygienist' were to produce their own 'sites of resistance'. As Friedan (1965, p. 9) put it, 'there was a strange discrepancy between the reality of our lives as women and the image to which we were trying to conform'. In addition to Friedan's work, *The Female Eunuch* (Greer, 1970) and *The Second Sex* (De Beauvoir, 1972, p. 72) spoke passionately to women's experience across the boundaries of nation and class.

Though not solely or even predominantly concerned with *sexual* liberation, these hugely influential books and the equally influential grassroots responses they engendered, collectively and individually cleared the ground for the airing of women's experiences *by women*, not by men or male experts. By opening the floodgates to women who spoke the language of sexual autonomy, they confronted the male-defined and male-centred sexuality integral to the system that had produced the 'problem which had no name'.

The unintended consequence of liberalizing heterosexuality was that the process produced its own central contradiction (or antithesis), embodied in the feminist challenge and critique of liberalized sex. Second-wave feminism challenged assumptions about women's sexual, social and political roles in the public and private spheres. The centrality of patriarchy as the form of domination central to women's oppression led directly to a challenge to patriarchal sexual relations. The issue of abortion as a woman's choice, and the campaigns against pornography and sexual violence against women, all had as their centre the predominance of the assumptions about male sexuality and its expression, whether this took place in the privacy of the bedroom or on cinema screens. These assumptions, which gave male sexuality primacy, had not, feminists argued, been eroded with the apparent dismantling of old prudish and repressive views about sex. The availability of contraception and the relaxation of sexual mores likewise did not free women to a world of sexual autonomy. The changes simply made women more sexually available and more vulnerable to exploitation in the name of (male-defined) sexual freedom. Feminism sought to reclaim women's bodies from the male-orientated medical spheres, which continued to monitor women's reproductive capacities. Women were also reclaiming their *sexual* bodies by gaining dominion over their erotic potentials. Just as sexual politics were central to patriarchy, so sexual politics were mobilized to confront it. Women were encouraged to explore and celebrate their sexual autonomy, independently of men.

The trajectory this took was complicated, and at times contradictory. The work of Masters and Johnson has been suggested to have been of central importance in the promotion of a *woman's* sexuality, as defined by, and in relation to, women (Robinson, 1976, p. 158). Yet their promotion of sexual and more importantly orgasmic equality with men never really escaped from the directive quality of earlier sex manuals (Segal, 1993, pp. 98ff.). For Masters and Johnson, there remained in the celebration of women's sexuality, the strong suggestion of a duty in the pursuit of the holy grail of the orgasm – a sort of sexual housekeeping that implicitly retained the primacy of male-defined sexuality. Yet Segal also argues that, following Masters and Johnson, there appeared a body of 'feminist sex research' that called on the language of bodily sovereignty: 'Over and over again, women were told by one expert after another "it's *your* choice, *your* body, *your* responsibility" ... These women experts were also confident that women's sexual independence and fulfilment, seen as a type of learned competence would spread to other areas of a woman's life' (Segal, 1993, p. 103).

Despite the fact that the much vaunted sexual freedom of women was circumscribed by, and retained deference to, a male-defined coital imperative, the active promotion of this 'freedom' provided a space within which women could speak to women about sex. The pioneers of this trend were Shere Hite and Nancy Friday, whose books charted in respondents' own words the sexual landscapes in reality and fantasy of thousands of women. However, evaluation of the content and effectiveness of these books is complicated. In one respect, they were ground-breaking in that the voices of the experts (for the most part male) appeared to have been, at least temporarily, silenced. While meticulously researched and presented, *The Hite Report* (Hite, 1976) and *My Secret Garden* (Friday, 1976) offered many women a sexual sphere of their own, through which, possibly for the first time, they could explore their sexual bodies. Yet, at the same time, as Segal has pointed out, women's sexual responsiveness remained closely associated with the behavioural models of mainstream sexology. Moreover, though opening up a sexual sphere for women, their enthusiastic exhortations to explore and achieve self-attained sexual pleasure fed the commercialization of women's sexuality by retaining the sexual, if not coital, imperative as an almost compulsory central element in their sexual citizenship. Finally, there was, despite some inclusion of same-sex desire, an implicit prioritization of heterosexual sexual choice, an aspect of the liberalization of heterosexuality that was the focus of radical feminist challenges.

The apparent creation of an autonomous sexual sphere for women had duped women into seeing as freedom what was in fact a more sophisticated form of sexual slavery. The situation called for radical measures to be taken and, given the analysis, the logical response was the sexual rejection of men. Women who emulated male heterosexual freedoms were colluding in their own repression and in that of their sisters. For women, liberalized heterosexuality was 'sleeping with the enemy', and a real challenge to patriarchal domination required the rejection of heterosexuality as its most effective script for sexual regulation (Onlywoman Press, 1981; Coveney et al., 1984). The processes involved in the uncoupling of sex indirectly opened up a space for the affirmation of fully autonomous sexuality that consciously rejected heterosexuality itself. This development is discussed as an element in a movement of sexual resistance in Hawkes (1996, chapter 8).

The uncoupling of sex thus had both operated to reinforce and to provide the basis for a challenge to the heterosexual hegemony. But it was also a crucial element in the shaping of late twentieth-century discourses around sex: one which was directly related to the emerging centrality of individual choice in the context of flexible accumulation and the accompanying manipulation of consumption.

From Sex as Production to Sex as Consumption

A second element in the conditional liberalization of heterosexuality was the promotion of individual choice as an almost moral imperative. In the logic of Fordist mass production, the issue of choice was secondary to that of availability and usefulness. The famous maxim, 'Any colour provided it is black', testifies to this. The manipulation of demand for manufactured goods entailed the promotion of the use value of the products. People were encouraged to buy washing machines, cookers, toasters and vacuum cleaners because they made domestic labour less physically onerous. Other goods were promoted for their contribution to the quality of life or the maximization of pleasure. There was, in promotional advertising, a direct relationship made between the product and the outcome of its purchase. Fordist mass production demanded 'appropriate consistencies of individual behaviours with the schema of reproduction...*a mode of regulation*' (Harvey, 1989, p. 122). This mode of regulation extended to spheres beyond the immediate site of production. Gramsci suggested that the regulation of sexuality and of sexual behaviour in specific ways was a necessary element in the sustenance of the mass production techniques of Fordism. Specifically, he argued that the sexual lives of workers cannot be left to the vagaries of whim or desire. Just as the activities of the worker in the work process must be carefully shaped towards the given end, so their appetites outside the workplace must reflect the prevailing ideology of ordered rational action.

> It is worth drawing attention to the way in which industrialists (and Ford in particular) have been concerned with the sexual affairs of their employees and with their family arrangements in general. One should not be misled, any more than in the case of prohibition, by the 'puritanical' appearance assumed by this concern. The truth is that a new type of man demanded by the rationalization of production and work cannot be developed until the sexual instinct has been suitably regulated and until it too has been rationalized. (Gramsci, 1971, p. 297)

Changes in the organization of production, from mass production to flexible accumulation, brought with it a new organization of the work process and an accompanying new mode of regulation. Just-in-time delivery systems, small-batch production, intensification of the labour process and the re-skilling and restructuring of the workforce process to adapt to both new technologies and the requirements of the rapidly changing consumption demands, marked the distinctiveness of flexible work processes.

Gramsci's essay, *Americanism and Fordism*, draws attention to the symbiotic relationship between the economic, political and social processes in the capitalist mode of production, and to the myriad of threads, often unseen, which connect them. A world dominated by the requirements of flexible accumulation demands another 'new type of person', achieved through the ideological shaping of expectations and motives in the life spheres beyond the workplace. Harvey has argued that in relation to the consumption patterns of goods and services, the distinctive feature is one of short-lived and ephemeral demands:

> The dynamics of 'throwaway society', as writers like Alvin Toffler (1970) dubbed it, began to be evident during the 1960s. It meant more than just throwing away produced goods...but also being able to throw away values, lifestyles, stable relationships and attachments to things, buildings, places, people, and received ways of doing and being. (Harvey, 1989, p. 286)

The significance of the product in relation to the individual self-identity is the central dynamic of the rapid changes in demands. At the centre of a 'culture of imagery' lies the advertising industry, whose effectiveness is dependent on the communicability of images and what they signify. 'Given the ability to produce images as commodities more or less at will, it becomes feasible for accumulation to proceed at least in part on the basis of pure image production and marketing' (ibid.: p. 289). Harvey argues that the distance of the images from the 'reality' of the product from which they are derived, gives the consumer the illusion that purchase of the goods is, in fact, an indication of free choice and individual distinctiveness.

Bauman (1989) points out there is a more depressing dimension to this marketing of delusion. Consumers have become dependent on the very endlessness of choices in the purveyance of imagery. The selling of products as a panacea for sexual insecurity, anxieties about parenthood, even the effectiveness of our ability to communicate socially, bind us to the values of the system in more insidious ways. The very failure of the goods to deliver these promises keeps alive, Bauman argues, the hope that the next 'improved version' will:

> The role of new products consists mainly in outdating the products of yesterday; together with the 'old' goods disappears the memory of their unfulfilled promises...Jean Baudrillard said of fashion that it 'embodies the compromise between the need to innovate and the other need to change nothing in the fundamental order'. We would rather shift the emphasis: fashion seems to be the mechanism through which the 'fundamental order' (market dependency) is maintained by a never ending chain of innovations; the very perpetuity of innovation renders their individual (and inevitable) failures irrelevant and harmless to the order. (Bauman, 1989, p. 165)

For Bauman, market dependency occurs at three different levels. First, new commodities create their own necessities' (ibid.: p. 164). Second, market dependence is created by the 'progressive destruction of social skills...the ability and willingness of men and women to enter social relations, maintain them and repair them in case of conflicts'. In place of stable long-standing social relationships, which may run the gamut from friend to lover or life-partner, this element of market dependency leads us to seek fulfilment, distraction and self-discovery in products of the market, be they sound production systems, therapy or exotic holidays. In this bleak landscape, our relationships with people are increasingly restricted to their 'bit-player' roles in this highly 'individualized' market-led process. Finally, the dependence on goods and services deepens to a dependence on the market itself, a belief that

> for every human problem there is a solution waiting somewhere in the shop, and that the one skill men and women need more than anything else is the ability to find it. This conviction makes consumers still more attentive to the goods and their promises, so that dependency may perpetuate and deepen. (Ibid.)

With these insights in mind, re-examining the liberalization 'thesis' suggests its equation with what amounts to a market of heterosexual sex. Products, imagery, how-to-do-it directives, expert advice in magazines, newspapers or on television, 'special-interest' sex guide videos and books have all proliferated since the mid-twentieth century. The outstanding feature of all of these is the simultaneous emphasis on individual choice and the advantages of conformity to the 'latest fashion' in sexual expression. It might be argued that this market in sex, with its increasing promotion of disembodied eroticism evident in the short-lived almost vicarious nature of the discourses, has replaced that of sex in stable, fixed, more socially embedded relationships. The market in sex presents an ever-changing panorama of choices in which the individual is encouraged to construct their own identity through a form of erotic 'window-shopping'. One possible consequence of a market dependency in relation to sexuality would be that involvement in the choice of, and identity with, sexual imagery would become more significant than what is *done* sexually.

The liberalization of heterosexuality in the context of the transition from 'sex as production' to 'sex as consumption' is more illusion than reality. The choices that are for some the indicators of freedom are in fact a more subtle form of regulation through the myth of individual autonomy inherent in consumer choice. Belief in the disentanglement of individual sexual expression from the constraining contexts of permanency or monogamy, as erotica is increasingly expropriated by the directors of the 'image culture', is central to the effectiveness, both economic and cultural, of 'choice'.

Lifestyle Sex and the 'Reflexive Project of the Self'

In the introduction to his *Modernity and Self-Identity*, Giddens (1991) tells us that late modernity offers us, and perhaps can even be defined by, a proliferation of 'lifestyle choices', through which we reflexively constitute our self-identity:

> The reflexive project of the self, which consists in the sustaining of coherent, yet continuously revised, biographical narratives, takes place in the context of multiple choice as filtered through abstract systems. In modern social life the notion of lifestyle takes on a particular significance. (Giddens, 1991, p. 5)

The crucial characteristic of the dynamics of the project of self and lifestyle choice lies not just in its reflexivity, but in the degree to which we are conscious agents of those choices. 'All human beings continuously monitor the circumstances of their activities as a feature of doing what they do and such monitoring always has discursive features' (ibid.: p. 35). While Giddens concedes that such activities and perceptions take place within, and are in part reflective of, the material conditions of late capitalism, he suggests that the outcome of the choices and discursive practices are not structured by these in orthodox ways:

> In some circumstances of poverty, the hold of tradition has perhaps been more thoroughly disintegrated than elsewhere.... Lifestyle habits are constructed through the resistance of ghetto life as well as through the direct elaboration of distinctive cultural styles and modes of activities. (Ibid.: p. 86)

For Giddens, one distinguishing feature of high modernity is the dissolution of the hierarchically ordered distinction between experts and lay audience. In this former arrangement, there was a one-way channel of knowledge and experience from the active 'educators' to the passive 'educatees'. In high modernity, the relationship becomes reflexive, a two-way process. This reflexivity lies in the proliferation of expertise associated with all aspects of daily life on the one hand, and the active participation of the agent engaged in the project of the 'self' on the other.

The second particularity of late modernity is that while the individual is confronted with a 'complex diversity of choices' (ibid.: p. 80), these exist independently of a more traditional context that might shape or influence the choices along more traditional lines (e.g. class trajectories). In one sense, then, the 'choice' is not a choice in that one cannot choose between inaction (leaving things 'as they are') and the alternative(s) on offer. For there is no meaningful state of 'things as they are'. Late modernity lacks the traditional frameworks that allow for the inheritance of lifestyle. In these conditions, lifestyles must be adopted through choice (ibid.: p. 81). In a commonsense understanding, 'lifestyle' is defined by consumer choices. In Giddens's work, lifestyle is not an endpoint but a process, one which entails the *creation* of self in the context of a multiplicity of choices. It is not just the act of choice but the process of getting there that lies at the core of self-identity.

Lifestyle choices are constituted, first, by the existence of the context in which they are to be made. For example, to choose to smoke cigarettes in the context of evidence relating to ill-health is a 'lifestyle choice'. Second, they are constituted through our existence in a multiplicity of parallel worlds: work-place, family, friendships, sexual relationships. The domains of the public and private are no longer recognizably distinct but, to a greater or lesser degree depending on the context, overlap. Third, post-Enlightenment certainties about the permanency of scientifically legitimated knowledge have been replaced with a much less secure notion of 'until further notice' contingencies. Finally, choice takes place against a background of 'mediated experience', an increasingly virtual reality made possible by globalization of images and information. These conditions apply to the phenomenon of lifestyle choice irrespective of the individual capacity to participate.

The universality of these conditions which Giddens emphasizes, constitutes the structural conditions under which choice in late modernity is constituted. The absence of the more fixed, traditional frameworks within which we *experienced* rather than *created* our identity, has conferred upon the body a new role and meaning. In a context in which our identity, sexual or in other contexts, is not a given:

> Body regimes and the organization of sensuality in high modernity become open to continuous referential attention against the backdrop of a plurality of choice. Both life-planning and the adoption of lifestyle become (in principle) interpreted within bodily regimes. (Ibid.: p. 102)

In what has been said so far, the body has been a constant presence. Sometimes eroticized, sometimes dissected, ignored or celebrated, hidden or exposed, the body in modernity has been, to use Foucault's terminology, both the 'object of knowledge' and the 'subject of power'. In high modernity, Giddens argues, the body itself has been disengaged from the fixities and certainties of the 'categories of givens'. It has become an integral and flexible element in the process of the self, both in the way we experience living in it and the ways in which we deploy it as identity in material form. This potential for active use of the body in the shaping of self can be seen in the management of appearance, of dress and adornment, and of how and in what ways we choose to experience pleasure (or pain). This experience and presentation of self draws from, and feeds back into, the proliferation of regimes – the ever-present guides for the proper management of self. What is distinctive about these regimes, Giddens's work suggests, is that they no longer operate as regulatory blueprints, underpinned by fixed notions of either/or, right or wrong, pathological and normal.

Illustrating Consumer Sex

The lifestyle journals that line the walls of newsagents might be seen as evidence of the ever-widening choices made available by the march of technological advance. In these 'bibles' of ever-increasing range, the distinction between advertisement and feature articles becomes increasingly blurred.

The tone in which the 'advice and guidance' is communicated lays stress, explicitly or implicitly, on choice – a curious mixture of the unique individual, released from gender-, class- or age-based constraints in a carnival of consumption, and the dedicated follower of fashion. One striking feature is the way in which 'the body' has emerged as a central focus for this making of self through choice. Whether through fashion, diet, make-up, cosmetic surgery, reflexology, aromatherapy, detailed and obsessive shaping of the body in gymnasia, potions for internal and external application to nourish, shape and defoliate, the body has become the most fertile ground for the cultivation of self. But the extent to which 'choice' in late modernity offers a mode of self-expression that is significantly independent from the linchpin values of social order is problematic.

The symbiotic relationship between discourses of self-expression and the maintenance of dominant ideologies can be seen in the seemingly inexhaustible fascination with sex in women's monthly magazines. To exemplify this connection, a sample of leading women's magazines on the shelves of British newsagents between 1992 and 1994 was taken. All those randomly selected featured prominent articles on sex. In one respect, these often highly explicit and detailed discussions are evidence of the 'every-dayness' of sex in late modernity:

> Wednesday night we tried alfresco nookie just west of the barbecue. Thursday we tried a vertical perspective, I wore high heels. Friday we were shagged out... Saturday massaged each other followed by a vigorous workout in the cutlery position, Sunday was exclusively oral. (*Cosmopolitan*, 1994)

Giddens (1992, p. 2) has suggested that in late modernity, sexuality has been freed from 'the rule of the phallus, from the overweening importance of the male sexual experience'. Yet the tone of the articles surveyed continues to prioritize male-centred erotic practice. The following is from a feature entitled 'How to handle a manhood', subtitled 'The user's guide to manual *sex*' (*Cosmopolitan*, 1994). The general tone is typical 'Cosmo', a series of cartoon 'willies' manipulated by determined looking cartoon women, with the only real visual image that of a half-peeled upward curving banana. There follows twenty increasingly explicit descriptions of how to handle the penis, for the pleasuring of the man, and of course to ensure that the reader increases her sexual proficiency. One example will suffice:

> After your man has been tied up for a while, sit astride his chest with your back to his face. Firmly grasp the root of his penis with the one hand and with the other, stroke upwards very rapidly and sharply. Wait for the space of one heartbeat and repeat. Do this 10 times. Then give him ten more strokes, but this time perform them in rapid succession, allowing yourself no time to pause in between. Alternate these two stroking groups for five to eight minutes until he screams for mercy. Finally, give him a spectacular orgasm by way of your hand, mouth or vagina. Be sure to untie him quickly... then just let him lie there basking in the glory of you. (*Cosmopolitan*, 1994)

Despite the frivolous and humorous imagery (the article ends with the erect cartoon penis saying 'Got that? Now put down the magazine and come here.'), the distinctions between this copy and that of what is marketed as 'pornography' are blurred.

Given the emphasis on flexibility in late modernity, one might expect a low profile or even absence of fixities like normal/abnormal, and of a sense of anxiety about correct performance, in which the performance of the woman in heterosexual relationships is the focus of expert attention. Dr Ruth Westheimer, an American media sexologist, gives the following advice to women:

> The secret is to encourage desire. Functional sex can be technically satisfying but it's boring. Every relationship needs an erotic atmosphere between you even when sex is the last thing on your mind. When you phone from work, slip in a comment on what you'd like to do to him. Brush up against him. Undressing can be solitary and forgettable, or you can ask him to undress you, both times can be private and sexless, or shared and arousing. (Westheimer, quoted in *She*, 1994)

The implication is that all aspects of the woman's day could (and should) be sexualized in order to avoid the dreaded sexual boredom. A sense of autonomy of self, particularly for women, is negated in the exhortations to stoke the fires of desire. One can never let up sexually. Similarly, in an article apparently devoted to exploring alternative sexual practices in the same issue of *Cosmopolitan*, a number of women interviewees indicated their unease about partner's requests for oral or anal sex, dressing-up, domination or role-playing. The editorial response to these misgivings illustrates the tensions in the notion of women's sexual self-determination. On the one hand, their reluctance is validated: 'Our likes and dislikes in bed are just as legitimate as our likes and dislikes out of bed ... everyone's been made to feel as if she has a moral obligation to fulfil every one of her and her partner's fantasies'. On the other, saying no – *choice* – has troubling consequences: 'So if your partner asks should you just say no? Obviously you have the right to refuse anything that you find unappealing, stupid or offensive, but bear in mind that "no" is a harsh word to hear in bed from someone you love'.

The principle of the right to say 'no' is now qualified by engendering anxiety about *how* you say no. And we must even be wary of *why* we say no. 'We're insecure about change. Sex has become a comfortable habit for many of us. But comfortable can easily become dull', and sex must not be 'dull' at any costs, even if we must now not lie back and think of England but go and tog up in rubber.

In this brave new age of sex, the greatest sin is sexual boredom. And there is more than a hint of 'old' ideas about women's sexual roles and the process of their continued construction. The ubiquity of articles about sex in *women's* magazines underlines the persistence of the view that good sex, like good housekeeping, is the woman's responsibility. 'Sexual problems arise when one of you feels frustrated or censored in bed' (*New Woman*, September 1994). The answer is to *learn* the correct way to talk about sex. When is important: 'during a romantic dinner, on a weekend morning or afternoon, taking a walk together or having a picnic'. How is even more crucial: 'never say "never" or "always". Avoid judgemental phrases or personal attacks... instead of saying "you're too rushed", tell him how pleasurable it is if he goes slowly.' During actual love-making use the 'caring sandwich':

> A caring sandwich gives you a positive way to verbalize exactly what you need whenever something's not working in love-making without criticism or personal attacks. Gloria was trying to tell Rick how uncomfortable it was for her when he grabs her breast during love-making. Instead of saying 'ouch!', 'Watch out!' or 'Don't be so rough!' as she had in the past, she said softly 'Sweetheart I love you' (the supporting statement), 'and I need you to be gentle with my breasts' (the 'no'), 'because I really am enjoying the rest of what you are doing' (the supportive statement). This caring sandwich was the first time Gloria could express a dislike to Rick without his getting defensive or sulking. (*Woman*, September 1994)

Speaking about sex is so difficult it must be done in the right way (in case he sulks), in the right place (when you are both relaxed) and following an ordained pattern. The self-monitoring involved in these exercises is truly breathtaking in its depth and breadth. 'Work as Partners Choreographing a Dance' it exhorts as its final instruction, to ensure synchronous pleasure, the right buttons touched, but avoiding, at all costs, 'threatening his delicate ego'.

This article is followed immediately by another, 'X-Stasy – Legitimate sex aid or degrading pornography? Women are split about the value of erotic videos' (*Woman*, September 1994). It's not enough, it argues, for women to have sex because they are in love or because they want a family: 'There's more to feeling and consciousness, and not to be aware of them leaves one feeling vulnerable and not very confident'. This sets the stage for an 'ignorance anxiety'. 'How does sex work? What are my desires? How does my body respond? What are my boundaries? Should I do this just because everybody thinks I should? What really turns me on?' (ibid.). The heavy implication that lies in both the question and the solution is that the reader cannot trust herself, nor does she possess the capacities to overcome these induced doubts. Such strategies are familiar in other commercial spheres – selling insurance, health foods and childcare products, for example – in which anxieties can be easily mobilized and commodified. So,

> Erotica can be very useful at showing people's behaviours, styles, and tonalities which they are not familiar or comfortable with.... People are simply not aware of the tremendous diversity in style – not position, *style*. And, other than reading erotica you can't get that too much any other place except watching people have sex. (*Woman*, September 1994)

This is unequivocally language of the contemporary market-place, where lifestyle is all. Erotica is the equivalent of a fashion show, or a travelogue, devoid of any affective content, its role being to communicate breadth of

choice. The endless advice, guidance, warnings and enthusiastic encourage-
ments for new and different sex consciously seek to entice us out from behind
the disenabling screens of embarrassment, boredom or just downright ignorance, and to fearlessly make statements, through our willingness to experiment,
about our sexual individuality. 'Sex as lifestyle' presents sex as a consumer
product. Additionally, the sex as lifestyle discourses seek to *create* a desire for
these commodities in endless variations of 'choices', through which one
expresses the self. The omnipresence of sex in the highly competitive and
advertising revenue-dependent monthly magazines are testimony to the economic viability of such a project. Yet manipulation of consumption patterns
depends not just on the 'showing of the wares', but, crucially, of engendering
anxiety about the effectiveness and success of the sexual self we choose to be.

There is no question but that sex will be 'had' in these discourses of lifestyle
sex. Desire (and heterosexual desire, at that) is assumed. So we are caught in a
pincer movement: on the one hand, a moral imperative to have sex, since this is
the central dynamic of a 'relationship'; on the other, if we 'have' it, then we are
honour bound to avoid sliding down into the abyss of boredom. This is a
lifetime project, and one for which we cannot be prepared too soon. 'Sex by
numbers.... Get set to multiply your orgasms', 'Find his G-spot by the second
date' (*More!*, November 1994). This twice-monthly journal read by young
women aged fifteen to nineteen years has a regular feature entitled 'Position
of the fortnight'. An illustration of the copulating couple is accompanied by
detailed instructions as to its achievement, and a 'sizzle' rating from 1 to 5.

The emphasis in this 'sex as leisure' is not only on how to speak about it, how
often, where and in what positions, but is implicitly on coital sex as the summit
of sexual experience. While the difference between male and female propensities
for the pleasures of coital sex are acknowledged, their resolution in mutual and
simultaneous coital orgasm is a matter of careful planning, education and
execution.

> The most blissful act in the known universe practically guarantees the man a flight
> to heaven, while women are put on standby and must sometimes take other means
> of transport. If someone could come up with a new position, then maybe this
> orgasmic inequality would disappear. Well, they have. A Manhattan
> psychotherapist has devised an innovative method of intercourse – a variation of
> the missionary position – that not only increases the chances of orgasm in women
> but also tends to bring on that ecstasy of ecstasies, the mutual orgasm. (*Cosmo-
> politan*, August 1992)

In the promotion of lifestyle sex, anxieties about inadequacy and boredom
are partially clothed in guidelines to attain orgasmic bliss. Hidden within both
are assumptions about the primacy of heterosexual coital sex and the masculin-
ist bias this rests on, despite the consistently reiterated theme of erotic equality.

The high-profile promotion of individual freedom does not just mask a
commercial agenda, but more effectively dissembles an agenda that silently
but no less effectively promotes and maintains key hegemonic ideas. Good

housekeeping has been replaced by 'good sex-making' – the how-to-do-it manuals now instruct, direct and cajole the uses of female sexuality where once they instructed and directed in the use of the cooker, sewing machine or duster. Concerns about hygiene and culinary proficiency have been replaced by concerns about orgasmic efficiency and the management of erotic pleasures. While appearing to represent the final severance of connections between domesticity and womanhood, the destruction of the 'Berlin Wall' that separates the spheres, there are significant sectors left standing. For the parameters of sexual and erotic success are derived from those of heterosexual coitus. This signals the extent to which women continue to occupy a differential position in 'the sexualization of modern societies' (Evans, 1993, p. 240).

> Just as male homosexuals could not be effectively commodified or politically incorporated as long as they remained illegal, passive nonobjectifying subjects…so too actively consuming public women need to be reconstituted in commensurate sexually active forms, and this indeed is what they have become. (Ibid.: p. 266)

The widely trumpeted sexual freedom has, in fact, been turned on its head. The key to this, the clitoris, has been commodified through the promotion of women's multi-orgasmic capacity. Possession of these capacities becomes the imperative to use them:

> A commodity is, in the first place, an object outside us, a thing that by its properties satisfies human need of some sort or another. The nature of such wants, whether, for instance they spring from the stomach or from fancy, makes no difference. (Marx, in McLellan, 1977, p. 421)

But there is a price to be paid for the legitimation of sexual pleasures, a tariff which loosens none of the regulatory fetters. Sexual desire, and the means to assuage it, now appears to us, as Marx would put it, in fantastic form. The constitution of individual sexual desires, derived from our imagination and our capacity for sensual pleasure, is expropriated in a sexual market-place of commodified pleasures. The 'real sensual qualities' are obscured by objectified mechanistic manipulation, in which the real sensuality is not just assumed but occluded.

Sex as lifestyle is not, literally, selling sex, exchanging sex for money. This at least is more straightforward. In such a case, there is 'a physical relationship between physical objects' (Marx, in McLellan, 1977, p. 434). In the marketing of lifestyle sex, what is being exchanged has no material form. It is not packaged, nor is there a visible exchange of money for sexual pleasure. Moreover, lifestyle sex is of doubtful worth in the enhancement of human satisfaction or governance of our sexual selves. Yet it is clearly one which has almost guaranteed appeal. For this particular commodity appears in a highly commercialized competition for advertising revenue, without which such ventures could not survive. Marketing strategies cannot 'get it wrong'. There is too much at stake. This is a strictly commercial outlet for talking about sex, on the face of it far removed from the clinical texts and laboratories of the sexologists – Alex Comfort's 'anxiety-makers'. Nor does it, despite appearances to the contrary, offer the same promise as erotica. These are not texts to encourage exploration of sensuality. There is an imperative quality to lifestyle sex, which seeks to fix a sexual agenda through mobilization of anxieties about physical performance.

In this respect, there are parallels with the masturbation anxieties engendered and promoted in the eighteenth and nineteenth centuries. In the context of the dissolution of reproduction from sexuality, where the latter is promoted as *the* principal marker of the individualized self, a new rationale for normative frameworks has emerged. The anxiety now is not about the essential dangers associated with allowing free rein to our sexual drives, and the threat to physical health which this represents. In late modernity, lifestyle sex contains rather than enables choice. The new 'anxiety-makers' monitor attempts at sexual self-realization through 'choice', through the reiteration of 'old' messages from experts who hold the key to sexual fulfilment.

Conclusion

The 'liberalization of heterosexuality' is a complex idea because it is both a truth and a non-truth. Considered chronologically, there has been a considerable loosening of sexual mores that can be related to a particular historical epoch or particular decades. Viewed 'from above', there has been a shift from sex-as-danger to sex-as-pleasure. From the interwar years of the twentieth century, a reluctance to promote sex in any form publicly has apparently been exchanged for its enthusiastic promotion. Taking a variety of indices of social change – extramarital sex, divorce, onset of sexual activity, availability and use of contraception, censorship patterns of literary and visual material, legal statutes – the twentieth century may be seen by future historians of Western culture as the century that liberalized heterosexuality. Yet a cursory contrast between this and the last century would reveal some striking similarities. In both we might accurately speak of a preoccupation with sex and a compulsion to speak about it. The equally striking difference is that at the end of the twentieth century, we are enveloped in a post-liberation environment in which the 'specialness' of sex – the anxieties, ambivalences, fears and preoccupations reflected in the overt regulation of sexuality we associate with the bourgeois model – appears to have been dissolved.

Such a characterization would be as misleading as the 'repressive thesis' of the previous century. It has been argued that liberalization cannot be understood either as a linear or evolutionary process, sweeping away all 'old' ideas in its wake. The valorization – attaching a positive rather than a negative value to sex and sexuality – has, on the contrary, been halting and highly contingent on particular circumstances and participants. This chapter has criticized the contention that there has been a liberalizing of heterosexuality from the fetters of past regulatory frameworks, which equated sex with duty rather than pleasure, with prudery rather than celebration, with stratified gender inequalities. The complexity lies in the fact that one cannot deny that these 'old' ideas are, if not wholly dissolved, at least marginalized and unfashionable. But just as historians challenged the notion of the repressive hypothesis, which applied to bourgeois sexual ideology, in their critical examination of both its form and content, applying a similar evaluation to the twentieth-century 'liberalization hypothesis' reveals similar intricacies. Proposing the notion of liberalization presumes the question 'from what?' If from the past, then the bird's-eye view reveals an affirmative answer. We are no longer Victorians.

This chapter has examined the processes by which heterosexuality was 'uncoupled', in which sex was legitimately disconnected from the pillars of monogamy and conjugality, while retaining the stabilizing connections with patriarchal sexual relations. It has also explored the promotion of lifestyle sex, as heterosexuality became a vital component in the dynamics of flexible accumulation. This incorporation depended for its viability on the overt pro-motion of sexual freedom as the mark of the liberated individual consumer, and was arguably one of the major influences in our largely uncritical acceptance of the superficial picture. The notion of liberalization of heterosexuality suggests the release from regulation which stifles individual self-expression. It suggests the attainment of a 'sexual adulthood' in which the paternalistic 'anxiety-makers' are rendered redundant. And it suggests that the high-profile 'special-ness' of sex associated with modernity has, in late modernity, been levelled to the status of just another lifestyle choice. Looked at another way, these shifts are illustrative of the elasticity of the heterosexual imperative, a capacity for adaptation that parallels and, it has been argued, is indirectly related to the processes by which strategies for capitalist accumulation have manoeuvred to retain their primary driving force.

REFERENCES

Bauman, Z. (1989), *Legislators and Interpreters: On Modernity, Post-modernity and Intellectuals*, Cambridge: Polity Press.

Campbell, B. (1982), 'A feminist sexual politics: now you see it, now you don't', in M. Evans (ed.), *The Woman Question: Readings on the Subordination of Women*, Oxford: Fontana.

Coveney, L. et al. (1984), *The Sexuality Papers: Male Sexuality and the Social Control of Women*, London: Hutchinson.

Davies, C. (1980) 'Moralists, causalists, sex, law and morality', in W. H. G. Armytage, R. Chester and J. Peel (eds), *Changing Attitudes to Sexual Behaviour*, London: Academic Press.

De Beauvoir, S. (1972), *The Second Sex*, Harmondsworth: Penguin.

Evans, D. (1993), *Sexual Citizenship: The Materialist Construction of Sexualities*, London: Routledge.

Friday, N. (1976), *My Secret Garden: Women's Sexual Fantasies*, London: Quartet.

Friedan, B. (1965), *The Feminine Mystique*, Harmondsworth: Penguin.

Gavron, H. (1966), *The Captive Wife*, Harmondsworth: Pelican.

Giddens, A. (1991), *Modernity and Self-Identity: Self and Society in the Late Modern Age*, Cambridge: Polity Press.

Giddens, A. (1992), *The Transformation of Intimacy: Sexuality, Love and Eroticism in Modern Societies*, Cambridge: Polity Press.

Gramsci, A. (1971), *Selections from the Prison Notebooks of Antonio Gramsci*, eds and trans. Q. Hoare and G. Nowell Smith, London: Lawrence and Wishart.

Grant, L. (1993), *Sexing the Millennium*, London: Harper Collins.

Greer, G. (1970), *The Female Eunuch*, London: MacGibbon and Kee.

Gurley Brown, H. (1962), *Sex and the Single Girl*, New York: Geis.

Harvey, D. (1989), *The Condition of Postmodernity: An Enquiry into the Conditions of Cultural Change*, Oxford: Blackwell Publishers.

Hawkes, G. (1996), *A Sociology of Sex and Sexuality*, Buckingham: Open University Press.

Hite, S. (1976), *The Hite Report*, London: Pandora.

Kinsey, A., Pomeroy, W. and Martin, C. (1948), *Sexual Behaviour in the Human Male*, London. W. B. Saunders.

Kinsey, A. et al. (1953), *Sexual Behaviour in the Human Female*, London: W. B. Saunders.

McLellan, D. (1977), *Karl Marx: Selected Writings*, Oxford: Oxford University Press.

Masters, W. and Johnson, V. (1966), *Human Sexual Response*, Boston, MA: Little Brown.

Masters, W. and Johnson, V. (1970), *Human Sexual Inadequacy*, London: J. & A. Churchill.

Mitchell, J. (1971), *Women's Estate*, Harmondsworth: Pelican.

Onlywoman Press (ed.) (1981), *Love Your Enemy? The Debate Between Heterosexual Feminism and Political Lesbianism*, London: Onlywoman Press.

Robinson, P. (1972), *The Sexual Radicals: Reich, Roheim, Marcuse*, London: Paladin.

Robinson, P. (1976), *The Modernization of Sex: Havelock Ellis, Alfred Kinsey, William Masters and Virginia Johnson*, New York: Harper and Row.

Schofield, M. (1965), *The Sexual Behaviour of Young People*, Harmondsworth: Penguin.

Segal, L. (1987), *Is the Future Female? Troubled Thoughts on Contemporary Feminism*, London: Virago.

Segal, L. (1993), *Straight Sex: The Politics of Pleasure*, London: Virago.

Weeks, J. (1985), *Sexuality and its Discontents*, London: Routledge.

Westheimer, R. (1994), Contributor to 'How to have hot sex again', in *She*, London: National Magazine Company.

3

The One and the Many: Modernity and Postmodernity

David Cheal

Changes in family theories often follow changes in family life. As one observer noted about the 1980s: 'studies and research on the family carried out in the last decade may be interpreted as an answer – in the area of knowledge – to the transformations that have occurred in the structure of society' (Sgritta, 1989, p. 90). We see this in the ways the increased tendency for wives to seek employment challenged theories that equated women's roles with domestic labour. Those difficulties prompted social scientists to develop alternative approaches to studying relations between family, work and gender – ones that emphasize historical variation (Jallinoja, 1989). Summarizing the new work, Laslett and Brenner state that 'In the most recent scholarship the accent is on variation and human agency, and particularly on the ways in which women have constructed their own worlds of activity' (1989, p. 384).

Other changes in everyday life have had a related effect upon family theory, which is more profound. In recent years living arrangements have become more diverse (Rapoport, Fogarty and Rapoport, 1982). This new social pluralism was accompanied by the questioning of established images of family life. In particular, the dominant tendency in the sociology of the family – to seek theoretical integration through one coherent model of a specifically modern type of family – has been severely criticized (Denzin, 1987; Rapoport, 1989).

Such critiques create a degree of fluidity, and uncertainty, in family theory that is unsettling. The sociology of the family is not alone in this awkward situation. It is part of a much larger problem in social theory, which Alain Touraine (1984) refers to as 'the waning sociological image of social life'. What he means by this is that established theoretical approaches in sociology are less and less able to provide comprehensive and coherent accounts of how contemporary social forces are connected. More specifically, Touraine (1988) explains, it has become increasingly difficult to reconcile the cultural principles of modernity (i.e. reason, progress) with modernization (i.e. ceaseless change, constant revolutionizing of means of production and social forms). Touraine claims that the current state of sociological theory – which he refers to as a crisis – reflects a fundamental dislocation in social life, namely the passage from one culture to another. This *crisis of modernity* appears in sociology as the failure of monolithic theories of history (i.e. of historicism). Touraine comments that 'What is disappearing is social evolutionism, the idea of a natural modernization, commanded by laws of historical development' (1984, p. 38).[1] In this chapter we will explore the thesis of the waning of monolithic theories of social change, with respect to its implications for theories of change in family life.

Family Changes Revisited: Standardization or Diversification?

In standard sociological theory a model of family life is held out as a progressive standard, to which everyone is thought to aspire sooner or later. It is believed that all groups converge towards that standard, though they realize it to different degrees according to their unequal capacities to do so. Since the process of modernization brings about a general increase in capacities, this theory of family life assumes that modernization is accompanied by the standardization of family role behaviour.

The theory of modernity has had a deep and lasting effect upon standard sociological theory. In the theory of modernity, powerful institutions that are central to modern society are held to transform everyday life in regular and predictable ways. This process of *institutionalized transformation* shapes and controls social life at the same time as it changes it, so that the result is an increased regularity of social behaviour. As Touraine (1988, p. 443) explains:

> The history of modernization is seen as that of the gradual obliteration of cultural and social differences in favour of an increasingly broad participation of everyone in one and the same general model of modernity, defined by applying the general principles of reason to the conduct of human affairs.

An interesting and sophisticated application of modernization theory to the standardization of family life is the argument presented by Michael Young and Peter Willmott (1974) for a trend toward the 'symmetrical family'. They advance a thesis of social change that they refer to as the *principle of stratified diffusion*. This states that, due to the tendency of lower status groups to emulate those above them, important changes always begin high up in the status hierarchy and are gradually diffused downwards. Applying the principle to family history in England, Young and Willmott hypothesize that, as technology replaces the more physically arduous and less interesting jobs, so the greater attachment to work of middle-class people will extend downwards. They believe that this affects the choices between home and employment made by working-class women, who will increasingly choose occupational careers.

According to this thesis, the occupational commitments of husbands and wives will become more similar, or in their terminology 'symmetrical'. At the same time, Young and Willmott expect that the impact of feminism will mean the redistribution of housework, in proportion to occupational demands on time. The result is that the familial division of labour should also become symmetrical. Young and Willmott therefore believe that the segregation of marriage roles will decline.[2]

An earlier thesis of the class-based standardization of family life was Parsons's theory of the modern family. Writing about the United States, Parsons argued that the cultural standard for American family life was that of the urban middle-class family. It defined for practical purposes the 'normal American family' (Parsons, 1971). The major exceptions to this pattern, Parsons thought, were families in the lower class. Parsons stated that 'family disorganization' was particularly prevalent in this class, as a result of its being rejected by those who were economically more successful. With that important exception, Parsons claimed that the general trend of development in America was 'a massive upgrading of standards in many respects and the inclusion of much higher proportions of the population in the groups enjoying the higher standards' (ibid.: p. 63). Parsons believed that as a result of this upgrading, there had been a very substantial homogenization of patterns of life in the population. The consequence of this, he thought, was that there had 'emerged a remarkably uniform, basic type of family' (ibid.: p. 53).

Ellen Gee (1986) has presented evidence for women in Canada that broadly supports Parsons's interpretation of family change. She concludes that the principal changes in the occurrence and timing of life-course transitions over the last 100 or 150 years involve increased standardization. This pattern is due to widespread improvements in the quality of life. The decline in mortality levels has reduced the prevalence of disrupted family relationships, such as early widowhood. As Gee points out, this increases the predictability of family living. Also, greater economic affluence has made it possible for most of those who wish to marry to do so. By comparison with earlier periods of economic difficulty, the result has been an increased standardization of marital status.

The relevance of modernization theory to family studies includes the historical subjection of domestic activities to the rationalization of means and ends. This was done in order to achieve greater efficiencies in the use of time and money, and in order to bring about an upgrading of moral and physical standards of care. Reiger (1985, 1987) has shown how in Australia, between the 1880s and the Second World War, women's traditional chores of cooking, cleaning, sewing, childcare and generally servicing the needs of others became subjected to rational scientific management. Informal practices that were passed on from mothers to daughters were considered to be inadequate. Instead, attempts were made to replace unhealthy and inefficient practices through formal instruction in models produced by the new domestic sciences. Experts from the human service professions played a considerable role in this cultural redefinition, in a self-conscious attempt to improve the quality of family life. This professionally engineered social change extended to redefining the naturalness of mothering, and a major effort was made to teach women how to rear their children more effectively.

The exposure of contemporary populations to family roles and to cultural definitions of levels of family performance has become in certain respects more uniform. But these are not the only changes that have taken place. It also seems to be the case that family interactions have become more diverse. This diversity is not easily described by standard sociological theory, which sees social relationships as governed by a system of roles. In its narrowest form, standard sociological theory conceives of the 'normal family', or 'conventional family', as consisting of the nuclear roles of husband and wife, and their children. In the work of Parsons (1943, 1971) the norms regulating interactions between family roles require the following:

1   Marriage between adult partners (more specifically, monogamy).
2   Superiority of the conjugal bond over other social commitments.
3   Fulfilment of the marriage bond through the raising of legitimate children.
4   Co-residence.
5   The employment of one or more adult members outside the home.
6   The unrestricted sharing of incomes between adult members.

The Parsonian model of family life was always an abstraction from reality, like any other ideal type. However, in recent years its links to observed reality have become increasingly tenuous in a number of countries. Furstenberg and Spanier (1984, pp. 51–2), writing about the United States, conclude:

> In general, the pathways of family formation have become less normatively prescribed insofar as behavioral regularities reveal social rules. Individuals have greater leeway to tailor family arrangements to their personal needs and desires. Hence, the early part of the life course has become more discretionary in both the timing and the order of family-related transitions, at least compared to a generation ago.

There is evidence (in the United States) of a growing percentage of teenage births occurring to unmarried women (Furstenberg, Brooks-Gunn and Morgan, 1987) and more generally of increased cohabitation before or independent of marriage (Trost, 1977; Cotton, Antill and Cunningham, 1983) and of 'commuter marriages' between partners who live in different cities (Gross, 1980; Gerstel and Gross, 1984). Increased divorce rates and single parenthood by choice indicate that the marriage bond is less binding, and perhaps less important, than it once was (Renvoize, 1985; Ahrons and Rodgers, 1987). This would also seem to be confirmed by the way in which never-married and voluntarily childless lifestyles have come to be recognized as viable forms of social life, that are not necessarily devoid of family ties (Veevers, 1980; Allen, 1989). It also appears that when husbands and wives both earn large incomes they may decide not to pool them (Hertz, 1986).

Finally, there continue to be significant differences between industrial nations in family patterns, which are not entirely explicable by modernization theories

(Boh, 1989). Important cultural differences remain in the modern world. This includes ethnic differences within many industrial societies, especially those which had significant post-Second World War immigration. It has therefore been argued that greater attention should be paid to ethnic variations in family arrangements (Rosenthal, 1983).

The present situation is in many ways ambiguous. It appears to permit interpretations of both familial standardization *and* lifestyle diversification. Martin Kohli (1986) has described this situation as one of a long-term trend (of approximately 300 years) towards increased standardization, and a short-term trend (of approximately the last twenty years) towards increased diversification. Until the early 1970s, the secular trend was that of strengthening the normative pattern, of getting married, having children and surviving until at least age fifty in an intact first marriage (Uhlenberg, 1978). However, since the beginning of the 1970s in most Western countries, several of the processes that resulted in the standardization of the family life cycle have either stopped or gone into reverse. As a result, there is now an increasing proportion of household configurations and sequences that depart from the normative pattern of family life.

The immediate consequence of the increased prevalence of lifestyle diversity has been a decline in the utility of sociological approaches that rely upon a concept of the 'normal family' (Bernardes, 1986). Katja Boh emphasizes this point with a play on words. She states that the only common feature in the evolution of family life patterns in Europe is *convergence to diversity* (Boh, 1989, p. 296). She concludes that:

> There is no indication in our analysis that the evolution of family life patterns in European societies would follow a certain pattern to become the model for family modernization in Europe. Not one but a variety of family patterns have emerged, have become legitimate and practised by people in accordance with their needs and living conditions. And just because the living conditions and the social forces that influence them are so different in the different European countries, we are inclined to believe that the development will not go in one and the same direction, but will lead to a still greater diversification of family patterns in Europe. Nevertheless, there is at least one uniform trend in the overall development of family patterns, and this is the trend towards a recognition of diversity. (Ibid.: pp. 295–6)

The recognition of diversity, which is so easy as a matter of empirical observation, poses a real challenge for social theory in its positivistic forms. This is because in any scientific field of study there must be some agreement about what the objects of investigation are, so that they can be included in a common theoretical discourse, and so that comparable observations can be generated for the purposes of repeat hypothesis testing. This concern leads to the defining of units of analysis. At present, increased awareness of diversity in family life is leading a number of social scientists into a conscious concern with *redefining* units of analysis, in ways that are appropriate to contemporary conditions. It is this challenge we must take up next.

Rethinking What We Study

Defining the object of investigation, or unit of analysis, is an important activity in the social sciences. It is necessary for purposes of clarification, because theorists often have different ideas about what it is that they are studying. The principal unit of analysis is often not the same in different theoretical approaches, even when a common term such as 'family' is employed. The term 'family' is often used to mean different things by different theorists, and in some cases 'the family' has been replaced by other units of analysis in family studies. Current issues include whether 'the family' is a basic unit or a derived unit, or if it is simply one unit of analysis among a number of plausible possibilities (Cheal, 1989a). More fundamentally, the reflexive questions raised by family experts include whether or not we know what 'family' is, and whether or not such a thing as 'the family' even exists at all (Bernardes, 1985b). Trost (1990) has shown that this state of confusion among family experts is a reflection of the enormous variety of family classifications that are employed by lay members of society. He concludes that 'Evidently no one "knows" what a family is: our perspectives vary to such a degree that to claim to know what a family is shows a lack of knowledge' (ibid.: p. 442).

There is much at stake in current debates about definitional problems. Professionally speaking, its consequences include whether or not the scientific study of something called 'the family' is possible. It follows directly from this that the very existence of a specialized discipline of 'the sociology of the family' is called into question. In addition to potential effects upon the organization of academic life, the current debate about definitions also has implications for views on social structure. If there is no concept of 'the family' that can be the subject of general agreement, then how *should* we define the recurring forms of private life? This in turn raises a further question, concerning how to theorize about issues of behavioural uniformity and diversity. Finally, is all the recent concern about theory definitions and models just a temporary phase of intellectual confusion? Or is it symptomatic of larger shifts in the field of social scientific knowledge, and in contemporary culture?

There are four broad approaches to answering these questions which are being actively pursued today. They are: concept specification, concept abandonment, concept displacement and concept expansion.

Concept specification

Standard sociological theory has regarded the family as a cultural universal. That is to say, it assumes that the culture of any society will contain a general normative expectation that all adults who are mentally and physically capable of doing so should marry and should have children. Clearly, in the contemporary Western societies that expectation has been breaking down for some time. But it has not yet disappeared. The 'normal' family continues to be a cultural model for many people, although their precise numbers may be a matter of dispute. Taubin and Mudd (1983) refer to these people as living in 'contemporary traditional families'. For such people, the traditional cultural model of 'the family' continues to be a lived reality, even though it is no longer a cultural universal.

Separation of the concept of 'the family' from any assumption of cultural universality makes possible certain developments in modern social theory that are of some interest. Contemporary traditional families can be seen as shaped not so much by fixed cultural traditions as by the ongoing process of modernization. Ralph Linton's (1936) anthropological theory of cultural change can help to explain why this is so. Linton pointed out that when new cultural elements (such as cohabitation) are introduced into a society, previous cultural universals (such as marriage) become alternatives, about which individuals must now make a conscious choice – to follow the traditional model, or not. Linton thought that in the long run one of two things would happen. One possibility is that if enough people cease to opt for the traditional model, it will drop out of the culture completely. The other possibility is that some people may continue to choose the traditional model, but as a specialized solution to particular requirements. Linton referred to the altered contexts of such cultural elements as 'specialties'.

The fact that 'the family' today may be a 'specialty', in Linton's sense, is one conclusion to be drawn from Nave-Herz's (1989) work on family and marriage in Western Germany. Nave-Herz continues to use the 'normal' definition of 'the family', as a unit made up of an adult couple and their children living together in the same household. The findings from her research lead her to conclude that the social significance of the family has changed, due to the continuing trend toward increased functional specialization in modern societies. Whereas cohabitation is tending to be adopted by young Germans as the social basis for companionship and emotional gratification, the family is adopted as the context in which to bring up children. There is, Nave-Herz argues, a marked shift in attitudes taking place, towards child-oriented marriage as a rational choice that is based on instrumental reasons.

'The family', considered as a contemporary traditional group, remains the focus of useful sociological investigation, as we have just seen. Nevertheless, many sociologists are not likely to be satisfied with an approach that is limited to studying only one narrowly defined social form. Therefore, other approaches to rethinking what we study have been developed.

Concept abandonment

The most radical solution to difficulties in defining what is meant by 'family' is to abandon the term for all theoretically significant purposes. This is the approach recommended by John Scanzoni (1987). Scanzoni is concerned that emerging forms of everyday living cannot any longer be subsumed under the rubric of 'alternatives' to the normal family. As patterns such as cohabitation and single parenthood become more widespread, so they take on a cultural reality of their own that is no longer definable simply in terms of difference from the benchmark of the conjugal family. Scanzoni therefore argues that a new image or paradigm is needed for the study of structured interpersonal ties. He finds this image in the concept of 'close relationships' (ibid.), and the related concept of 'primary relationships' (Scanzoni et al., 1989).

Scanzoni and his colleagues recommend that the concept of 'the family' should no longer be used by social scientists, because it is too 'concrete', or in other words too historically and culturally specific. Instead they recommend using the 'higher order' concept of *primary relationships*, under which various kinds of tie that are conventionally defined as family relationships may be subsumed. For example, legal marriages would be included here, along with other kinds of sexual couplings that are not defined in law, under the general heading of 'sexually based primary relationships'.

Scanzoni and his associates state that multifarious and ambiguous meanings of the term 'family' are in fact viable in everyday life, because they help ordinary people to apprehend 'the slippery realities' of families and to communicate lay conceptions of reality effectively (ibid.: p. 37). However, they insist that a sharp distinction must be drawn between lay and scientific concepts. In particular, they claim that scientific concepts should not be shaped by the 'prevailing symbol-system' (i.e. culture), since the latter is both value-laden and infused with the emotions of ordinary people. Scanzoni et al. seek to 'escape' from the distractions and confusions that inevitably accompany lay discourse about families, by using the term 'primary relationships' in its place (ibid.: p. 44).

The approach taken by Scanzoni and his colleagues is open to some important objections. It is questionable whether it is either possible or desirable to avoid bringing culture into social theory, through the deliberate use of esoteric words and phrases. Indeed, the attempt to do so may simply serve to mask the nature of cultural influences, and thereby make analyses and debates of theoretical issues more difficult.

Clearly, the term 'primary relationship' is not a common phrase in ordinary conversation. Social scientists can therefore realistically expect to control the meanings they give to it, in ways that are not possible with a term such as 'the family'. However, the concept of primary relationships does not stand alone; it is not a pure term. It, too, has a social context, or more precisely a sociosemiotic context. Together with the contrasting term of 'secondary relationships', the use of the term 'primary relationships' reflects an historically specific division between public (i.e. secondary) and private (i.e. primary) spheres of action in industrial societies. The division between private and public powerfully affects family life and profoundly influences how social scientists think and talk about it. The cultural contradiction between the private world of families and the public world of institutions, such as the state, has a significant but unacknowledged influence upon the theorizing of Scanzoni and his colleagues.

Scanzoni's view of social theory is positivistic in its notions of scientific detachment and conceptual purity. It differs from ideas of the post-positivists in family studies, who seek to uncover the previously unacknowledged influences of everyday common sense upon social science. Post-positivists do not try to escape from lay concepts of reality, but rather attempt to confront them directly, within social theory. It is to approaches of this sort that we turn next.

Concept displacement

Post-positivist theorists in family studies recognize that the term 'family' is first of all an element in the everyday stock of knowledge about the social world. They set out to make that knowledge an object of investigation for the social sciences. Here, lay views are not ignored but considered to constitute one part of the subject matter of sociology. There are two broad streams of work in this intellectual tradition, one primarily cognitive, the other primarily discursive.

The cognitive thrust in post-positivist family studies envisages lay ideas about the family as a system of morally charged beliefs, which represent and misrepresent economic and political interests in concrete social relations. 'The family' is described as a mental construct that is the product of a *familial ideology* (Beechey, 1985). This is the approach taken by Jon Bernardes (1985a, 1985b). He argues for a *new* family studies, that will displace 'the family' from its status as a reality that is taken for granted (Bernardes, 1988). This departure from standard sociological theory is important, he claims, because it is necessary for us to recognize how far commonsense knowledge is incorporated into public language, which is in turn taken up by social theory.

A focus on language as the object of social investigation is most characteristic of the second branch of post-positivism that will be considered here. In *discourse theory* the terms with which people describe the world are studied in their practical uses for purposes of communication. Cheal (1988a) states that there is no universal form of 'the family', and that 'family' is a term used by lay actors to label those ties which they believe to involve enduring intimate relations. In a similar manner, Gubrium and Holstein (1990) have drawn attention to the use of language in the social construction of the family. In their words, 'The term "family" is part of a particular discourse for describing human relations in or out of the household' (ibid.: p. 13). They state that family discourse is a mode of communication, which assigns meanings to actions that are both substantive and active. In its substantive dimensions, family discourse names and makes sense of interpersonal relations. In its active dimensions, it communicates the attitudes which actors intend to adopt towards others, as well as the courses of action which they propose to take.

Post-positivist theorists of all persuasions are very sensitive to the multiple forms and multiple meanings of family life, as these emerge from different social contexts. Bernardes is especially concerned with the way in which talking about *the* family may obscure much real diversity in family situations. He therefore admonishes social theorists that 'This term can and must only have one possible use in future: specifically we must relegate the term "the Family" to denoting only the usage of everyday actors' (Bernardes, 1985b, p. 210). Notwithstanding

Bernardes's position, other social theorists who do use the term 'the family' have attempted to make use of some of the multiple meanings of everyday life, in complex sociological models of family structures (Wilson and Pahl, 1988). The basic question to ask about their line of work is how many such models we will need in order to understand contemporary societies.

Concept expansion

Structural sociologists have worked for some time to produce family concepts which would enable them to apply established theories to emerging phenomena. One solution has been to extend the definition of 'the family' into a normal form and at least one secondary form that is a transformation of it. The work of Harris (1983) is a good example of this approach. In a manner that is influenced by social anthropology, Harris speaks of 'the family' as a class of groups. It is all those groups which are formed by extension from the elementary relations of the nuclear family; namely relations between spouses, between parents and children and between siblings.

A related, but simpler, approach was deployed by Ahrons (1979) and later taken up by Ahrons and Rodgers (1987). Ahrons was concerned with the reorganization of the nuclear family after divorce, which frequently results in the formation of two households. Because of the connections between these households, through their shared rights over children in common, Ahrons argued that they form one family system – a 'binuclear family system'. Ahrons therefore defines family life as consisting of the pre-divorce structure of the nuclear family, and the post-divorce structure of the binuclear family.

Jan Trost, too, is concerned with definitional problems that arise in part from the increased prevalence of divorce. In an elegant theoretical model, he has demonstrated in principle how a wide variety of living arrangements can be generated from a limited number of fundamental social properties (Trost, 1980). Trost is particularly interested in two types of group which he defines as families. They are the parent–child unit, consisting of one parent and one child related to each other, and the spousal unit, consisting of two cohabiting adults, either married or unmarried (Trost, 1988). Both these types are in effect theoretical reductions of the nuclear family that reflect contemporary conditions of social fragmentation.

Rather than proliferate types which are transformations of the normal family, Rhona Rapoport has recommended that we adopt a generalized 'diversity model'. She describes this approach as follows: 'With the diversity model, each particular family form – conventional, dual-worker, single-parent, reconstituted, etc. – is seen as providing the structure for a lifestyle' (Rapoport, 1989, p. 60). Rapoport justifies this position on two grounds: first, because there are so many unknowns today that a new intellectual flexibility is required; and second, because past ideologies about family forms have proved inadequate for understanding contemporary changes. She does, however, note one potential problem with the diversity model. This is the tendency to reduce analysis to a micro-sociological level. In this approach large-scale social structural factors may be ignored, in favour of individual and small-scale interpersonal analyses.

Individualization

In so far as the sociology of the family has been moving in the direction of more individual-focused analyses, it may be because structural changes in society have made relations between autonomous individuals the principal basis for everyday social life. Observations of increased cultural diversity and heightened individuality are closely related in contemporary family theory, because the loosening of social controls that accompanies diversification allows individuals to choose between alternative lifestyles. This *destandardization* of the family increases the freedoms that are open to individuals, and expands their sense of individuality and personal autonomy (Buchmann, 1989). Boh (1989, p. 296) expresses this point as follows:

> Whatever the existing patterns are, they are characterized by the acceptance of diversity that has given men and women the possibility to choose inside the boundaries of the system of available options the life pattern that is best adapted to their own needs and aspirations.

Modernist social theorists are inclined to believe that increased individualism is a logical extension of the long-term trend of structural differentiation. This is the *individualization* thesis of modernity, which has been especially popular in recent German social theory (Kohli, 1986; Buchmann, 1989). It is thought that in the process of modernization, individuals become differentiated from each other as autonomous social units. This point was made by Parsons in one of his later works, although it is little known. Parsons noted that 'a strong case can be made that the trend of modern society, because it has become so highly differentiated and pluralistic, is positively to favor individuality' (Parsons, 1977, p. 198). More recent theories have also pointed to the important role of the state in the public institutionalization of individual rights, and in under-mining the powers of traditional groups such as families, which are con-sequently less able to act as corporate units (Meyer, 1986; Mayer and Schoepflin, 1989).

Cheal (1988a) has argued that contemporary family relations take the principal form of a *moral individualism*, due to the increased indeterminacy of cultural codes under conditions of social pluralism. Acquired rights to individual autonomy are aligned with commitments to others mainly through interpersonal bonding that is socially constructed. Characteristic consequences of this situation for family interactions include the search for intersubjective agreement about members' biographies (Berger and Kellner, 1970), and increased sentimentality and increased ritualization of family ties (Cheal, 1988a, 1988b). The combination of the last two features produces an expanded significance of symbolic media for communicating to significant others the message that they are loved (Cheal, 1987a).

Luhmann (1986) claims that love should be understood not as a natural feeling, but as a generalized medium of communication. He argues that this code of communication, with its rules for expressing, forming and stimulating feelings, has become an increasingly important means for the management of intimate relationships. Luhmann attributes the origin of this state of affairs to functional differentiation in social systems. Progressive system differentiation has produced a great variety of specialized structures. Since individuals participate in a number of these they are no longer firmly located in any one of them. As a result, individuals now believe themselves to possess unique combinations of experiences, which they attribute to their unique personal qualities. Stable interaction between individuals requires that they confirm each other's personal, inner experiences. The code of love has evolved, Luhmann argues, as a mode of *interpersonal interpenetration*, which relies upon the internalization of another person's view of the world.

Interest in inner, subjective views of the objects that individuals perceive as relevant to them is an important theme in the theoretical approach known as *phenomenology*. This approach has its origins in the philosophy of human experience, and it is intensely individualistic. For example, in the sociology of the family McLain and Weigert (1979, p. 187) have objected to any assumption that 'some construct called family actually behaves'. Instead, they claim that only individuals behave.

The theme of individualization which runs through much modern social theory revolves around issues of autonomy, personhood, choice and identity. Those themes have sometimes been set out as formal assumptions of sociological theories, particularly in the United States.

Exchange

One well-known approach to theorizing about individuals in families is *exchange theory* (Nye, 1979, 1980, 1982). With its origins in behavioural psychology and in micro-economics, exchange theory has often been a preferred basis for deductive theorizing about patterns of interaction in families (Aldous, 1977; Tallman, 1988). The heart of exchange theory is a model of rational choice. It is assumed that individuals choose between lines of action in such a way as to minimize their costs and maximize their rewards. Exchange theorists believe that individuals engage in interaction only if it is profitable for them to do so. It is therefore thought that family life takes the general form of an exchange of goods and services.

Most exchange analyses of family life have been concerned with relations between husbands and wives. Topics include the choice of marriage partner (Murstein, 1973), the quality of the marriage relationship (Lewis and Spanier, 1982), marital separation (Levinger, 1979) and remarriage (Giles-Sims, 1987). One of the best-known applications of this approach is Scanzoni's work on marital interaction as a bargaining process, in which failure to agree on the rules of exchange may result in open conflict (Scanzoni, 1972, 1978, 1979; Scanzoni and Szinovacz, 1980).

Exchange theory is the most single-mindedly individualistic of the recent approaches in sociology that emphasize human agency. As a result, it has a simplicity and clarity that is admired by positivist theorists. At the same time, exchange theory has been criticized for oversimplification.[3] Other approaches often seek to combine notions of individual agency with notions of collective agency. This combination opens up wider possibilities for sociological explanation, but it also leads to conflicting interpretations and the possibility of theoretical confusion. Examples of this can be found in discussions of the concept of 'strategy'.

Strategy

It has been noted that the boundaries between sociology and social history are no longer as strong as they once were. There is today greatly increased traffic of people and ideas between these two fields. For the most part, this traffic has taken the form of theories and concepts moving from sociology to history, and data and interpretations moving from history to sociology. Occasionally the process of cross-fertilization works the other way, when concepts developed by historians are introduced into sociological discussions. The emergence of the concept of strategy is an example of this (Modell, 1978; Moch et al., 1987; Morgan, 1989).

Many social historians and other social scientists have increasingly argued for a view of human beings as active strategists (Hareven, 1987; Lamphere, 1987). People are not seen as passively determined by their economic situations, but as actively adapting to them (Cheal, 1987b). They do this by setting long-term goals, and by weighing alternative means to achieve their ends within the possibilities existing in particular environments. The concept of strategy also conveys the idea that in evaluating alternatives open to them people adopt a comprehensive view of their situations, including taking account of the actions of others with whom they interact. If it is assumed that all the members of a group adopt an identical view of their situation, then there may exist not only individual strategies but also collective strategies, such as *family strategies* (Brenner and Laslett, 1986).

The concept of family strategy is thought to be particularly useful for analysing decisions about the allocation of persons to family positions – such as the timing of marriage, the number of children to have, co-residence with extended kin, and which family members should work outside the home and which should work within it (Hareven, 1987; Laslett and Brenner, 1989). However, the relationships between family interests and individual interests are often ambiguous, and sometimes conflicting (Crow, 1989). This can create some uncertainty as to which explanatory models are most appropriate for which kinds of data (Moch et al., 1987).

Interaction

The moral ideal that all members of a family should adopt an identical view of their collective situation has been explicitly incorporated into sociology, in the theoretical approach known as *symbolic interactionism*. The usual definition of the family employed here is that given by Burgess (1926), namely that the family is a unity of interacting personalities. By this Burgess meant, in the first instance, that family life is constituted by interactions, which maintain the relationships of husband and wife and parents and children. In addition, he believed that 'the family develops a conception of itself' (ibid.: p. 5). This conception includes a sense of the responsibilities that each member has to the others, as defined in family roles, and notions of what family life is or ought to be.

Burgess's emphasis on family unity was reflected in his concept of 'marital adjustment', which he saw as a precondition for a stable marriage.[4] He defined marital adjustment as involving processes of accommodation and assimilation, as follows:

> In certain of its phases, marital adjustment may be measured by accommodation, the mode of living that minimizes conflict and promotes harmony. Many, perhaps the majority of, marriages remain on the level of accommodation.
>
> From the standpoint of assimilation, adjustment is to be defined as the integration of the couple in a union in which the two personalities are not merely merged, or submerged, but interact to complement each other for mutual satisfaction and the achievement of common objectives. The emphasis is upon intercommunication, interstimulation, and participation in common activities.
>
> A well-adjusted marriage from the point of view of this study may then be defined as a marriage in which the attitudes and acts of each of the partners produce an environment which is favorable to the functioning of the personality of each, particularly in the sphere of primary relationships. (Burgess and Cottrell, 1939)

Burgess and his associates and followers were very interested in the relations between personality and marital interaction. It has been characteristic of the symbolic interactionist approach since then that attention is paid to the ways in which individuals' images of themselves are shaped by their interactions with others. Each person's sense of his or her identity is assumed to be derived from the communications that take place in everyday life, including family life. Stryker (1968) described this in terms of the 'familial identities' to which individuals are committed. These identities, he says, 'exist insofar as persons are participants in structured social relationships' (ibid.: p. 559).

Symbolic interactionism has been a diverse, complex and influential approach to the sociology of the family over many years (Turner, 1970; Hutter, 1985). Much of this symbolic interactionist work has been absorbed into the standard sociological theory of the family, in the form of social psychological *role theory* (Burr et al., 1979). Here the focus is typically upon how individuals 'take' family roles, in processes of socialization and identity formation (Mackie, 1987). Interactionists also study how individuals 'make' and sometimes break roles as they try to shape family life to fit their emerging definitions of themselves. Interactionist work on shifting patterns of family life thus includes studying ways in which behaviour is negotiated, and renegotiated, among family members (Backett, 1987; Finch, 1987).

From a feminist standpoint, the interactionist perspective has been criticized for obscuring asymmetry in relations between women and men, and for encouraging a benign view of family life that ignores the capacity of men to impose their definitions of reality upon women (Glenn, 1987). Prompted by emergent gender issues, symbolic interactionists have had to recognize that families are not always united. They have therefore extended their investigations to include conflict situations. This involves them in studying the interactive dynamics of control and domestic violence (Stets, 1988).

One sign of increased interest in gender issues by interactionists is the *microstructural theory* of gender (Risman and Schwartz, 1989). From this perspective, gendered behaviour is held to be the result of ways in which meanings are constructed within social relationships. Gender stereotypes are thought to be mapped onto the sexes from the typical activities in which men and women engage, as a result of their roles in the sexual division of labour. In turn, stereotypical behaviour is reproduced in cycles of interaction rituals (Cheal, 1989b). The consequences of this pattern include female dependence. Women's greater reliance on marriage gives them a stronger interest in respectability, which enables men to exercise greater control in premarital interactions (DiIorio, 1989).

A shift in emphasis has occurred within interactionist family studies, from an assumption of unity to looser models of individuals and their relationships. This shift has become more marked in recent years. Focusing on individuals rather than families has in turn meant an increased awareness of the fact that not all intimate interactions occur in family settings. Sociologists influenced by this emphasis upon methodological individualism stress the extent to which sexual encounters occur in non-family contexts. They have demonstrated how role commitments may be redefined, new relationships entered into and plural involvements sustained (Atwater, 1979, 1982; Richardson, 1988). All of this leads to increased questioning of developmental models of the changes that occur in individuals' family roles over time.

Life course

Interactionists' openness to the prevalence of social instability in modern societies was an important factor in the emergence of the interdisciplinary field known as 'life course dynamics' (Elder, 1984, 1985). The concept of the *life course* refers to the changes that occur in an individual's relationship to his or her environment over time. Like the concept of strategy, conceptualizations of the life course received much of their impetus from sociologically informed historical investigations (Elder, 1977; Hareven, 1978, 1982, 1987). However, it is the particular relevance of the life course concept to the analysis of present conditions that attracts the attention of many sociologists, who have become increasingly dissatisfied with notions of the family life cycle (Cheal, 1987b).

Family life cycle theory defines the existence of a universal set of family stages (marriage, birth, etc.), in terms of the evolution of the role system of the normal family. The underlying difficulty with family life cycle theory is the impossibility of fitting all the different sequences of domestic arrangements that exist today into any one set of stages (Trost, 1977; Murphy, 1987; Eichler, 1988).[5] Glen Elder (1984) has suggested that the notion of a normative sequence of family stages did in fact make some sense in the 1950s, which was an historically unusual era of marital stability and high fertility. But he believes that family life cycle models are no longer useful in the context of current behavioural diversity. He therefore recommends that we adopt the individual rather than the family as the basic unit of analysis for the purpose of studying changes in family relationships. Individuals' lives are followed across time, as they engage in family building and dissolving.

The focus in life course analysis is on the individual's passage through a sequence of social situations, and on how each individual is affected by the passages of others. The total sequence of an individual's situations is referred to as a life course 'trajectory' or 'pathway'. The passage from one situation to another is referred to as a 'transition'. Life course studies in the sociology of the family have dealt mainly with transitions, such as passages into and out of the married status (Wallace, 1987; Cheal, 1988c).

Life course studies exploded in the 1980s, when they had a considerable impact on the sociology of the family (Bernardes, 1986). From the life course perspective, a family is considered to be a set of 'interlocking trajectories'. Glen Elder (1985) points out that failed marriages and careers frequently lead adult sons and daughters to return to their parental household, and economic setbacks and divorce among parents of adolescents can impede their transition to adulthood. Each generation in the family is therefore seen as affected by decisions and events in the life courses of others. Among sociologists there has been particular interest in the extent to which 'problem behaviours' may result from the disadvantages caused by early experiences of other family members, especially parents, as in the case of adolescent childbearing (Elder, 1974; Elder, Caspi and Downey, 1986; Furstenberg, Brooks-Gunn and Morgan, 1987).

A major emphasis of life course research is the search for social patterns in the timing, duration, spacing and order of transitions. As studies on these issues have accumulated, it has become increasingly apparent that there is a great deal of variability and fluidity in life course trajectories. One advantage of the life course concept here is that it permits drawing comparisons between individuals and classes of individual in the degree of life course predictability and order (Rindfuss, Swicegood and Rosenfeld, 1987). An important conclusion to emerge from such studies is that women's lives are less predictable and less standardized than those of men. Two issues appear to be particularly important here.

First, it has been noted that the social dimensions of women's lives are more plural, and more finely balanced, than those of men. Glen Elder (1977) has stated as a matter of paradigmatic principle that any individual's life course is multidimensional. Individuals engage in multiple roles, such as work, marriage and parenthood, whose trajectories are affected by different events. The multi-dimensionality of the life course is especially important in accounts of women's lives. Men's life course trajectories are tied to and controlled by the institutions in which they are employed, and by related public regulatory bodies. Women's life course trajectories, on the other hand, are more influenced by their family roles, and so they are more affected by the transitions of other family members (Lopata, 1987). This is most obvious in the effects of having children upon women's employment patterns. However, it is also visible in patterns of caring for elderly dependents. Whereas caring by men usually takes the form of looking after their wives during the retirement phase of the life course, women occupy a wide variety of life course positions at the time when they begin caring (Ungerson, 1987).

The second point about female life course diversity stressed in recent socio-logical studies is that the normative identification of women with the private sphere, which was so important in the recent past, has become less strong. Women have increasingly taken up occupational careers, in combination with or as alternatives to domestic responsibilities. As they have done so, they have made different choices that reflect their particular circumstances and values. Gerson (1985, 1987), for example, has described the different ways in which women resolve the 'hard choices' between employment and family commit-ments. Women today make many different kinds of choice, ranging from the traditional model of domesticity, through rising employment aspirations and ambivalence about motherhood, to rejection of motherhood and homemaking in favour of a non-traditional career. This new diversification of women's roles, it is argued, reflects a trend toward increased individualization of the female life course (Buchmann, 1989). This trend is sometimes described as a long-term feature of modernity, and sometimes seen as inaugurating a new epoch of postmodernity.

Something is Happening

We have noted at several points, and most recently in the discussion of the life course approach, that changes in family theories often follow changes in family life. We have also seen that in the search for new understandings sociologists have explored a number of new approaches, including a variety of redefinitions of 'family'. In all this blooming, buzzing confusion there is no clear line of theoret-ical development, nor should we expect to find one. Nevertheless, there is a tendency in some of the most recent writings for discussions of theoretical possibilities to crystallize into two contrasting views of the state of theory (Buch-mann, 1989, pp. 70–5). These come together in the modernism/postmodernism debate over the future of social life and the future of the social sciences. In the remainder of this chapter we will be concerned with the future of family life.

The theoretical framework of modernism has provided the guiding thread for our discussions up to this point. It includes the theory of modernity, and related concepts of processes of modernization and anti-modernist reactions. The unifying theme here is that of the *rationalization* of social life. The progressive rational organization of human affairs is thought to be due to the emancipation of human beings from arbitrary limits of poverty and ignorance. As a result, people become free to order their activities guided by the powers of reason. Accounts of the standardization of the life course illustrate this idea very well. It is held that the timing and spacing of family transitions in the Western societies has become more orderly. It is also thought that this has occurred not so much because of intensified normative controls of the traditional sort, but because individuals have chosen common patterns of life course management under conditions of material improvement and institutional bureaucratization.

But we have noted too that this grand vision of human progress has been disturbed in recent years. There is a bewildering variety of alternative lifestyles. Also, disorderly sequences of transitions have become more prevalent. Parenthood may come before marriage, and individuals may cycle into and out of marriage and family formation many times, without ever completing the task of raising their children into independent adults.

In addition to the practical difficulty of providing explanatory models for these more complex patterns, there is a deeper problem for social theory. Are these recent changes simply a short-term interruption to the secular trend of Western modernization? Or are they the beginning of a cultural transformation, to which the classical sociological theories of social order will no longer apply?

Postmodernist theorists agree with the second of these statements. Höhn and Luscher (1988), for example, consider the ambivalent situation of the family in Germany today to be indicative of a societal transition that they think should be characterized by the term 'postmodernity'. Whatever social forms eventually emerge from this transition, Höhn and Luscher seem to think that they will involve a break with core ideas of modernity.

Modernist theorists generally disagree with claims of such a break. They do so by arguing for either a dualistic or a cyclical model of modernization. On the one hand, it is thought that there are secular tendencies toward greater collective control and social order, achieved through the expansion of powerful institutions such as the state. On the other hand, it is thought that the changes required by a modern society engaged in the progressive transformation of itself entail the frequent destruction of existing social forms, which have become outmoded. Too much destruction would, of course, render social life impossible. Tendencies towards disorganization are therefore held to be counteracted by creative forces of reorganization, which recombine the fragments of the old order in new and more advantageous ways.

Marshall Berman is a persuasive exponent of the idea that modernity is unstable. He states that in its destructive aspect, modern society 'pours us all into a maelstrom of perpetual disintegration and renewal, of struggle and contradiction, of ambiguity and anguish' (Berman, 1982, p. 15). The causes of these great upheavals include industrialization, urbanization, international migration, and violent swings in access to economic resources and in levels of economic security. These themes were in fact very prominent in American studies in the sociology of the family during the first half of the twentieth century (Elder, 1984). Although not presented in the terms that we today would want to call the theory of modernity, the work of Burgess and his colleagues none the less illustrates the nature of this approach very well.

In their justifiably famous book which summarized the best of American family sociology between the two world wars, Burgess and Locke (1945) argued that the American family was in a state of transition – from *institution* to *companionship*. In the past, they thought, a stable and secure family life was guaranteed by external pressures of law, custom and public opinion. Those controls were reinforced inside the family by the authority of the male family head, the rigid discipline exercised by parents over their children, and elaborate private and public rituals. That system of control, they argued, had broken down in America in the twentieth century. This was due to a complex combination of causes – economic deprivation among the lower classes, particularly during the Great Depression; individualism that permitted greater autonomy within and from families; a democratic ethos that loosened public controls over morality as well as internal authority relationships; the decline of domestic production and thus of an economic focus to family life; and migration and the growth of cities, with consequent exposure to new and shifting patterns of behaviour (ibid.; Burgess, 1973).

Burgess claimed that the result of all these changes was family disorganization; that is, a situation characterized by normative uncertainty, behavioural fluidity and relationship disintegration. But he was not pessimistic. Burgess believed that *disorganization* was always followed eventually by *reorganization*. Since he thought that the external, institutional supports for family life had declined, Burgess located the potential for reorganization in the desires and capacities of individuals to construct meaningful lives for themselves. Family life, he thought, was being reconstituted on the basis of interpersonal relationships of mutual affection and understanding. The result of that process would be the companionship family.

Significantly, Burgess seems to have believed it was unlikely that individuals could reconstitute family life on their own. He thought that individuals' limited resources of self-understanding and social skills would have to be supplemented and upgraded by the knowledge generated from social scientific research. Translated by family experts into practical techniques, this knowledge was to be communicated and implemented by a variety of social agencies. Burgess was deeply concerned with advancing the programmes of child guidance clinics, marriage counselling centres, psychiatrists and clinical psychologists in their efforts to treat the behaviour problems of children and adults. He also stressed the preventative value of family studies courses for college students.

Today it is the existence of the companionship family that is in question. Perhaps Burgess and Locke would not have been too surprised at this. They pointed out that ties of affection are not as strong as ties of duty, when the latter are publicly enforced. They also noted the greater vulnerability of the socially isolated companionship family, especially to the effects of economic insecurity (Burgess and Locke, 1945, p. 719).

All this is well known. What is new today – and what may justify applying the term 'postmodern' to our present condition – is that the human service programmes that Burgess recommended no longer work in precisely the way he envisaged. He seems to have simply assumed that therapeutic agencies would inevitably be committed to the values of familism, and in particular to the preservation of the family as a unity of interacting personalities. But today it is the values of individualism and emancipation from social limitations that are increasingly evident in the work of human service practitioners. Cheal (1991) notes how this is related to critical rethinking of social scientific theory and practice, especially in relation to abuse of women within their families. That rethinking is part of a trend which is not likely to reconstitute family life. Today, feminist therapists and workers in women's shelters often see it as their responsibility to provide women with personal resources with which to leave their families.

The Postmodern Family?

Postmodernist theorists have begun to grapple with the possibility that many of the features of social life that were taken for granted for a long time will have to be rethought. This is not simply a question of rethinking specific social arrangements, such as family life, or even the sex/gender role system. Rather, postmodernism poses the question of a general rethinking of 'the social' and of 'theory'. Postmodernism is an elusive approach to the study of human existence, which has only recently begun to be incorporated into the sociology of social life (Denzin, 1986; Bauman, 1988a, 1988b; Featherstone, 1988; Kellner, 1988; Murphy, 1988, 1989). The remarks that follow are therefore intended to be merely suggestive of current lines of development.

Postmodernist thought begins with experiences of pluralism, disorder and fragmentation in contemporary culture that are not predicted by the modern paradigm of universal reason. Postmodernists go on to argue that if modernity, and hence our concepts of reason and progress, have in some sense failed, then presumably a very different set of principles must be at work in the world. Unlike the modernist theorists, however, the postmodernists do not think these alternative principles will eventually produce a total reorganization of social life.[6] Rather, they are inclined to believe that what is most characteristic of the postmodern era is its continuous production of instability. This production of instability – in science, art and literature as well as in lifestyles and family relationships – is described by a set of ideas that are unlike the standard theories of social evolution (such as that of Talcott Parsons), which presupposed convergence to equilibrium. The following points deal with some current questions about the future of family life in postmodern society.

The end of progress

Faith in modernity has included the belief in a continuous upward path of improvement for all that leads to an ever more glorious future of popular well-being and social harmony. This romantic view of modernity has been severely eroded by recent events in the Western societies. There is a growing realization that economic growth and the expansion of the welfare state since the end of the Second World War did not solve all social ills. Many individuals remain trapped in poverty and ignorance, and for some social groups – such as American blacks – conditions have got measurably worse. Stories about increasing numbers of children growing up in poverty reach us from many different directions, like a bad echo from the nineteenth century.

Social change continues, of course – at an ever more rapid pace – but it is thought that it does so in ways that bring only dubious benefits, or benefits for some but not others, or benefits that have side-effects whose accumulation will eventually cost us dearly. It therefore appears to some observers that, in the Western societies at least, progress has come to an end and with it modernity (Vattimo, 1988). If that is the case, then what does the postmodern family look like?

Norman Denzin argues that the traditional concept of a family can no longer be applied to the postmodern situation. The modern nuclear family, in which children were cared for by two parents within a protective and emotionally secure environment, is no longer the norm in America, he believes. He therefore proposes a definition of a new type of family for the postmodern period. His bleak assessment is that 'It is a single-parent family, headed by a teenage mother, who may be drawn to drug abuse and alcoholism. She and her children live in a household that is prone to be violent' (Denzin, 1987, p. 33).[7]

In addition to these structural and interactional features, Denzin refers to two other aspects of postmodern family life. They have to do with the connections that family members have with the social environment. First, Denzin suggests that increasing numbers of children are now cared for by someone other than a parent. The daycare setting is therefore an important factor in contemporary child development. Second, there is the presence of the television set in the home, which is left on for up to seven hours a day. It is from television that children learn cultural myths today, Denzin insists. He concludes that the postmodern child 'is cared for by the television set, in conjunction with the day-care center' (ibid.). The mass media and daycare providers also figure prominently in other accounts of postmodernization.

Simulations and the death of the subject

Postmodernist theories of popular culture attach considerable importance to the ways in which mass-mediated meanings penetrate all corners of contemporary social life. Jean Baudrillard, especially, argues that the media's insatiable urge to communicate creates an excess of cultural products. This excess of meanings erases all boundaries, and it produces a de-differentiated mass society (Baudrillard, 1983a).[8] One aspect of this situation, in Baudrillard's (1983b) view, is the disappearance of any separation between public and private spheres. This is because intimate details of private lives are picked up by journalists and talk-show hosts, processed through electronic networks, and relayed into millions of homes through television and newspapers.

Denzin (1987) is concerned that 'television set family myths', which are portrayed in soap operas and situation comedies, are out of touch with the realities of family life for most people. They are 'cultural fantasies', which do not provide practical guidelines for how to live today. The television 'families' that fascinate mass audiences are, in Baudrillard's (1988) terminology, *simulations*. These images are not real families, nor are they signs that refer to real families. Nevertheless, these imaginary families are 'real' to millions of viewers, who discuss the events of their lives at work the next day just as they discuss the details of their own lives. This is, Baudrillard says, 'the generation by models of a real without origin or reality: a hyperreal' (ibid.: p. 166).

Hyperreal mediated fantasies are of particular interest to feminist theorists, who detect in them sites for the ideological construction of male-dominated heterosexual couples. Popular romance narratives, such as the Harlequin Romance paperbacks, have drawn especial attention (Ebert, 1988; Finn, 1988). The precise subjective effects produced by reading these texts are important issues in contemporary social theory. Postmodernist interpretations of romance narratives see them as constituting the 'subjectivity' of the individual, or in other words as creating the individual's sense of self. Of course, romance stories are only one source of subjectivity. They are therefore described as existing in (partially) contradictory relations to other constitutive sources, such as everyday family life. These other sources are also thought to contain contradictory experiences, such as love and fear, submission and autonomy, sexual desire and asexual care-giving. The self, or 'subject', produced by this complex of experiences is seen not as a coherent, stable essence, but as a fragmented participant in various discourses. Ebert (1988, p. 38), for instance, holds that today,

> gender instability and identity confusion threaten to undermine the individual's imaginary sense of a whole self. As a result, individuals readily seek out and embrace those ideological representations that symbolically resolve these contradictions and produce the illusion of a unified, stable subjectivity.

The claim that individuals do not now (and perhaps never did) possess a stable inner identity is sometimes expressed in the phrase 'the death of the subject'. Behind this phrase lies the argument that individuals who do not possess a coherent sense of their own identity will not be able to act consistently upon, or especially against, their environment. It is at this point that the sociology of the family comes back in. The shifting contexts of childhood socialization in postmodern society are sometimes thought to contribute to subjective instability. It is here that current research into the experiences of children in daycare acquires its theoretical relevance.

Chaos

Leavitt and Power (1989) question whether children can develop authentic understandings of their emotions in daycare interactions, if the care-givers' own lack of emotional investment in them results in a failure to legitimize children's emotional expressions. Dencik (1989) considers such anxieties to be themselves indicative of the postmodern condition of a quickening 'social acceleration'. Old patterns have been abandoned, but the new ones are not stable. Dencik argues that in Denmark, parents and other care-givers distance themselves from their own experiences as children, which they consider to be invalidated as models for childhood today. But at the same time they lack confidence in the alternative models proposed by experts, since their effects are unknown and they are subject to endless revision. In Dencik's words:

> Modern parents know a lot about children and child development as compared with previous generations. Still, many of them simply feel at a loss at what to do. They listen eagerly to the advice of experts, but soon discover they often change their minds and prove themselves to be unreliable. One year we hear the children absolutely must eat at regular times, next year they must be allowed to eat whenever they feel hungry. One year the children must have as much freedom as possible, the next year strict rules of behaviour must be enforced. Nobody can give hard and fast advice, the know-how changes just as quickly as the development itself. Uncertainty is chronic. (Dencik, 1989, p. 174)

Forced to make decisions in a much shorter time than that needed to assemble the requisite information, people may panic and abandon reason in favour of simplified codes. The resulting social structure is not a product of social reorganization, but a temporary order within a constant instability. It is this instability of knowledge, uncertainty of judgement and lack of confidence in experts that make the present era merit the description 'postmodern' (Bauman, 1987). Lack of confidence pervades all expert systems now, since they are continuously being outmoded, scrapped, broken down and reassembled. This is notoriously the case with computer technology, as Dencik notes. It is also the situation in social theory.

NOTES

1   Touraine has criticized as outmoded the dominant sociological view of the relationship between social life and social history, which he says was 'based on the unity between the stage of evolution of a society and its form of social and cultural

organization; this is an idea that S. M. Lipset has defended with great talent through a series of influential books beginning with *Political Man'* (Touraine, 1984, p. 41). For an empirical critique of Lipset's hypotheses along these lines see Cheal (1978).

2 Young and Willmott's hypothesis of a trend toward the symmetrical family has been subjected to close scrutiny, from which mostly negative conclusions have been drawn. See Hunt and Hunt (1982), Lupri and Symons (1982) and Finch (1983, 1985).

3 Critics include Cheal (1984) and Glenn (1987). Hartsock (1985) argues that exchange theory is incompatible with a feminist standpoint. First, she says that the prevalence of empathy in women's self-definition contradicts the key assumption in exchange theory, that individuals are fundamentally separate and concerned only with their own interests. Second, women's experiences do not support the view that all social relations are voluntaristic. Women who are responsible for small children typically have little choice over whether or not to accept them. And third, unlike the opposition of interests in competitive market relations, conflict is not at the core of the relationships between most mothers and their children.

A relevant example of the issues here can be seen in Ivan Nye's (1982) discussion of transactions between parents and their children. Nye points out that in an industrial society children provide few material benefits which would compensate their parents for the enormous costs of their upbringing. This leads him to question why parents continue to shoulder heavy costs on behalf of their children, when they can expect to get few rewards in return. In searching for ways to deal with this problem in exchange theoretic terms, Nye suggests that parental support might be induced by non-material rewards from children, and by social rewards from the larger community. The possibility that family life might be a complex relational nexus constituted by mixed motives is not even considered.

4 Marital adjustment has been a topic of enduring interest among American family scientists, particularly in relation to the concept of 'marital quality' (Spanier, 1976; Lewis and Spanier, 1979; Vannoy-Hiller and Philliber, 1989).

5 One option for family life cycle theory in the 1980s was to follow the route of concept expansion, outlined above. This involved identifying a normal model of the family life cycle, and one or more secondary models. Expanded family life cycle models have sometimes been proposed as a means of adapting family life cycle theory to contemporary conditions of social diversification (Stapleton, 1980; Mattessich and Hill, 1987). Reuben Hill (1986), for example, took this approach towards the end of his career, when he outlined a complex model of the paths of development of three types of single-parent family. The principal disadvantage of this approach is the proliferation of typologies and models. Eventually this reaches the point at which the originally simple and powerful idea of the family life cycle becomes too unwieldy to be of practical value for social scientific explanation. At that point more or less arbitrary typological reductions must be carried out (Höhn, 1987).

6 Reorganization is a possibility in postmodern society, but it is likely to appear only in patches, in unique configurations that emerge under particular, local conditions.

7 There are some striking similarities between the postmodernist critique of the failure of modern institutions and the anti-modernist critique of modernity as cultural decline. For example, anti-modernists and postmodernists are generally highly critical of welfare bureaucracies, which they believe provide only partial solutions to some problems, while creating new problems which they cannot solve. This similarity is one of the most controversial aspects of postmodernism. Some observers claim

that postmodernism is simply a new form of conservatism in disguise (Habermas, 1981; Sangren, 1988). Denzin's postmodernism does not identify with anti-modernist calls for a return to tradition. He insists that 'We must stop defining problems in terms of a middle-class morality', and we must avoid 'proposals that take freedom away from those they are intended to serve' (Denzin, 1987, p. 35).

8   The process of cultural de-differentiation in postmodernization is the opposite of the process of structural differentiation in modernization (e.g. as described by Parsons).

REFERENCES

Ahrons, C. (1979), 'The binuclear family', *Alternative Lifestyles*, 2.

Ahrons, C. and Rodgers, R. (1987), *Divorced Families*, New York: W. W. Norton.

Aldous, J. (1977), 'Family interaction patterns', *Annual Review of Sociology*, 3, Palo Alto: Annual Reviews.

Allen, K. (1989), *Single Women / Family Ties*, Newbury Park: Sage.

Atwater, L. (1979), 'Getting involved', *Alternative Lifestyles*, 2.

Atwater, L. (1982), *The Extramarital Connection*, New York: Irvington.

Backett, K. (1987), 'The negotiation of fatherhood', in C. Lewis and M. O'Brien (eds), *Reassessing Fatherhood*, London: Sage.

Baudrillard, J. (1983a), *In the Shadow of the Silent Majorities*, New York: Semiotext(e).

Baudrillard, J. (1983b), 'The ecstasy of communication', in H. Foster (ed.), *The Anti-Aesthetic*, Port Townsend: Bay Press.

Baudrillard, J. (1988), *Selected Writings*, Stanford: Stanford University Press.

Bauman, Z. (1987), *Legislators and Interpreters*, Ithaca, NY: Cornell University Press.

Bauman, Z. (1988a), 'Is there a postmodern sociology?', *Theory, Culture and Society*, 5: 217–37.

Bauman, Z. (1988b), 'Sociology and postmodernity', *Sociological Review*, 36: 790–813.

Beechey, V. (1985), 'Familial ideology', in V. Beechey and J. Donald (eds), *Subjectivity and Social Relations*, Milton Keynes: Open University Press.

Berger, P. and Kellner, H. (1970), 'Marriage and the construction of reality', in H. Dreitzel (ed.), *Recent Sociology No.2*, New York: Macmillan.

Berman, M. (1982), *All That Is Solid Melts Into Air*, New York: Simon and Schuster.

Bernardes, J. (1985a), '"Family ideology": identification and exploration', *Sociological Review*, 33: 275–97.

Bernardes, J. (1985b), 'Do we really know what "the family" is?', in P. Close and R. Collins (eds), *Family and Economy in Modern Society*, Basingstoke: Macmillan.

Bernardes, J. (1986), 'Multidimensional developmental pathways: a proposal to facilitate the conceptualization of "family diversity"', *Sociological Review*, 34: 590–610.

Bernardes, J. (1988), 'Founding the *new* "family studies"', *Sociological Review*, 36: 57–86.

Boh, K. (1989), 'European family life patterns – a reappraisal', in K. Boh, M. Bak, C. Clason, M. Pankratova, J. Qvortrup, G. Sgritta and K. Waerness (eds), *Changing Patterns of European Family Life*, London: Routledge.

Brenner, J. and Laslett, B. (1986), 'Social reproduction and the family', in U. Himmel-strand (ed.), *Sociology: From Crisis to Science?*, vol. 2, London: Sage.

Buchmann, M. (1989), *The Script of Life in Modern Society*, Chicago: University of Chicago Press.

Burgess, E. (1926), 'The family as a unity of interacting personalities', *The Family*, 7: 3–9.

Burgess, E. (1973), *On Community, Family, and Delinquency*, Chicago: University of Chicago Press.

Burgess, E. and Cottrell, L. (1939), *Predicting Success or Failure in Marriage*, New York: Prentice-Hall.

Burgess, E. and Locke, H. (1945), *The Family*, New York: American Book Company.

Burr, W., Leigh, G., Day, R. and Constantine, J. (1979), 'Symbolic interaction and the family', in W. Buff, R. Hill, F. I. Nye and I. Reiss (eds), *Contemporary Theories About the Family*, vol. 2, New York: Free Press.

Cheal, D. (1978), 'Models of mass politics in Canada', *Canadian Review of Sociology and Anthropology*, 15: 325–38.

Cheal, D. (1984), 'Transactions and transformational models', in N. Denzin (ed.), *Studies in Symbolic Interaction*, vol. 5, Greenwich, CT: JAI Press.

Cheal, D. (1987a), '"Showing them you love them": gift giving and the dialectic of intimacy', *Sociological Review*, 35: 150–69.

Cheal, D. (1987b), 'Intergenerational transfers and life course management', in A. Bryman, B. Bytheway, P. Allatt and T. Keil (eds), *Rethinking the Life Cycle*, Macmillan: Basingstoke.

Cheal, D. (1988a), *The Gift Economy*, London: Routledge.

Cheal, D. (1988b), 'The ritualization of family ties', *American Behavioral Scientist*, 31: 632–43.

Cheal, D. (1988c), 'Relationships in time: ritual, social structure and the life course', in N. Denzin (ed.), *Studies in Symbolic Interaction*, vol. 9, Greenwich, CT: JAI Press.

Cheal, D. (1989a), 'The meanings of family life', in K. Ishwaran (ed.), *Family and Marriage*, Toronto: Wall and Thompson.

Cheal, D. (1989b), 'Women together: bridal showers and gender membership', in B. Risman and P. Schwartz (eds), *Gender in Intimate Relationships*, Belmont: Wadsworth.

Cheal, D. (1991), *Family and the State of Theory*, Hemel Hempstead: Harvester Wheatsheaf.

Cotton, S., Antill, J. and Cunningham, J. (1983), 'Living together', in A. Burns, G. Bottomley and P. Jools (eds), *The Family in the Modern World*, Sydney: Allen & Unwin.

Crow, G. (1989), 'The use of the concept of "strategy" in recent sociological literature', *Sociology*, 23: 1–24.

Dencik, L. (1989), 'Growing up in the post-modern age', *Acta Sociologica*, 32: 155–80.

Denzin, N. (1986), 'Postmodern social theory', *Sociological Theory*, 4: 194–202.

Denzin, N. (1987), 'Postmodern children', *Society*, 24: 32–6.

DiIorio, J. (1989), 'Being and becoming coupled', in B. Risman and P. Schwartz (eds), *Gender in Intimate Relationships*, Belmont: Wadsworth.

Ebert, T. (1988), 'The romance of patriarchy', *Cultural Critique*, 10: 19–57.

Edelman, M. (1987), *Families in Peril*, Cambridge, MA.: Harvard University Press.

Eichler, M. (1988), *Families in Canada Today*, Toronto: Gage.

Elder, G. (1974), *Children of the Great Depression*, Chicago: University of Chicago Press.

Elder, G. (1977), 'Family history and the life course', *Journal of Family History*, 2: 279–304.

Elder, G. (1984), 'Families, kin, and the life course', in R. Parke (ed.), *Review of Child Development Research*, vol. 7, Chicago: University of Chicago Press.

Elder, G. (1985), 'Perspectives on the life course', in G. Elder (ed.), *Life Course Dynamics*, Ithaca, NY: Cornell University Press.

Elder, G., Caspi, A. and Downey, G. (1986), 'Problem behavior and family relationships', in A. Sorensen, F. Weinert and L. Sherrod (eds), *Human Development and the Life Course*, Hillsdale, NJ.: Lawrence Erlbaum.

Featherstone, M. (1988), 'In pursuit of the postmodern', *Theory, Culture and Society*, 5: 195–215.

Finch, J. (1983), *Married to the Job*, London: Allen & Unwin.

Finch, J. (1985), 'Work, the family and the home', *International Journal of Social Economics*, 12: 26–35.

Finch, J. (1987), 'Family obligations and the life course', in A. Bryman, B. Bytheway, P. Allatt and T. Keil (eds), *Rethinking the Life Cycle*, Basingstoke: Macmillan.

Finn, G. (1988), 'Women, fantasy and popular culture', in R. Gruneau (ed.), *Popular Cultures and Political Practices*, Toronto: Garamond.

Furstenberg, F., Brooks-Gunn, J. and Morgan, S. P. (1987), *Adolescent Mothers in Later Life*, Cambridge: Cambridge University Press.

Furstenberg, F. and Spanier, G. (1984), *Recycling the Family*, Beverly Hills: Sage.

Gee, E. (1986), 'The life course of Canadian women', *Social Indicators Research*, 18: 263–83.

Gerson, K. (1985), *Hard Choices*, Berkeley: University of California Press.

Gerson, K. (1987), 'How women choose between employment and family', in N. Gerstel and H. Gross (eds), *Families and Work*, Philadelphia: Temple University Press.

Gerstel, N. and Gross, H. (1984), *Commuter Marriage*, New York: Guilford Press.

Giles-Sims, J. (1987), 'Social exchange in remarried families', in K. Pasley and M. Ihinger-Tallman (eds), *Remarriage and Stepparenting*, New York: Guilford Press.

Glenn, E. N. (1987), 'Gender and the family', in B. Hess and M. Ferree (eds), *Analyzing Gender*, Newbury Park: Sage.

Gross, H. (1980), 'Dual-career couples who live apart', *Journal of Marriage and the Family*, 42: 567–76.

Gubrium, J. and Holstein, J. (1990), *What Is Family?* Mountain View, CA.: Mayfield.

Habermas, J. (1981), 'Modernity versus postmodernity', *New German Critique*, 22: 3–18.

Hareven, T., (ed.) (1978), *Transitions*, New York: Academic Press.

Hareven, T. (1982), 'The life course and aging in historical perspective', in T. Hareven and K. Adams (eds), *Aging and Life Course Transitions*, New York: Guilford Press.

Hareven, T. (1987), 'Historical analysis of the family', in M. Sussman and S. Steinmetz (eds), *Handbook of Marriage and the Family*, New York: Plenum Press.

Harris, C. (1983), *The Family and Industrial Society*, London: Allen & Unwin.

Hartsock, N. (1985), 'Exchange theory', in S. McNall (ed.), *Current Perspectives in Social Theory*, vol. 6, Greenwich, CT: JAI Press

Hertz, R. (1986), *More Equal than Others*, Berkeley: University of California Press.

Hill, R. (1986), 'Life cycle stages for types of single parent families', *Family Relations*, 35: 19–29.

Höhn, C. (1987), 'The family life cycle: needed extensions of the concept', in J. Bongaarts, T. Burch and K. Wachter (eds), *Family Demography*, Oxford: Clarendon Press.

Höhn, C. and Luscher, K. (1988), 'The changing family in the Federal Republic of Germany', *Journal of Family Issues*, 9: 317–35.

Hunt, J. and Hunt, L. (1982), 'The dualities of careers and families', *Social Problems*, 29: 499–510.

Hutter, M. (1985), 'Symbolic interaction and the study of the family', in R. S. Perin Banayagam (ed.), *Studies in Symbolic Interaction*, Supplement 1, Greenwich, CT: JAI Press.

Jallinoja, R. (1989), 'Women between the family and employment', in K. Bob, M. Bak, C. Clason, M. Pankratova, J. Qvortrup, G. Sgritta and K. Waerness (eds), *Changing Patterns of European Family Life*, London: Routledge.

Kellner, D. (1988), 'Postmodernism as social theory', *Theory, Culture and Society*, 5: 239–69.

Kohli, M. (1986), 'The world we forgot: a historical review of the life course', in V. Marshall (ed.), *Later Life*, Beverly Hills: Sage.

Lamphere, L. (1987), *From Working Daughters to Working Mothers*, Ithaca NY: Cornell University Press.

Laslett, B. and Brenner, J. (1989), 'Gender and social reproduction', in W. R. Scott (ed.), *Annual Review of Sociology*, vol. 15, Palo Alto: Annual Reviews.

Lerole, R. and Powel, M. (1989), 'Emotional socialization in the postmodern era', *Social Psychology Quarterly*, 52: 35–43.

Levinger, G. (1979), 'A social exchange view on the dissolution of pair relationships', in R. Burgess and T. Huston (eds), *Social Exchange in Developing Relationships*, New York: Academic Press.

Lewis, R. and Spanier, G. (1979), 'Theorizing about the quality and stability of marriage', in W. Burr, R. Hill, F. I. Nye and I. Reiss (eds), *Contemporary Theories About the Family*, vol. 1, New York: Free Press.

Lewis, R. and Spanier, G. (1982), 'Marital quality, marital stability, and social exchange', in F. I. Nye (ed.), *Family Relationships*, Beverly Hills: Sage.

Linton, R. (1936), *The Study of Man*, New York: Appleton-Century.

Lopata, H. (1987), 'Women's family roles in life course perspective', in B. Hess and M. Ferree (eds), *Analyzing Gender*, Newbury Park: Sage.

Luhmann, N. (1986), *Love as Passion*, Cambridge: Polity Press.

Lupri, E. and Symons, G. (1982), 'The emerging symmetrical family: fact or fiction?', *International Journal of Comparative Sociology*, 23: 166–89.

Mackie, M. (1987), *Constructing Women and Men*, Toronto: Holt, Rinehart and Winston.

McLain, R. and Weigert, A. (1979), 'Toward a phenomenological sociology of family', in W. Burr, R. Hill. F. I. Nye and I. Reiss (eds), *Contemporary Theories About the Family*, vol. 2, New York: Free Press.

Mattessich, P. and Hill, R. (1987), 'Life cycle and family development', in M. Sussman and S. Steinmetz (eds), *Handbook of Marriage and the Family*, New York: Plenum.

Mayer, K. and Schoepflin, U. (1989), 'The state and the life course', in W. R. Scott (ed.), *Annual Review of Sociology*, vol. 15, Palo Alto: Annual Reviews.

Meyer, J. (1986), 'The self and the life course', in A. Sorensen, F. Weinert and L. Sheffod (eds), *Human Development and the Life Course*, Hillsdale, NJ: Lawrence Erlbaum.

Moch, L., Folbre, N., Smith, D., Cornell, L. and Tilly, L. (1987), 'Family strategy: a dialogue', *Historical Methods*, 20: 113–25.

Modell, J. (1978), 'Patterns of consumption, acculturation, and family income strategies in late nineteenth-century America', in T. Hareven and M. Vinovskis (eds), *Family and Population in Nineteenth-Century America*, Princeton, NJ: Princeton University Press.

Morgan, D. H. J. (1989), 'Strategies and sociologists', *Sociology*, 23: 25–9.

Murphy, J. (1988), 'Making sense of postmodern sociology', *British Journal of Sociology*, 39: 600–14.

Murphy, J. (1989), *Postmodern Social Analysis and Criticism*, New York: Greenwood.

Murphy, M. (1987), 'Measuring the family life cycle', in A. Bryman, B. Bytheway, P. Allatt and T. Keil (eds), *Rethinking the Life Cycle*, Basingstoke: Macmillan.

Murstein, B. (1973), 'A theory of marital choice applied to interracial marriage', in I. Stuart and L. Abt (eds), *Interracial Marriage*, New York: Grossman.

Nave-Herz, R. (1989), 'The significance of the family and marriage in the Federal Republic of Germany', in P. Close (ed.), *Family Divisions and Inequalities in Modern Society*, Basingstoke: Macmillan.

Nye, F. I. (1979), 'Choice, exchange, and the family', in W. Burr, R. Hill, F. I. Nye and I. Reiss (eds), *Contemporary Theories About the Family*, vol. 2, New York: Free Press.

Nye, F. I. (1980), 'Family mini theories as special instances of choice and exchange theory', *Journal of Marriage and the Family*, 42: 479–89.

Nye, F. I. (1982), 'The basic theory', in F. I. Nye (ed.), *Family Relationships*, Beverly Hills: Sage.

Parsons, T. (1943), 'The kinship system of the contemporary United States', *American Anthropologist*, 45: 22–38.

Parsons, T. (1971), 'The normal American family', in B. Adams and T. Weirath (eds), *Readings on the Sociology of the Family*, Chicago: Markham.

Parsons, T. (1977), *Social Systems and the Evolution of Action Theory*, New York: Free Press.

Rapoport, R. (1989), 'Ideologies about family forms: towards diversity', in K. Boh, M. Bak, C. Clason, M. Pankratova, J. Qvortrup, G. Sgritta and K. Waerness (eds), *Changing Patterns of European Family Life*, London: Routledge.

Rapoport, R. N., Fogarty, M. and Rapoport, R. (eds) (1982), *Families in Britain*, London: Routledge & Kegan Paul.

Reiger, K. (1985), *The Disenchantment of the Home*, Melbourne: Oxford University Press.

Reiger, K. (1987), 'All but the kitchen sink: on the significance of domestic science and the silence of social theory', *Theory and Society*, 16: 497–526.

Renvoize, J. (1985), *Going Solo*, London: Routledge & Kegan Paul.

Richards, L. (1989), 'Family and home ownership in Australia – the nexus of ideologies', in K. Boh, G. Sgritta and M. Sussman (eds), *Strategies in Marriage, Family and Work: International Perspectives*, New York: Haworth Press.

Richardson, L. (1988), 'Secrecy and status: the social construction of forbidden relationships', *American Sociological Review*, 53: 209–19.

Rindfuss, R. C., Swicegood, G. and Rosenfeld, R. (1987), 'Disorder in the life course', *American Sociological Review*, 52: 785–801.

Risman, B. and Schwartz, P. (1989), 'Being gendered: a microstructural view of intimate relationships', in B. Risman and P. Schwartz (eds), *Gender in Intimate Relationships*, Belmont: Wadsworth.

Rosenthal, C. (1983), 'Aging, ethnicity and the family: beyond the modernization thesis', *Canadian Ethnic Studies*, 15:

Sangren, S. (1988), 'Rhetoric and the authority of ethnography: "postmodernism" and the social reproduction of texts', *Current Anthropology*, 29: 405–35.

Scanzoni, J. (1972), *Sexual Bargaining*, Englewood Cliffs, NJ: Prentice-Hall.

Scanzoni, J. (1978), *Sex Roles, Women's Work, and Marital Conflict*, Lexington: D. C. Heath.

Scanzoni, J. (1979), 'Social processes and power in families', in W. Burr, R. Hill, F. I. Nye and I. Reiss (eds), *Contemporary Theories About the Family*, vol. 1, New York: Free Press.

Scanzoni, J. (1987), 'Families in the 1980s: time to refocus our thinking', *Journal of Family Issues*, 8: 394–421.

Scanzoni, J., Polonko, K., Teachman, J. and Thompson, L. (1989), *The Sexual Bond*, Newbury Park: Sage.

Scanzoni, J. and Szinovacz, M. (1980), *Family Decision-Making*, Sage: Beverly Hills.

Sgritta, G. (1989), 'Towards a new paradigm', in K. Boh, M. Bak, C. Clason, M. Pankratova, J. Qvortrup, G. Sgritta and K. Waerness (eds), *Changing Patterns of European Family Life*, London: Routledge.

Spanier, G. (1976), 'Measuring dyadic adjustment', *Journal of Marriage and the Family*, 38: 15–28.

Stapleton, C. (1980), 'Reformulation of the family life-cycle concept', *Environment and Planning A*, 12: 1103–18.

Stets, J. (1988), *Domestic Violence and Control*, New York: Springer-Verlag.

Stryker, S. (1968), 'Identity salience and role performance', *Journal of Marriage and the Family*, 30: 558–64.

Tallman, I. (1988), 'Problem solving in families', in D. Klein and J. Aldous (eds), *Social Stress and Family Development*, New York: Guilford Press.

Taubin, S. and Mudd, E. (1983), 'Contemporary traditional families', in E. Macklin and R. Rubin (eds), *Contemporary Families and Alternative Lifestyles*, Beverly Hills: Sage.

Touraine, A. (1984), 'The waning sociological image of social life', *International Journal of Comparative Sociology*, 25: 33–44

Touraine, A. (1988), 'Modernity and cultural specificities', *International Social Science Journal*, 40: 533–42.

Trost, J. (1977), 'The family life cycle: a problematic concept', in J. Cuisenier (ed.), *The Family Life Cycle in European Societies*, The Hague: Mouton.

Trost, J. (1980), 'The concept of one-parent family', *Journal of Comparative Family Studies*, 11: 129–38.

Trost, J. (1988), 'Conceptualizing the family', *International Sociology*, 3: 301–8.

Trost, J. (1990), 'Do we mean the same by the concept of family?', *Communication Research*, 17: 431–43.

Turner, R. (1970), *Family Interaction*, New York: Wiley.

Uhlenberg, P. (1978), 'Changing configurations of the life course', in T. Hareven (ed.), *Transitions*, New York: Academic Press.

Ungerson, C. (1987), 'The life course and informal caring', in G. Cohen (ed.), *Social Change and the Life Course*, London: Tavistock.

Vannoy-Hiller, D. and Philliber, W. (1989), *Equal Partners*, Newbury Park: Sage.

Vattimo, G. (1988), *The End of Modernity*, Cambridge: Polity Press.

Veevers, J. (1980), *Childless By Choice*, Toronto: Butterworth.

Wallace, C. (1987), *For Richer, For Poorer*, London: Tavistock.

Wilson, P. and Pahl, R. (1988), 'The changing sociological construct of the family', *Sociological Review*, 36: 233–66.

Young, M. and Willmott, P. (1974), *The Symmetrical Family*, New York: Pantheon.

Part II

Marriage, Intimacy and Power

In Part II of this book, the focus shifts from a broad concern with the changing order of family relationships to the narrower question of how contemporary marriage and partnerships are structured. Clearly, many models of family change reflect the ways in which 'blueprints' of marriage (Cancian, 1987) have altered. Some of these were discussed in Part I, particularly in chapter 1 by Finch and Summerfield. In general the belief that marriage has become more expressive, more egalitarian and more democratic is a culturally powerful one. Moreover, people's increased willingness to recognize separation and divorce as a solution to marital disputes and unhappiness has helped foster the perspective that gender inequalities within marriage are much less pervasive than they were in previous eras. The chapters in Part II address these types of issue. Together they demonstrate that while marital expectations and ideologies may be shifting, within marriage (and other heterosexual partnerships) men remain powerful and continue to have privileged access to resources.

Chapter 4 by Jean Duncombe and Dennis Marsden, first published in *Sociology*, is explicitly concerned with the expression of intimacy within contemporary marriage. A strong theme within popular accounts of the changing character of marriage and partnership is that couples are now far more willing than they were in the past to confide in each other and to share feelings, hopes and fears. The expression of intimacy has become a hallmark of contemporary coupledom. Without this, without emotional communion, many would now hold a marriage to be incomplete; it might be the marriage that many have but it is not the ideal people seek. Although based on a small sample of marriages, Duncombe and Marsden's chapter explores these issues with both wives and husbands. What their chapter shows, in line with other research (e.g. Mansfield and Collard, 1988; Rubin, 1990; Wood, 1996; Harrison, 1998), is that only rarely are these ideals met to any great extent in practice. More specifically, just as there is a highly gendered division in the domestic work done within the home, so too men and women acquire different responsibilities for — and different skills in — the emotional labour involved in sustaining their relationship. It is women far more than men who manage emotionality within the home. While this fits in with other aspects of gender identity and socialization, it none the less leaves many wives dissatisfied with their husbands' apparent inability to validate their relationship through an appropriate expression of emotions and feelings. Giddens's *The Transformation of Intimacy* (1992) discusses the growth of 'confluent love' in late modernity – a love based on an 'equality in emotional give and take' (ibid.: p. 62) – but this is clearly some way removed from the love being constructed and experienced in the marriages Duncombe and Marsden examine.

Chapter 5 by Jeffrey Weeks, Brian Heaphy and Catherine Donovan – written especially for this volume – also addresses issues of intimacy and equality. As its title indicates, its focus is on gay partnerships rather than heterosexual ones. The research on which the chapter is based is particularly important, as it is one of the very few British studies to examine the dynamics of domestic life in gay households. The chapter is especially concerned with how issues of personal commitment and domestic organization are managed in these 'families of choice'. In analysing the ways in which gay couples construct their domestic relationships, the authors explicitly contrast the pleasures and tensions found in these partnerships with those arising in heterosexual ones, and in particular marriage. Among other issues, they highlight the strong emphasis placed on equality within these relationships. Of course, at an ideological level such an emphasis can also be found in marriage, though the reality is usually different as a consequence of the systematic gender inequalities inherent in contemporary social and economic organization. However, among gay couples there is a greater reflexivity about the construction or 'fashioning' of their relationships and, consequently, a higher degree of monitoring of activities, tasks and responsibilities within them to ensure that significant differentials do not arise. This level of reflexivity and concern for equality is in marked contrast to that sustained in most marriages and other long-term heterosexual partnerships. As noted, comparatively few studies of gay couples have been published; however, the studies by Blumstein and Schwartz (1983) and Dunne (1997) are relevant to this chapter.

Chapter 6 by Caroline Vogler and Jan Pahl is concerned with the ways in which money is allocated within heterosexual partnerships. Like the issue of intimacy, a key theme in contemporary visions of marriage (and other equivalent relationships) is that resources are distributed more 'fairly' than in the past. The sharing of money within marriage is particularly significant within this. Building on Pahl's earlier work (Pahl, 1980, 1983, 1989), Vogler and Pahl's chapter, originally published in *Sociological Review*, demonstrates the complexities there are in understanding the idiosyncratic practices which couples evolve. However, notwithstanding the variations which exist, it is evident that access to and control over money are gendered, and that the implications of this vary depending on the level of income in the household. Putting it somewhat simply, men seem to be advantaged in terms of access to money for personal spending, no matter what system of money management is used in the household. Thus, even when women exercise control over household income and expenditure, usually the result is that in balancing the household budget they skimp on themselves, prioritizing husbands' and children's needs above their own. Readers wanting to explore these matters more should read Vogler and Pahl's (1993) companion article to this one, as well as Wilson (1987) and Pahl (1989). Other aspects of resource distribution within households are raised in Part III.

Chapter 7 by James Nazroo is concerned with a more direct form of control and power: physical violence. Until the 1970s domestic violence received remarkably little attention from sociologists or others interested in family patterns. It was only towards the end of that decade that studies into domestic violence began to be published (e.g. Martin, 1978; Dobash and Dobash, 1980; Pahl, 1985). In Britain much of the research was informed by a feminist perspective and based on studies of women living in refuges. Nazroo's chapter, originally published in *Sociology*, is particularly interesting both because it is based on a randomly generated sample of couples who were not previously known to have used violence, and because it contrasts a feminist model of domestic violence with the 'family dysfunction' model dominant in the United States. This latter posits that domestic violence is perpetrated by both husbands and wives, and consequently should not be viewed principally as an aspect of male control. However, Nazroo's data offers little in support of this argument. In particular, he found that while some women were violent to their partners, they very rarely were so to an extent that threatened the man or left him fearful. In contrast, when men were violent the women involved were far more likely to be seriously hurt and to be frightened by the prospect of future attacks. In other words, family violence is an element of male power and not solely the result of dysfunctional family dynamics. It is a means by which a number of men – and rather more than is usually recognized – intimidate and control the women in their lives. Other studies of domestic violence are included in Pahl (1985), Hanmer and Maynard (1987) and Dobash and Dobash (1992). *Violence Against Wives* by Dobash and Dobash (1980) remains an important study, even though it is now quite old.

REFERENCES

Blumstein, P. and Schwartz, P. (1983), *American Couples*, New York: William Morrow.

Cancian, F. (1987), *Love in America: Gender and Self-Development*, Cambridge: Cambridge University Press.

Dobash, R. E. and Dobash, R. P. (1980), *Violence Against Wives*, London: Open Books.

Dobash, R. E. and Dobash, R. P. (1992), *Women, Violence and Social Change*, London: Routledge.

Dunne, G. (1997), *Lesbian Lifestyles*, London: Macmillan.

Giddens, A. (1992) *The Transformation of Intimacy*, Cambridge: Polity Press.

Hanmer, J. and Maynard, M. (1987), *Women, Violence and Social Control*, London: Macmillan.

Harrison, K. (1998), 'Rich friendships, affluent friends: middle-class practices of friendship', in R. Adams and G. Allan (eds), *Placing Friendship in Context*, Cambridge: Cambridge University Press.

Mansfield, P. and Collard, J. (1988), *The Beginning of the Rest of Your Life? A Portrait of Newly-Wed Marriage*, London: Macmillan.

Martin, J. (1978), *Violence and the Family*, Chichester: Wiley.

Pahl, J (1980), 'Patterns of money management within marriage', *Journal of Social Policy*, 9: 313–35.

Pahl, J. (1983), 'The allocation of money and the structuring of inequality within marriage', *Sociological Review*, 31: 237–62.

Pahl, J. (1985), *Private Violence and Public Policy*, London: Routledge & Kegan Paul.

Pahl, J. (1989), *Money and Marriage*, London: Macmillan.

Rubin, L. (1990), *Erotic Wars: What Happened to the Sexual Revolution?*, New York: Farrar, Strauss and Giroux.

Vogler, C. and Pahl, J. (1993), 'Social and economic change and the organization of money in marriage', *Work, Employment and Society*, 7: 71–95.

Wilson, G. (1987), *Money in the Family*, Aldershot: Avebury.

Wood, J. (1996), *Gendered Relationships*, Mountain View, CA: Mayfield Publishing.

4

Love and Intimacy: The Gender Division of Emotion and 'Emotion Work': A Neglected Aspect of Sociological Discussion of Heterosexual Relationships

Jean Duncombe and Dennis Marsden

Sociologists' Neglect of the Expressive or Emotional Aspects of Intimate Personal Relationships

Increasing expectations of close couple relationships as a 'haven in a heartless world' will place a premium on the ability to communicate and to 'do' intimacy – a phrase we use to emphasize that emotional states may entail forms of emotional action or 'emotion work' rather than mere being (Hochschild, 1975). Yet there is various evidence (which we explore below) to suggest that conflict arises because individuals' capacities to express emotion are socially regulated or 'managed' in such a way that men and women have a differing ability or willingness to think and talk in terms of 'love' and 'intimacy' and to make the emotional effort which appears (to many women at least) necessary to sustain close heterosexual relationships. This raises sociologically important questions: what is the nature and validity of women's emotional demands of men; and even if men's behaviour in relation to housework, financial management and caring services may change, how far can and should men change emotionally as many women are now demanding?

It is not our purpose here to discuss the historic and cultural dimensions of this current stress on intimacy in personal relationships (Morgan, 1990). Rather we wish first to establish the existence and sociological importance of gender divisions in emotional behaviour in relation to love and intimacy, and then to attempt to place such differences in the context of gender and labour market inequalities, patterns of socialization and alternative sexualities.

Despite the importance of intimate emotion in people's lives, it is only relatively recently that a case has been made for including emotion as a fit topic for sociological discussion (Hochschild, 1975; James, 1989). The causes of such sociological neglect are complex and overlapping, intellectual, political and personal. Emotions such as love tend to be experienced as uniquely personal events, so that 'the very idea that social forces...might have shaped the form of one's love seems like an infringement of personal liberty' (Sarsby, 1983, p. 1). Some feminist sociologists maintain that 'male-stream' sociologists find emotion *personally* threatening, to be relegated to the irrational, unquantifiable and therefore essentially untheorizable (Safilios-Rothschild, 1976), leaving a sociology which is about 'rational men' rather than 'sentient persons' (Eichler, 1981, p. 206). Seidler has argued that the contrast between rationality and emotion which is a central part of the development of the European masculine intellectual tradition has helped to shape sociology and heterosexual masculinity itself, with the result that male academics 'prefer theories which make the reality of our own experience unreachable', and 'men can analyse the state of the international capitalist economy better than issues in their personal life' (Seidler, 1985, pp. 178, 172).

Actually, it is not strictly true that sociologists have entirely neglected emotion. Talcott Parsons's discussion of the ideal nuclear family provided an early (albeit sexist and overly functionalist) sketch of what we call below 'the gender division of emotion', contrasting the instrumental role of the male breadwinner in the public sphere of work with women's expressive responsibility for providing emotional warmth, stability and tension-free relationships for the whole family in the private sphere of home (Parsons and Bales, 1956). And by the 1970s, sociologists of the family had began to explore what was argued to be a move from marriage as an 'institution' to marriage as an intimate conjugal 'relationship' of equals (Berger and Kellner, 1970; Young and Willmott, 1974). However, in neither of these models of complementary or companionate heterosexual relationships was the emotional content explored (Cheal, 1991; Mansfield and Collard, 1988; Morgan, 1975, 1982).[1]

Indeed, this somewhat too cosy enterprise – and 'family sociology' itself – was soon blown apart under the impact of changing demographic patterns and feminism (Gavron, 1968; Oakley, 1976). In Britain, discussion of the role of emotion in personal relationships was further inhibited by the powerful backlash against what had often been too simplistic an emphasis on the individual and the personal at the expense of the political (Seidler, 1989). Lee Comer argued the need to change not only monogamous relationships but the associated imagery where, 'like so much butter, romantic love must be spread thickly on (only) one slice of bread' (Comer, 1974, p. 219). And many feminists turned away from explorations of romantic love, seen as merely an aspect of male hegemony, towards explorations of sexuality and separatism (a notable exception to this trend died with the death of one of its authors (Cartledge and Ryan, 1983)).

Recently there has been a revival of interest in theorizing relationships in the private sphere. However, discussions of 'households' in terms of how members arrange their finances and participate in paid and domestic labour remain primarily economistic and work-oriented in their view of power in relationships (Brannen and Wilson, 1987; Morris, 1990; Pahl, 1984; Pahl, 1989), because early attempts to incorporate issues like marital satisfaction apparently proved difficult and were not followed up (Edgell, 1980; Pahl, 1989). A notable exception is discussion of women's role in caring for elderly kin (Finch and Groves, 1983; Land and Rose, 1985), although here again academic research and discussion has focused mainly on the exploitation of women's labour rather than the emotional strain of the caring relationship which women themselves may find more distressing (Marsden, 1987).

Some Recent British Sociological Evidence on Gender Differences in Emotional Behaviour in Heterosexual Relationships

Despite what we have argued to be British sociologists' neglect of the issue of emotion in relationships, there is some local survey evidence which we will use here to illustrate a key aspect of intimacy, the gender difference or 'asymmetry' in intimate emotional behaviour.

In the best recent study of intimate heterosexual relationships (based on sixty newly-wed couples), Penny Mansfield and Jean Collard found that on the whole husbands and wives tend to meet as 'intimate strangers'. When 'the false romantic images which are part of "falling in love"' (Mansfield and Collard, 1988, p. 87) have been broken down, it turns out that couples seek incompatible emotional goals in marriage: 'Most (though not all) men seek a *life in common* with their wives, a home life, a physical and psychological base; somewhere to set out from and return to'. In contrast, the wives wanted '*a common life* with an empathetic partner... a close exchange of intimacy which would make them feel valued as a person not just a wife'. As a result, although most wives accepted inequality in domestic tasks as counterbalanced by their husbands' work-demands, only three months into marriage they expressed deep disappointment with the emotional asymmetry of their relationships: they felt they were the ones who reassured and were understanding and tender to their husbands, but their husbands failed to reciprocate by being equally intimate and open in 'disclosing' their emotions (ibid.: pp. 178–9). For example, many wives reported that to enjoy sex they needed to be talked to in a loving and gentle way – 'Sex doesn't make me feel warm and secure. I'd rather he give me a cuddle, that makes me warm and secure, more than anything else. I tell him I love him, but *he* don't tell *me*'. Many husbands talked of love only in the context of sex or resisted romantic expression altogether: 'Sometimes she asks, "Do you love me?" I say, "I married you", something like that. She knows she's not going to get a direct answer so she don't bother no more' (ibid.: pp. 168, 178–9).

An earlier study of a more selective sample (twenty-four couples receiving marital counselling) also found that major disagreements arose from women feeling they had not got a 'companionate marriage' because of their husbands' unwillingness or incapacity to disclose (Brannen and Collard, 1982, pp. 33–4).

Indeed the authors argue that for these men non-disclosure was 'a central, unchanging and fervent part of their identity'.[2] (In contrast, Brannen and Moss (1991) report that working wives who do perceive their relationships as conforming to the emotional ideal of 'companionate love' will condone, excuse or even misreport their husbands' inadequate sharing of domestic tasks – a finding these authors interpret as a form of 'false consciousness'.)

Significantly, Mary Ingham comments how her interviews with forty middle-aged and middle-class husbands appeared at first unrevealing because male disclosure was so limited (Ingham, 1984). With friendships based on leisure activities or their wives' social networks, most of these husbands found it difficult to articulate their feelings and talk personally to other men. They seemed emotionally isolated and uncertain, and they revealed that they felt hollow and empty inside. A few of these husbands would confide in their wives but most suppressed much of what they felt, and Ingham pictures them as 'psychic celibates' who may participate in childcare and domestic tasks more than their fathers did but who still fail to take any deep *emotional* responsibility for marriage and fatherhood.

In view of the lack of comprehensive data on the role of emotion in relationships, we here venture to include some preliminary findings from our own ESRC-funded research on the role of ideologies of love in the social construction of coupledom. Our interest in this area was stimulated by work with the British Household Panel Study's pilot project on Household Allocative Systems (Pahl, 1989), where we noted that couples tended to give the rationale for their financial arrangements as, 'because we're a couple' or 'we're not a real couple'; that is, ideologies with a component of *emotional* sharing influenced the way couples presented their finances and, we would argue, to some extent shaped the actual financial arrangements themselves. It seemed to us that recent attempts to theorize complex affective relationships merely in terms of 'households' and the instrumental aspects of work, domestic labour and finance were missing out this powerful emotional component. Our own research has therefore been designed to explore the interrelationships between the emotional and the economic in the lives of sixty mature married or cohabiting couples, the main sample being mature heterosexual couples (interviewed both together and individually) but with subsamples of gay male and lesbian couples. We are particularly concerned with emotional change in longer-term relationships, for example, how do couples negotiate the transition between what are conventionally assumed to be two phases of 'love' – the early, heady romantic stage of being 'in love' and the conventional image of a mature and stable 'companionate' love.

We should stress that (at the time of writing) we had completed the pilot stage of this research,[3] but we were still interviewing the main sample of heterosexual couples, so this chapter makes no claims concerning the distribution of the phenomena we describe (for example, possible variations with social class and educational levels). We are here making illustrative suggestions – mainly on the basis of our pilot research but confirmed in the work so far undertaken with the main sample – as to how gender differences in emotional behaviour emerge in the ongoing dynamic of everyday lived relationships, and how the negotiation of intimacy may change over the life-course (Plummer, 1983). We were particularly struck in group discussions by the way some women discovered, apparently for the first time, that the emotional loneliness within coupledom which they had regarded as a personal failing was shared by other women. Indeed, although we did not set out with this as our main focus, it emerged that the dominant pattern of our female respondents' experience of coupledom was an *asymmetry* of emotional response:

> I think I always loved him too much. I didn't really have a 'falling in love' ... but I had a deep love for him, but it was all very unequal ... I never felt really very loved, and I think that for every one of the sixteen years of my marriage, it was a struggle to make him love me more and to get the relationship equal. (Divorcee: group discussion)

Most of our women respondents felt their male partners were lacking in what might be called 'emotional participation' in their relationships – a lack which women who were mothers feared was also a feature of men's relationships with their children (Duncombe and Marsden, 1992, 1995; Lewis and O'Brien, 1987).

Most of the women described an initial disorientating and overtly sexual stage of 'falling in love'. Contrary to the stereotype of male courtship, they felt they had usually made the emotional running, sometimes urged on by feelings they had later come to regard as treacherous – 'wanting to be in love – am I? Aren't I? I must be!' or 'wanting-to-be-married-and-have-two-children'. A very few women reported they still got occasional 'flashbacks' to this early sense of intimacy. However, overwhelmingly women reported that their male partners had seemed to 'psychically desert' them by giving priority to work, becoming 'workaholics' and working long hours or bringing work home. As some wives bitterly observed, 'he wanted the picture' (wife, house and two children) rather than the emotional intimacy for which they had hoped.

Women with children mostly reported that they had again made the emotional running in persuading men to father their children, but with the unforeseen result that some men had then abrogated physical and *emotional* responsibility, treating their children as belonging to their wives alone. The couple's emotional commitment to one another became less intense ('more stretched' as one woman expressed it), much of their conversation now being about their children, and it was noticeable how parents in second marriages made a deliberate attempt to defend their relationship against the encroachment of children (although a childless woman felt that she and her husband were 'too much a couple – always just the two of you together, forever').

Women in longer relationships had accommodated to men's emotional distance in various ways. A few women insisted they were 'ever so happy really', and even here there was sometimes overt evidence that all was not well (for example, descriptions of husbands' bouts of violent temper when crossed). Perhaps they were attempting to manage the public image of their coupledom to conform to the ideal of companionship, but several reported that behaving companionably in public actually made them feel more intimate in their private lives. However, a more common response was that – comparing their relationships with worse possible scenarios and finding that their partners were good providers, didn't drink, weren't violent and so on – women came to blame themselves for wanting too much. While denying that there were any general differences in men's emotional behaviour, they felt that their particular partner couldn't be expected to be emotionally intimate (recalling the flour advert, 'McDougals never varies', one woman said she had come to think of her husband as like a bag of flour!).

These women described how, initially very reluctantly and with great difficulty, they had been forced to build an emotional life apart from their husbands, through children, part-time work and relationships with other women: one woman reported uneasily that her husband's frequent absence had caused her to become a 'sort of couple' with her eldest son. Sometimes women had then come to value and feel jealous of their emotional space and to see close coupledom, as one said, as 'a "caughtness", a "trappedness"'. They foresaw problems when husbands naively anticipated that the earlier, more intimate coupledom would automatically return after the children left or upon retirement: 'He had his chance. I wanted to be a couple at the start but he didn't. Now he's retiring he talks of nothing but the cosy couply life we can have – but it's too late!'

In this chapter we have not set out to provide detailed evidence of the relative influences of intimate emotion and economic power, but we would stress how changes in couples' financial arrangements sometimes clearly *followed* (rather than *caused*) shifts in perception of the emotional climate of their relationships. For example, moves from separate to 'associative' budgeting and then to joint accounts overtly mark (and also reinforce) stages of growing emotional commitment. And one divorcee explained her otherwise puzzling provision of housing and financial support for her alcoholic ex-husband by saying, 'I don't love him "love him", if you know what I mean, but I do still *love* him'. Equally, some women's insistence on going out to work and having their own bank account was the *result* of 'giving up on' the project of fully sharing emotionally as well as financially in a companionate relationship, although their working might then reinforce the couple's emotional separation.

There was evidence in our pilot that women's accommodation to low levels of intimacy might be fragile. For although couples tend to reinforce their image of themselves as normal by mixing with others at a similar stage of development, nostalgic and unsettling memories might be aroused by chance sightings of happier couples. For example, a twenty-years married woman observed the joy of a recently remarried friend when the new husband rang to say he could escape the office for an hour or two: 'Ooh, *yes! Do* come home!' Realizing that she herself never now felt like that, our respondent said she experienced severe pangs of jealousy, and went home for a row with her husband which led to their going for counselling. Similarly, the woman who had become a couple with her son felt displaced when he fell in love ('gazing into her eyes, and "snogging" all over the place'), and she began to challenge her emotionally distant husband because he didn't make her 'feel special any more'.

However, she and the other women in our pilot who had attempted such challenges found that their partners could not respond because they appeared simply not to understand. Women were looking for some sort of *validation*. They might want recognition of their domestic role: 'It's not that you necessarily want *them* to do the housework; it's that you want them to understand that *you* do it'. But they also wanted to feel emotionally 'special', and what made such 'demands' peculiarly difficult for men was that they were largely unspoken and required a response that was essentially spontaneous: women said that if they had to ask, then men's response of flowers, cuddles or loving talk seemed empty.

On the whole, the men in our pilot couples tended to respond to women's largely unspoken demands with incomprehension, but disagreements followed several courses. Some men became so violently angry that women gave up the attempt to communicate. Other men tried to exercise control by steadfastly avoiding arguments altogether, to the extent that they moved into another room or went out of the house. Alternatively, they tried to win arguments by deploying a calculatedly cool and verbally articulate logic, focusing tightly on immediate issues (Rubin, 1983). However, women were further irritated by what they saw as men 'intellectualizing' – speaking without experiencing emotion. So, much to the men's disgust, they threw in unresolved issues from previous disagreements, 'everything including the kitchen sink and his mother'. Eventually out of frustration the women might weep, and the men would then be reduced to the baffled question, 'What do you want me to do, or say?' But the women reported that what they wanted was empathy with how they were *feeling*. Some arguments had lasted for days, with the man periodically attempting to pretend nothing was happening, until the women felt their emotion was spent and they had received emotional acknowledgement. Ideally at this stage women said they would have liked the men to 'kiss and make up' and offer loving reassurance, but a typically unsympathetic male response was, 'You must be joking!' If these men had ever learned to relate as intimately as women wanted, it seemed to be only with great difficulty and some reluctance.

Yet men do respond to women's challenges, albeit often in a puzzled and angry way. Our male respondents tended to argue that they *did* have feelings but their feelings were *theirs* and not to be disclosed. To varying degrees, these men felt pulled apart by the contradictory demands of coupledom and work. In fact, a few unhappy men acknowledged to us that their partners' views were justified: some didn't know what to do in the face of the genuinely pressing demands of their jobs, but others acknowledged that the pressure of work was self-generated yet they continued to work longer hours than they needed to – as one said, 'I want to change but I don't know how'. Most men perceived themselves as working harder and harder, but essentially on behalf of their wives and families. Consequently, when they returned from a hard day's work, either bringing work home or wanting only to relax with the newspaper, women's emotional 'demands' (as men thought of them) could too easily be seen as unreasonable, undermining and basically disloyal or even threatening.

From men's perspective, women's dissatisfaction over intimacy was apt to emerge in the form of sexual difficulties, for while some women adapted to their partner's sexual 'demands' as a matter of duty or to avoid conflict, others could no longer hide their distaste for sex without intimacy. Holiday times seemed particularly likely to bring conflict, with men's expectations that romantic foreign settings would bring a renewal of intimacy (and with it sex) likely to be disappointed by women's feeling that the emotional barriers which they had reluctantly built up over a period ('like putting up a wall against him') could not be breached so quickly and easily, even had they themselves wished it. Characteristically, some men tended to hint at underlying sexual conflict through 'jokes' or asides: 'I've given up smoking and now I've had to give up sex as well!'

It will be evident that this preliminary account of our research has largely focused on women's 'complaints' of what they perceive as men's failure to relate emotionally. However, this is in line with other research, and we make no apologies for the way our account mirrors the phenomena of male non-disclosure and gender asymmetry in emotional behaviour. For further discussion of this asymmetry we will now turn to the literature from other discourses.

Other Discussions of Gender Differences in Relation to Love and Intimacy

In this part of the chapter we wish to draw attention to the continuity in descriptions of emotional differences between men and women, allied however to a remarkable diversity in perceptions of how they arise, whether or not they constitute a problem, and what can and should be done about them. In contrast to the relative neglect of this issue in British sociology, discussion of gender differences in intimate emotional behaviour has been extensive in some other countries (particularly the USA) and other academic specialisms and in more popular or polemical forms (indeed, the gender stereotypes are so deeply embedded that the difficulty of separating out 'academic' from more popular levels of discourse is a major obstacle to gaining acceptance for this area as a valid topic for sociological study).

In the psychological literature, the main finding from a diligent search for innate gender differences has been similarity in terms of individual attributes. In any case interpretation of psychological test-findings needs care because rather than measuring innate 'masculinity' and 'femininity', tests tend to work projectively to reflect 'the cognitive constructs derived from sex roles which we use to organize our perceptions and our social world' (Segal, 1990, p. 67). Alternative social psychological approaches have viewed gender difference as learned sex-role behaviour, but US male writers have tended to perpetuate the sexism of Parsons's original model (Morgan, 1975), seeing women as well-adjusted to their emotionally expressive domestic roles in contrast to men whose modern bureaucratic work role is said to condemn them to being 'inexpressive', 'emotionally constipated' and hence 'emotionally incompetent' in relationships with women and children (Ballswick and Peek, 1975; Farrell, 1974; Pleck, 1982; Pleck and Sawyer, 1974). Blame is placed on early socialization in the harsh and competitive world of school and the male peer group, and in family settings where a boy 'never hears his father say "I love you"...never feels his father's arm around his shoulder hugging him' (Ballswick, 1974, p. 59). Men are also pictured as lonely, lacking the close emotional friendships formed by women (although somewhat puzzlingly, they are said to conceal their unhappiness and to continue to strive to fulfil their ambiguous and emotionally unrewarding role). The message of this literature has been 'pity poor men', and there has emerged the 'male confessional' which might be paraphrased as: 'I was once an inexpressive man but you too can learn to express yourself with the help of other men – and a liberated woman' (e.g. Farrell, 1974, p. 75). Not surprisingly, these writers have shunned feminism.

Sex role theory has been criticized because it cannot explain change and 'abstract opinions about "difference" replace the concrete changing power relations between men and women' (Segal, 1990, p. 69). Moreover, whatever emotional capacities men may reveal under test conditions, in real-life relationships with women they may simply 'not bother' (Cline and Spender, 1987). Nevertheless, cautious interpretation of test-findings may offer some clues to gender difference in how men and women relate emotionally (Cohen, 1990; LaFrance and Banaji, 1992). Men *say* they care more about relationships than work, but their tendency to prioritize work may come from a higher need to achieve, which stems in turn from early fears of failure. In close relationships they tend to be less prepared than women to disclose their intimate emotions, again apparently from fears instilled by early socialization when any signs of vulnerability might be exploited.[4] (We here imply nothing in relation to expressions of anger which seem likely to be differently governed.) Men seem less skilled at labelling or *expressing* their emotions, and less likely to perceive and therefore be influenced by the emotions of others. In contrast, women disclose weaknesses more readily and reveal emotions more clearly both facially and bodily (so it has been suggested that women's 'intuition' may be partly their more skilled perception of mismatches between speech and facial expression).

Recent psychoanalytical literature also suggests that all men have a deeply embedded fear of intimacy, but this stems from much earlier childhood experience when – in the emotional (and often physical) absence of their fathers – they are reared by envied and powerful mothers from whom they must distance themselves if they are to become truly masculine (Chodorow, 1978; Vogel, 1986). However, while such psychoanalytical models have achieved a fair degree of acceptance, it has been argued that they need to be placed in a societal and comparative context, and deliberate policies to give fathers greater involvement in childrearing might promote greater emotional openness (Segal, 1990).

Discussions of gender difference in emotional expression also appear in the extensive US feminist literature. For example, Gloria Emerson describes men as 'emotional cripples', unable to handle women's need for love because they have 'substituted duty for genuine feeling' (Emerson, 1985, p. 285); men seem 'distant and inattentive . . . they're always in disguise', and 'their vague congeniality which they affect so often (is) as useful as a concrete overcoat' (ibid.: pp. 30–1). Eakins and Eakins claim men can't even *sound* intimate, they merely 'growl' endearments which get misunderstood; and Carol Gilligan pictures men as spending 'their lives out on the edge of their personal space patrolling its boundaries, having grown up to interpret most infringements . . . as a personal attack' (both quoted in Ingham, 1984, pp. 227, 243). Significantly, Shere Hite (1988) has followed her writings on sex with a study which highlights men's failure to disclose emotionally and to express love and intimacy. However, as in Britain, some US feminists have criticized the importance which women attach to love, as mere 'romanticizing' of what is essentially an exploitative economic bond between men and women (Ehrenreich, 1983, p. 3). In various ways, these writers often suggest that women give up trying to have fuller relationships with men under current societal conditions.

Other writers, however, have called for women to have a greater tolerance of the way men are. Francesca Cancian argues that women are unfairly assessing men by a feminine ruler which overstresses emotional expressions of love and undervalues the way men show their love instrumentally through shared physical activity and DIY: we must seek to reduce the polarization between male work and female caring, in order to achieve a love which gives equal status to the expression of feelings and to instrumental activities (Cancian, 1989). Deborah Tannen calls for more understanding of what she regards as the culture gap between men's mode of 'report-talk' – which results from their socialization into status-striving, mastery over problems, 'being right', and emotional defensiveness – contrasting with the 'rapport-talk' through which women seek communication and emotional connectedness (Tannen, 1991). Robin Norwood's argument that the problem is really *Women Who Love Too Much* (1985) has found perhaps too-ready a response from women apt to blame themselves for men's lack of emotional reciprocity.[5]

A recent US development is men's response to this debate, which reinforces suggestions of gender differences in emotional behaviour. In *Iron John*, Robert Bly (1990) argues that – partly because of unresponsive fathers – men have lost touch with their emotions and they need to find their true inner selves through learning to communicate with other men. Numerous men's groups have been set up in response, but unfortunately for Bly's message they tend to be hijacked by another movement (celebrated by David Mamet) where men reaffirm traditional masculinity by literally going back to the woods and engaging in hunting and fishing, drinking and gambling.

Compared with this flood of US literature, British writers have shown less interest in exploring gender differences in emotion. Some feminists have argued that any discussion of masculinity diverts attention from the key issue of women's exploitation (Leonard, 1982). Recent talk of emotional change towards 'the New Man' is mistrusted as a mere softening of the face of patriarchy: the future may be 'feminine' but it will still be male (Chapman and Rutherford, 1988). Alternatively, the New Man has been pictured as a leech, prepared to use women as an emotional sponge but not disposed in turn to listen; or as the 'New Lad', deploying the new language of disclosure but only instrumentally with a view to traditional sexual conquest! Such attacks have helped to censor discussion of change at the ideological level of gender relationships in Britain as mere 'false consciousness' or futile.

Nevertheless, with rare optimism Segal has recently argued that men have changed and they are vulnerable to further change because 'power struggles in the home heighten... as conflicts between women and men deepen, strengthening at least the possibilities for further movement' (Segal, 1990, p. xi). She sees hope in the range of masculinities now available as alternatives to 'the oppressiveness of traditional "masculinities"... men's wretched fear of... intimacy and closeness' (ibid.: p. 317). But she admits that 'the difficulty of changing men is, in part, the difficulty of changing political and economic structures' (ibid.: p. 309), and not all men who want to change will be able to. She sees a further basic obstacle in the idealized images of love to which many women (including some feminists) still cling: 'the object of romantic desire is, by definition, he (or she) who dominates and disappoints' (ibid.: p. 274; Oakley, 1984, 1988).[6]

Evidence that men may be reluctant and slow to change comes from the surveys quoted earlier. Ingham found it was rare for men to admit that their lives had been affected by changes happening to women: 'If there was a quiet movement of British men, they were keeping very quiet indeed' (Ingham, 1984, p. 7). It also seems significant that the newly emerging 'masculinity' literature, some from men who self-consciously struggle to be personal, is most unrevealing, as if it has no 'emotional subject'.

Yet a few of these masculinity authors do manage to convey their own emotional experience of a crisis of male heterosexual identity – of 'roofs being blown off many family homes' (Metcalf and Humphries, 1985, p. 8) as feminists 'swept through the suburbs' (Cohen, 1990, p. 5; see also Jackson, 1990; Seidler, 1989). With a touch of the 'male confessional', these writers describe their puzzlement, guilt and resentment as women challenged their emotional behaviour in intimate relationships. Seidler recounts how his immersion in political activity and a series of difficulties in personal relationships led him to the view that men have power only at the considerable cost of the loss of emotional life: 'a fear of intimacy has held men in terrible isolation and loneliness' (Seidler, 1985, p. 158). In order to maintain control, men repress and compartmentalize emotion to such an extent that they have no way of identifying, nor even a language for discussing, their own needs and their expectation of women's emotional support:

> I have been constantly challenged for not giving enough of myself in my relationships, though it has taken time to grasp what this means.... We resent it if demands are made on us to respond more openly.... Sometimes it is easier to 'help' more in domestic work and childcare than it is to change the tone and character of our emotional and sexual relationships. (Ibid.: pp. 157–8)

Cohen also reports that he found it easier to help more with tasks than to change emotionally, seeing his wife's emotional 'demands' as a disloyal undermining of the hard work that he convinced himself he was doing for her. In rows she pointed out where he had 'made one "big mistake" after another, as if living with her required one to pass a series of emotional and sexual exams'. He reports ruefully, 'My marks were very low' (Cohen, 1990, p. 62).

These writers argue that in their questioning of the emotional deficiencies of current heterosexual masculinity they represent many men who need and want to change, but any overall societal progress towards equality of the sexes will not be enough to bring about personal development. Jackson, coming from a literary background, argues for a form of autobiography through which the past can be critically examined and the self radically reconstructed (see also Giddens, 1991). Metcalf and Seidler suggest a political form of group therapy/consciousness raising ('Red Therapy'). But they confess that men's unwillingness to engage with one another or with feminism is an obstacle: faced with feminist challenges in their personal lives, men commonly react by denying they have a problem, a way out being to seek validation in another heterosexual relationship with a 'less demanding' woman of more traditional views, and to resent and reject feminism (Seidler, 1985, p. 172). A further recent twist in popular discourse is the amount of coverage given by popular women's magazines to books by men expressing resentment at feminism's criticisms and attempting to reassert men's 'needs' and rights (Lyndon, 1992; Thomas, 1992) – perhaps the minor British counterpart of America's 'backlash' (Faludi, 1991).

Theorizing the Role of Emotion in Intimate Personal Relationships: The Gender Division of Emotion and 'Emotion Work'

The stereotypical and controversial nature of the discourses which we have just described, allied to sociological neglect, makes it difficult even to guess at the incidence or degree of gender difference in emotional behaviour. Nevertheless, we would argue that the various survey evidence and the weight of the above discussion possibly points to widespread gender differences of two kinds: 'susceptibility to', or the valuation of, romantic discourse and intimate emotion; and the ability or willingness to disclose emotionally and to 'do' intimacy in personal relationships.

We have noted the tendency in British sociology to ignore or dismiss discussion of emotional difference and change as ultimately dependent upon, or undesirable without, broader progress towards equality. And indeed it does seem likely that any long-term shifts in economic and political power would have broad consequences at the emotional level, for example in terms of the way men and women express their needs and dependencies in relation to one another. Yet our own interest is in exploring the here and now, where (as we argued above) gender differences in emotional behaviour seem likely to become a greater source of friction and unhappiness among heterosexual couples as the 'institution' of marriage is transformed by ideologies of the personal 'relationship' which call for greater emotional communication. Men's difficulties in expressing intimate emotions will emerge as a major source of the 'private troubles' underlying the 'public issues' of rising divorce and family breakdown, or the instability of cohabitation among couples who may often be parents. Such emotional difficulties are similarly apparent in fatherhood, and they will also intrude in any subsequent relationships between men and their ex-partners and children, particularly under the new draconian legal proposals which stress biological fathers' rights to continued participation in children's upbringing along with increased financial liabilities and responsibilities for the support of children and ex-spouses.

In these circumstances we regard the sociological study of emotion in intimate personal relationships as a valuable part of the attempt to promote a dialogue between the sexes, provided of course that discussion is securely located in the context of the structure and ideology of gender inequalities of power and alternative sexualities (Maynard, 1990, pp. 234–5). In fact, currently sociological interest in intimate personal relationships seems to be quickening. For example, research on the realms of the personal and the private and their links with the public sphere, has been argued to be urgently necessary in order to revitalize theories of 'marriage' and new household or quasi-family forms, or as an essential basis for broader theories of society (Cheal, 1991; Clark and Haldane, 1990; Morgan, 1985, 1990). Indeed even some male theorists of society (Alberoni, 1983; Giddens, 1991, 1992; Luhmann, 1986) – possibly in a disguised and abstract version of the 'confessional' mode! – have come to recognize the importance of the study of love and intimacy in the changing forms of interpersonal relationships.[7]

One fruitful initial approach to theorizing intimate relationships appears to lie in recent work on the social management of emotion. Elias has argued that in 'the civilizing process', the social regulation and management of emotion becomes concentrated in the nuclear family (James, 1989). However, gender segregation in the labour market has meant that responsibility for the domestic sphere has fallen largely on women, and as a result the gender division of labour results in a gender division of emotion: '"emotional" becomes part of a major cluster of other adjectives by which "masculine" and "feminine" are differentiated and through which the emotional/rational divide of female/male is perpetuated' (ibid.: p. 23). Hochschild (1983) has further argued that emotional life is largely socially regulated by ideologies of feeling, operating through a series of 'feeling rules' which prescribe how individuals *ought* to feel in various situations: an individual who does not happen to feel spontaneously in accord with a particular rule (or who wants others to feel in a particular way) will engage in a form of 'emotion work' to try to *act* the appropriate emotion or to influence the way others feel. Women's assigned role in recognizing and meeting the emotional needs of household members therefore calls for considerable 'emotion work' – a sort of 'emotional housework' or 'invisible domestic labour'.[8] Possibly at least, this entails the development and exercise of a range of emotional *skills*, and women able to fulfil this role will possess valuable skills which men lack. In male-dominated society, however, such 'emotion work' remains invisible and unacknowledged and the skills undervalued, although Hochschild (1983) and James (1989) have documented how such skills may be commercially exploited in service industries or state caring services.

We believe that the concepts of the gender division of emotion, emotion work and emotional skills also offer further insights into the private sphere of intimate personal relationships. Such an approach accepts that there probably are significant gender differences in emotional behaviour, but it recognizes that these are complex products of processes of social interaction between the individual's biology and psyche and societal institutions, in the context of gender inequality. The model is therefore essentially sociological, whilst not pre-empting discussion of psychological or psychodynamic processes in socialization and inter-generational and cultural transmission (Hochschild, 1983, pp. 201–22). Clearly, we must beware the potentially too-rigid (Parsonian) functionalism of this model, which does not provide a universal specification of actual heterosexual behaviour, still less the innate possibilities or aspirations of men and women who currently occupy the emotionally differentiated spheres of work and home (a similar caution must be exercised in relation to the dogmatic structuralism of Delphy and Leonard, who have recently embraced the concept of emotional housework but merely as further evidence of women's exploitation by men (Delphy and Leonard, 1992; Duncombe and Marsden, 1995)). It might be argued that the persistence of the gender division of emotion and emotion work over time has led to the social reproduction of broadly separate emotional cultures for men and women. However, further empirical research will be needed to map the actual degree of matching between the emotional behaviour of individuals and their work and domestic activities, or how emotional behaviour changes when individuals move from home to work or vice versa. (Although we are here primarily concerned with heterosexual relationships, clearly this model has implications for attempts to theorize coupledom among gay men and lesbians.)

How can this model of the gender division of emotion help us to understand the asymmetrical expression of emotional 'needs'? One argument might be that women search for emotional 'validation' in intimate relationships with men only because they are excluded from the work and rewards through which men gain confirmation of their identity and status. It seems possible that women's expression of their emotional needs may change if they gain greater equality through paid work (although women's paid work often entails unacknowledged emotion work). Yet individuals' emotional needs of one another hardly seem reducible to the lack of a satisfying source of identity in work: rather, it tends to be argued that the increasing complexity of modern life leads individuals of both sexes to place greater emphasis on intimate and loving relationships as a 'haven in a heartless world'. A more plausible explanation of gender asymmetry in the expression of emotional needs is that men too *value* and *need* their intimate personal relationships – indeed men consistently say that personal relationships are the most important thing in their lives, and there is some evidence that they tend to fall apart emotionally after divorce and in consequence remarry more quickly than women (Ingham,

1984, p. 220). But as a consequence of the gender division of emotion, men may devalue and be less ready to acknowledge and express their own needs at an emotional level.

Such inequalities of actual or expressed emotional need for intimacy are integrally related to gender inequalities of power, for true intimacy between men and women would imply an equal emotional reciprocity. It has been suggested by exchange theorists that the balance of emotional power may be seen as residing precisely in asymmetry – that is, the extent to which one partner wants something which the other withholds, whether unwittingly or deliberately (Cancian, 1989; Eichler, 1981; Safilios-Rothschild, 1976). So men's withholding from women of the emotional validation which they seek through intimacy may become a source of male power, and indeed some women reported that they experienced men's usual emotional 'remoteness' as a form of power. In a mysterious way, the giving or withholding of emotion and intimacy thus becomes one kind of 'carrier' of gender power.

However, to imply that men more often have all the emotional power in relationships is clearly over-simple. Apart from the dimension of sexual desire, the literature cited above suggests that men have powerful if unacknowledged needs of the emotion work which women perform for them. So women too could be said to have the *possibility* of exercising emotional power over men – if they choose deliberately to withhold their emotional 'services'. In such an exercise of female power could lie the answer to the question of why men should ever change when they benefit so substantially from current inequalities in domestic labour and emotional housework. But whether, in practice, women have such power if they themselves mainly fail to recognize and use it – indeed if women primarily *collude* with the exercise of male power – is a more complex theoretical issue than we can enter into here (for further discussion see: Duncombe and Marsden, 1995; Connell, 1987; Coward, 1992; Segal, 1990, p. 287). It seems to us an important empirical question how far women's *emotional* behaviour towards their husbands – and husbands' emotional response – changes unconsciously or deliberately when they gain alternative emotional validation and economic power through work (Hochschild and Maching, 1990).

The asymmetrical expression of emotional needs may also underlie gender differences in 'susceptibility' to, or the employment of, the discourses of love and intimacy. Again Hochschild's discussion of 'feeling rules' offers insights as to how such discourses – which embody ideologies of feeling – may influence intimate emotional states and behaviour. In our research there was clear evidence of emotion work devoted to attempts at managing the emotions of 'the beloved' – for example, the woman who spent sixteen years struggling to make her husband love her. But there is also a form of emotion work that may be entirely devoted to managing the individual's own emotional state – as captured in the situation of 'wanting to be in love – am I? Aren't I? I *must* be!' This suggests that Hochschild's model is over-simple in lumping together 'emotion work' devoted to managing the individual's own emotions and that directed at changing the emotions of 'the beloved'.

Hochschild's discussion of emotion may also help to throw light on the processes whereby women try to adapt to disappointment of their expectations of intimate and companionate relationships with men. She suggests that, depending on the situation and the degree to which they have internalized the feeling rules, individuals engage in different levels of acting effort: surface acting does not obscure what is 'really' felt, but under more powerful pressure 'deep acted' feeling obscures the authentic, even for the actors themselves. We suspected this was the case with wives in our study who claimed to feel happy despite overt evidence to the contrary. And Vaughan (1987) has argued that in coupledom there are strong internal pressures on each partner to suppress consciousness of any embryo criticism of the other lest even individual private acknowledgement becomes a secret which drives a wedge between the couple.

This suggestion raises difficult methodological and ethical questions about researching emotion in the private sphere (Duncombe and Marsden, 1996). A key part of emotion work where the couple relationship is old or shaky may be the couple's management of their image to outsiders – including interviewers – so as to present a picture of companionate love. What *is* 'the private sphere', if partners keep secrets from one another and even from themselves? And what ethical justification can there be for probing in an attempt to expose the couple's shared secrets or trying to persuade one partner to articulate feelings about the other which may give a push to the process of 'uncoupling'? Are we interested in the 'real' feelings about the partner or the 'acted' feelings, what might be called the 'false consciousness' in the relationship? (This attempted distinction between authentic and 'acted' emotions also raises questions which we cannot discuss here about the nature and different levels of the self.)

In this chapter we have attempted to make a preliminary case that the study of emotions in intimate personal relationships is a topic of major sociological importance. We are not arguing for the primacy of emotional over economic power; rather, sociologists need to study the *relationship* between the two (and indeed sexual power also), instead of focusing on the economic as they do at present. For although romantic imagery may often disguise exploitation, people experience feelings of love as powerfully 'real' in ways which have very real consequences for their lives. In some ways, women's demands for the emotional reciprocity of intimacy may be seen as the next frontier of the battle for gender equality. To study intimate emotional behaviour is therefore not merely to collude in the mystification of women's economic exploitation; it is to gain a deeper understanding of the lived experience of a great many women and men today and in the foreseeable future.

ACKNOWLEDGEMENTS

We gratefully acknowledge ESRC funding for this study (ROOO232737), and the comments of Dr Lydia Morris on an early draft of the chapter.

NOTES

1   Berger and Kellner refer to the ideology of love as a resource in the construction of couple relationships but fail to explore it. Blumstein and Schwarz (1983) also fail to deal with love, and they see emotional states as dependent on behaviour rather than possibly influencing actions. Denzin (1984) discusses emotion but abstracted from particular relationships (a failing of much social psychological literature, e.g. Duck and Gilmour, 1981).

2   To the extent that their problems are related to work, men may often choose not to disclose because they don't think wives can help or should be worried. Reviewing the literature, Brannen and Collard (1982, pp. 31–2) comment how disclosure is taken simplistically as unequivocally a good thing, neglecting social constraints and issues of privacy. Seen in this light, it may be questioned whether the counselling 'industry' purveys a 'feminine' ideology of disclosure.

3   The pilot stage of our research consisted of lengthy intensive interviews with half a dozen couples (seen together and individually), plus discussions conducted with groups drawn from FE students (mostly mature women but with some men, at different stages of coupledom), covering in all the current and past experience of around forty mainly middle-class couples.

4   Gender differences in expressions of intimate emotion are already apparent in teenage (Jackson, 1982; Lees, 1986; Sarsby, 1983).

5   *Women Who Love Too Much* also received a ready response in Britain, where many groups have been set up. There is a rapidly growing genre of books aimed at helping women in relationships with unresponsive men, e.g. *Men Who Hate Women and the Women Who Love Them; Men Who Can't Love: How to Recognize a Commitment-Phobic Man Before He Breaks Your Heart; What To Do When He Won't Change; Why Men Don't Get Enough Sex and Women Don't Get Enough Love: With a Ten-Step Great Love, Great Sex Programme To Transform Your Relationship – and Your Life; If This Is Love Why Do I Feel So Insecure; Why Do I Think I Am Nothing Without A Man.*

6   The tension between women's difficulties in romantic relationships with men and the feminist pursuit of equality has been well-caught by Ann Oakley, although significantly she appears to have felt that in the current sociological climate she could only explore love in fiction (Oakley, 1984, 1988), and even so she has been strongly condemned by feminists.

7   In his first discussion of intimacy, Giddens uses Hite's findings to support claims that individuals are increasingly searching for 'the pure relationship' expressed through intimacy, but intriguingly (perhaps as a man?) he ignores Hite's argument that men often appear incapable of intimacy (Giddens, 1991, p. 91). Subsequently, he has acknowledged that men's unreconstructed possessive and controlling sexuality presents a major obstacle to women's pioneering search for intimacy through the pure relationship (Giddens, 1992; Duncombe and Marsden, 1995).

8   Hochschild distinguishes 'emotional labour' sold for a wage and therefore with exchange value, from 'emotion work' in a private context which has use value (Hochschild, 1983, p. 7). James, however, defines emotional labour as dealing with other people's feelings (James, 1989). More expressive terms for 'emotion work' are 'emotional housework' or Jean Baker Miller's (1976) 'invisible domestic

labour' (which, however, includes taking responsibility for the practical tasks of buying flowers, cards and presents for emotionally significant occasions).

REFERENCES

Alberoni, F. (1983), *Failing in Love*, New York: Random House.
Ballswick, J. (1974), 'Why husbands can't say "I love you"', in D. David and R. Brannan (eds), *The 49 per cent Majority: The Male Sex Role*, New York: Addison-Wesley.
Ballswick, J. and Peek, C. (1975), 'The inexpressive male: a tragedy of American society', in J. Petras (ed.), *Sex Male: Gender Masculine*, New York: Alfred Publishing.
Berger, P. and Kellner, H. (1970), 'Marriage and the construction of reality', in H. Dreitzel (ed.), *Recent Sociology*, no. 2, New York: Macmillan.
Blumstein, P. and Schwarz, P. (1983), *American Couples: Money, Work and Sex*, New York: Wm. Morrow.
Bly, R. (1990), *Iron John: A Book About Men*, Shaftesbury: Element Books.
Brannen, J. and Collard, J. (1982), *Marriages in Trouble: The Process of Seeking Help*, London: Tavistock.
Brannen, J. and Moss, P. (1991), *Managing Mothers*, London: Unwin Hyman.
Brannen, J. and Wilson, P. (1987), *Give and Take in Families: Studies in Resource Distribution*, London: Allen & Unwin.
Cancian, F. (1987), *Love in America: Gender and Self-Development*, Cambridge: Cambridge University Press.
Cancian, F. (1989), 'Gender and power: love and power in the public and private spheres', in A. S. Skolnick and J. H. Skolnick (eds), *Family in Transition: Rethinking Marriage, Sexuality, Child Rearing and Family Organization*, London: Scott Foresman.
Cartledge, S. and Ryan, J. (1983), *Sex and Love: New Thoughts on Old Contradictions*, London: The Women's Press.
Chapman, R. and Rutherford, J. (1988), *Male Order: Unwrapping Masculinity*, London: Lawrence and Wishart.
Cheal, D. (1991), *Family and the State of Theory*, London: Harvester Wheatsheaf.
Chodorow, N. (1978), *The Reproduction of Mothering: Psychoanalysis and the Sociology of Gender*, London: University of California Press.
Clark, D. and Haldane, D. (1990), *Wedlocked? Intervention and Research in Marriage*, Cambridge: Polity Press.
Cline, S. and Spender, D. (1987), *Reflecting Men*, London: Deutsch.
Cohen, D. (1990), *Being a Man*, London: Routledge.
Comer, L. (1974), *Wedlocked Women*, Leeds: Feminist Books.
Connell, R. W. (1987), *Gender and Power*, Cambridge: Polity Press.
Coward, R. (1992), *Our Treacherous Hearts: Why Women Let Men Get Their Way*, London: Faber.
Delphy, C. and Leonard, D. (1992), *Familiar Exploitation*, Cambridge: Polity Press.
Denzin, N. K. (1984), *On Understanding Emotion*, New York: Jossey Bass.
Duck, S. and Gilmour, R. (eds) (1981), *Personal Relationships 2: Developing Personal Relationships*, London: Academic Press.
Duncombe, J. and Marsden, D. (1992), Unpublished paper presented to the Annual Conference of the BSA at Canterbury.

Duncombe, J. and Marsden, D. (1995), '"Workaholics" and "whingeing women": theorising intimacy and emotion work: the last frontier of gender inequality?', *Sociological Review*, 43: 150–69.

Duncombe, J. and Marsden, D. (1996), 'Can we research the private sphere? Methodological and ethical problems in the study of the role of intimate emotion in personal relationships', in L. Morris and E. S. Lyon (eds), *Gender Relations in Public and Private: New Research Perspectives*, London: Macmillan.

Edgell, S. (1980), *Middle-class Couples: A Study of Segregation, Domination and Inequality in Marriage*, London: George Allen & Unwin.

Ehrenreich, B. (1983), *The Hearts of Men: American Dreams and the Flight from Commitment*, London: Pluto Press.

Eichler, M. (1981), 'Power, dependency, love and the sexual division of labour: a critique of the decision-making approach to family power', *Journal of Women's Studies Quarterly* 4: 201–19.

Emerson, G. (1985), *Some American Men and Their Lives*, New York: Simon and Schuster.

Faludi, S. (1991), *Backlash: The Undeclared War Against Women*, New York: Crown.

Farrell, W. (1974), *The Liberated Man: Beyond Masculinity: Freeing Men and Their Relationships with Women*, New York: Random House.

Finch, J. and Groves, D. (eds) (1983), *A Labour of Love: Women, Work and Caring*, London: Routledge & Kegan Paul.

Fogel, G., Lane, F. and Liebert, G. (eds) (1986), *The Psychology of Men: New Psychoanalytical Perspectives*, New York: Basic Books.

Gavron, H. (1968), *The Captive Wife*, Harmondsworth: Penguin.

Giddens, A. (1991), *Modernity and Self-Identity: Self and Society in the Late Modern Age*, Cambridge: Polity Press.

Giddens, A. (1992), *The Transformation of Intimacy: Love, Sexuality and Eroticism in Modern Societies*, Cambridge: Polity Press.

Hite, S. (1988), *The Hite Report: Women in Love*, London: Viking.

Hochschild, A. R. (1975), 'The sociology of feeling and emotion. selected possibilities', in M. Milkman and R. Kanter (eds), *Another Voice*, New York: Anchor.

Hochschild, A. R. (1983), *The Managed Heart: Commercialization of Human Feeling*, London: University of California Press.

Hochschild, A. R. and Maching, A. (1990), *The Second Shift: Working Parents and the Revolution at Home*, London: Piarkus.

Ingham, M. (1984), *Men*, London: Century.

Jackson, A. (1990), *Unmasking Masculinity*, London: Unwin Hyman.

Jackson, S. (1982), *Childhood and Sexuality*, Oxford: Basil Blackwell.

James, N. (1989), 'Emotional labour: skill and work in the social regulation of feelings', *Sociological Review*, 37: 15–42.

Lafrance, M. and Banaji, M. (1992), 'Towards a reconsideration of the gender emotion relationship', in M. S. Clark (ed.), *Emotion and Social Behaviour*, London: Sage.

Land, H. and Rose, H. (1985), 'Compulsory altruism for some or an altruistic society for all?', in P. Bean, J. Ferris and D. Whynes (eds), *In Defence of Welfare*, London: Tavistock.

Lees, S. (1986), *Losing Out: Sexuality and Adolescent Girls*, London: Hutchinson.

Leonard, D. (1982), 'Male feminists and divided women', in S. Friedman and E. Sarah (eds), *On the Problem of Men*, London: Women's Press.

Lewis, C. and O'Brien, R. (eds) (1987), *Fatherhood Reassessed*, London: Sage.

Luhmann, N. (1986), *Love as Passion*, Cambridge: Polity Press.

Lyndon, N. (1992), *No More Sex War*, London: Sinclair Stevenson.

Mansfield, P. and Collard, J. (1988), *The Beginning of the Rest of Your Life?*, London: Macmillan.

Marsden, D. with Abrams, S. (1987), '"Allies", "liberators", "intruders" and "cuckoos in the nest": a sociology of caring relationships over the life cycle', in P. Allatt, T. Keil, A. Bryman and B. Bytheway (eds), *Women and the Life Cycle*, London: Macmillan.

Maynard, M. (1990), 'The re-shaping of sociology? Trends in the study of gender', *Sociology*, 24: 269–90.

Metcalf, A. and Humphries, M. (1985), *The Sexuality of Men*, London: Pluto Press.

Miller, J. B. (1976), *Towards a New Psychology of Women*, Boston: Beacon Press.

Morgan, D. H. J. (1975), *Social Theory and the Family*, London: Routledge & Kegan Paul.

Morgan, D. H. J. (1982), *Berger and Kellner's Construction of the Family*, University of Manchester, Department of Sociology, Occasional Paper No. 7.

Morgan, D. H. J. (1985), *The Family, Politics and Social Theory*, London: Routledge & Kegan Paul.

Morgan, D .H. J. (1990), 'Institution and relationship within marriage', paper presented at the ISA World Congress in Madrid.

Morris, L. (1990), *The Workings of the Household*, Cambridge: Polity Press.

Norwood, R. (1985), *Women Who Love Too Much*, Los Angeles: Jeremy P. Tarcher.

Oakley, A. (1974), *The Sociology of Housework*, London: Martin Robertson.

Oakley, A. (1984), *Taking It Like a Woman*, London: Jonathan Cape.

Oakley, A. (1988), *The Men's Room*, London: Virago.

Pahl, J. (1989), *Money and Marriage*, London: Macmillan.

Pahl, R. E. (1984), *Divisions of Labour*, Oxford: Blackwell Publishers.

Parsons, T. and Bales, R. F. (eds) (1956), *Family, Socialization and Interaction Process*, London: Routledge & Kegan Paul.

Pleck, J. (1982), *The Myth of Masculinity*, Boston: MIT Press.

Pleck, J. and Sawyer, J. (1974), *Men and Masculinity*, Englewood Cliffs, NJ: Prentice-Hall.

Plummer, K. (1983), *Documents of Life*, London: George Allen & Unwin.

Rubin, L. B. (1983), *Intimate Strangers: Men and Women Together*, New York: Harper & Row.

Safilios-Rothschild, L. (1976), 'A macro- and micro-examination of family power and love: an exchange model', *Journal of Marriage and the Family*, 38: 355–62.

Sarsby, J. (1983), *Romantic Love and Society*, Harmondsworth: Penguin.

Segal, L. (1990), *Slow Motion: Changing Masculinities, Changing Men*, London: Virago.

Seidler, V. J. (1985), 'Fear and intimacy', in A. Metcalf and M. Humphries (eds), *The Sexuality of Men*, London: Pluto Press.

Seidler, V. J. (1989), *Rediscovering Masculinity*, London: Routledge.

Tannen, D. (1991), *You Just Don't Understand: Women and Men in Conversation*, London: Virago.

Thomas, D. (1992). *Walk Like a Man*, London: Weidenfeld.

Vaughan, D. (1987), *Uncoupling*, London: Methuen.

Young, M. and Willmott, P. (1974), *The Symmetrical Family*, Harmondsworth: Penguin.

Partners by Choice: Equality, Power and Commitment in Non-heterosexual Relationships

Jeffrey Weeks, Brian Heaphy and Catherine Donovan

Introduction

Across the Western world in the 1990s a new claim to rights forcefully emerged: for the recognition of same-sex partnership arrangements. Beginning with the campaign for the right to register lesbian or gay partnerships (as in Scandinavian countries from the late 1980s – see Bech, 1996), by the mid 1990s it had emerged in countries such as the USA and the Netherlands as a full-scale effort to promote same-sex marriage on the same terms as heterosexual marriage. Not all, perhaps not even most, non-heterosexual men and women are prepared to go all the way with this (see Sullivan, 1997), but the impetus behind the various campaigns betokens a significant cultural trend: a claim for the equal validity of non-heterosexual with heterosexual relationships. In terms of the traditions of Western societies, with their firm institutionalization of the heterosexual norm in family life, legal discourse, social policy and popular assumptions, this is a radical departure. Yet it can be argued that despite the often frenetic energy of the debates, the new claim to rights and recognition is in large part simply a product of long-term changes which had already transformed intimate life, virtually under the eyes of most observers. The political froth hides a more important development: the coming of age of non-heterosexual ways of life.

The new concern with partnerships' rights can be seen as an aspect of a wider reshaping of non-heterosexual patterns of relationships, and the emergence of what we describe as 'families of choice': flexible but often strong and supportive networks of friends, lovers and even members of families of origin which provide the framework for the development of mutual care, responsibility and commitment for many self-identified non-heterosexuals (lesbians and gays, bisexuals, homosexuals, 'queers': the self-descriptions vary) (Weeks, Donovan and Heaphy, 1998). The key terms used by members of such elective networks to refer to their relationships are 'choice' and 'created': many non-heterosexuals have a strong sense that opportunities now exist on a greater scale than ever before for the construction of relationships that have some at least of the qualities attributed (in ideology at least) to the traditional family: continuity over time, mutual support, a focus for identity and for loving and caring relationships. This is not to say that such supportive networks of marginalized non-heterosexuals, female and male, did not exist in earlier periods (see Porter and Weeks, 1990). What we would argue, however, is that families of choice can be seen as indices of something new: positive and creative responses to social and cultural change, to 'detraditionalization', which are genuine 'experiments in living' (Giddens, 1992). The regular, though not invariable, deployment of the language of family, which suggests continuity, should not be allowed to obscure the emergence of an important change in the social geography of intimate life. Within this evolving broad framework of relationships, same-sex partnerships (usually, but not invariably, couple relationships) both propel a new claim to rights, and reveal evolving patterns and rituals, through which commitment and trust are affirmed and confirmed.[1]

The sections that follow, based on interviews with self-identified non-heterosexual men and women conducted in 1995 and 1996, will explore three aspects of non-heterosexual relationships: attitudes to equality in, and social recognition of, partnerships; issues of power which arise in such relationships; and the working out of commitment. The aim is to show emerging patterns of non-heterosexual life, and to relate these to wider changes in patterns of intimacy.

Equal Partnerships

Non-heterosexual subjects tell two related stories: one which affirms difference, which roots lesbian and gay relationship patterns in a distinctive history; and another which asserts a claim to equivalence, equality and ultimately similarity. On the one hand, there is a passionate affirmation of difference:

> To me the whole basis of lesbian and gay relationships are different from heterosexual relationships... I don't know whether it's good or bad, but I mean, that's a fact. It is blatantly different. And trying to tailor heterosexual laws and understanding towards gay relationships is bound to fail. (M012)

> I do not, as a black lesbian, want to be seen as the same as a heterosexual couple. I do not want to marry my lover, nor do I want to do anything that even remotely looks like that. I don't want to make a commitment publicly. I'm quite content with the fact that I can make a commitment privately, and that's just as important. (F02)

On the other hand, there is an equally forceful assertion of similarity, at least in the claim to rights:

I feel that people should have equal rights whatever, and it all comes...under equal opportunities. Equal opportunities doesn't exist, particularly for gay and lesbian people...I believe that people should have them. (F13)

The contradiction between these two positions is more apparent than real. Overwhelmingly, our subjects feel that being lesbian and gay opens opportunities for more equal and fulfilling relationships than are available to most heterosexuals. This echoes wider historical studies which have indicated that the twentieth century has seen a significant shift in the traditional pattern of homosexual interactions for men and women, with forms of inter-generational or cross-class relationships amongst men, or 'romantic friendships' amongst women, being replaced by an explicitly egalitarian model (Abelove et al., 1993; Dunne, 1997). There are also significant sociological accounts, of course, which indicate that this is increasingly true for relations between men and women, largely as a result of the changing role of women and the 'transformation of intimacy' (Giddens, 1992; Beck and Beck-Gernsheim, 1995). The interesting feature, however, is that many lesbians and gay men have consciously shaped their relationships in opposition to assumed heterosexual models, and especially the power imbalance they are seen as shaped by.

A number of women, particularly, see their lesbianism as empowering them to move beyond heterosexuality, offering opportunities for co-operation and egalitarian relationships that do not require marriage (cf. Dunne, 1997). For many women, the idea of marriage is itself loaded:

As far as I'm concerned, marriage or partnership rights, or whatever you want to call it, is about ownership – and I do not want to own another person. I don't want that at all. I'll be responsible for my own relationship but I will not own someone. And I think it's very strange that there are women who think that this is a good thing. Because marriage has never been in women's interests – ever. (F02)

Less strongly, but making a similar point, a male subject who is not averse to some sort of legalization of gay partnerships remarks: 'I think that marriage is not a word that I would like – because it is still wrapped up in the heterosexual bigotry' (M04).

The assumption, amongst men as well as women, is that, 'it's much easier to have equal relations if you're the same sex' (M31), because this equalizes the terms of the intimate involvement. As one of our lesbian subjects says: 'The understanding between two women is bound to be on a completely different wavelength' (F33). Equal standing means that issues around, for example, the division of labour in the household, are seen to be a matter for discussion and agreement, not *a priori* assumption, because of 'being able to negotiate, being on an equal level to be able to negotiate in the first place' (M04); 'Everything has to be discussed, everything is negotiable' (F29; cf. McWhirter and Mattison, 1984; Blumstein and Schwartz, 1983; Tanner, 1978; Dunne, 1997).

Equality is also seen as integral to intimacy:

I think there is... less a kind of sense of possession, or property, in same-sex relationships, and more emphasis on... emotional bonding... that's not quite what I mean, but they're less ritualized really... I think that kind of creates a necessity for... same-sex relationships to kind of find their own identity. (M39)

Or in the words of a lesbian respondent:

I think there is a kind of empathy that I can't ever remember having with a man. (F06)

There is a strong emphasis amongst lesbians and gays on the importance of building intimate involvement: 'being in a relationship helps to affirm one as a person and we all need that' (M44); 'I love the continuity... I like the sex. I like doing some things jointly.... A sense that you are loveable' (F06). Affirmation through involvement in a democratic, egalitarian relationship appears to be the dominant non-heterosexual norm, conforming closely to Giddens's (1992, p. 58) definition of the 'pure relationship':

A situation where a social relation is entered into for its own sake, for what can be derived by each person from a sustained association with another; and which is continued only in so far as it is thought by both parties to deliver enough satisfaction for each individual to stay within it.

Given this, it is not surprising there is an ambivalence about the idea of legal partnerships or marriage:

I think if we were fighting for equal rights for lesbians and gay men, and we got those rights, then that [partnership rights] would automatically follow. What I don't agree with is the fact that... it's like taking a short cut to equal rights, and it's not going to give equal rights to everyone – it's only going to give equal rights to people who are in long-term relationships. And that doesn't seem fair to me. ... And what bothers me about it that it's kind of like, we want to be seen as the same as heterosexuals, therefore... it has to be legal on paper what we're doing... (F02)

Many, like this gay subject, want:

minimal interference by the state in the way people live their lives... I think that people should be able to make a contract between them saying exactly what their relationship is... I also think that it is no good trying to apply laws that apply to heterosexual couples to homosexual couples. (M44)

On the other hand, there is strong hostility to what is widely seen as a discriminatory and homophobic legal system, and it is in this context that some sort of framework of partnership rights is seen as (often reluctantly) desirable:

I suppose the things I object to about marriage, in the legal sense, are the social security and tax implications which always seem to end up one person less equal than the other... I would like social security reform to be in the direction of everybody having an independent income, regardless of marital or cohabitation status or gender. And I think that is the way to go with heterosexual couples, so that lesbian and gay couples aren't any worse off... it shouldn't be on a marriage model, it should be more on a sort of legal contract model – and there should be varying kinds of legal contract for what people want. (F29)

I think we should be equal in the eyes of the law. I think we should have... well, equal age of consent and also equal rights around tax and the sort of benefits that straight people get for being married and having children. And I think if people want to get married they should be allowed to – but I wouldn't. (F36)

Two issues particularly appear to be the focus of the wish for equal partnership rights: in relationship to parenting; and in relationship to property, especially when facing the ultimate disaster of illness and death. With regard to parenting, it is noticeable that most of the existing European legislation on lesbian and gay partnerships explicitly excludes rights to adoption (for example, see Bech, 1996): non-heterosexual parenting rights remain a taboo. Not surprisingly, many lesbians and gays are particularly concerned with legal access to parenting rights. In this extract, a man involved in caring for his (biological) daughter with his male partner remarks that when he first heard arguments for partnership registration and marriage: 'I just thought there were so many more important things that we ought to be addressing and dealing with that it irritated the shit out of [me]'. But:

If our relationship could be registered, and the fact that we are co-parents could be registered, then... when B.[his daughter] was younger it would have made me feel more secure. As it was I had a certain amount of paranoia... about social workers barging into your life and deciding that this is not proper, and taking the child away... there was a fair amount of paranoia on my part. So I suppose if those rights existed, then it would remove some of the paranoia, but part of me is just suspicious that it's trying to be normal and trying to be 'Look, we're as good as heterosexuals'. And I don't actually care. It's got to the point in my life where I don't give a stuff. (M17)

With property issues, there are recurrent problems about access to pensions, mortgages, spousal rights and so on. But the most emotive issues are around illness and bereavement:

You should have a right to have a say in each other's health care. If your partner was hospitalized you should have the same rights as any other partner would have... we should all be able to have a say in what happens, say with funeral things. I mean, S...'s funeral was horrific. His parents completely took it over; his boyfriend was hardly mentioned or... spoken to, and it was a very Christian burial. It was hideous. Absolutely nothing to do with his life – the preacher didn't know a thing about him and just stood reading from a piece of paper. And because his parents preferred his female friends, they had a bigger say in what happened than his partner did. And you just think, 'No way...' (F14/15)

For many respondents, then, the questions of partnership recognition and lesbian and gay marriage are essentially pragmatic ones: ensuring legal rights and protection, without surrendering what are seen as the real core of non-heterosexual partnerships – the possibilities of more democratic relationships, and the possibility of creating something different.

The main purpose of legal change is seen as protection of this possibility. For prejudice, discrimination and stigma in various forms, despite all changes that have taken place in social attitudes, is always a potential experience of lesbians and gays, however 'respectable' the relationship:

> Because it's monogamous, because we live together in a stable unit with a child, it sometimes feels in that sense that it's like [a marriage]. But I only have to walk out into the street to know that it's not. (F36)

The presence of children tends to accentuate the social pressure, dictating sometimes careful strategies of avoidance. As the male co-parents of young B. observed, it is possible to come out as parents in small circles; coming out as gay parents at her school is quite another matter, not least because of the likely embarrassment to their daughter: 'it's like the difference between being out personally and the fact that you're out as a family. I think we're out as individuals, but the family isn't' (M17/18). Similarly, two lesbian parents, when asked what they most feared about being openly homosexual, replied it was 'the crap' their daughter would get (F04/05).

Achieving recognition, and with it respect, is therefore a crucial goal. In striving for this, the attitudes of friends are crucial, and it is here that the wiser family of choice can be vital, especially if relations with the family of origin are difficult or non-existent. But in the end, what matters are the dynamics of the relationships themselves. Several American studies have attempted to investigate what might be called the 'natural careers' of lesbian and gay couples. Harry and DeVall (1978) suggest the absence of predictable patterns because of the lack of institutional expectations. Others, however, have attempted typologies. Laner (1977) divides homosexual couples into 'parallel' and 'interactional' types, the former suggesting independent lives, while the latter share a single world. Bell and Weinberg (1978) divide their male partnerships into 'closed couples' and 'open couples', while Silverstein (1981) offers 'excitement seekers' and 'home builders'. Tanner's (1978) study of lesbian couples suggested three prototypes: the 'traditional-complementary', the 'caretaking' and the 'negotiated-egalitarian'. McWhirter and Mattison (1984), in their study of 156 male couples, present the most extensive typology, with a six-stage model of relationship careers, from 'blending' and 'nesting' to 'releasing' and 'renewing'.

Whilst each of these models no doubt exists, we would argue both that no single model can capture the complexity and fluidity of lesbian and gay patterns, and that the norm is the democratic-egalitarian model, which in fact suggests diversity of life choices within a common framework. The critical point is that each of these forms of commitment has to be negotiated, and though these negotiations may follow relatively well-defined pathways, the end result is not predetermined. The will and wish to go on is the most vital component.

Negotiating Power

There is, however, a widespread awareness that the creation and maintenance, or fashioning, of equal relationships necessitates a considerable amount of labour, in a context where power imbalances are omnipresent. Such labour particularly that involved in the constant need for discussion and negotiation, is, as we saw above, perceived as inherently easier for non-heterosexuals than that involved in striving for equality in heterosexual relationships:

> With lesbian relationships everything has to be – well, the lesbian relationships I've had – there are no assumptions about how you will relate, what you will do, who does what... with relationships with straight men, certain things seem to be assumed and then you have to fight to get something else. That has been my experience. (F29)

In looking out at heterosexual relationships the accounts of our female respondents particularly are consistent with those provided in Dunne's (1997) research on the lesbian lifestyle. Dunne (ibid.: pp.181–2) highlights two main aspects of heterosexual relationships which are seen to pre-empt an egalitarian outcome. The first are structural inequalities, which relate to the different material resources available to men and women. In our own research this was most often articulated in terms of there being 'an essential power imbalance' (F34) between women and men. The second relates to the gendered assumptions guiding the actual operation of heterosexual relationships. Many of the women we interviewed place a strong emphasis on the unequal expectations and assumptions about the labour women perform in heterosexual relationships and family forms:

> When I look at other people's relationships [heterosexuals], yeah, there's differences. I think they're much more role-defined, although they would like to think that they've moved on a lot from where they were, I don't see it very often. It may be hidden, but it's still very role-defined. I still see the women doing the majority of the housework and looking after the children and the men going out doing their leisure time. (F36)

> I just found the family and heterosexuality really oppressive. I constantly, constantly had battles about my rights to any sort of equal status in terms of cleaning,

cooking, washing, child care, going out to work, having friends, having a life of my own. I think from beginning to end it was a struggle and a battle and I hadn't realized that they were battles and struggles. (F28)

Importantly, in some of the women's accounts it is not so much individuals who are 'blamed' for the operation of unequal relationships, but rather the institution of heterosexuality itself is perceived to be bound up with the disempowerment of women. As is evident in the quotation above (F28) for some women, heterosexuality is experienced as being productive of pressures to conform to hegemonic notions of 'appropriate' gender behaviour:

> For me, they're [lesbian relationships] based on trying to kind of – find some equality between two people and they're based on freedom and they're based on not owning a person and not dictating to the person what they can do and what they can't do...[in heterosexual relationships] there is a role that is ascribed to the man and a role that is ascribed to the woman. And I don't mean roles as in housework and breadwinner – I mean roles as in – you know – game playing, manipulation, being passive, being victimy – whatever. (F03)

In many such accounts it is clear that 'the feminist value system' (Benjamin and Sullivan, 1996, p.229; cf Dunne, 1997) is influential as a personal resource in making sense of the power in interpersonal relationships. On the surface this could be said to be the case also for some of the men interviewed. The quotation from a male respondent below brings together many of the themes addressed above and focuses explicitly on the relationship between heterosexuality, roles and hegemonic forms of masculinity and femininity:

> I suppose I would have to relate it to my experience of having been in a heterosexual relationship, really. And I mean, it's something to do with how I think we're socialized as men and the way that we think we can be.... You know, I think the kind of macho male bit is very destructive and you know – there's an awful lot of it about really. As there is the stereotype of the kind of passive, the passive female. But I mean, those are kind of stereotypes, but you can see them being acted out. (M39)

It is, however, notable that while many male respondents talk of the potential that same-sex relationships offer for going beyond gendered roles, this does not, in the main, refer to the *structural* differences between men and women or address questions of unequal labour that women undertake. Rather, the emphasis tends to be placed on the 'entrapments' of the male role as they related to the pressure to conform to hegemonic notions of masculinity (Connell, 1987, 1995). While women focus on both the material and the emotional, in men's responses the primary focus appears to be the extent to which heterosexuality and heterosexual relationships are bound up with particular notions of masculinity – and particularly the various 'possibilities of being' in emotional lives. Comments are often framed by reference to the extent that homosexuality and same-sex relationships provide ways of imagining being men that do not have to conform to notions of 'hegemonic masculinity':

I think partners in a gay relationship are much more honest and open about what they feel for each other; what they want from a relationship; I think they're much more honest about expressing feelings of like or dislike or whatever and I just think there's much more forum for discussion. (M23)

I'm not at all sure how heterosexual men of my age get emotional support. I think a lot of them don't. That's a tragedy for them... I mean, to be a heterosexual former public schoolboy. I mean, can you imagine how they cope with life? I mean, I just don't think they know who they are or who anybody else is ever. I don't think they get beyond a certain level of knowledge of people. (M03)

In such accounts it is not women who are located as problematic, but rather the extent to which heterosexual patterns are implicated in the reproduction of particular types of masculinity. A notion of equality emerges in these accounts as primarily focused on reciprocal emotional relationships.

So while women are likely to place a greater emphasis on the unequal divisions of labour within heterosexual relationships, both gay men and lesbians equally emphasize the emotional possibilities opened up by same-sex relationships. The 'egalitarian ideal' is common to both men and women (Peplau, Venigas and Miller Campbell, 1996; Dunne, 1997). For both, the key to equality is the extent to which dichotomous gender scripts and 'roles' are avoided in same-sex relationships. When looking in at their own relationships the notion that couples might organize their own domestic lives in accordance with male/female (or 'butch/femme') roles, or that they might be perceived by others as doing so, is sometimes seen as shocking, and almost always refuted. In the few cases where respondents themselves suggested that their household division of labour could appear to match such roles, the notion of choice is emphasized:

I occasionally look and think 'My God! We're a 1950s butch/femme couple' with what who is doing round the house, sort of thing. Uhm, there are aspects of that. I'm reasonably comfortable with that – so it's ok. I would worry – in some ways it feels less of a problem in a lesbian relationship than it would in a heterosexual relationship where one would be working harder at getting rid of gendered roles...as I've got older I've got easier about the fact that actually I do like cooking and I really don't like hammering nails into fences... I'm less bothered because I don't... because the fact that two adults of the same gender choose to do different things within the house, doesn't give kids a message that says 'Men are only supposed to do this one' or 'Women are only supposed to do that one'. (F21)

Conflicts can, of course, occur. The extract from one respondent below, who is retired and lives with a male partner who is over twenty years younger, highlights that tensions around domestic labour may arise where a partner is not in paid employment:

We very rarely get angry with each other. He still complains I don't do enough housework.... Well, we didn't have a row, we had a discussion the other day and

I said 'All right look', he was busy and he couldn't clean the bathroom for a fortnight and because he hadn't done it he thought that I should have done it. 'Right, we'll sit down and we'll make a list of the jobs that need doing and we'll write a list of who is going to do what and then, we're not going to have these misunderstandings'... because in a way I feel that I'm... this is my retirement when I should have leisure and the time to do things and what not... well I feel as if I don't really benefit very much from being retired... and he's got a very exacting job. (M44)

The following quotation from a woman who is temporarily unemployed and who lives with a partner who is in paid employment, highlights this further:

I think until I'm working and earning the same amount of money that she is, it can never be equal... and yet it can be, in other ways. But I think as individuals we probably make it difficult to be equal because there's, even if she was perfectly fine, and said, even if we had a joint bank account and, which we don't at the present time, and I could take any of her money whenever I wanted it, or whatever, I wouldn't feel equal. Because I wouldn't feel that I was making an equal contribution. So, I would make myself feel unequal. (F43)

These respondents indicate that there are limits to negotiation. These limits are emphasized where there is a lack of emotional reciprocity and mutual commitment to the relationship, or when the grounds on which the commitment was based change. While many respondents have successfully negotiated the shifting from monogamy to non-monogamy, or even the shift from a sexual relationship to a non-sexual one, such negotiations are only perceived to be possible where the changed relationship is mutually desired:

He said 'I don't... I don't want us to have sex any longer'. And I said 'Erm... that's not so easy for me, because I do see sex as a very important part of our relationship'. And he didn't want to stop seeing me but he didn't want to have sex with me and I didn't want to necessarily see him if it wasn't going to be that kind of relationship... I wrote him a really angry letter which he'd never received one like that before from me. And I think it had quite shocked him... I think he was more frightened than angry and realized that... we had to negotiate around this somehow, but at the same time I was seeing this as fairly untenable because you can't kind of say to someone 'I don't care if you don't want to have sex with me – you've got to have sex with me...'. You know, you can't do that. (M25)

Finding what you can and cannot do is the ultimate challenge to the reciprocal relationship:

It's a downward spiral, because my response to feeling threatened by her loving someone else more than me, is to behave in a way which makes her feel controlled and so, therefore, she doesn't love me as much – or can't express her love so much. And I know it's a vicious circle. You know, the only way out for me is to let go. . . .

It doesn't feel equal because I think there's a level on which I need her more than she needs me and I don't like that. (F29)

Forms of Commitment

A key question arises in relation to how we make sense of the 'egalitarian ideal' that has been outlined above. Previous attempts to address the equality of lesbian and gay male relationships has suggested that they can be understood to be structured around 'best-friend' models of relating (Harry and DeVall, 1978; Harry, 1984; Peplau, 1981; Kehoe, 1988). As Peplau, Venigas and Miller Campbell (1996, p. 403) suggest:

> A friendship script typically fosters equality in relationships. In contrast to marriage, the norms of friendship assume that partners are relatively equal in status and power. Friends also tend to be similar in interests, resources, and skills. Available evidence suggests that most American lesbians and gay men have a relationship that most closely approximates best friendship.

Friendship scripts also imply a substantial degree of autonomy for each partner. While the friendship model is not universally employed, there is broad agreement that friendship has a large role to play in the structuring of these relationships. Indeed, Blumstein and Schwartz (1983) in their study of same-sex and heterosexual couples have argued that lesbians and gay men appear to combine the need for friendship and romantic love in one person to a greater extent than heterosexuals. From our own research it is clear that for many lesbians and gay men friendship is seen as central to the operation of 'successful' couple relationships:

> No. I would say it's very much more a friendship... I think we have a very stable relationship. Sex is obviously part of it, but... I wouldn't say our relationship was based on sex. (M12)

> I'm back again on my friendship kick, I'm afraid, I think that underpinned everything... I'm stuck in the groove on that... I think that, as they say, was the sort of rock, the underpinning, whatever you want to call it. (F47)

The notion of friendship has also been employed with regard to same-sex relationships in other ways that are worth noting here. The term 'intimate friendships' is used by Dunne (1997) to denote the reciprocal nature of lesbians' emotional relationships. This is in contrast to the notion of 'intimate strangers' that is employed by Mansfield and Collard (1988) to refer to the different emotional goals that husbands and wives may have in marriage. Blasius (1994) also focuses on friendship, though in his scheme it is termed 'erotic friendship' which 'is characterized by reciprocal *independence* (not interdependence based upon complementarity)' (ibid.: pp. 219–20):

> Erotic friendship is an ethico-erotic relationship productive of equality; the participants (whatever they name themselves – lovers, ex-lovers, fuckbuddies, partners) are inventing themselves and become the conditions for such self-invention of each other. (Ibid.: p. 221)

The key to equality in erotic friendship, Blasius suggests, is that it is based on *reciprocal* giving and receiving of pleasure. Echoing some of our interviewees' accounts as outlined earlier, he argues the power to shape the other in such relationships is limited by the freedom of that other to remain in or leave the relationship. As Weston (1991, p. 149) notes in her discussion of the extent to which her own respondents located equality as a distinguishing feature of relations within lesbian and gay couples, 'The portrayal of lovers as a union of equals rather than a relation of subjugation has clear ties to romantic ideologies of heterosexual marriage'.

Duncombe and Marsden (1993, 1996) note that a key influence in heterosexual couples' stories may be the desire to conform to the model of the happy companionate relationship: 'A key part of emotion work where the couple relationship is old or shaky may be the couple's management of their image to outsiders – including interviewers – so as to present a picture of companionate love' (Duncombe and Marsden, 1993, p. 237).

However, a key aspect of the romantic narrative that is not present in the accounts of our non-heterosexual respondents is the notion of 'together for ever' – rather one of the 'freedoms' identified is precisely the perceived freedom to leave. In this sense we are presented with a story more in keeping with what Giddens (1992) terms 'confluent love',which cuts across the homosexual/heterosexual dichotomy:

> Confluent love is active, contingent love, and therefore jars with the 'for ever', 'one-and-only' qualities of the romantic love complex (i.e. less the 'special person' that counts and more the 'special relationship').... Love here only develops to the degree to which intimacy does, to the degree to which each partner is prepared to reveal concerns and needs to the other and to be vulnerable to that other. (Ibid.: pp. 61–2)

Superficially, this would appear to leave contingent love without cultural guidelines. However, there is strong evidence that a whole set of local norms and patterns have emerged in the non-heterosexual world, closely conforming to what Blasius (1994, p. 206) calls the lesbian and gay ethic, a type of existence that is the consequence of coming out, and which is bound up with a set of knowledges about the possibilities of being lesbians and gay men. Such knowledges are potentially accessed through 'coming out' of the heterosexual selves that are socially ascribed and 'into' non-heterosexual 'communities'. In this context, coming out can be seen to necessitate 'reskilling' in the sense that it is employed by Giddens (1991) with regard to 'fateful moments' – times where individuals are faced with an alerted 'set of risks' (ibid.: p. 131). Coming out can allow for (if not necessitate) reskilling as an engagement with community knowledges that are informed by various analyses of power – including feminist value systems and lesbian and gay politics. From Blasius's (1994, p. 212) account we can locate some of the possible sources that might be accessed in this reskilling:

> A way of life produces knowledge needed in order to exist in the world at a particular historical moment. This ethos necessitates the production of knowledge, understood not just as theory, but including practical guides to and reflections upon living – such as self-help manuals (concerning medicine, the law, relationships, etc.), fiction, autobiography and scientific research.

Other important sources are what Plummer (1995) refers to as 'sexual stories'. Such stories, often concerning 'new ways of living', circulate in and through developing interpretative communities, providing informal scripts or narrative structures by which individuals can reflexively shape their intimate lives. These local knowledges and stories provide the resources which can be deployed in managing everyday life, particularly where traditional guidelines are absent.

Bauman (1993, p. 98) has argued that there are two characteristic strategies for dealing with the perceived flux of modern relationships, what he calls 'fixing' and 'floating'. Fixing takes place when the potential openness of what Giddens (1992) calls 'confluent love' is set firmly in place by the demands of duty. Floating occurs when the labour of constant negotiation on the terms of a relationship leads to people cutting their losses, and starting all over again. This is often, of course, the case in non-heterosexual as well as heterosexual relationships: 'A lot of lesbians and gay men split up more often than heterosexuals because they're not necessarily conventionally married, and they don't have to go through all the hassle, so it is easier to split up, I think, in some cases' (F44).

This is not, however, the only pathway. Many work through the vicissitudes of their relationship, constantly remaking it, trying to 'make a go of it' by affirming their long-term commitment. Inevitably, given the absence of an institutional framework, there is a recognition of a certain contingency in lesbian and gay relationships, but many see this as a positive rather than negative factor:

> I think it's an advantage for lesbian relationships that there isn't a kind of whole structure built around them, like marriage or whatever, because it allows you to be freer within the relationship to build the relationship that you want. And that's why I don't want public recognition in the way of any kind of ceremony or anything like that for lesbian relationships. (F06/07)

But a recognition that relationships do not last for ever does not mean they cannot be worked at 'as if' they will last:

> We've never, ever said that – you know – till death us do part. But we do plan...while the relationship is going well, we will be planning long term.

> Because you can't keep planning short term and expect long-term things to sort themselves out. (F06/07)

Commitment based on mutual trust is seen as the key to sustaining a relationship (cf. Weeks, 1995), and this is not dependent on any institutional backing:

> Why do I need a licence to commit myself to somebody? The very idea is really quite abhorrent. (F43)

> We were very insistent when we had our meeting of thankfulness, that this was not a form of marriage and it was not creating a relationship or commitment because the commitment had been there for nine years. (M44)

The commitment takes many forms, from sexuality to domestic involvement, and there appears to be no common pattern. Sexual attraction may be the first step towards mutual involvement, but it is not necessarily the decisive factor: '[Intimacy] is about closeness really. And there's different degrees of it. It's about trust...friendship, right through to sexuality. It's about being close and trusting' (F40/41).

Similarly, living together may be an essential for many partners, but something to be avoided by others. Commitment broadly for our respondents means two basic things: a willingness to work at difficulties, which implies a constant process of mutual negotiation; and a responsibility to care, and 'emotional labour' (cf. Johnson, 1990; Marcus, 1992).

This is not dissimilar to wider trends. Finch and Mason (1993), for example, suggest that although ties to family of origin remain highly significant, they cannot be assumed, and are as much a product of 'working out' as of blood. The authors prefer to use the concepts of 'developing commitments' and of a sense of responsibility that is worked out over time, so that while kin relationships remain distinctive, the extent to which they differ from other relationships, particularly friendships, is blurred. Commitments, they suggest, are likely to feel particularly strong precisely because they are developed in negotiation with specific others. This is clearly of great significance in relationship to non-traditional commitments.

It is striking that many of our respondents avoid the language of obligation, which they see as being about duty, something imposed from outside. Duty is 'Like some kind of moral code that people use to put on you... I don't think I need that kind of external thing put on me' (F04/F05). These terms were compared unfavourably with the concepts of responsibility and mutual care and commitment:

> Responsibility is something I decide to do and I keep to; obligation is when I feel I have to. (F01)

> Duty is something that is imposed on you...if you feel responsible for someone...then you do that because you feel you want to, not because somebody else feels you ought to. (M44)

If commitment, mutual responsibility and care are the defining characteristics of partnerships, then many feel these need to be confirmed in demonstrable ways.

In his self-help book for lesbians and gay men, Uhrig (1984) suggests that many are looking for four things in their relationships: affirmation, celebration, symbolization, and something that goes beyond traditional ways of doing things. In practice, Driggs and Finn (1991) argue, this often takes place through two processes: the creation of couple traditions, and the creation of couple rituals as symbolic ways of affirming bonds and deepening attachments.

Our own research suggests that these two processes are usually merged: rituals become part of the traditions of a relationship, though not unproblematically. Partners seek ways of confirming their involvement, but are often reluctant to do anything that seems too 'heterosexual'. So many find ways of celebrating with irony, or play with traditional modes, balancing ambivalence with an underlying seriousness. Anniversaries can be particularly important: of first meeting, first sex, when they moved in together or made a commitment (cf. Johnson, 1990; Marcus, 1992).

Similarly, partners may celebrate St Valentine's Day, with flowers or gifts. Others, however, are made of sterner stuff: 'I'm very anti-Valentine's Day because I've always thought it was heterosexual' (F22). For some people, anything can be an excuse for celebration: 'anything we can think of, we celebrate' (F33). Traditional 'family' feast days and holidays can be a particular trial for many partners, making for tensions between a sense of obligation to family of origin and current commitments (cf. Tanner, 1978):

> We did celebrate Christmas together as a family...that was quite difficult. Well, I found it a bit difficult because my mum and dad saw it as a rejection of them...after Christmas she did actually say... 'Yes, you've got your family now'. (F05)

Lesbian and gay events, however, such as the annual Pride celebrations, can offer alternative foci for 'family' celebration. In the end, however, perhaps what is chosen as a focus for celebration is less important than the fact that many people do feel the need for celebration or symbolism, as cement for a relationship.

The growth of a self-help literature (for example, Driggs and Finn, 1991; Uhrig, 1984) suggests the developing importance for many lesbians and gays of finding ways of publicly and privately affirming commitment, without necessarily following traditional heterosexual modes. Early in the 1980s, in a study of gay male couples, McWhirter and Mattison (1984) commented on the absence of set rules and of ways of formalizing relationships. In the late 1990s it is clear that this situation is rapidly changing as the narratives of non-heterosexual relationships circulate ever more widely.

Conclusion

We have highlighted three aspects of non-heterosexual partnerships as they have emerged in recent years. There are many more sides to such arrangements, of course, for they are potentially as variegated as heterosexual arrangements. The point we would want to emphasize is that the non-heterosexual patterns represent a creative juncture between a specific history (that of homosexuality) and wider social developments (particularly changes in family life and in patterns of intimate involvement). Out of this complex background there have developed forms of everyday life, 'ways of being in the world', which stress the importance of the egalitarian relationship as the focus for intimate life.

NOTE

1   This chapter is based on research conducted for a project funded by the Economic and Social Research Council, entitled 'Families of choice: the structure and meanings of non-heterosexual relationships' (reference no. L315253030). The research took place between 1995 and 1996, as part of the ESRC's research programme on Population and Household Change, and was based in the School of Education, Politics and Social Science, South Bank University, London. The director of the project was Jeffrey Weeks, with Catherine Donovan and Brian Heaphy as the research fellows. The core of the research involved in-depth interviews with 48 men and 48 women who broadly identified as 'non-heterosexual' (a term we use throughout the following discussion to encompass a range of possible self-identifications: as gay, lesbian, homosexual, 'queer', bisexual). All the first-person quotations in this chapter come from these interviews. All female interviews are denoted by 'F', the male interviews by an 'M', each followed by a number. The numbers reflect the order in which the interviews took place. On the methodology used see Heaphy, Donovan and Weeks (1999).

REFERENCES

Abelove, H. et al. (eds) (1993), *Lesbian and Gay Studies Reader*, London: Routledge.
Bauman, Z. (1993), *Postmodern Ethics*, Oxford: Blackwell Publishers.
Bech, H. (1996), *When Men Meet: Homosexuality and Modernity*, Cambridge: Polity Press.
Beck, U. and Beck-Gernsheim, E. (1995), *The Normal Chaos of Love*, Cambridge: Polity Press.
Bell, A. P. and Weinberg, M. S. (1978), *Homosexualities: A Study of Diversity among Men and Women*, London: Mitchell Beazley.
Benjamin, O. and Sullivan, O. (1996), 'The importance of difference: conceptualizing increased flexibility in gender relations at home', *Sociological Review*, 44: 225–51.

Blasius, M. (1994) *Gay and Lesbian Politics: Sexuality and the Emergence of a New Ethic*, Philadelphia: Temple University Press.

Blumstein, P. and Schwartz, P. (1983), *American Couples*, New York: William Morrow.

Connell, R. W. (1987), *Gender and Power*, Cambridge: Polity Press.

Connell, R. W. (1995), *Masculinities*, Cambridge: Polity Press.

Driggs, J. H. and Finn, S. E. (1991), *Intimacy Between Men: How to Find and Keep Gay Love Relationships*, London: Plume.

Duncombe, J. and Marsden, D. (1993), 'Love and intimacy: the gender division of emotion and emotion work', *Sociology*, 27: 221–4.

Duncombe, J. and Marsden, D. (1996) 'Can we research the private sphere? Methodological and ethical problems in the study of the role of intimate emotion in personal relationships', in L. Morris and S. Lyons (eds), *Gender Relations in Public and Private: Research Perspectives*, London: Macmillan.

Dunne, G. (1997), *Lesbian Lifestyles: Women's Work and the Politics of Sexuality*, London: Macmillan.

Finch, J. and Mason, J. (1993), *Negotiating Family Responsibilities*, London: Routledge.

Giddens, A. (1991), *Modernity and Self-Identity*, Cambridge: Polity Press.

Giddens, A. (1992), *The Transformation of Intimacy*, Cambridge: Polity Press.

Harry, J. (1984), *Gay Couples*, New York: Praeger.

Harry, J. and DeVall, W. B. (1978), *The Social Organization of Gay Males*, New York: Praeger.

Heaphy, B., Donovan, C. and Weeks, J. (1999), 'Methodological issues in research into non-heterosexual relationships', to be published in *Sexualities*.

Johnson, S. E. (1990), *Staying Power: Long Term Lesbian Couples*, Florida: Naiad Press.

Kehoe, M. (1988), 'Lesbians over 60 speak for themselves', *Journal of Homosexuality*, 16: 1–111.

Laner, M. R. (1977), 'Permanent partner priorities: gay and straight', *Journal of Homosexuality*, 3: 119–72.

McWhirter, D. and Mattison, A. M. (1984), *The Male Couple: How Relationships Develop*, Englewood Cliffs, NJ: Prentice-Hall.

Mansfield, P. and Collard, J. (1988), *The Beginning of the Rest of Your Life? A Portrait of Newly-wed Marriage*, London: Macmillan.

Marcus, E. (1992), *The Male Couples' Guide: Finding a Man, Making a Home, Building a Life*, New York: Harper Perennial.

Martin, A. (1993), *The Guide to Lesbian and Gay Parenting*, London: Pandora.

Mendola, M. (1980), *The Mendola Report: A New Look at Gay Couples in America*, New York: Crown Publishers.

Peplau, L. A. (1981) 'What homosexuals want in relationships', *Psychology Today*, March, 28–38.

Peplau, L. A., Venigas, R. C. and Miller Campbell, S. (1996), 'Gay and lesbian relationships', in R. C. Savin-Williams and K. M. Cohen (eds), *The Lives of Lesbians, Gays, and Bisexuals*, New York: Harcourt Brace College.

Plummer, K. (1995), *Telling Sexual Stories: Power, Change, and Social Worlds*, London: Routledge.

Porter, K. and Weeks, J. (1990), *Between the Acts: Lives of Homosexual Men 1895–1967*, London: Routledge.

Silverstein, C. (1981), *Man to Man: Gay Couples in America*, New York: Morrow.

Sullivan, A. (ed.) (1997), *Same-Sex Marriage: Pro and Con. A Reader*, New York: Vintage Books.

Tanner, D. M. (1978), *The Lesbian Couple*, Lexington, MA: Lexington Books.

Uhrig, L. J. (1984), *The Two of Us: Affirming, Celebrating and Symbolising Lesbian and Gay Relationships*, Boston, MA: Alyson Publications.

VanEvery, J. (1995), *Heterosexual Women Changing the Family: Refusing to be a 'Wife!'*, London: Taylor and Francis.

Weeks, J. (1995), *Invented Moralities: Sexual Values in an Age of Uncertainty*, Cambridge: Polity Press.

Weeks, J., Donovan, C. and Heaphy, B. (1996), *Families of Choice: Patterns of Non-Heterosexual Relationships: A Literature Review*, Social Science Research Papers No. 2, South Bank University.

Weeks, J., Donovan, C. and Heaphy, B. (1998) 'Everyday experiments: narratives of non-heterosexual relationships', in E. Silva and C. Smart (eds), *The New Family?*, London: Sage.

Weston, K. (1991), *Families We Choose*, New York: Columbia University Press.

6

Money, Power and Inequality in Marriage

Carolyn Vogler and Jan Pahl

Introduction

There is now a considerable body of research which suggests an association between money and power in marriage. In general the partner with the larger income is likely to play a more dominant part in decision-making: wives who have paid employment are likely to have greater power than those who only work at home (see, for example, Safilios Rothschild, 1970; Cromwell and Olson, 1975; Scanzoni, 1979; McDonald, 1980). However, in general the literature on marital power has considered money in terms of income entering the household. More recently there has been a surge of interest in the intra-household economy and, in particular, in the financial arrangements of married couples. The growing body of research on the intra-household economy is casting new light on the sociological literature on marital power, as well as questioning the economists' assumption that the household is an unproblematic economic unit (see, for example, Edwards, 1981; Blumstein and Schwartz, 1983; Hertz, 1986; Wilson, 1987; Blumberg, 1988; Dwyer and Bruce, 1988; Pahl, 1989; Zelizer, 1989; Rogers and Schlossman, 1990; Treas, 1991). In a recent review article, which appeared in the *Journal of Marriage and the Family*, Ferree suggested that 'Control over money and how it is used are important dimensions of power inside the household'. She concluded: 'More work on what happens to women's and men's money, once it enters the household, is desperately needed' (Ferree, 1990, pp. 877–8).

Most existing research on the intra-household economy has been based on relatively small samples, which has made it impossible to carry out satisfactory statistical analyses to explore the complex interrelationships between money, power and inequality within marriage. This article uses a major, new, British data set to examine some of the questions which the topic raises. For example, how do married couples manage and control their finances and what are the implications, for individual married people, of different systems of financial allocation? We know that marital power, as measured by decisions made, reflects each partner's financial contribution to the household; does it also reflect, or affect, patterns of financial allocation within the household? Can there be differences in living standards between husband and wife within the same household, and if so, do these reflect the access of each partner to household resources? These are the questions which we shall try to answer.

This is the second of two articles on the control and allocation of money within households. The first article (Vogler and Pahl, 1993) examined the determinants of allocative systems, focusing especially on the interrelationships between allocative systems and employment patterns, social class, gender ideologies and other variables. It showed that shifts to greater equality in household financial arrangements depend, not only on women's full-time participation in the labour market, but also on effective challenges to the husband's traditional status as the main breadwinner in the family. This article describes the methods couples use to organize money and explores the links between power and access to money within the household.

The Methods of the Study

This article draws on data from the Social Change and Economic Life Initiative, a British study funded by the Economic and Social Research Council (Gallie, 1988). The initiative focused on six urban labour markets with contrasting experiences of economic and social change. Three areas – Swindon, Aberdeen and Northampton – had experienced relatively low rates of unemployment for most of the 1980s, while Coventry, Rochdale and Kirkcaldy had experienced prolonged recession and above-average rates of unemployment. An initial set of interviews was carried out in 1986 with 1,000 people in each locality, focusing on their attitudes to work and their work histories. Respondents were randomly selected from the overall non-institutional population aged between 20 and 60. Fieldwork was conducted by Public Attitude Surveys Research Limited. In 1987, there was a subsequent phase of interviewing in which, in each locality, 300 of the original respondents were re-interviewed about their household circumstances. In households where respondents were living with a spouse or partner (approximately 200 in each locality) partners were also interviewed.

Interviews were conducted jointly with both partners; however, in order to reduce the risk of consensus answers a large proportion of questions were answered by means of self-completion booklets. Each partner was given a self-completion booklet in which they ticked their own answers, without conferring with each other. For a large proportion of questions we thus obtained independent answers from both husbands and wives. This chapter is based on the second, follow-up survey and is restricted to the 1,211 cases of partnership or couple households. Whenever possible analysis is based on both husbands' and wives' answers.

In terms of their economic and demographic characteristics the 1,211 house-holds corresponded broadly to a national sample. They were spread across the ages between 20 and 60 reasonably evenly and 70 per cent had children living at home with them. Among the men, 87 per cent were in full-time employment, while 8 per cent were unemployed and 4 per cent non-employed, mainly retired. Among the women, 29 per cent were in full-time employment and 37 per cent in part-time employment, while 34 per cent were unemployed or non-employed, most of whom were housewives. A more detailed report is presented in Vogler (1989).

Previous Research on Financial Allocation within Households

There have been few large-scale studies of individuals within households focus-ing specifically on the extent to which social inequalities can be said to exist between members of the same household. Quantitative sociology has a long tradition of theoretical and empirical analysis focusing on social inequalities deriving from the labour market. In the area of households, however, assump-tion has often played a more powerful role than empirical analysis. Households have been assumed to be similar to each other, operating as redistributive units within which resources are shared equitably, so that there are no significant inequalities between husbands and wives within them. Social economists, and most sociologists from Parsons onwards, have all conceptualized households as collective units operating on the basis of common household values and goals. Spouses are assumed to have equal access to financial resources.

More qualitative studies, however, have questioned these assumptions, often showing both significant differences between individuals in the same household, as well as significant differences between different types of household. In a review of the studies which investigated the topic in the first half of the twentieth century, Pahl showed how particular patterns of financial allocation could be associated with inequalities both between and within households (Pahl, 1980). In low-income households women typically managed the money, a situation in which money management is more accurately seen as a chore rather than as a source of power. In households with higher incomes, or in communities where gender roles were highly segregated and married women were economically inactive, husbands were likely to take control of finances; typically wives were given a housekeeping allowance. This pattern could lead to considerable conflict, as husbands could enjoy greater power over decision-making, and a higher standard of living than their wives and children (Klein, 1965). If housekeeping allowances were not increased when wages or prices rose, or when additional children were born, the additional financial burden fell on the women and children, instead of being shared equally. In a review of interwar and postwar poverty studies, Young concluded by warning about the dangers of using total household income as a guide to the living standards of women and children, especially when wives received their share of household resources in the form of a fixed housekeeping allowance (Young, 1952).

While two subsequent studies of the family claimed to show a long-term trend to greater equality in marriage consequent upon women's increased labour market participation, they failed to collect data either on inequalities in access to money or on inequalities in financial decision-making (Bott, 1957; Young and Willmott, 1973). They were thus unable to show how far financial decision-making was genuinely becoming more consensual, rather than dominated by one partner, or how far financial resources were genuinely shared more equally. Many small-scale studies undertaken during the 1970s and 1980s questioned the extent to which women's part-time work was capable of fundamentally altering traditional inequalities between male breadwinners and female childrearers/secondary earners. In a review of these studies, Morris (1988, 1989) concluded that while the ideology of sharing and joint partnership certainly seemed more prevalent now than in the past, actual practices of financial allocation did not appear to have changed to such a large degree and that this in turn had important implications for women's labour market behaviour.

A Typology of Household Allocative Systems

It seems clear, then, that the relative positions of individuals within households need to be analysed empirically, rather than assumed *a priori*. We therefore focus in detail on differences between households in the methods used to organize household money, before going on to analyse the extent to which these in turn entail inequalities between individuals within the same household, both in financial decision-making and in access to money as a resource. Our first aim was to classify the main ways in which couples organized their household money. For this purpose we have used Pahl's (1989) typology of household financial allocative systems. These are systems of money management which vary according to whether spouses have separate or joint spheres of responsibility for managing household money. Where responsibilities are segregated, Pahl's systems specify which spouse has responsibility for organizing different parts of the household budget. Pahl identifies five basic systems of money management, four of which can be thought of as involving separate spheres of responsibility for household money – the female whole-wage system, the male whole-wage system, the housekeeping allowance system and the independent management system, while the remaining pooling system involves joint or non-segregated spheres of responsibility for household finances.

In the *female whole-wage system* wives have sole responsibility for managing all household finances. Husbands hand over the whole of their wage packet, minus their personal spending money, to wives, and the husband's responsibility for budgeting or making ends meet ends with the handing over of the wage. In Oakley's (1974) sample this was resented by wives, on the grounds that they were the ones who had to worry about paying bills, while husbands could spend without worrying. This system has traditionally been associated with low income, working-class households and a strict division of labour between husbands and wives (Dennis, Henriques and Slaughter, 1956; Land, 1969; Wilson, 1987; Pahl, 1989). Wives usually have no personal spending money separate from collective funds and husbands using this system have been found to be less inclined to work overtime, since all additional money is allocated for collective expenditure (Gray, 1979). In the *male whole-wage system*, however, husbands have sole responsibility for managing all household finances, which may leave non-employed wives with no personal spending money. This system has been found particularly in studies of abused women (Evason, 1982; Pahl, 1985).

The *housekeeping allowance system* involves separate spheres of responsibility for household expenditure. Husbands give their wives a fixed sum of money for housekeeping expenses, while the rest of the money remains in the husband's control and he pays for other items. Husbands have traditionally had the final say over the amount of the housekeeping allowance, as well as over the purchase of other items. Additions to the husband's pay packet may not necessarily find their way into collective expenditure, since they may be seen as additions to his personal spending money rather than as contributions to domestic expenditure. Various studies have found that since basic pay is often allocated for collective expenditure, whereas bonuses are regarded as personal spending money, husbands have often preferred increases in bonuses rather than rises in basic pay (Mays, 1954; Zweig, 1961; Tunstall, 1962). Wives who do not earn may have no personal spending money separate from the housekeeping money, which is allocated for collective expenditure. This system has traditionally been associated with higher paid workers and middle-class couples in which the husband is the only earner (Oakley, 1974; Edgell, 1980; Zweig, 1961; Dennis, Henriques and Slaughter, 1956; Klein, 1965; Edwards, 1981; Gray, 1979; Pahl, 1989).

In the *pooling system*, however, financial responsibilities are in principle non-segregated. Both partners have access to all or nearly all household money and both are thought to be responsible for management and expenditure from the common pool. This system is found across all income levels, especially where wives are in employment (Hunt, 1980; Wilson, 1987; Land, 1969; Edwards, 1981; Pahl, 1989). It is often associated with a joint bank account and a more egalitarian relationship, although the mechanisms by which it operates on a daily basis are unclear. The ways in which management and control are exercised and the processes of conflict resolution are unspecified. Finally, in the *independent management system*, both partners have independent incomes and neither has access to all the household money. Each partner is responsible for specific items of expenditure and while these may change over time, the principle of keeping flows of money separate within the household is maintained. This system is typically associated with dual-earner households.

In the study reported in this article respondents were asked to say which of Pahl's allocative systems came closest to the way in which they currently organized their own household finances. Table 6.1 shows that the most commonly used system was undoubtedly the pool, chosen by a full half of all our respondents, with the remaining half selecting one of the segregated systems.

Table 6.1   Household allocative systems: a comparison of different studies

	Family finances group 1983 N – 250 %	Pahl (1989) N – 102 %	SCEL initiative* N – 1211 %
Female whole wage	18	14	26
Male whole wage	–	–	10
Housekeeping allowance	24	22	12
Pool	54	56	50
Independent management	4	9	2
	100	100	100

* Social Change and Economic Life Initiative: these percentages are based on the full sample, from which the household survey respondents were drawn as a subsample

The next most frequently used segregated system was the female whole-wage system, used by more than half of those using a segregated system, or 26 per cent of the overall sample. The male whole-wage and housekeeping allowance systems were used by 10 per cent and 12 per cent respectively of the overall sample, and the independent management system by only 2 per cent. The last was too small for independent analysis and has thus been omitted from the subsequent discussion.

Three Different Forms of Pooling

As can be seen in table 6.1, these findings differ slightly from those of other studies using the same or similar categories. Our results show a higher incidence of both the male and female whole-wage systems and a lower incidence of the housekeeping allowance system, although the proportions using the pooling system are very similar. This raises two questions. First, how far were the budgetary categories with which respondents were presented meaningful to them and second, how far did selection of the pooling option simply reflect, as Pahl has suggested, a generalized ideological commitment to sharing and equality, as opposed to any real practice of joint financial management? We were able to answer both questions by means of a separate indicator of money management which we were able to cross-check against responses to the budgetary categories. The independent measure of money management asked both respondents and their partners to say who in their household had ultimate responsibility for organizing household money and paying the bills: the male partner, the female partner or both equally. Each couple's responses were combined into a single five-point scale showing both partners' perceptions of money management, as well as the extent of agreement or disagreement between them.[1]

This independent indicator of financial management clearly validated Pahl's segregated systems, but confirmed our hypothesis that the pool was in fact very heterogeneous in terms of management practices. Only 39 per cent of pooling couples *both* perceived finances as jointly managed, with almost as many disagreeing with each other; 16 per cent disagreed over whether they were jointly or husband-managed and 18 per cent over whether they were jointly or wife-managed. A substantial minority of pooling couples also agreed that finances were managed by only one partner, the wife in 14 per cent of pooling households and the husband in the remaining 13 per cent of pooling households. In short, in as many as 61 per cent of pooling households, at least one and often both partners nominated one or the other of them as ultimately responsible for management. These results clearly indicate that the general 'pool' category masks the existence of three analytically different forms of pool – the male pool, the female pool and the jointly managed pool – which need to be analysed separately, rather than assumed to be similar or the same as each other. It may be, for example, that in practice husband- and wife-managed pools are rather more similar to the male and female segregated systems than they are to the joint pool. Pooling couples have therefore been subdivided into three categories on the basis of both partners' responses to the management indicator. Those in which one or both partners claimed husbands were responsible for management have been classified as using a *male-managed pool*, and those in which one or both partners claimed wives were responsible for management were said to be using a *female-managed pool*, thus reserving the term *joint pool* for households in which both partners agreed that both were equally responsible for management. This produced the sixfold classification of allocative systems shown in table 6.2. As can be seen in the table, the real or joint pool now accounts for only 20 per cent of the overall sample with the male- and female-managed pools accounting for a further 15 per cent each.

Two points should be noted about the allocative categories. First, while there were no statistically significant differences between male and female respondents, male respondents were initially more likely than female respondents to classify their system as a joint pool (55 per cent and 50 per cent respectively), whereas female respondents were more likely than male respondents to claim they used the female whole-wage system (29 per cent and 24 per cent

Table 6.2   Household allocative systems showing different forms of pooling

	%
Female whole wage	27
Female managed pool	15
Joint pool	20
Male managed pool	15
Male whole wage	10
Housekeeping allowance	13
Total %	100
N	1235

respectively). In practice, however, the excess of male over female respondents selecting the pool all turned out to be using male-managed pools (18 per cent of male respondents as compared with 13 per cent of female respondents). The implication then is that male respondents were slightly more likely than female respondents to mask their own management of finances under the label of 'pooling'.

A second point was that the prevalence of different allocative systems varied slightly by labour market. If we divide the budgetary categories into those involving female management, those involving male management and the jointly managed pool, the male-managed systems, especially the male whole-wage system, were most prevalent in Coventry – traditionally a skilled working-class area with no historical tradition of married women's employment. The joint pool, on the other hand, was most prevalent in Kirkcaldy – traditionally a coal-mining area which also provided good opportunities for women's employment, initially in linoleum and textiles and later in electrical engineering. Finally, traditionally low-wage Aberdeen was marked by a slightly higher proportion of female-managed systems.

Systems of Financial Allocation and Inequalities within the Household

Systems of financial allocation provide some indication of the different ways in which money is managed within households, but in themselves tell us little about inequalities, either in financial decision-making or in access to money as a resource. Systems of money management may be related to differences in living standards between individuals in the same household through the way in which they are related to inequalities in power over financial decision-making. Inequalities in power over financial decision-making may facilitate inequalities in access to money as a resource, which may in turn culminate in differences in living standards between spouses in the same household. We therefore need to distinguish between *strategic control* over household finances and financial *management* as an executive function, recognizing that the person exercising strategic control may be different from the person responsible for implementing decisions on a day-to-day basis. Our previous question on ultimate respons-ibility for organizing household money and paying bills was an indicator of executive management. Strategic control, however, can be thought of as refer-ring to control over infrequent but important decisions, such as which allocative system should be used, how much should be spent on collective domestic expenditure as opposed to personal spending money, and who has the final say over big financial decisions. Previous studies have shown that while wives are more likely to manage household finances, control is more often a male prerogative, associated with the breadwinning, primary earner status (Edwards, 1981; Wilson, 1987; Pahl, 1989).

Inequalities in Decision-making

Our main indicator of financial control involved asking respondents to say whether the male partner, the female partner, or both equally had the final say in *big financial decisions*. In the sample as a whole 70 per cent of respondents indicated that financial decision-making was joint, nearly a quarter (23 per cent) reported that the husband had the final say and 7 per cent that the wife had the final say. There were no significant differences between male and female respondents. As table 6.3 shows, strategic control varied markedly with the type of allocative system used in the household. The joint or female-managed systems were much more likely to be jointly controlled than the male-managed systems: 81 per cent of couples using the joint pool, 79 per cent of couples using the female pool and 74 per cent of those using the female whole wage system claimed to have joint control over finances, as compared with only 61 per cent of couples using the male pool, 56 per cent of couples using the male whole-wage system and 50 per cent of couples using the housekeeping allowance system.

An interesting difference emerged between male and female respondents using the female whole-wage system. Male respondents in households using this system were twice as likely as female respondents to see wives as exercising financial control, whereas female respondents were slightly more likely to see financial control as joint or as exercised by husbands. Wives using the female whole-wage system thus felt they had less independent control over finances than husbands perceived them as having. This raises a question mark over the extent to which wives using this system really controlled, as opposed to simply managing the finances, and tends to support findings in the literature emphasizing the constraints on women using this system (Wilson, 1987; Pahl, 1989). We shall return to this issue later.

A very similar picture emerged from our more general indicator of control, which concerned the *most important decisions* made in the household. Respondents and partners were both asked who in their households had the most say over important decisions: the male partner, the female partner or both equally.

Table 6.3   Household allocative systems by financial control

	Female whole wage %	Female managed pool %	Joint pool %	Male managed pool %	Male whole wage %	Housekeeping allowance %
Female control	17	7	3	1	–	1
Joint control	74	79	81	61	56	50
Male control	9	14	16	36	44	48
Total	100	100	100	100	100	100
N	343	205	249	186	117	150

Sig < 0.001

Table 6.4 brings together both partners' answers to the question about important decisions. When partners disagreed this typically took the form of one person claiming that control was joint, whereas the other partner saw control as either male or female dominated: when this sort of disagreement took place the answer was coded as 'male control' or 'female control' respectively. In the sample as a whole, 7 per cent of couples were characterized as 'female control', 67 per cent of couples agreed that important decisions were jointly controlled and 27 per cent were characterized as 'male control'. Table 6.4 shows that cross-tabulating both partners' answers by the type of budgetary system used in the household shows a very similar pattern of results to the financial decision-making indicator. Joint or female-managed systems were much more likely to be associated with equal control over decision-making. Spouses had an equal say over decision-making in 78 per cent of female pool households, 73 per cent of joint pool households and 70 per cent of female whole-wage households, as compared with 67 per cent of male pool households, 54 per cent of male whole-wage households and only 46 per cent of housekeeping allowance households. The two explicitly male-managed systems – the male whole-wage and the housekeeping allowance systems – were also associated with higher levels of disagreement between partners over who exercised control than was the case with households using the more egalitarian joint or female-managed systems.

In order to construct a rough summary index of power within the household, which would take account of both spouses' answers as well as decision-making in both the financial and the general spheres, respondents' answers to the financial control question were combined with couples' responses to the general decision-making question. Households in which husbands exercised control in both spheres were said to be characterized by strong male power, those in which wives exercised control in both spheres were said to be characterized by strong female power and those in which both partners exercised equal control in both

Table 6.4 Household allocative systems by control over important decisions: both partners' answers

	Female whole wage %	Female managed pool %	Joint pool %	Male managed pool %	Male whole wage %	Housekeeping allowance %
Female control	15	7	4	4	2	2
Joint control	70	78	73	67	54	46
Male control	16	16	23	30	44	52
Total	100	100	100	100	100	100
N	338	203	248	189	117	153

Sig < 0.001
Note 'Female control' includes couples where one partner described control as joint, but the other described decisions as female-dominated. 'Male control' includes couples where one partner described control as joint, but the other described decisions as male-dominated.

spheres were characterized by strong equality. Households in which husbands (or wives) exercised control in one sphere while decisions were made jointly in the other sphere were said to be characterized by weaker male or female power. Just over half of all households (59 per cent) could be said to be egalitarian on both measures. This may well be less than orthodox economists and sociologists have assumed. One third of households were characterized by some degree of male control and 9 per cent by some degree of female control. As can be seen in table 6.5, the method of financial allocation a couple used was quite a good predictor of the distribution of power within the household. Couples using the joint or female-managed systems were markedly more egalitarian than those using the male-managed systems.

Finally, management and strategic control were quite clearly related to each other within each of the allocative systems. When husbands managed finances, as in the male whole wage, the housekeeping allowance system and to a lesser extent the male pool, they were also most likely to control them. When wives managed finances, however, or when finances were equally managed as in the joint pool, they were most likely to be jointly controlled. In short, both wife and joint management were subject to joint control. The implication is that *male control is in fact exercised through male management, whereas other forms of management, notably joint or wife management, are almost invariably circum-scribed by joint control.*

In conclusion, systems of financial allocation were clearly associated with inequalities in power over decision-making. These were smallest in households using the joint or female-managed systems and greatest in households using the explicitly male-managed systems – the male whole-wage and housekeeping allowance systems. The male-managed pool fell between the two extremes,

Table 6.5 Household allocative systems by the index of power*

	Female whole wage %	Female managed pool %	Joint pool %	Male managed pool %	Male whole wage %	Housekeeping allowance %
Strong female power	4	–	1	–	–	–
Weaker female power	18	9	4	2	2	2
Equality	61	69	69	56	45	37
Weaker male power	13	17	21	31	35	39
Strong male power	4	4	5	11	18	22
Total	100	100	100	100	100	100
N	(334)	(202)	(248)	(183)	(116)	(150)

* The index of power combines respondents' answers to the financial control question with respondents' and partners' answers to the general decision-making question

being less male dominated than the other male-managed systems. How far then can inequalities in power over financial decision-making, in turn, be seen as laying the basis for inequalities in access to money as a resource?

Inequalities in Access to Money as a Resource

Individuals living in the same household may experience two rather different kinds of inequalities in access to money as a resource. First, they may experience different levels of financial deprivation and, second, there may be inequalities in access to personal spending money.

In order to provide a general picture of the experience of financial deprivation, respondents and partners were asked to indicate which economies 'you yourself have had to do over the last two years to make ends meet when your household was short of money'. The focus of the question was clearly on the individual. The list which was presented to individuals included fourteen different items, running from having missed a meal or turned down the heat, to borrowing money or selling the car. The commonest things on which people had cut back were social activities, buying clothes and holidays. Much rarer were reductions in heating and expenditure on food, together with measures such as getting into debt and borrowing. The chief differences between partners were that wives were much more likely than husbands to have experienced cuts in spending on meals (28 per cent and 14 per cent respectively) and clothing (54 per cent and 37 per cent respectively). This is likely to reflect both gendered responsibilities for expenditure, as well as the tendency for wives to protect husbands from the effects of reductions. Charles and Kerr (1987), for example, found that when husbands were in low-paid employment wives deliberately tried to shield them from the effects of reductions in food spending by cutting back on the quality of their own food so that husbands received a disproportionate share of what was available. When husbands were unemployed, however, reductions tended to be shared more equally. In short then, the husbands in our sample may have been genuinely less aware than wives of reductions in food expenditure and also less subject to the effects of cutbacks in this respect.

Differences between husbands and wives in their experiences of financial deprivation were found to vary substantially with the allocative system used in the household. The most intensive cuts and the largest differences between spouses emerged in households using either the housekeeping allowance system or the two female-managed systems. In these households the brunt of inequalities in financial deprivation fell clearly on wives, who were more likely than husbands to have experienced cutbacks across a broad range of items. Wives using the female pool had cut back more than husbands on meals expenditure, social life, clothing and savings, while those using the female whole-wage system had cut back more than husbands on meals expenditure, clothing and savings. Finally, wives using the housekeeping allowance system had cut back more than husbands on meals expenditure, clothing and holidays.

Table 6.6   Differences between husbands and wives in financial deprivation*

Allocative systems	Differences between spouses in financial deprivation (mean .33)
Female managed pool	.55
Female whole wage	.52
Joint pool	.07
Male managed pool	.11
Male whole wage	.15
Housekeeping allowance	.44

Sig < .01

* To obtain a measure of the difference in financial deprivation between individual husbands and wives, husbands' financial deprivation scores were subtracted from those of their own wives. A minus score would indicate that husbands experienced higher levels of financial deprivation than wives, whereas a positive score indicates that wives experienced higher levels of financial deprivation than husbands. The scale ranged from −7 to +9 with a mean of .324 and a standard deviation of 1.9.

To provide a rough summary index of the experience of financial deprivation we gave people a score of one for each action that they had taken to cope with financial difficulty. A measure of the difference in financial deprivation between husbands and wives living in the same household was then obtained, by subtracting husbands' financial deprivation scores from those of their own wives. A minus score would indicate that husbands experienced higher levels of financial deprivation than wives, whereas a positive score would indicate that wives experienced higher levels of financial deprivation than husbands. As table 6.6 shows, all the scores were positive, indicating that wives generally experienced greater financial deprivation than husbands, but the extent to which this was the case varied markedly with the type of allocatory system. The largest differences between spouses emerged among couples using the female pool, the female whole-wage and the housekeeping allowance systems, with index scores of .55, .52 and .44 respectively. Those using the male whole-wage system scored .15 and those using the male pool system scored .11. Differences between spouses were smallest among couples using the jointly managed pool (.07).

It might be argued that these differences occur because allocative systems vary according to household income. For example, does the relative financial deprivation of women in female whole-wage households reflect the relative poverty of these households? In order to answer this question we controlled for income, dividing households between high, medium and low income according to standard conventions. Table 6.7 shows the results, and also describes the techniques used in the analysis. It is clear that patterns of inequality between husband and wife persist, even when income is held constant. The greatest inequalities, in terms of financial deprivation, are found in households with the female whole-wage system, the female managed pool and the housekeeping allowance system. Thus wives in medium- and low-income households, with

Table 6.7 Differences between husbands and wives in financial deprivation by allocative system and controlling for household income*

Household income	Female whole wage	Female managed pool	Joint pool	Male managed pool	Male whole wage	Housekeeping allowance
High	.3	.4	−.04	−.04	.4	−.02
Medium	.7	.7	−.2	.2	−.2	.5
Low	.7	.7	.3	.I	−.04	.7

Sig. of allocative system < .0I
Standardized household income not sig.
Sig. of whole table < .007

* Total household income was standardized according to DHSS conventions, by the number of adults and children in the household, and then split into three equal categories, viz. high, medium and low.

female-managed or housekeeping allowance systems, were doubly disadvantaged: financial constraints emanating from outside the household were reinforced by gender inequalities in access to financial resources within the household.

Inequalities in Access to Personal Spending Money

The second way in which allocative systems may be associated with inequalities between spouses in access to money is through their relationship with personal spending money. Access to personal spending money was measured by asking both respondents and partners who in their household had the most personal spending money: the male partner, the female partner or both equally. Given the strong normative emphasis on the importance of sharing and equality in marriage, people may have been reluctant to admit to having different amounts of personal spending money, which means we may be underestimating possible inequalities in this respect. In the sample as a whole, just over half (58 per cent) of all couples both perceived personal spending money as equally distributed. A further 12 per cent agreed that the husband had the most personal spending money, a tiny 4 per cent agreed that the wife had most personal spending money, while the rest disagreed. In the analysis couples who disagreed over whether the wife had more personal spending money or whether they had equal amounts were coded as 'female more PSM'; disagreement over whether the man had more or whether personal spending money was equally shared were coded as 'male more PSM'. As table 6.8 shows, inequalities in access to personal spending money varied markedly with the type of allocative system used in the household. Couples using the joint and male pools were characterized by the highest level of equality: 67 per cent of joint and 70 per cent of male pool couples agreed they had the same amount of personal spending money

Table 6.8 Household allocative systems and differences between spouses in personal spending money (PSM)

	Female whole wage %	Female managed pool %	Joint pool %	Male managed pool %	Male whole wage %	Housekeeping allowance %
Male more PSM	34	24	18	20	26	42
Equal PSM	50	61	67	70	55	47
Female more PSM	15	15	15	11	20	13
Total	100	100	100	100	100	100
N	324	196	232	179	109	138

Sig < 0.0001

compared with 61 per cent of those using the female pool, 55 per cent of those using the male whole-wage, 50 per cent of those using the female whole-wage and 47 per cent of those using the housekeeping allowance system. In households using the two female managed and the housekeeping allowance systems, husbands thus clearly had greater access to personal spending money than wives. These differences were remarkably persistent within income groups and within classes. Similar results were found by Pahl (1989).

Inequalities between spouses in financial deprivation and personal spending money thus tended to hang together. The housekeeping allowance system and the two female managed systems were clearly associated with the largest inequalities between husbands and wives, both in terms of financial deprivation and in access to personal spending money. The joint, and to a lesser extent, the male managed pools, on the other hand, were associated with greater equality both in financial deprivation and in access to personal spending money.

Patterns of Equality and Inequality within Households

How far, then, were inequalities in strategic financial control in turn associated with inequalities in access to money as a resource? Patterns of financial control and management suggested *three* main types of household.

First, there was a group of households who used the joint pool: these comprised about a fifth of the total sample. Joint pooling households stood out from others in the extent to which joint management was associated both with equal strategic control over finances and also with equal access to money as resource. Differences between husbands and wives in terms of financial deprivation were least in these households.

Second, there were households using one of the three male managed systems: the male managed pool, the male whole wage and the housekeeping allowance. Together, these comprised nearly two fifths of the sample. In these households husbands were more likely to control finances and had more power in the making of important decisions. Inequality between the partners was particularly marked in the case of allowance system households: here finances were both controlled and managed by husbands, who suffered less financial deprivation than wives, while having markedly more personal spending money. This implies that the allowance system has changed little since Young's warning in 1952. Far from having slowly evolved into a more egalitarian system, as some have suggested, the separation of responsibilities for household expenditure continues to privilege husbands at the expense of wives. In male whole-wage and male pool households, where male control of finances was associated with greater equality in access to money, wives' access to financial resources may still have been more conditional on the husband's good will, by comparison with the joint pooling couples, who were likely to control their finances jointly.

Third, there were households using one of the two female managed systems, which made up just over two fifths of the sample. In households using the female whole wage or the female managed pool there was a disjunction between control over finances and access to money as a resource: this was particularly marked in middle- and low-income households. Despite their control over finances and their greater power in decision-making, wives in these households experienced significantly higher levels of personal deprivation than husbands, while husbands were likely to have more personal spending money than wives. These findings raise questions about the real meaning of female control, especially in low-income households, suggesting that it may be more nominal than real. Where the opportunities for exercising financial power are heavily circumscribed by low income and by the husband's expectation of personal spending money, 'responsibility' may be a more appropriate term than 'control'! As Wilson (1987) has argued, equal control of finances in these households may serve an important ideological role in masking the real extent of inequality in access to money as a resource.

Allocative Systems and Household Income

Previous research has indicated that patterns of allocation of money vary according to the total income of the household. It has been suggested that wives are more likely to manage money in low-income households, when money management is more of a chore than a source of power, while husbands are more likely to manage the finances of higher-income households (Edwards, 1981; Pahl, 1989; Wilson, 1987). Was this pattern confirmed in the study described here and did this account for the differences between households in terms of deprivation and access to personal spending money?

Table 6.9 shows the mean standardized household income for each allocative system. The two female managed systems were associated with the lowest income levels, while the male managed pool and the male whole wage were associated with relatively high household incomes. Thus the study confirmed that in low-income households women are more likely to have to undertake the

Table 6.9 Mean standardized household income for different allocative systems

	Standardized income: £s per month
Female whole wage	624
Female managed pool	658
Joint pool	719
Male managed pool	728
Male whole wage	755
Housekeeping allowance	697

difficult task of making ends meet. In households where women controlled the finances, the male respondents were more likely to be classified as low paid (Low Pay Unit, 1990) and the household was more likely to have fallen into arrears with rent, gas and electricity bills. Thus the higher levels of deprivation among women in households with female managed pools and female whole-wage systems may simply reflect the lower total income available in these households.

It was interesting to compare households using the joint pool with those using the housekeeping allowance system. In terms of income these two groups were very similar, having neither very high nor very low standardized incomes. However, in terms of intra-household inequality the differences were quite great. This implies that the higher levels of financial deprivation and reduced access to personal spending money experienced by wives with housekeeping allowances reflected the allocation of money within the household rather than the total household income. As Morris (1989) has argued, the rigid demarcation of financial responsibility in these households has traditionally served to protect the husband's personal spending money and limit the wife's access to the husband's earnings.

Thus there was an interlocking pattern of class and gender inequalities which had the effect of increasing the differences between men and women. In low-income households the wife's responsibility for household finances served to protect the husband from the level of deprivation which she was experiencing and to guarantee his access to some personal spending money. At higher income levels there was greater equality as husband and wife shared the benefits of a larger income. However, particular allocative systems could decrease or increase inequalities within the household, as exemplified by the contrast between the joint pool and the housekeeping allowance systems.

Conclusion

In this article we have tried to advance our understanding of the relationships between money, power and inequality within marriage. We have shown that there are important differences between couples in the ways they control and manage their money. The orthodox model of households as egalitarian decision-making units, within which resources are shared equally, applied to only one fifth of the households in the sample, those using the joint pool system. In other households the system of financial allocation served to exacerbate, or to diminish, inequalities between men and women in a way which was related to, but separate from, broader inequalities within and between households.

Thus there was an interlocking pattern of class and gender inequalities which had the effect of increasing differences between men and women. In low-income households the wife's responsibility for household finances served to protect the husband from the level of deprivation which she was experiencing and to guarantee his access to some personal spending money. At higher income levels there was greater equality as husband and wife shared the benefits of a larger income. However, particular allocative systems could decrease or increase inequalities within the household, as exemplified by the contrast between the joint pool and the housekeeping allowance systems. Inequality between husband and wife was least in households with joint control of pooled money and greatest in either lower-income households or in higher-income households with male control of finances.

NOTE

1   Disagreement was of two types, which we term 'short' and 'long' range. Short-range disagreement occurred when one partner claimed financial management was undertaken jointly, while the other partner claimed it was undertaken by only one partner. Long-range disagreement, however, occurred when one partner claimed management was undertaken by one spouse while the other partner claimed it was undertaken by the other spouse. In practice virtually all disagreement was of the short-range type. In the sample as a whole, 70 per cent of couples gave exactly the same answer to the management question, while the remaining 30 per cent gave different answers, all disagreement being of the short-range type.

REFERENCES

Blumberg, R. L. (1988), 'Income under female versus male control: hypotheses from a theory of gender stratification and data from the Third World', *Journal of Family Issues*, 9: 51–84.

Blumstein, P. and Schwartz, P. (1983), *American Couples*, New York: William Morrow.

Bott, E. (1957), *Family and Social Network*, London: Tavistock.

Charles, N. and Kerr, M. (1987), 'Just the way it is: gender and age differences in family food consumption', in J. Brannen and G. Wilson (eds), *Give and Take in Families*, London: Allen & Unwin.

Cromwell, R. E. and Olson, D. (1975), *Power in Families*, New York: Sage.

Dennis, N., Henriques, L. and Slaughter, C. (1956), *Coal is Our Life*, London: Eyre and Spottiswoode.

Dwyer, D. and Bruce, J. (1988), *A Home Divided: Women and Income in the Third World*, Stamford, CA: Stamford University Press.

Edgell, S. (1980), *Middle Class Couples*, London: Allen & Unwin.

Edwards, M. (1981), *Financial Arrangements within Families*, Canberra: National Women's Advisory Council.

Evason, E. (1982), *Hidden Violence: A Study of Battered Women in Northern Ireland*, Belfast: Farset Press.

Ferree, M. M. (1990), 'Beyond separate spheres: feminism and family research', *Journal of Marriage and the Family*, 52, 866–84.

Gallie, D. (1988), *The Social Change and Economic Life Initiative: An Overview*, Oxford: Nuffield College.

Gray, A. (1979), 'The working-class family as an economic unit', in C. C. Harris (ed.), *The Sociology of the Family*, Sociological Review Monograph, University of Keele.

Hertz, R. (1986) *More Equal than Others: Women and Men in Dual Career Marriages*, Berkeley: University of California Press.

Hunt, P. (1978), 'Cash transactions and household tasks', *Sociological Review*, 26: 555–71.

Hunt, P. (1980), *Gender and Class Consciousness*, London: Macmillan.

Klein, J. (1965), *Samples from English Cultures*, vol. 1, London: Routledge & Kegan Paul.

Land, H. (1969), *Large Families in London*, London: Bell.

Low Pay Unit (1988), *The Poor Decade: Wage Inequalities in the 1980s*, London: Low Pay Unit.

McDonald, G. W. (1980), 'Family power: the assessment of a decade of theory and research, 1970–1979', *Journal of Marriage and the Family*, 42: 841–54.

Mays, J. B. (1954), *Growing up in the City*, Liverpool: Liverpool University Press.

Morris, L. (1988), 'Employment, the household and social networks', in D. Gallie (ed.), *Employment in Britain*, Oxford: Basil Blackwell.

Morris, L. (1989), *The Workings of the Household*, Cambridge: Polity Press.

Oakley, A. (1974), *The Sociology of Housework*, London: Martin Robertson.

Pahl, J. (1980), 'Patterns of money management within marriage', *Journal of Social Policy*, 9: 313–35.

Pahl, J. (1985), *Private Violence and Public Policy*, London: Routledge & Kegan Paul.

Pahl, J. (1989), *Money and Marriage*, London: Macmillan.

Rogers, B. L. and Schlossman, N. P. (1990), *Intra-household Resource Allocation: Issues and Methods for Development Policy and Planning*, Tokyo: United Nations University Press.

Safilios Rothschild, C. (1970), 'The study of family power structure: a review 1960–1969', *Journal of Marriage and the Family*, 32: 539–52.

Scanzoni, J. (1979), 'Social processes and power in families', in W. Burr, R. Hill, I. Nye and I. Reiss (eds), *Contemporary Theories about the Family*, New York: The Free Press.

Treas, J. (1991), 'The common pot or separate purses? A transaction cost interpretation', in *The Triple Intersection: Household, Gender and the Economy*, Newbury Park, CA: Sage.

Tunstall, J. (1962), *The Fishermen*, London: MacGibbon and Kee.

Vogler, C. (1989), *Labour Market Change and Patterns of Financial Allocation Within Households*, Oxford: Social Change and Economic Life Initiative, Nuffield College.

Vogler, C. and Pahl, J. (1993), 'Social and economic change and the organization of money in marriage', *Work, Employment and Society*, 7: 71–95.

Wilson, G. (1987), *Money in the Family*, Aldershot: Avebury.

Young, M. (1952), 'Distribution of income within the family', *British Journal of Sociology*, 3: 305–21.

Young, M. and Willmott, P. (1973), *The Symmetrical Family*, London: Routledge & Kegan Paul.

Zelizer, V. (1989), 'The social meaning of money: "special monies"', *American Journal of Sociology*, 95: 342–77.

Zweig, F. (1961), *The Worker in an Affluent Society*, London: Heinemann.

7

Uncovering Gender Differences in the Use of Marital Violence: The Effect of Methodology

James Nazroo

Introduction

One of the central areas of debate in the marital violence literature concerns whether women are as violent as men in marriage (in which I include cohabiting relationships) and, consequently, whether marital violence should be understood as a problem of male violence against women within a patriarchal structure, or whether it should be viewed as a problem of violent spouses. In this chapter I first review these contrasting approaches to an understanding of marital violence. I then go on to use data from a community sample of couples to illustrate that gender-neutral approaches, which claim women are as violent as men in marriage, are misled by their use of a structured questionnaire methodology which simply focuses on acts of physical aggression. This obscures the meaning of such acts, which leads to an inability to demonstrate crucial differences between male and female violence in marriage.

Current Approaches to the Study of Marital Violence

Academic, social and political interest in marital violence increased in the 1970s as the feminist movement exposed and publicized the plight of battered wives. Amidst growing concern, the first refuge for battered women was opened in Britain in 1972 and the first specifically for battered women in the USA in 1974 (Dobash and Dobash, 1987). The academic community's approach to the investigation of this problem has broadly followed one of two routes. The first is that taken by feminist researchers, the second is one followed by family sociologists with a deliberate (in order to avoid any possible bias in a scientific inquiry) gender-neutral perspective.

Feminist researchers demonstrated that husband to wife violence was common, frequently severe and persistent, and often resulted in serious physical and psychological injury and social and personal consequences (e.g. Dobash and Dobash, 1979; Pagelow, 1984). These researchers also pointed out that all segments of the community, including the police and healthcare workers, often failed to respond effectively to such violence (e.g. Dobash and Dobash, 1979; Stark and Flitcraft, 1983). Lying behind this research is a desire to further expose the extent of patriarchy. This has led to an examination of how marital violence, together with other forms of male to female violence, acts as a form of social domination through which women can be subordinated and controlled for the benefit of men (Hanmer and Maynard, 1987). Of course, other forms of social control and coercion are recognized as being important to patriarchy; however, violence is seen as playing a central role in its maintenance: 'As with subservience based on social class, ethnic group or third world country, that of sex, too, rests ultimately on force and its threat' (Hanmer, 1978, p. 219). This perspective on the relationship between violence and power is by no means unique. For example, Lenski sees force as the ultimate power resource: 'there is no appeal from force in a given situation except the exercise of superior force' (Lenski, 1986, p. 243). Others have pointed out that power maintained through force runs the risk of losing its legitimacy (see Arendt's (1986) comments on the difficult relationship between a government's use of force and its attempts to maintain a legitimate authority). It seems that feminists have had some success in raising questions about male authority in marriage by demonstrating its links with husband to wife violence.

The feminist approach to the study of husband to wife violence has mainly involved in-depth interviews with relatively small samples of women who were usually selected into the research because of their experience of marital violence. This has produced detailed descriptive data on these women's experiences. However, the sampling methods and the use of qualitative data in these studies has led to criticism from more survey-orientated researchers. A typical comment is: 'this descriptive approach does not promote a thorough understanding of the problem, and in fact, may generate even more unfounded speculation about its extent and causes' (Hornung, McCullough and Sugimoto, 1981, p. 676). Another drawback of this research is that, in their desire to expose the oppression of women, men's experience of marital violence, both as perpetrators and victims, has been largely ignored. However, knowledge of such experience is essential to an understanding of men's use of violence and to an exploration of the differences between male and female perpetrated violence.

The gender-neutral research carried out by family sociologists on the topic of marital violence is typically based on the use of fixed-format questionnaire surveys, which have the supposed advantages of being more objective and flexible research tools as well as being cheaper than less structured interviews. The main instrument used in this research is the Conflict Tactics Scale (CTS), a measure of interpersonal violence that asks the respondent to tick the number of times s/he has used a variety of tactics during a dispute, ranging from calm discussion to the use of a knife or gun (Straus, Gelles and Steinmetz, 1980). The popularity of the CTS can be seen from its use in the majority of published surveys of marital violence. The first national postal survey of both men and women (but not couples) in the USA revealed a high prevalence of physical violence between spouses: 28 per cent of respondents reported using violence at some point in their marriage to resolve a conflict and 12.6 per cent had used violence which could cause serious injury (ibid.). However, even more surprising than these high rates of violence was their finding that rates of female and male perpetrated marital violence were similar across all categories of violence. When this study was repeated in 1985 using a telephone survey, very similar results were found, the only trend being a possible increase in the relative use of marital violence by women compared to men (Straus and Gelles, 1986). Also surprising was the discovery that very little of this female violence appeared to have been carried out in self-defence (Stets and Straus, 1990; Straus, 1993). This evidence has led to and reinforced the belief amongst family sociologists that the problem is not one of violence to *wives* but of violence towards *spouses*, which they see as justifying their gender-neutral approach. This has resulted in a concern with uncovering reasons for an ungendered rather than a gendered individual's use of violence in marriage and a consequent focus on reasons for individual psychopathology (see Rosenbaum and O'Leary, 1981; O'Leary and Vivian, 1989; Sugarman and Hotaling, 1989).

Despite the evidence they have produced, these and other researchers using similar methodologies and obtaining similar results have sometimes recognized that there must be differences between male and female perpetrated marital violence (O'Leary et al., 1989). However, they appear to have been largely unable to uncover this difference in their assessment of acts of aggression using structured questionnaires. This has led to a repeated claim that men are also and possibly more often than women victims of violence from their spouses (McNeely and Mann, 1990). In fact, as a result of this research there has developed both a media and research interest in 'battered husbands' (e.g. Steinmetz and Lucca, 1988).

In the light of the feminist belief in a link between marital violence and power, it is interesting to note that family sociologists have also linked wives' marital dependency and the distribution of marital power with marital violence (Straus and Gelles, 1990). The link appears to be between a power imbalance and the use of violence. However, according to these researchers, who used a decision-making measure of power, this power imbalance in marriage seems to occur rarely with only 9.5 per cent of marriages being male dominated and 7.5 per cent being female dominated (Coleman and Straus, 1990). This finding and the assumptions that underlie it are also clearly at odds with feminist research which typically takes men's power over women as given. For example, Barker sees marriage as 'a particular, exploitative relationship between men and women in which the wife provides unpaid domestic and sexual services, child-bearing and rearing, and wage-earning and contribution to the household income when convenient' (Barker, 1978, p. 239).

These two differing approaches to the study of marital violence have, inevitably, come into conflict and, not surprisingly, this conflict has focused on the reports of high rates of female perpetrated violence (for example, Berliner, 1990). Feminists have argued that the survey approach using structured questionnaires to assess acts of aggression has serious theoretical, methodological and evidential problems (see Dobash et al. (1992) for a comprehensive critique). Most of these problems have resulted from the approach's reliance on CTS material which has resulted in two major flaws. First, like all such questionnaires, it is respondent-rated which means that the job of measurement is handed over to the respondent who interprets how terms such as 'very much' are to be used. This results in it confounding patterns of response within different groups with the variable measured. For example, women may include a different class of acts within a 'beat partner up' category to those men may include. Second, because the CTS simply measures acts of aggression, it obscures the context in which any violence occurs (e.g. whether it occurs with other forms of abuse) and the effects it has (e.g. whether it produces fear of a recurrence).

Such problems are aggravated by a gender-neutral perspective which means that differences in the social and personal meaning of male and female perpetrated marital violence are even more difficult to investigate. This inability to uncover meaning is a result of one of the apparent strengths of structured questionnaires, their measurement of acts without allowing for contamination by potentially biased interpretations. However, this can easily result in the social and personal significance of acts being ignored and apparently equivalent, but fundamentally different, acts being placed in the same broad category. This problem has also arisen in the context of life events research, which attempts to explore the links between stress and health. In this work, structured questionnaire measures typically give a standard stress score to events such as the birth of a baby. However, it is immediately apparent that the birth of a baby in the context of overcrowded housing, or marital problems, or unemployment and financial difficulties, or a combination of these features, is very different in its social and personal consequences from a birth that does not occur in these contexts (see Brown (1989) for a detailed discussion).

Straus, the developer of the CTS, and others have defended their approach. First, they have claimed that the high rates of female violence detected are the result of effective random sampling instead of relying on self-selected or clinical samples: 'Studies that find gender differences are generally based on clinical samples, while studies that find no gender differences are based on non-clinical samples' (Stets and Straus, 1990, p. 151; see also Straus, 1993). Second, they have claimed that feminist researchers have failed to ask women about violence they may have perpetrated and have suppressed data that shows how violent women are in marriage (Straus, 1993). Third, they have claimed that most of the important context has been taken into account by adding questions such as 'who started the physical conflict, you or your partner?' (Stets and Straus, 1990, p. 153) and by including measures of the effects of marital violence, in particular physical and psychological injury. However, only the measures of physical injury have revealed differences between male and female perpetrated violence and the act-based structured questionnaire approach has remained unable to explain why this difference might exist beyond the observation that a male punch might be more damaging than a female one. It seems clear that we should take seriously the feminist argument that an understanding of the apparently similar rates of marital violence perpetrated by women and men requires knowledge of the context, meaning and effects of the violence.

Methodology

This research used a semi-structured, open-ended approach to interviewing which allows a topic such as marital violence to be explored in depth so that context and meaning can be collected. It also allows the respondent to raise issues that s/he considers important. Introductory questions encouraged the respondent to talk spontaneously and in detail about his or her experiences. Directive questions were only used when the account did not cover certain predetermined topics, such as how frequently violent incidents occurred, or if the narrative did not quite hold together. However, rather than producing purely descriptive data, this was linked to a *systematic and quantitative* approach to investigator-based measurement based on rating scales. This kind of investigator-based approach to measurement has been used to measure a variety of social phenomena where progress could not be made without assessing meaning. For example, family activity and expressed emotion (Brown and Rutter, 1966), life events and difficulties (Brown and Harris, 1978) and self-evaluation and social support (O'Connor and Brown, 1984). Brown (1992, p. 252) describes this approach, somewhat indulgently, as

> one with an epidemiological base, but still able to deal with case-history material; one that emphasizes systematic measurement, but retains the ability to develop new measures once material has been collected; one that deals with what respondents say about relevant phenomena, but also uses the investigator to judge what has taken place; and one that recognizes the possibility that special precautions have to be made if its empirical generalizations are not to be threatened by bias, and yet allows the respondent to talk at length and develop narrative and stories about relevant phenomena.

The advantage of this methodology for the purposes of this research is that it allows three approaches to be used in the measurement of marital violence. First, sufficient information is collected for any incidents of marital violence to be explored in a *qualitative* way. Second, this information is collected in a systematic but detailed enough way for it to be *quantitatively coded in the context-specific way* recommended by Brown (1992), though, rather than using full biographical material, only the immediate context of the violence is considered. Third, the systematic collection of basic information allows it to be *quantitatively coded in a purely act-based way* similar to that used by the CTS. The coding schemes used in this chapter are fully described in the appendix.

The Sample

The sample consists of 96 cohabiting couples below retirement age who were recruited from questionnaires sent to individuals on GP patient lists for a study investigating gender differences in the experience of stress. Consequently, all the respondents had recently experienced a severely stressful event. The response rate for the questionnaire was 46 per cent, with no difference between men and women. Those couples who were approached for an interview were offered £50 to participate and two thirds agreed. Most refusals seemed to be a result of either the partner of the person approached for interview not being interested in participating, or their relationship being so poor that the respondent would not approach his/her partner about the interview. This means that this sample probably under-represents, though it does include, severely abusive and very distant relationships.

None of the couples were recruited on the basis of having experienced any form of marital violence; however, the stressful event for about 10 per cent of the couples did involve marital problems. The members of the couple were separately interviewed by different interviewers. Both a male and a female interviewer were involved, but interviews were *not* gender matched – just under half the female interviews were carried out by the male interviewer. Respondents were asked and questioned in detail about any incidents of physical aggression that occurred at any time in their relationship. Any incident of physical aggression, no matter how minor, that was mentioned by either member of the couple, and that was not used in a playful manner, was included in the analysis. This probably contributes to the high rates of marital violence reported, though the use of couple data, rather than using aggregated male and female data or using data collected from women only, also results in more marital violence being detected. For example, Szinovacz (1983) claimed that using couple data increases the estimated numbers of violent marriages by 20 per cent in the case of interviewed women and 50 per cent in the case of interviewed men. If we assume that when a respondent reports an incident s/he is telling the truth, the threat to data collection comes from respondents failing to report incidents, so the use of couple data also has the benefit of increasing the validity of the data.

The sample was recruited from a relatively deprived inner-city area and 70 per cent of the sample were working class. The mean age of the men was 38 (ranging from 22 to 61) and of the women was 36 (ranging from 19 to 55): 77 per cent of the sample had children at home and the mean length of cohabitation was 11 years (ranging from 9 months to 35 years), and 18 per cent of the men and 15 per cent of the women had had one or more previous cohabiting relationships.

Results[1]

Table 7.1 uses an act-based measure of marital violence to look at rates of violent acts in much the same way as the CTS does. In fact the table uses similar categories collapsed in a similar way to those used by the CTS. (Definitions of the categories used can be found in the appendix.) Nothing regarding the *context* of these incidents of violence is considered. It should be remembered that the table includes any incidents of violence and does not consider the frequency of the violence. For example, no attempt is made to exclude one-off incidents of gentle hitting.

From this table it appears that 38 per cent of men and 55 per cent of women have been violent in their current relationship. If both possible perpetrators of physical aggression are considered, 61.5 per cent of these couples report one or more acts of physical aggression in the history of their relationship. The table also shows that women are significantly more likely than men to be violent in marriage. This difference is, if anything, more surprising than the results reported by Straus and his colleagues, where rates of male and female perpetrated acts of marital violence are broadly similar, and it does appear to confirm that marital violence is not a gender issue.

This conclusion is challenged by table 7.2, which explores the *immediate context* of the violence rather than simply recording acts of aggression. A full definition of the categories used is found in the appendix, but they are all quantitative assessments of how dangerous the violence is, the 'danger' category combining the other three, taking into account exactly what happened and how it happened. All these types of violence have a strong and significant relationship with the act-based measure of severity of violence in the expected direction.

These results show that across a variety of dimensions male violence is far more likely to be dangerous than female violence. However, comparing numbers rather than percentages shows that the 'injurious' category does not have a particularly large gender difference in base rates. Eighteen men compared to twelve women used this type of violence. Even so, the gender differences in rates of 'danger' violence amongst the whole sample (n = 96) are large and significant (20 per cent of men and 6 per cent of women used 'danger' violence, $p < 0.01$, relative risk for men to use dangerous violence = 3.2 (1.3 < 95 per cent < 18)).

The one immediate context of the violence that I have not yet explored is self-defence. Again a full definition of my usage of the term 'self-defence' can be

Table 7.1   Level of physical aggression in marriage by gender

Level of violence	Women N	Women %	Men N	Men %	Probability 2 d.f.
Severe	28	29	20	21	
Moderate or mild	25	26	16	17	< 0.05
None	43	45	60	63	
Total	96	100	96	101	

Relative risk for women compared to men to use marital violence = 1.5 (1.1 < 95% < 2).

Table 7.2 Type of physical aggression used in marriage by gender

Type of violence	Women (N = 53)[1]		Men (N = 36)[1]		Probability 1 d.f.	Relative risk
	N	%	N	%		
Undefendable[1]	9	17	26	79	< 0.001	4.5 (2.5 < 95% < 8.5)
Intimidating	4	8	12	33	< 0.005	4.4 (1.5 < 95% < 12.6)
Injurious	12	23	18	50	< 0.01	2.2 (1.2 < 95% < 4)
Danger	6	11	19	53	< 0.001	4.7 (2 < 95% < 10.5)

1 For undefendable violence the N is slightly lower, 52 women and 33 men.

found in the appendix. I have included only dangerous violence that is not in self-defence in a category termed 'threatening'. Again, gender differences in the use of threatening violence are large and significant, 19 per cent (18/96) of men compared to only 4 per cent (4/96) of women used threatening violence (p < 0.005, 1 d. f., relative risk for men to use threatening violence = 4.5 (1.6 < 95 per cent < 12.8)).

These quantitative data exploring the immediate context of the violence show that, contrary to the conclusions that may be drawn from table 7.1, men's violence in marriage is very different from women's. It is far more likely to be dangerous and threatening. What is crucial about the difference between these data and those used in table 7.1 is that they include information about the social and personal meanings of the acts of aggression. So, if meaning is excluded from the measurement system, women compared to men appear to be about one and a half times more likely to physically abuse their partners. However, if the meaning of acts of aggression is included in the measurement system, men are found to be considerably more likely than women to physically abuse their partners.

I later explore the broader context of the violence using a more descriptive approach, which shows that using the immediate context is still not sufficient if we want to understand marital violence. However, before I do this I examine two outcomes of marital violence which lend strong support to the belief that it is better understood in the light of a gender-based analysis. The first outcome, explored in table 7.3, is level of injury. (Definitions of the different levels of injury can be found in the appendix.)

Table 7.3 shows very clearly one important and different consequence of male and female violence. If the total sample is considered, only 1 out of 96 men has been severely injured by his partner, compared to about 10 per cent (9 out of 96) of the women.

Table 7.3   Level of injury by gender of the target of the violence

Level of injury	Women		Men		Probability 3 d.f.
	N	%	N	%	
Severe	9	25	1	2	
Moderate	11	31	8	15	} < 0.001
Mild	0	0	4	8	
None	16	44	40	75	
Total	36	100	53	100	

Relative risk for women compared to men to be severely injured − 13.3 (1.8 < 95% < 100).

The other outcome is the psychological effect of marital violence. The psychological outcomes the literature suggests need to be considered for both men and women are depression and anxiety (Andrews and Brown, 1988; Gelles and Harrop, 1989; Maiuro et al., 1988). Unfortunately the selection criteria for the sample means the respondents are at very high risk for depression for reasons other than the experience of marital violence. This means that I can only concentrate on anxiety symptoms.[2] In the current context, assessing anxiety has an additional advantage, because investigations exploring the aetiology of anxiety have suggested it is a response to the experience of dangerous situations (Finlay-Jones and Brown, 1981; Finlay-Jones, 1989). Obviously marital violence is potentially such a situation. Levels of anxiety were assessed using a semi-structured clinical interview, the present state examination (Wing, Cooper and Sartorious, 1974). The cut-off point used, medium borderline anxiety, involves significant disability (see the appendix for full details). The relationship between experiencing physical aggression in marriage, gender of respondent and current anxiety is shown in table 7.4. In this analysis I have assumed that physical aggression from previous cohabiting partners may play an important role in predicting current anxiety, so I have included physical aggression from any cohabiting partner.

For women, but not for men, there is a strong relationship between having experienced partner violence and having anxiety symptoms. This suggests that male-perpetrated marital violence has a completely different meaning from female-perpetrated marital violence. As expected, there is also a strong relationship between gender and anxiety (see the 'Total' row). However, a close examination shows that this relationship is entirely accounted for by the higher rate of anxiety amongst women who have had a partner who was or is violent (the top left). Those women without partner violence have a very similar rate of anxiety to both groups of men. This raises the possibility that male acts of physical aggression in marriage are not only categorically different from female acts of physical aggression, but also account for the greater rates of anxiety found amongst women compared to men. In order to explore this further, I carried out a logistic regression with medium borderline or worse anxiety as the dependent variable and gender, experience of moderate or severe partner

Table 7.4 Rates of anxiety by severe or moderate partner violence and gender

| | Medium borderline anxiety or higher | | | | | |
| | Women | | Men | | | |
	N	%	N	%	Probability 1 d.f.	Relative risk
Any violent partner	22/38	58	8/45	18	< 0.001	3.3 (1.6 < 95% < 6.5)
No violent partner	11/58	19	8/51	16	n.s.	n/a
Total	33/96	34	16/96	17	< 0.005	2.6 (1.2 < 95% < 3.5)

Probability for women with compared to women without partner violence to have anxiety < 0.001, 1 d.f., Relative risk = 3 (1.7 < 95% < 5.6).

violence and the interaction between these two as the independent variables. The logistic regression confirms the conclusions drawn from table 7.4. First, being female alone does not increase risk of anxiety (odds ratio = 1.26, wald = 0.2, p < 1). Second, experiencing marital violence alone does not increase risk of anxiety (odds ratio = 1.16, wald = 0.08, p < 1). However, being a woman and experiencing marital violence from a male partner dramatically increases the risk of anxiety (odds ratio = 5.1, wald = 5.05, p < 0.03), so this increase in risk is sufficient to explain the gender differences in rates of anxiety. Whether women's experience of marital violence directly leads to anxiety or increases women's vulnerability to anxiety is beyond the scope of these data, but the link between the two seems clear.

While these tables have done much to explode the myth that women are equally or more violent than men in marriage, their dependence on only the *immediate* context of the violence and the effects of the violence means they do not tell the whole story. If the broader context of the violence is explored, the difference between male and female violence is found to be even more dramatic. However, in order to do this I will use a more descriptive approach to analysis, rather than the quantitative approach used so far. A starting point is to compare the types of male with the types of female violence that are included in the 'threatening' and 'self-defence' and other 'non-threatening' categories. Table 7.5 groups the men and women in these categories and shows clear differences between those that are in apparently similar categories.

Of the four women who are included in the 'threatening' category, only one has beaten her partner and she has only done this twice whilst suffering from a 'psychotic' breakdown. (As a result of these incidents she was institutionalized.) Although her partner was repeatedly punched and kicked, he was not injured and during the worst of these assaults was quite easily able to 'escape' and get help. In comparison, eight of the men in this category terrorized their wives with *frequently repeated protracted and severe beatings* which usually resulted

Table 7.5   Male and female marital violence compared

'Threatening' violence

Male – total 19	Female – total 4
• 8 repeatedly severely beat up their partners.	• 1 twice repeatedly punched and kicked her partner during a psychotic breakdown.
• 2 severely beat up their partners, but only once or twice.	• 2 threw a heavy object at their partners, one blow only and on one occasion.
• 1 less severely beat his wife, but also repeatedly sexually assaulted her.	• 1 punched her partner, he would punch back and she always came off worse.
• 6 repeatedly assaulted their partners, but not at the beat up level.	
• 2 repeatedly slapped and pushed their partners in a coercive manner.	

Violence used in self-defence

Male – total 2	Female – total 8
• 2 slapped their partners across the face while being punched on the chest. Both stopped her assault.	• 2 seriously assaulted their partners with weapons on one occasion after suffering repeated severe beatings. Both stopped any further assaults.
	• 6 punched and kicked their partners while being beaten-up. None stopped his assault.

Other 'non-threatening' violence

Male – total 15	Female – total 41
• 6 slapped or violently pushed their partners to stop them nagging or when they 'got out of order' or refused to have sex. They all intimidated their partners and often changed her behaviour.	• 17 either punched, kicked or threatened their partners with weapons. Usually only one or two blows were used and the men always easily defended themselves.
• 9 occasionally slapped or pushed their partners, 3 of these either frightened or seriously injured her.	• 24 occasionally slapped or pushed their partners, none caused him any concern.

in serious injury. The kinds of incidents common in this group are: the man repeatedly kicking and punching the woman; or choking her until she is unconscious; or banging her head repeatedly against the wall. A further two of these men engaged in a similar level of violence but only on one or two occasions. One used less severe violence, but also repeatedly sexually assaulted his wife. This was the only incident of marital rape reported by these couples.

A further six of the men in this category also repeatedly assaulted their wives, but not so badly. Nevertheless these were severe assaults which included things like: swinging the woman around the room by her hair; or repeatedly slapping the woman hard across the face; or punching or kicking her body; or grabbing her by the throat sufficiently hard to leave bruising and choke her, but not long enough for her to lose consciousness. The remaining two of these men used less severe but repeated violence and did this in an intimidating and coercive manner, one of them smashing furniture at the same time. Of these men, only one has not injured his partner and many of their partners have sustained broken bones and severe bruising from the violence they have received.

The two most serious assaults perpetrated by women were carried out in self-defence, one woman stabbing her partner and the other hitting her partner with a chain. Both of these incidents were one-offs and occurred after the women had been repeatedly and badly beaten. Interestingly, both of these incidents ended the beatings these women suffered at the hands of their partners. However, in all the other cases where women used violence whilst being beaten by their partners, this violent response was ineffectual, their partners easily being able to continue. In contrast, both the men who used violence only in self-defence (in both cases this was a one-off slap across the face) stopped their partners' assaults immediately and one of these men left his partner 'shook up'.

One contradictory result is the large number of women who are rated as having used severe violence according to the CTS type act-based measure, but who are also rated as having used 'non-threatening' violence. The violence perpetrated by these seventeen women has usually only occurred once or twice and usually only involved one or two blows. What is immediately apparent when listening to accounts of this violence is that the men were easily able to defend themselves from attack. They grab their partners by the arm and hold them off, or pick them up and put them in another room to calm down, or disarm them. They will also not respond at all to their partners' attacks and they will frequently laugh at the audacity of their partners. Some of these men respond in a threatening way, for example one man, describing his response to being slapped, says: 'I shouted and she ran'. None of these men appear to have been intimidated in the least. The ease with which the men appear to be able to defend themselves is undoubtedly partly a result of their greater physical strength. However, it is also partly a result of the nature of the assaults carried out by the women in this group. Unlike the men who used severe violence, the women rarely seem to be seriously intent on harming their partners, never really pushing their attacks home even if they have the advantage of a weapon or surprise. So, it appears that the 'non-threatening' group of women genuinely consists of women who have not frightened and intimidated their partners and very often did not want to. In contrast, well over half of the men in the 'non-threatening' category succeeded in intimidating or seriously injuring their partners (see table 7.5).

Discussion

These results demonstrate that context is crucial to understanding marital violence, because without it the social and personal meaning of the violence cannot be tackled. If context and meaning are ignored, as they are in purely act-based measures like the CTS, it appears that women are as likely, or more likely, than men to be violent in marriage. However, if context and meaning are included in either a quantitative or qualitative measurement system, it is immediately apparent that male violence in marriage is far more likely than female violence to be dangerous and threatening.[3] The importance of meaning to the measurement of marital violence is also confirmed if the outcomes of any violence are explored. Male violence is considerably more likely than female violence to result in serious physical injury and adverse psychological consequences. In fact, the data presented suggests that gender differences in rates of anxiety could be a result of the physical abuse that women experience in marriage.

If a detailed examination of these couples' experiences of marital violence is carried out, gender differences in the use of violence in marriage become even more stark. While a significant number of the men repeatedly and severely physically abused, intimidated and humiliated their partners, none of the women carried out similar attacks. In fact the women who were violent towards their partners appeared to have very different motives from the men who were violent. The women who were severely violent usually only hit their partners once or twice during an attack and, if they were successful in gaining some kind of physical advantage over their partners, would stop their assault. In contrast, the men in similar situations continued their assaults no matter how defenceless their partners were. The only two women who can genuinely be said to have persevered with their assaults once getting the better of their partners, did so in self-defence after having suffered years of severe physical abuse. Less severe violence is also a common feature of these couples' relationships. Those women who used less severe violence never seemed to cause any concern amongst their partners. However, a significant number of those men who used less severe violence did succeed in intimidating and injuring their partners, even if the violence did not obviously have this motive, was mild and a one-off incident.

These data strongly support the criticisms that feminists and others have levelled at the use of instruments such as the CTS (for example, Dobash et al., 1992; Kurz, 1993). Although throughout this chapter I have implied that the choice of methodology is central here, there is, of course, more than this to the feminist/family sociologist debate around marital violence. Some have argued that the problem *is* one of methodology and that bridges can be built if both sides become aware of the benefits of and perhaps use the other's methodologies (Murphy and O'Leary, 1994), and my own use of quantitative data suggests that this is possible. However, a careful reading of various proponents' defences of their approaches reveals that the choice of methodology reflects a more fundamental divide. For example, Straus's recent robust defence of his approach and perspective on female-perpetrated marital violence reveals that his interest is based on 'the intrinsic moral wrong of assaulting a spouse' (Straus, 1993, p. 80). This leads to the conclusion that all violence is equally wrong and the failure to condemn female perpetrated as much as male perpetrated marital violence leads to 'the unintended validation of the traditional cultural norms tolerating a certain level of violence between spouses' (ibid.). In contrast, it is clear that feminist interest in marital violence is part of their exploration of patriarchy and is explicitly linked to other forms of male violence to women (for example, Dobash and Dobash, 1979; Hanmer and Maynard, 1987; Kurz, 1993). From this position female-perpetrated marital violence simply does not have the same meanings and consequences as male-perpetrated marital violence, consequently the two cannot be equated.

Both the quantitative and qualitative data presented here support the feminist position in two ways. First, they clearly demonstrate that male and female perpetrated marital violence are very different in both their meanings and consequences, and there does appear to be a link between much of men's use of violence in marriage and their (successful) attempts to dominate their partners. Second, it appears that almost all of the female violence described here does not carry that sense of intrinsic 'wrongness' that Straus attributes to all violence, because it is clearly not intimidating and nowhere near dangerous. If anything it reflects the powerless position of these women. Considering the extent of the differences in the meaning and consequences of male and female marital violence again, it seems that it is extremely unlikely that female violence in some sense legitimates the use of marital violence by men in the way Straus (1993) suggests.

Having reached these conclusions, I would not like to imply that men are *never* physically abused in marital relationships. Media interest in this issue has clearly allowed such men a voice. However, two points regarding this issue need to be considered. First, although this sample is small and not truly random, it is immediately apparent that men in such a position are considerably rarer than women. Second, the differences between the resources of men and women in marriage suggest that the experiences of men who are physically abused by their partners are very different from those of women in an apparently similar situation. They are far more likely to have access to the resources necessary to escape from their abuse. For example, I am reminded of a man recently interviewed on British television who described how his wife seriously assaulted and injured him with a saucepan. However, despite this assault he was able to pick up his wallet and car keys and leave. How many women in such a situation would have the resources to be able to do the same, even if they did not have children to consider?

Some limitations of this sample need to be considered. First, it is relatively small and questionnaire response rates and acceptance of the interview demonstrate that it is not fully representative. Consequently, conclusions drawn need to be treated cautiously. In particular, the relationship between anxiety and marital violence would benefit from further exploration. Second, the sample consists of couples who have a good enough relationship to co-operate in a detailed research interview. This undoubtedly means that the most abusive relationships were less likely to be included in this sample. Third, the sample is drawn from a particular population, members of an inner-city community all of whom had experienced severe stress, which means that in certain other respects it may be unrepresentative. Having said this, the sample has two important advantages. First, it is a sample of couples, which means that both female and male accounts of the marriage can be explored and contrasted. Second, it is a community sample that was not selected on the basis of having experienced marital violence. This means it is not a self-identified population with all the possible bias this may incur and is not, consequently, sensitive to the criticisms of samples that are unrepresentative in that way (see Straus, 1993).

Conclusion

These data suggest that purely act-based measures of marital violence, such as the CTS, are highly misleading and that this is a result of their failure to consider the context in which violence is used and the meaning of the violence. Introducing the immediate context of the violence into a quantitative measurement system improves the quality of the data obtained. However, even this benefits from being used alongside a more detailed descriptive analysis where the broader context of the violence can be considered. A more detailed exploration of men's and women's accounts emphasizes that men's experience of violence in marriage is not as victims, even when they are being hit, while women's experience of violence is almost always as a victim. This confirms that it is dangerous to use quantitative approaches which do not tackle meaning without considering the insights obtained through more descriptive approaches. This returns us to the crucial context that feminist researchers have highlighted, which is the relationship between marital violence and patriarchal power. While I have not provided a detailed account of the men's and women's experiences in this sample, a cursory description of their accounts of husband to wife violence shows that it involves a significant degree of intimidation, humiliation and control. This suggests that the relationship between marital violence and marital power should be explored, bearing in mind that violence is one of a variety of resources that men have access to in their attempts to dominate women.

NOTES

1   Where appropriate, significance is assessed using chi-square tests (with Yates's correction applied if any expected cell frequency is less than ten, or 2–tailed Fisher tests if any expected cell frequency is less than five in a two by two table). To assess the strength of associations I have used relative risk, which is simply the relative chance of one population compared to another having a particular attribute or outcome: 95 per cent confidence limits can be found after the relative risk score. All these statistics were computed using the Epi Info statistical package for personal computers.

2   Of course, anxiety and depression are highly related (Brown, Harris and Eales, 1993). However, the use of the present state examination (Wing, Cooper and Sartorious, 1974) to assess psychiatric symptoms allowed a clear distinction between the two to be drawn. Finlay-Jones et al., (1980) use discriminant function analysis to show that anxiety and depression have unique clusters of key symptoms. Also the different nature of life events that provoke episodes of anxiety and depression, 'danger' events for the former and 'loss' events for the latter (ibid.), suggests that they can be treated as separate outcomes despite the high level of co-morbidity.

3   Despite their similarities, there is an interesting comparison to be made between the act-based measure used here and the CTS. According to respondent-rated structured questionnaire measures, women are only slightly more likely than men to use acts of physical aggression in marriage (Straus and Gelles, 1986). However, according to this chapter's investigator-rated act-based measure, women were one and a half times more likely than men to use acts of physical aggression in marriage. This difference is possibly a result of the importance of meaning to *any* measurement system. A respondent-rated structured questionnaire involves the respondent in interpreting and therefore applying meaning to the categories used. In terms of acts of physical aggression, part of this attributed meaning will inevitably involve its abusive potential or reality. Consequently, in the light of this chapter's finding that female violence in marriage is considerably less likely than male violence to be abusive, it is not surprising that respondent-judged rates of physical aggression that implicitly include meaning will tend to underplay acts of physical aggression perpetrated by women, when compared to quantitative investigator-judged rates of physical aggression that explicitly exclude meaning. This lends support to the criticisms of such measures that were made earlier, being respondent-rated they do not achieve the objective status they aspire to.

APPENDIX: DEFINITIONS

1   *Act-based categories of level of violence*

a   Severe: punching, kicking, beating up, hitting with objects that potentially cause severe injury, potentially lethal force and use or threatened use of knives or guns.
b   Moderate: slapping around head or face.
c   Mild: pushing, shoving, gentle hitting anywhere except head or face and gentle hitting with an object that is unlikely to cause injury.

2   *Level of injury*

a   Severe: broken bones, severe bruising, deep cuts and burns.
b   Moderate: black eyes, bruising, superficial cuts, scratches and scrapes.
c   Mild: short-term weals.

3   *Undefendable violence:* violence that the other cannot easily defend him/herself from. Severe violence is only excluded from this category if the other succeeds in defending him/herself. *Mild* violence is only included in this category if the other fails to defend him/herself. Some incidents are not obviously rated in this dimension or cannot be appropriately rated in this dimension, e.g. the respondent slapping his/her partner once and then walking away and another incident never occurring. Consequently, not all respondents are rated here.

4   *Intimidating violence:* violence that is used to intimidate or frighten the other. It does not include violence that is mildly coercive, such as gently slapping the other on the arm while arguing. It does include violence that is repeatedly used until the other gives in or until the other is frightened. It does not include self-defence.

5   *Injurious violence:* violence that has a definite possibility of causing physical injury to the other.

6   *Danger violence:* violence that is undefendable and is either intimidating or injurious.

7   *Self-defence:* violence that is *only* used to defend against the other's violence. In this sample all occurrences of this have involved defence against contemporary violence from a partner, though I would not in principle exclude violence that is used to defend from anticipated acts of aggression from a partner.

8   *Threatening violence:* danger violence which is not in self-defence.

9   *Minimum requirements for medium borderline anxiety are:*

a   Severe situational anxiety, e.g. in tubes, buses, lifts, crowded shops and being alone, but *not* specific phobias, for example like those of cats and dogs.
or

b   Severe free-floating anxiety unattached to any particular situation, e.g. while lying in bed at night.
or

c   Panic attacks, such as having to run out of an anxiety-provoking situation or call for help.
and

d   Avoidance of the anxiety-provoking situation where possible.
and

e   Physical symptoms of anxiety such as difficulty getting breath, choking, dizziness, dry mouth, sweating, trembling, palpitations and butterflies.

ACKNOWLEDGEMENTS

I am grateful to Graham Scambler, Bernice Andrews and *Sociology*'s anonymous referees for comments on an earlier draft of this chapter, and to Angela Edwards who helped with the interviewing and June Thomas for secretarial support. I would also like to thank the respondents who participated in this research.

REFERENCES

Andrews, B. and Brown, G. W. (1988), 'Marital violence in the community: a biographical approach', *British Journal of Psychiatry*, 153: 305–12.

Arendt, H. (1986), 'Communicative power', in S. Lukes (ed.), *Power*, Oxford: Basil Blackwell.

Barker, D. L. (1978), 'The regulation of marriage: repressive benevolence', in G. Littlejohn, B. Smart, J. Wakeford and N. Yuval-Davis (eds), *Power and the State*, London: Croom Helm.

Berliner, L. (1990), 'Domestic violence: a humanist or feminist issue?', *Journal of Interpersonal Violence*, 50: 128–9.

Brown, G. W. (1989), 'Life events and measurement', in G. W. Brown and T. Harris (eds), *Life Events and Illness*, London: Unwin Hyman.

Brown, G. W. (1992), 'Social support: an investigator-based approach', in H. Veiel and U. Baumann (eds), *The Meaning and Measurement of Social Support*, London: Hemisphere.

Brown, G. W. and Harris, T. (1978), *Social Origins of Depression*, London: Tavistock.

Brown, G. W., Harris, T. and Eales, M. J. (1993), 'Aetiology of anxiety and depressive disorders in an inner-city population. 2. Comorbidity and adversity', *Psychological Medicine*, 23: 155–65.

Brown, G. W. and Rutter, M. (1966), 'The measurement of family activities and relationships: a methodological study', *Human Relations*, 19: 241–63.

Coleman, D. H. and Straus, M. A. (1990), 'Marital power, conflict, and violence in a nationally representative sample of American couples', in M. A. Straus and R. J. Gelles (eds), *Physical Violence in American Families*, London: Transaction.

Dobash, R. E. and Dobash, R. P. (1979), *Violence against Wives: A Case Against the Patriarchy*, New York: Free Press.

Dobash, R. E. and Dobash, R. P. (1987), 'The response of the British and American women's movements to violence against women', in J. Hanmer and M. Maynard (eds), *Women, Violence and Social Control*, London: Macmillan.

Dobash, R. P., Dobash, R. E., Wilson, M. and Daly, M. (1992), 'The myth of sexual symmetry in marital violence', *Social Problems*, 39: 71–91.

Finlay-Jones, R. (1989), 'Anxiety', in G. W. Brown and T. Harris (eds), *Life Events and Illness*, London: Unwin Hyman.

Finlay-Jones, R. and Brown, G. W. (1981), 'Types of stressful life event and onset of anxiety and depressive disorders', *Psychological Medicine*, 11: 803–15.

Finlay-Jones, R., Brown, G. W., Duncan-Jones, P., Harris, T., Murphy, E. and Prudo, R. (1980), 'Depression and anxiety in the community: replicating the diagnosis of a case', *Psychological Medicine*, 10: 445–54.

Gelles, R. J. and Harrop, J. W. (1989), 'Violence, battering, and psychological distress among women', *Journal of Interpersonal Violence*, 4: 400–20.

Hanmer, J. (1978), 'Violence and the social control of women', in G. Littlejohn, B. Smart, J. Wakeford and N. Yuval-Davis (eds), *Power and the State*, London: Croom Helm.

Hanmer, J. and Maynard, M. (1987), *Women, Violence and Social Control*, London: Macmillan.

Hornung, C., McCullough, B. and Sugimoto, T. (1981), 'Status relationships in marriage: risk factors in spouse abuse', *Journal of Marriage and the Family*, 43: 675–92.

Kurz, D. (1993), 'Physical assaults by husbands: a major social problem', in R. J. Gelles and D. R. Loseke (eds), *Current Controversies on Family Violence*, London: Sage.

Lenski, G. (1986), 'Power and privilege', in S. Lukes (ed.), *Power*, Oxford: Basil Blackwell.

McNeely, R. L. and Mann, C. R. (1990), 'The truth about domestic violence: a falsely framed issue', *Social Work*, 32: 485–90.

Maiuro, R. D., Cahn, T. S., Vitaliano, P. P., Wagner, B. C. and Zegree, J. B. (1988), 'Anger, hostility, and depression in domestically violent versus generally assaultive and nonviolent control subjects', *Journal of Consulting and Clinical Psychology*, 56: 17–23.

Murphy, C. M. and O'Leary, K. D. (1994), 'Research paradigms, values, and spouse abuse', *Journal of Interpersonal Violence*, 9: 207–23.

O'Connor, P. and Brown, G. W. (1984), 'Supportive relationships: fact or fancy?', *Journal of Social and Personal Relationships*, 1: 159–75.

O'Leary, K. D., Barling, J., Arias, I. and Rosenbaum, A. (1989), 'Prevalence and stability of physical aggression between spouses: a longitudinal analysis', *Journal of Consulting and Clinical Psychology*, 57: 263–8.

O'Leary, K. D. and Vivian, D. (1989), 'Physical aggression in marriage', in F. Fincham and T. Bradbury (eds), *The Psychology of Marriage: Conceptual, Empirical and Applied Perspectives*, Hove: Guildford.

Pagelow, M. D. (1984), *Family Violence*, New York: Praeger.

Rosenbaum, A. and O'Leary, K. D. (1981), 'Marital violence: characteristics of abusive couples', *Journal of Consulting and Clinical Psychology*, 49: 63–71.

Stark, E. and Flitcraft, A. (1983), 'Social knowledge, social policy, and the abuse of women: the case against benevolence', in D. Finkelhor, J. Gelles, G. Hotaling and M. A. Straus (eds), *The Dark Side of Families*, Beverly Hills, CA: Sage.

Steinmetz, S. and Lucca, J. (1988), 'Husband battering', in V. Van Hasselt, R. Morrison, A. Bellack and M. Hersen (eds), *Handbook of Marriage and the Family*, New York: Plenum Press.

Stets, J. E. and Straus, M. A. (1990), 'Gender differences in reporting marital violence and its medical and psychological consequences', in M. A. Straus and R. J. Gelles (eds), *Physical Violence in American Families*, London: Transaction.

Straus, M. A. (1993), 'Physical assaults by wives: a major social problem', in R. J. Gelles and D. R. Loseke (eds), *Current Controversies on Family Violence*, London: Sage.

Straus, M. A. and Gelles, R. J. (1986), 'Societal change in family violence from 1975 to 1985 as revealed by two national surveys', *Journal of Marriage and the Family*, 48: 465–79.

Straus, M. A. and Gelles, R. J. (1990), *Physical Violence in American Families*, London: Transaction.

Straus M. A., Gelles, R. J. and Steinmetz, S. (1980), *Behind Closed Doors: Violence in the American Family*, New York: Anchor.

Sugarman, D. B. and Hotaling, G. T. (1989), 'Violent men in intimate relationships: an analysis of risk markers', *Journal of Applied Social Psychology*, 19: 1034–48.

Szinovacz, M. E. (1983), 'Using couple data as a methodological tool: the case of marital violence', *Journal of Marriage and the Family*, 45: 633–44.

Wing, J., Cooper, J. and Sartorious, N. (1974), *The Measurement and Classification of Psychiatric Symptoms: An Instruction Manual for the Present State Examination and CATEGO Program*, London: Cambridge University Press.

Part III

Domestic Organization

Part III is concerned with aspects of domestic organization. The arguments developed in the chapters included here follow on very naturally from those in Part II, especially the ones by Vogler and Pahl and by Nazroo. A key issue in debates in family and household sociology in recent years has concerned the distribution of work within the family – both paid and unpaid work. Much attention has been directed at who does what around the home, who carries responsibility for different types of activity, and how couples come to decide on these matters. The chapters in Part III address these concerns, and are particularly useful for showing just how structural 'decisions' about family and household organization are. In other words, while individual couples are undoubtedly active in constructing the patterns around which their family life is built, equally in practice most organize domestic matters in a broadly similar – and highly gendered – fashion, clearly reflecting gender divisions located outside the domestic sphere. In particular, as is now well understood, parenthood – and in particular, motherhood – is especially important in informing the respective roles of men and women within families. A good deal of research has analysed the social and economic circumstances of full-time mothers and shown how motherhood dominates social identity and generates strong feelings of dependence (e.g. Gavron, 1968; Oakley, 1974, 1976; Boulton, 1983; Phoenix, 1991; Phoenix, Woollett and Lloyd, 1991; Richardson, 1990).

Chapter 8 is concerned with motherhood, though in a different way to most other studies. It is taken from Susan McRae's *Cohabiting Mothers: Changing Marriage and Motherhood* (1993). As the title indicates the focus of this research is on mothers who were cohabiting before their children were born. At the time of the interviews – four years after the child's birth – some of the mothers had married, but others had continued to cohabit. McRae is consequently able to compare these groups of mothers with one another, in terms of household organization as well as cohabitation experiences, and analyse what they saw as the benefits and disadvantages of cohabitation. Of course, because they are mothers, the women in

McRae's study are not typical of all cohabiting women. Although cohabitation is now extremely common both as a prelude to marriage, and as a form of partnership in its own right, there remain surprisingly few studies of the sociological – as distinct from demographic (Haskey and Kiernan, 1989; Haskey, 1995) – characteristics of cohabitation. If we are to understand contemporary partnerships, there is a need for far more research into the ways in which cohabitation is structured – how it differs from marriage; what domestic divisions of labour are negotiated; when, if at all, does it become routinized; to what degree a greater sense of freedom is sustained; how resources are distributed; and so forth. McRae's chapter – and the book it comes from – provides answers to some of these questions. None the less, there is a clear need for more studies of different cohabiting couples, especially given the extent to which cohabitation has now become such a common life-course experience.

As the studies of motherhood referenced above have shown, child care considerations play a major part in shaping the division of labour established by a couple, a point also emphasized by Mansfield and Collard (1988) in their study of the first few months of marriage. But equally child care and motherhood are part of a broader package of activities and responsibilities which are socially constructed as essentially feminine and consequently routinely allocated to women. These include a wide range of housework tasks, not the least of which is meal production. As Charles and Kerr indicate in chapter 9, meal production involves far more than preparing and cooking meals. Indeed in many respects it symbolizes women's role in household reproduction. If the family collectively is to thrive, the management and production of food is a core activity, and one which needs attending to frequently and regularly. Similarly, meal times often come to symbolize family solidarity, notwithstanding the growth of convenience food and of snacks or meals taken in front of the TV rather than round the dining-room table. The organization and management of food – from shopping for it to ensuring balanced diets – is seen culturally as a central element of nurturing and thus as a key component within the wife/mother complex. By focusing on the symbolism of 'a proper meal', Charles and Kerr's chapter, which is taken from their book *Women, Food and Families*, highlights both the significance of food consumption within the family and the ways in which food production – which Land (1978) refers to rather aptly as 'the tyranny of meals' – impacts on women's experiences and identities.

The same broad division of responsibilities applies equally to other spheres of domestic labour. Some husbands/fathers may now be more fully involved than they were in selected domestic tasks, especially child care ones, but domestic organization continues to be framed predominately around gender. However, like so many features of family life, patterns established within the home do not arise in isolation from non-domestic aspects of social and economic organization. In particular, the responsibilities held and the work done by men and women within the household are strongly patterned by the gendered character of much employment. In chapter 10, Lydia Morris addresses this relationship between the division of labour inside and outside the home. In this chapter from *Family, Economy and Community* edited by Chris Harris, she draws on the idea of 'household strategies' to emphasize the importance of differences in male and female labour markets for understanding the decisions couples come to about the division of paid and unpaid work within their marriage. In particular, she shows that when men are unemployed, there is only rarely any significant renegotiation of domestic responsibilities, despite popular ideas that male unemployment might encourage couples to think about a 'role-swap'. Not only is the notion of employment, rather than domestic labour, strongly internalized by men as part of their masculine identities, but the generally low level of pay of women's employment, compounded by the disincentives built into the benefits system, often results in there being little economic advantage to be gained by any role-reversal. As long as there continues to be marked gender differentials in pay, compounding the impact of earlier socialization, there is little prospect of any real change in the division of labour within the home. Those interested in following up the ideas in this chapter should read Lydia Morris's *The Workings of the Household*. Brannen and Moss (1991), Crompton and Sanderson (1990), Delphy and Leonard (1992) and Mansfield and Collard (1988) also contain diverse material relevant to the arguments in this chapter.

REFERENCES

Boulton, M. (1983), *On Being a Mother*, London: Tavistock.

Brannen, J. and Moss, P. (1991), *Managing Mothers: Dual Earner Households after Maternity Leave*, London: Unwin Hyman.

Charles, N. and Kerr, M. (1988), *Women, Food and Families*, Manchester: Manchester University Press.

Crompton, R. and Sanderson, K. (1990), *Gendered Jobs and Social Change*, London: Unwin Hyman.

Delphy, C. and Leonard, D. (1992), *Familiar Exploitation*, Cambridge: Polity Press.

Gavron H. (1968), *Captive Wife*, Harmondsworth: Penguin.

Harris, C. C. (1990), *Family, Economy and Community*, Cardiff: University of Wales Press.

Haskey, J. (1995), 'Trends in marriage and cohabitation: the decline in marriage and the changing pattern of living in partnerships', *Population Trends*, 80: 5–15.

Haskey, J. and Kiernan, K. (1989), 'Cohabitation in Great Britain', *Population Trends*, 58: 23–32.

Land, H. (1978), 'Who cares for the family?', *Journal of Social Policy*, 7: 257–84.

McRae, S. (1993), *Cohabiting Mothers: Changing Marriage and Motherhood*, London: Policy Studies Institute.

Mansfield, P. and Collard, J. (1988), *The Beginning of the Rest of Your Life? A Portrait of Newly-Wed Marriage*, London: Macmillan.

Morris, L. (1990), *The Workings of the Household*, Cambridge: Polity Press.

Oakley, A. (1974), *The Sociology of Housework*, London: Martin Robertson.

Oakley, A. (1976), *Subject Housewife*, Harmondsworth: Penguin.

Phoenix, A. (1991), *Young Mothers?*, Cambridge: Polity Press.

Phoenix A., Woollett, A. and Lloyd, E. (eds) (1991), *Motherhood: Meanings, Practices and Ideologies*, London: Sage.

Richardson, D. (1990), *Women, Motherhood and Childrearing*, London: Macmillan.

8

Cohabitation or Marriage? – Cohabitation

Susan McRae

A central reason for studying cohabiting mothers was to gain some understanding of the apparent weakening of the link between motherhood and marriage. There is a tendency to treat cohabitation as if it does not differ from marriage in any important respects. This response was apparent in the early 1970s, when very few couples lived together outside marriage. For example, in a highly influential contribution to the study of marriage, Jessie Bernard likened cohabitation to marriage as simply one of many forms through which marital commitment may be manifested.

> One fundamental fact underlies the conception of marriage itself. Some kind of commitment must be involved. Without such commitment a marriage may hardly be said to exist at all... The form of the commitment is less important than the emotional contents it underlines. It may be a written contract or simply vows and promises made before witnesses or even simply an 'understanding' or consensual arrangement. (Bernard, 1978, pp. 87–8)

Twenty years later, when rates of cohabitation have grown to encompass about 1 in every 12 couples, the tendency to treat it as essentially identical to marriage remains. In an expansive review of marriage and the family by Delphy and Leonard, discussion of cohabitation is sparse, while a final comment suggests that *cohabitation is no longer very different from marriage* (Delphy and Leonard, 1992, p. 265). Of course, this view may be accurate; but it is based on little empirical evidence either about cohabitation which does not end in marriage or about premarital cohabitation. Indeed, what evidence there is suggests that in the past cohabiting and marital relationships have differed in at least one important respect: durability.

Recent demographic analyses have suggested that couples who lived together before marriage were more than twice as likely to experience divorce or separation within 15 years of marriage as couples who did not premaritally cohabit. That is, the risk of divorce was found to be significantly greater for marriages preceded by premarital cohabitation, even when the start of living in a consensual union was treated as the start of the 'marriage' (Haskey, 1992). However, it is important to note the possibility that couples who began to cohabit in the sixties and seventies (the generations covered by these analyses) are likely to have been fairly unconventional and as such, may have been more prone to marital disruption than other, non-cohabiting couples. Whether the association between premarital cohabitation and marriage breakdown will continue to hold when over half of all men and women cohabit for at least some part of their early years remains to be seen.

However, research has shown that important differences exist between the economic circumstances and life chances of women who continue to cohabit long after becoming mothers and those of women who marry. Accordingly, it seems reasonable to assume that other differences between women who marry and those who cohabit may exist which have hitherto been obscured by a lack of primary research.

To begin to uncover such differences, we explored the following issues: what influenced the initial decision of women who had cohabited to set up home together with their partners. Why women who ultimately married chose to cohabit first rather than marry straight away; why they decided to marry. Why women who continued to cohabit had chosen not to marry; and what might influence their decision to marry. What were considered to be the advantages and disadvantages of cohabitation (if any). Whether women who had had a child while cohabiting had ever felt pressure to marry, and if so, from whom.

Of course, the women who participated in our research had differing experiences of cohabitation. For one group of women, cohabitation had not (yet) ended, and these women recorded the longest duration of cohabitation, averaging 7.8 years, Another group of women had never cohabited and had been married, on average, for 11 years. Among women who had cohabited premaritally and married their partners *before* becoming mothers, cohabitation had been fairly short-lived, averaging just less than 2 years, and had ended at least 4 years before our research was carried out. Cohabiting women who married their partners after becoming mothers had cohabited for just over 4 years on average; and for some, cohabitation had ended only a few months before our interviews. It seemed reasonable at the outset of our analyses to expect that these different histories of cohabitation and marriage would have implications for women's views about their living arrangements – an expectation that is amply confirmed below.

Living Together

What reasons do people give for their decisions to set up home together? According to a recent study of men and women in six British cities, the large majority of women in all social groups begin to live together or get married because they are in love (the Social Change and Economic Life Initiative – SCELI). Having enough money to set up an independent household also enters in, as does being at a suitable point in one's working life; but love appears largely unrivalled and over three-quarters of SCELI's female respondents gave this as the reason why they had set up home with a partner or married (Anderson et al., n.d., pp. 21–2).

SCELI was not intended to focus directly on respondents' marital histories and thus did not distinguish between the decision to live together and the decision to marry. Burgoyne (1985) focused exclusively on cohabitation and identified three avenues to living together among her largely middle-class, childless couples. Such couples may undertake to live together as a test of their relationship – a trial marriage. Alternatively, they may live together with little expectation of permanence: the arrangement suits them at the moment. Thirdly, a stable cohabiting relationship may evolve from an earlier, more temporary relationship or from sharing the same accommodation.

All of these reasons for cohabitation find resonance in our own study of cohabiting and married mothers. For cohabiting mothers, however, pregnancy also was a major precipitating factor. Among SCELI's respondents, 1 in 10 women reported that being pregnant influenced their decision to set up home or get married (Anderson et al., n.d., p. 22). Among the mothers we interviewed who were *continuing* to cohabit, however, the proportion was 1 in 5 – rising to 1 in 2 among mothers whose cohabitation *after* the birth of a baby had culminated in marriage. These figures are shown in table 8.1, which summarizes the range of factors which influenced the point in life when *cohabiting* women first set up home with their partners.[1]

Table 8.1   Factors influencing the decision to cohabit

Column percentages

	Long-term cohabiting mothers	Cohabited premaritally	
		Married after baby	Married before baby
Fell in love	51	51	65
Pregnancy	23	49	12
Wanted regular sexual partner	31	33	23
Wanted a child*	13	6	7
Rented accommodation available	21	24	25
Could afford a house	18	18	14
Previous household split up	10	6	14
Couldn't stand previous household	14	12	9
At suitable point in working life	0	2	7
Base:	77	51	57

* Excluding those who also indicated that pregnancy was a precipitating factor in their cohabitation decision.
Sums to more than 100 per cent because multiple reasons possible.

Apart from pregnancy, few differences separated the three groups of women shown in table 8.1.[2] Somewhat surprisingly, perhaps, the only other major difference concerned the extent to which falling in love figured as a response. For two-thirds of women who cohabited but married *before* giving birth, cohabitation had been triggered by falling in love; for the other two groups, pregnancy and the desire for a regular sexual partner had been as important as falling in love.[3] It seems reasonable to suggest that, in the absence of pregnancy, falling in love represents the spontaneous and romantic ideal which is supposed to govern all our lives and lead us to becoming part of a couple. After all, if you were not pregnant, why else would you have lived with the man you ultimately married?[4]

Table 8.1 also shows the influence of housing on the decision to establish a cohabiting relationship. Housing availability may have a marked influence on the decisions of young couples to establish a home together. A recent Rowntree Foundation (1992) study of the effects of housing costs on young people's lifestyles reported that about 1 in 7 18–35-year-olds in the Southeast had delayed setting up a home with their partners because of the high cost of housing. However, no substantial differences among women in relation to the impact of housing decisions emerged from our analyses. Nor were there any substantial differences in relation to the timing of cohabitation in terms of the women's working lives, although it might fairly be supposed that the slightly greater tendency for women who cohabited but married *before* giving birth to cite a work-related reason reflects their generally higher occupational standing.

But it remains in relation to pregnancy that differences are most pronounced between women who cohabited after giving birth (whether or not they ultimately married) and those who married before giving birth. Women who cohabited after giving birth were substantially more likely to establish a household with their partner *because they were pregnant*. Further: their pregnancies were largely unplanned. Unexpected first pregnancies were reported by 71 per cent of mothers who premaritally cohabited after a birth and 58 per cent of mothers who continued to cohabit. This contrasts with 32 per cent of women whose premarital cohabitation ended before they became mothers and 27 per cent of women who did not cohabit before marriage (and 34 per cent of female SCELI respondents).

Of course, differences existed between mothers who were *continuing* to cohabit and those who married sometime *after* a birth: indeed, twice as many of the latter (49 per cent) as the former (23 per cent) reported that they were pregnant when they first set up home with their partners. This is likely to reflect in part at least the higher proportion of second marriages among women who married after a birth: waiting for a divorce affected the (re)marriage timing of about 1 in 5 of these women. But, in addition, it seems that for some of these women pregnancy was not only a precipitating reason for living with their partners, it was the reason they chose *not* to marry, thus bringing them into our category of cohabiting women who married after giving birth. That is, it was the fact of pregnancy itself that stopped them from marrying – at least until after the baby was born.

Reasons for Delaying Marriage

Table 8.2 summarizes the reasons why cohabiting women who married did not do so straight away but instead lived with their husbands for a period.[5] Almost 1 in 5 (18 per cent) of those who had had a baby *before* they married reported that they had not married because they were pregnant:

> We thought it better to wait till our son was born. I didn't want to get married when I was all fat. (201/1460)

> At the time I was expecting a baby and I didn't want to get married when I was pregnant, I preferred to wait. I would say basically because [then it would have seemed as if] I was pressurized into it, so I thought it was better to wait. (075/5535)

> I wanted everyone to celebrate our marriage because we were in love and not because I was pregnant. I felt it would have spoilt the day and it was the wrong reason to get married at that time. (091/4263)

For these women at least, the idea of a *shotgun wedding* was an anathema: better to wait until their child was born and then consider getting married. Indeed, more than one woman suggested that they had no wish to give hostages to fortune by appearing to use their pregnancy to force their partners into marriage.

The fact that pregnant women might choose to cohabit rather than to marry is itself one measure of the changes that have occurred in British society since

Table 8.2 Reasons for premarital cohabitation

Column percentages

	Cohabited premaritally	
	Married after baby	Married before baby
One or both did not want to marry	27	16
Trial marriage	27	25
Waiting for a divorce	18	14
Couldn't afford it	14	14
Didn't want to marry while pregnant	18	0
Other reasons	12	32
Accommodation became available	0	9
Base:	51	57

Note: Sums to more than 100 per cent because more than one reason possible.

the 1960s. So too is the fact that almost 1 in 5 (18 per cent) of the women who did not marry until after they had become mothers postponed marriage because they or their partners were still legally married to someone else. Research by Haskey (1992, p. 12) shows that premarital cohabitation is particularly likely before second marriages: *the prevalence of premarital cohabitation before second marriages is always higher than that before first marriages, when comparing those marrying for the second time at the same age and from the same birth cohort.* In other words, an important ingredient of the rise in cohabitation is an increase in the rate of divorce and remarriage. Living together is a way of becoming part of a couple again, of testing the water, without the complications of marriage:

> We had both been married before so we were not in a hurry to get embroiled again – once bitten, twice shy! We got married after our son was born. (204/3494)

> Well, we both had been married before and we knew of some of the complications that can happen and we just didn't think it was the time to get married. We thought we would wait and see if things would work out. (188/4794)

> [We wanted] to find out whether we could get on together. My husband didn't want to get married again until he was ready, so I waited for him. If you live together you can find out whether you can stand being in the same place as that person. (156/5596)

Moreover, as the words of the last woman suggest, there is often more than one reason why a couple postpones marriage:

> It seemed silly having two places and both paying out [rent] for them. We just did not feel the need to get married straight away and also his divorce wasn't through. (121/1389)

> We couldn't afford it and never thought about marriage and we had both been married before. That's it really. (240/0327)

The preceding two quotations, which come from women who married after a period of cohabitation but *before* becoming mothers, do more than illustrate the multiplicity of influences on women's decisions to marry or not. They show also the common ground between the two groups of women included in table 8.2. Few large differences were found in the reasons these women offered for not marrying straight away. Women who married *before* becoming mothers were less likely to report that they cohabited because one or the other did not want to marry, and more likely to offer a long, straggling tail of reasons. This accounts for the fact that about one-third of the reasons given by these women fell into an 'other' category. Included here were two women who felt they were too young to marry (but not to cohabit), two women who wanted to finish their education or training before marrying, two who reported problems finding the right time to get married, and one who began living with her husband because she had *nowhere else to go*:

> Because I was getting physically abused where I was living and we were engaged. I didn't want to go back home and he was moving North and asked me to come with him. We had a date set for getting married when we decided to live together. (137/0564)

This long tail of reasons notwithstanding, the explanations given by these two groups of women about why they chose first to cohabit rather than to marry have much in common, with one marked exception: their attitudes towards premarital pregnancy. Substantially fewer cohabiting women who married *before* becoming mothers experienced unplanned first pregnancies; but when they did so, their response was to marry:

> The only reason why we got married was because I was pregnant. We were quite happy living together, we had more freedom before marriage. (272/3262)

> We loved each other and I was pregnant and we wanted to get married before we had the child. (151/5645)

This view was shared also by women who married well before becoming pregnant:

> We both came from divorced parents. Looking back we realized that they got married before they knew each other. We decided to live together and see if we really got on well, and learn to live together. We then felt that we could live happily together and so got married. I would not have had children had I not been married. I don't think it would have been very good for the children, later on, to see on their birth certificates parents with different surnames. I do care about that. (110/2787)

Continuing to Cohabit

All of the women included in table 8.2 had married by the time we interviewed them in 1992: their period of cohabitation, in other words, had turned into a period of *premarital* cohabitation, and we examine later the reasons why they married. Women who were *continuing* to cohabit when we contacted them also were asked why they had not married. Because we wished to capture the full range of possible responses, our question to long-term cohabiting mothers was unprompted and open-ended.[6] Two points are worth noting, however, before we proceed to an examination of this critical issue.

First, we would emphasize that the views represented in table 8.3 come from a selection of highly unusual women: those who, by the early 1990s, were long-term cohabiting mothers. Their views may not be representative of all cohabiting mothers; but it seems likely that they signal the types of influences that might encourage increasing numbers of women in the future to become and to remain parents outside of formal marriage.

Table 8.3   Reasons why long-term cohabiting mothers have not married

Column percentages

	Long-term cohabiting mothers
Against marriage	21
No advantage in marriage	30
Weddings too expensive	26
Marriage delayed	19
Divorce as deterrent	30
No reason	6
Base:	77

Second, we would note that although our research asked long-term cohabiting mothers why they had chosen not to marry, we recognize that not marrying need not be the outcome of a deliberate or calculated decision. Rather, couples who live together (like married couples) simply may accept the day-to-day contours of their lives and not act to change them. Time passes surprisingly quickly, and unless there are compelling reasons to marry, marriage just might not happen. Of course, this is itself a 'choice', and one with specific (although diminishing) legal and social consequences, as we see below.

Indeed, implicit within the responses of several women was the sense that no decision had been taken about marrying or not marrying. They had simply not married. One woman made her position explicit:

> It isn't a decision we have made not to get married, we have just not made the decision to get married. You don't sit down and first say 'we are not getting married'. Now, having not chosen to not get married, I could not be less interested [in marriage]. (029/2152)

These views notwithstanding, most of the long-term cohabiting mothers we interviewed were able, when asked, to provide reasons for not having married. These reasons are summarized in table 8.3.

Avoiding marriage

A wish to avoid the institution of marriage, expressed either as opposition towards marriage or as apathy, was by far the most common reason given for continuing to cohabit over the longer term. Just over half of the long-term cohabiting mothers we interviewed said either that they were against marriage (21 per cent) or that they could see no advantage in getting married (30 per cent).

I don't particularly believe in the sanctity of marriage; having seen a lot of married couples and their carryings-on over the years made it seem irrelevant. Neither of us is religious. We did actually get engaged but never followed it through. We're both just happy as we are. (235/2235)

My partner does not really believe in marriage and we have lived so long together, very happily, that the matter has not been important. (221/1694)

I've just got no interest in being married. We live as a couple and we're quite satisfied with the way we are. I've been married and it's no different than living together. (324/4286)

Women giving these types of reason had lived with their partners longer than other long-term cohabiting mothers, averaging just over eight years together. About one-third had no qualifications (although 8 per cent had degrees) and almost half had household incomes of £12,000 or less. They were the most likely of long-term cohabiting mothers to be in paid work (60 per cent), and two-thirds had had an employed mother when they were growing up. Not surprisingly, a desire for personal independence often figured in their decisions not to marry:

I don't like the institution of marriage. I find it oppressive. It is a prison once you are married. I like living together, it suits my needs and feelings in life. (044/4365)

It's my decision rather than my partner's. I feel more independent not being married. I do not feel tied but am here by choice in this relationship. (206/1494)

The cost of weddings

Costly, big white weddings also deter cohabiting couples from marrying. Over one quarter of our long-term cohabiting mothers cited the expense of getting married as a reason for not marrying:

Neither of us are religious so we feel it would be hypocritical to be married in church. We also feel it's a great deal of expense which is wasted money when you think of the wedding dress and the reception and all that. You couldn't get married for under £4,000 and it's so much wasted money. (234/5531)

We were going to get married last year but couldn't because I got pregnant again, so we had to postpone it until we could afford it again. The local vicar was very good and understanding. We just couldn't afford the expense and things with another baby on the way. (020/5973)

Money for the wedding itself. (149/7275)

The words of these long-term cohabiting mothers underline the continuing symbolic importance of the big white wedding which, according to Gillis (1985,

p. 311), has never been so popular, particularly among working-class couples who spend as much if not more on getting married as the wealthy.

A big wedding has always been more than just a terrific party for family and friends. It is – or was – the major rite of passage for young women, when they passed through the door marked 'adult' and joined their mothers on the other side (Davidoff and Hall, 1987; Gittins, 1993). It seemingly no longer matters that today brides are rarely virgins; nor indeed, that many are now mothers when they walk down the aisle. It is the bride's big day. For many young women, it may be the *only* day when she is well and truly the centre of attention.

Elements of our characterization of the importance of the big wedding may be traced in the actions of cohabiting mothers who turn away from *marriage* because of the expense of a *wedding*. Tradition tells them what a proper wedding is: *popular custom dictated an elaborate event involving the huge expenditure of time and money* (Gillis, 1985, p. 84). Lacking money, such young women choose cohabitation over a registry wedding, sensing the inadequacy of the latter: *without all the festivities, no smallholder could consider himself or herself properly married* (ibid.). The question that remains for future research is whether these young cohabiting mothers, often with two or three children, are accepted as 'adults' by others, in the absence of the title 'wife'.

As it was the cost of a wedding which deterred these young cohabiting mothers from marrying, their comparatively poorer economic circumstances might have been expected. Among all long-term cohabiting mothers, those who cited the expense of marrying were the youngest (average age 28.6 years) and the most likely to be without qualifications (43 per cent). They were the least likely to be in paid work (29 per cent) or to own or be buying their own homes (38 per cent). One in three had an unemployed partner; over 40 per cent had household incomes of £12,000 or less. It was the case also that a small group of these mothers had higher-level qualifications (10 per cent) and household incomes above £24,000 (14 per cent), but these few apart, most long-term cohabiting mothers who had not married because of wedding costs were young, unqualified and unemployed women from working-class backgrounds.

Marriage delayed

In greatly different economic circumstances were the 1 in 5 women who were continuing to cohabit because they had not yet married:

> When we first moved in John wasn't divorced and we were happy the way we were. But now we have decided to get married in two months' time. (286/1680)

> We never seem to get the time. We keep saying we ought. We sometimes say we'll do it and go to town and say we are, but by the time we've done the shopping we've never got round to it. (197/1795)

> We always meant to. (183/1271)

There was little sense of antipathy towards marriage in the words of those women who remained unmarried because one partner was not yet divorced or because they had not yet got around to marrying or for some other, similar reason. Nor was there much indication that a lack of money was a deterrent. Rather, the dominant impression was that these women were likely to marry sooner or later.

The women who expressed such views had lived with their partners for the shortest period of time (6.3 years) among our long-term cohabiting mothers and 1 in 4 had been married before. As likely to come from working-class homes (44 per cent) as cohabiting mothers who could not afford a wedding (43 per cent), their current economic circumstances differed markedly. None lived in households with no earners and 44 per cent lived in households where both partners were in paid work. Consequently, women expressing these views included the highest proportion of owner occupiers (75 per cent); while about 1 in 7 had a joint income in excess of £24,000 per year.

Fear of divorce

The final major reason we examine for not marrying differed in kind from the preceding three explanations in that it was not antipathy or indifference towards marriage that perpetuated their cohabitation, but a strong dislike of divorce. One in three women who reported this view had been married before; but it was not only her own divorce that might inform her views, but that also of her partner, parents or friends:

> Everyone in my family that have been married are divorced. I don't think it's worth getting married. To me it's a lot of pain getting married and breaking up. (046/1917)

> I'm fairly anti-marriage – an awful lot of marriages end in divorce. I've not a lot of faith in the institution of marriage. My sister is divorced and a lot of friends are. It's not a lack of commitment to my partner, but I don't feel we need to be married. I take the idea of marriage very seriously. (196/2532)

> Having been married before, the length of time it took me to get divorced really. Also, I'm not a religious person, so I don't see the point. He doesn't want to get married at all. (281/1951)

Sometimes, fears raised by an earlier experience of divorce coexisted with worries about the stability of a current relationship:

> I was married before and it didn't work out. My first husband used to beat me up so I left him and he was also an alcoholic. We decided not just now – it's not suitable. We tend to fall out every so often and he goes back and stays with his mum so it's better the way it is. (084/0133)

The economic circumstances of these long-term cohabiting mothers most closely resembled those of long-term cohabiting mothers who could not afford to marry. They tended to be older than other long-term cohabiting mothers (average age 32.3 years) and included the highest proportion of cohabiting mothers (55 per cent) with household incomes of £12,000 or less, and the lowest proportion (5 per cent) with household incomes over £24,000 per year. One in three households had no one in paid employment; two in three of the women themselves were out of the labour force. Over half of their partners worked now – or last worked – in manual jobs. Their circumstances and attitudes bring to mind vividly Parker's (1990, p. 124) conjectural but seemingly accurate portrayal of modern-day cohabiting women:

> One can speculate that cohabitation might be attractive to   working-class men and women in, say, their late 20s or early 30s [who] may find that their marriages have broken down and [that] they are reluctant to make the sort of commitments traditionally required of marriage.... Working-class women who have been through a divorce might be prepared to form a new relationship but be slow to marry...income support may cease on cohabitation but at least the house is theirs.

The Advantages of Cohabiting

One of our research concerns was to identify the advantages and disadvantages of cohabitation perceived by women who had experienced a period of living with a partner outside marriage. To ensure a wide range of such experience, we questioned all women who had cohabited with the fathers of their four-year-old child for some period, whether or not they had married subsequently, or when that marriage might have taken place, about the advantages and disadvantages of cohabitation when compared with marriage.[7] This meant that women whose experience of cohabitation had ended in marriage some four or more years before our interviews were asked the same questions as women who were continuing to cohabit with their partners; their responses, moreover, suggested that women's perceptions are affected by the duration and outcome of their period of cohabitation.

Table 8.4 summarizes the advantages outlined by women who had cohabited with their partners for some period, and indicates the average duration of cohabitation experienced by each group. Advantages associated with cohabitation were reported by similar proportions of the three groups of women. Surprisingly, though, women who were *continuing* to cohabit were slightly less likely to say that there were advantages to cohabitation (40 per cent) than women who had subsequently married their partners (45 per cent).

Table 8.4   Advantages of cohabitation

Column percentages

	Long-term cohabiting mothers	Cohabited premaritally	
		Married after baby	Married before baby
No legal ties/more freedom	23	29	19
Able to test relationship/trial marriage	3	20	30
Do not take relationship for granted	6	2	4
Double MIRAS	5	2	4
Able to retain individuality	3	4	4
Cheaper than marriage	1	0	4
None	60	55	54
Average duration of cohabitation (years)	7.8	4.2	1.9
Base:	77	51	57

Note: More than one answer possible.

Trial marriage

The figures presented in table 8.4 suggest a link between the duration of cohabitation and the advantages that women perceive might inhere in such a relationship when compared with marriage. For women whose *premarital* cohabitation ended before the birth of any children, the primary advantage of cohabiting was to test their relationship with their partner before committing themselves to marriage. These women had lived with their husbands before marriage for a relatively short period – less than two years on average – and the benefit that many now recall about that period was that it was a trial marriage: a chance to

> get to know each other better. To get a better understanding of principles and attitudes to life, attitudes to children – fairly mundane things. (146/1843)

It matters little whether or not these women *entered* into a cohabiting relationship in order to test its durability or for some other reason; what is apparent from their responses is that an inclination to treat living together as a trial marriage is likely to be associated with shortened durations of cohabitation. As cohabitation lengthens, moreover, the perception that it acts as a practice run for marriage tends to disappear. For example, women who were *continuing* to cohabit when interviewed were highly unlikely to suggest that an advantage of living together was that it allowed opportunities to test relationships. At least some of these women initially began to live with their partners with the expectation that they would marry; and it seems likely that many eventually will marry (see below). Regardless, their views after many years' cohabitation suggest that the advantages of this living arrangement lie elsewhere than as a test for marriage.

A sense of freedom

Of rather more importance for mothers who were *continuing* to cohabit, but only cited by just over 1 in 5, was the sense of freedom associated with cohabitation. It is worth noting that in this regard, cohabiting mothers did not differ substantially in their views from women who had cohabited and married *before* having children, among whom also about 1 in 5 cited the lack of legal ties as an advantage of cohabitation.

> You're not perhaps feeling as committed; or at least that you can alter the arrangements and get out of it if you need to. It's more easily broken. (280/5215: married before baby born)

> You have not got to go through the courts if you are living together and anything goes wrong. You can just go your separate ways. My mum had two bad marriages and that's enough to put anybody off! (108/5438: long-term cohabiting mother)

> I've not got to go through the courts, etc. to get divorced. There's nothing stopping me, if I want to leave I can just leave. (046/1917: long-term cohabiting mother)

The inherent incompatibility between the notion of a trial marriage and a wish for freedom from legal ties is sufficient to render coherent the responses of women who had cohabited but chose to marry before becoming mothers. However, it seems surprising that so few cohabiting mothers cited the lack of legal ties as an advantage of cohabitation, despite it being the most commonly cited advantage. We examine later (in McRae, 1993) the extent to which legal ties had been established between the children and partners of long-term cohabiting mothers. Here it may suffice to suggest that some ties develop independently of the legal relationship between couples, and a wish for freedom and independence might not sit well with being a parent, an outcome that was recognized by at least two long-term cohabiting mothers:

> Personally I just feel more independent not being married. It would be easier to go if things went wrong. No, actually, it probably wouldn't be any easier now that we have a child – it would be just as traumatic as being married and breaking up. (021/2032)

> [There's a] greater *sense* of freedom – not a reality – you are no more free than if you were married. But you both know that there is no tie, so in a sense you are free. (044/4365)

The Disadvantages of Cohabiting

Table 8.5 summarizes the disadvantages of cohabiting in comparison with marrying as reported by women who had had some experience of living as part of a couple outside marriage. Women whose period of cohabitation was the most distant in time – those who cohabited but married *before* becoming mothers – were the least likely to report disadvantages associated with cohabitation (37 per cent); and women who had given up cohabiting for marriage more recently were the most likely to report disadvantages (45 per cent). These differences may reflect little more than the passage of time, as some women look backwards fondly towards that period of their lives when they had no children, no formal ties to their partners and few responsibilities, while others carry more recent memories of the problems that can attend unmarried family life. In any event, the differences were not large between these two groups of now-married women, and neither group differed markedly in their estimation of the disadvantages of cohabitation from mothers who continued to live outside marriage, among whom 43 per cent reported disadvantages.

Feelings of insecurity

The nature of the disadvantages cited by women with differing cohabitation and marital histories did not vary markedly, but here too links between the experience of cohabitation and perceived disadvantages were apparent. For example, cohabiting women who ultimately married were at least twice as likely as women who continued to cohabit to report feelings of insecurity or vulnerability – either their own or on behalf of their children – as a disadvantage of cohabitation. Nineteen per cent of women who married before becom-

Table 8.5   Disadvantages of cohabitation

Column percentages

	Long-term cohabiting mothers	Cohabited pre-maritally	
		Married after baby	Married before baby
No commitment/feel insecure	8	16	19
Socially unacceptable behaviour/stigma against unmarried mothers	14	10	5
Children affected/father has no rights	10	10	14
Better tax/benefits if married	5	2	2
Official forms awkward	5	0	0
None	57	55	63
Base:	77	51	57

ing mothers and 16 per cent of those who married afterwards cited insecurity or lack of commitment as a disadvantage, compared with only 8 per cent of currently cohabiting mothers.

> One can feel a little insecure if not married. It's perhaps the way one's brought up. You feel better when everything is legal and official. (049/0586: married after baby was born)

> Only where children are involved, I think. I think if you are not married and there are children, I think it is less secure for the children. (154/1000: married before baby was born)

> If you have children, it's just better for the child, to be married beforehand. It's easier to split up with children involved than to get divorced. My parents were not married and I didn't feel assured (010/0622: married before baby was born)

It is, of course, only reasonable that cohabiting women who feel vulnerable (personally or on behalf of their children) would be more likely than women who do not share these feelings to put an end to uncertainty by marrying. In this regard our findings are inherently plausible. But it is worth noting also that only a minority of women – whatever their cohabitation and marital histories – cited vulnerability or insecurity as a disadvantage; when they did so, moreover, they were more likely to be thinking of their children than themselves. It is perhaps a reflection of their increased presence in the public domain, through paid employment, that so few women felt insecure in their private lives simply by being unmarried.

Social unacceptability

Similar comments may be appropriate in relation to cohabitation as socially unacceptable or stigmatized behaviour, particularly for women with children. Table 8.5 indicates that this disadvantage was reported by only 5 per cent of women whose premarital cohabitation ended *before* they became mothers; that is, by the group of cohabiting women *least* likely to elicit the offending comments of others. Indeed, one such woman who had crossed both ethnic and religious lines when she chose to cohabit, married before having children in order to gain familial approval:

> Getting married wasn't a question then – it was the idea to get to know my partner and be sure I could live with him. Marriage just seemed a formality, a piece of paper. ... Acceptance by members of our families – particularly mine as he's not from the same ethnic group or religion as I. I am Asian and he is Catholic. I think it's best to be married if you're going to start a family. (059/5272)

In contrast, women whose behaviour had left them more open to the criticisms of others – those who had cohabited after becoming mothers, whether or not they ultimately married – were considerably more likely to refer to the social unacceptability of cohabitation after motherhood:

> People do accept you and view you a lot better if you are married and have a child. We were looked down on as we weren't married and had a child. Thirty to thirty-five-year-olds were surprisingly the worst. Childminders refused us as we weren't married. (054/3244: married after baby was born)

> Coming from a large international city to a small rural area, I found [I was] being constantly confronted with the expectation that you were married and then having to explain why you weren't. (233/3242: married after baby was born)

> Other people's attitudes – especially now we have children. Some of my family don't think it is permanent and there may be a stigma attached to the children's illegitimacy. (206/1494: continuing to cohabit)

It remained only a minority, however, who cited social or family disapproval as a disadvantage of cohabitation, encompassing 1 in 10 of cohabiting women who married *after* having children and 1 in 7 of long-term cohabiting mothers who had not (yet) married. Disapproval may rankle a few, but it seemingly does not deter the many.

Other disadvantages

The other main disadvantage recorded in table 8.5, that children may be affected by cohabitation and that fathers may have no rights, was cited about equally by the three groups of cohabiting women. Sometimes, this concern was expressed in relation to differing surnames, particularly by women who cohabited *after* motherhood:

> I was the only one with a different surname. We were worried about what the children would think when they grew up and realized they had different surnames. (030/6002: married after baby was born)

> Not having the same name as my children. I feel like an outsider sometimes. (159/5458: continuing to cohabit)

> Not having the same name. When the children go to school and when we go to school for reports and such like, and the children have my name – my partner must feel hurt. (234/5531: continuing to cohabit)

Other mothers worried about the financial disadvantages of cohabitation breakdown and how this might affect their children:

> If it breaks down, the woman might not be working or earning as much as she would have been, and so the children might suffer. (154/1000: married before baby was born)

The fact that fathers in cohabiting relationships might lack parental rights was mentioned by a small number of women in each group, and was seen as a potential disadvantage of cohabitation. (We discuss this issue more fully in McRae (1993) and do not here report the particular comments made by women who expressed a concern about legal relationships.) But before leaving the discussion of disadvantages, it is fair to note that at least some of the drawbacks to cohabitation mentioned by women who were *continuing* to cohabit appeared to rank higher as inconveniences than as serious impediments to living as a couple outside marriage:

> It makes filling in forms complicated because sometimes they count you as a couple and sometimes they don't. None other [disadvantages] that I've come across or anticipate. (225/5077)

> Just having to explain why and filling in forms. Just inconvenience, really. (230/6727)

> Introducing yourself to people, explaining what the relationship is. (277/5566)

It appears vexing that so far neither our language nor our bureaucracies have caught up entirely with changes in the way people organize their lives.

NOTES

1 Women who married straight away, without a period of premarital cohabitation, were not asked this question.
2 The responses shown in the table come from a question in the self-completion questionnaire which offered respondents pre-selected answers. Respondents were invited to tick as many of these answers as they wished and to write in any further answers. The question itself replicates one used in SCELI.
3 Among both long-term cohabiting mothers, and cohabiting women who married after having children, the previously married were more likely to suggest that they set up home together because they were in love. For long-term cohabiting mothers, this response was the only one given by more than four of the eighteen formerly married women. Eleven formerly married women gave this response.
4 Marrying for love, freely chosen, is said to be a hallmark of modern Western society, particularly when contrasted with (probably mythical) past times when marriages were social and economic unions (cf. Mansfield and Collard, 1988). We would argue that most women marry or establish relationships because they love a particular man, rather than some other man. As an explanation for becoming a couple, love is appropriate and socially acceptable, to oneself and to others. However, we would also agree with Delphy and Leonard (1992, p. 265), who reason that behind love lie the social and economic advantages of conforming to the norm and of allying oneself with a member of the dominant group: sharing his income and getting protection.
5 Respondents were asked the following open-ended question: 'We'd also like to know why you chose to live together as a couple, rather than get married straight away.

What things would you say were important in influencing your decision to delay getting married?' Up to twenty different responses were coded, and ultimately collapsed into the categories shown in table 8.2. Responses were analysed so that close meanings given by the same respondent were not double counted. The table sums to more than 100 per cent because respondents were able to give more than one answer.

6   Cohabiting respondents were asked the following open-ended question: 'We are also interested in why you and your partner have chosen not to get married. What things would you say were important in influencing your decision not to get married?' Fourteen different responses were coded and ultimately collapsed into the categories shown in table 8.3. Of the 77 cohabiting respondents, 44 gave one reason, 26 gave two reasons, 5 gave three reasons and 2 gave four reasons. Responses were analysed so that close meanings given by the same respondent were not double counted. The table sums to more than 100 per cent because respondents were able to give more than one answer.

7   Women were asked: 'Do you think there are any advantages (disadvantages) in living together as a couple, compared with being married?' Women who responded positively were then asked: 'What do you think the advantages (disadvantages) are?' Women who had separated from their partner by the time of our interviews were not asked these questions.

REFERENCES

Anderson, M., Bechhofer, F. and Kendrick, S. (n.d.), 'Individual and household strategies: some empirical evidence from the SCELI', unpublished manuscript.

Bernard, J. (1978), *The Future of Marriage*, New York: Bantam Books.

Burgoyne, J. (1985), *Cohabitation and Contemporary Family Life*, ESRC End of Grant Report, unpublished.

Delphy, C. and Leonard, D. (1992), *Familiar Exploitation: A New Analysis of Marriage in Contemporary Western Societies*, Cambridge: Polity Press.

Gillis, J. (1985), *For Better, For Worse: British Marriages, 1600 to the Present*, Oxford: Oxford University Press.

Gittins, D. (1993), *The Family in Question*, London: Macmillan.

Haskey, J. (1992), 'Pre-marital cohabitation and the probability of subsequent divorce', *Population Trends*, 68: 10–19.

McRae, S. (1993), *Cohabiting Mothers: Changing Marriage and Motherhood*, London: Policy Studies Institute.

Mansfield, P. and Collard, J. (1988), *The Beginning of the Rest of Your Life?*, London: Macmillan.

Parker, S. (1990), *Informal Marriage, Cohabitation and the Law 1750–1989*, London: Macmillan.

Rowntree Foundation (1992), 'The effect of housing costs on young people's lifestyles', *Housing Research Findings*, no. 68, York: Joseph Rowntree Foundation.

9

Women's Work

Nickie Charles and Marion Kerr

It is part of family ideology that 'a woman's place is in the home', while a man's task is to go out to work to earn the money to support his wife and children. This very specific division of labour along lines of gender (man the breadwinner, woman the homemaker) is enshrined in policies and practice at all levels of society, from the marriage service to social security legislation. Despite the contemporary rhetoric of equality between the sexes this ideology significantly influences women's experiences, particularly once they become mothers. If equality and an egalitarian sharing of domestic tasks exist between men and women within a household before the arrival of children, and we will explore the extent of this below, it is almost always the case that once children have arrived the allocation of tasks reverts to what comes 'naturally'. That is, it reverts to what is defined as natural within familial ideology; women take on the household and child-care tasks and men assume the mantle of breadwinner. What usually remains implicit in this 'different but equal' partnership is the differential allocation of power which is part and parcel of the gender division of labour. Women, on giving up paid work outside the home, relinquish the power and status that it confers upon them. Their partners, however, unless they are unemployed, retain their status, and the power differential between the sexes is thereby increased.

Women with young children are usually financially dependent on men, they are excluded from the world of paid work, the work they do within the home is devalued and they are marginalized by society. Despite this, or perhaps because of it, they usually shoulder the burden of responsibility for ensuring their partners and children are well fed and healthy. They take the day-to-day decisions about food purchase, how much money they can spend this week, what sort of food will keep the family happy and healthy. These tasks are women's work. But as we will show, having responsibility for these decisions does not necessarily mean that women enjoy power or that they control the food their families eat. They exercise their power in other people's interests, above all in the interests of their partners. Thus although women may have the day-to-day responsibility for food provision for their families, it is *men* who have the power and control. Women cook to please men, they decide what to buy in the light of men's preferences, they carry the burden of shopping for food and cooking food, but most of them carry out these tasks within a set of social relations which denies them power, particularly when they are at home all day with young children and are dependent for financial support on a man.

Responsibility for Cooking

Cooking has long been defined as one of women's major and most important tasks within the home. Let us therefore begin by exploring who it is who stirs the cooking pot in families which include young children. As we have already implied, in the majority of families in our sample (177–88.5 per cent) women were responsible for the regular day-to-day preparation of meals. In only two families was cooking shared equally between husband and wife, although in about a third of the families men, and occasionally children, would sometimes cook a meal. Men's culinary activities were usually confined to the preparation of non-main meals and 'snacks', a process which was not usually graced with the term 'cooking'. Apart from the two men who shared the cooking equally with their partners only twenty-three cooked on a regular basis, and even in these cases they did not cook daily or even every other day. And thirty-three men had never cooked a meal since the couple had been together. Most men only cooked when their partners were ill or otherwise unable to cook, or maybe cooked the breakfast on a Sunday. This type of cooking is obviously different from the regular provision of proper, family, meals which was what most women referred to when talking about cooking. This remained women's work in almost all the families we spoke to.

Most of the women accepted this division of labour, indeed they felt it was part of their 'job' as a wife and mother to do all the cooking:

> He would [help] if I wanted him to as I say but I'm here, it's my sort of job...if I'm ill, if I'm dying upstairs he might do a few chips for the kids. He just really doesn't like doing anything like that, he *will* do if I want him to but as I say I don't think he should have to.

And this was often justified by reference to the fact that men worked outside the home and could not therefore be expected to cook. A woman at home all day looking after demanding toddlers, however, could and should.

> He can't very well cook through the day, love, 'cos he doesn't come home until ten past five so I can't very well expect him to go and set to and cook a tea, I mean some wives do...he'd probably prefer to have me I'd think...but he's easy to please, he's not a bit faddy.

Some women, however, felt resentful that they were always the ones to prepare and cook meals:

> It's a bone of contention sometimes. He very, very rarely cooks anything. [When does he? What has to happen to make him cook?] Well me refusing to do so is really the only time he will, or if I'm ill, if I'm ill in fact he's very good, he's quite capable of doing so . . . but even if he makes a sandwich he asks you, 'What shall I put in it?' So no, he doesn't. Dreadful really isn't it? And he's not really a male chauvinist either . . . I always blame my mother-in-law for it, his upbringing.

Generally if men did cook they would cook at weekends or when they were on holiday. At these times the rigid sexual division of labour, which most women felt was dictated by the fact that their partners were out at work, could be slightly relaxed. But most men did not cook main meals at all and some were clearly considered to be totally incapable in the kitchen. One woman was asked whether her partner had ever cooked. She replied:

> No – can't even boil an egg. When I used to work I'd prepare about two meals in one – when I had the time I'd prepare it – and I remember leaving a casserole, you know, steak and kidney and potatoes and everything was in it and all he had to do was get some frozen peas out and put them in. He put the casserole on the top gas which promptly blew up and he put the frozen peas in a pan with no water would you believe. So that's how good a cook he is.

Women often reported that they had to instruct men on every step of meal preparation, or that if they were let loose in the kitchen the mess afterwards was more of an effort to clear up than if they hadn't been involved at all and the women had had to cook the meal themselves. The following descriptions make the situation abundantly clear:

> If he's cooking he's only having to cook snacks because it means I'm not here. He wouldn't know how to prepare a casserole. And if I go to work I've got to write on a piece of paper before I go, 'Put the oven on at such and such a time and such and such a temperature', and he should know by now. But I didn't do it one weekend. I prepared it all and I thought I'll just see what happens, and the telephone rang at 11 o'clock at work – 'What temperature do I put the oven on for the casserole? How long does it take?' I was waiting for that phone call.

> Well he can cook but I'd rather do it myself because he makes such a mess. When I was first married I went away for the weekend and when I came home I didn't recognize the kitchen, there was fat everywhere. He always cooks everything full blast – he doesn't sort of moderate it or anything – he just throws it in, turns it up high and hopes for the best. He's terrible. . . . It's more bother than it's worth, it's twice as hard work if he does it.

Possibly due to this kind of experience some women would not let their partners in the kitchen at all, they felt that it was *their* domain and they wanted to maintain control over it. One man who was present while his partner was being interviewed said: 'Susan doesn't really like me cooking but I mean I have cooked before'. His partner joined in:

> I must admit the kitchen is mine, I like to use my own cooker and you know I prefer it because I know that if something spills over, alright it's my fault. But if somebody else starts spilling things then I don't like it. But I mean on some occasions when I haven't been well you have done a little bit of cooking haven't you? If I'm late home, say I've got a parents' evening, Robert will perhaps do them a simple meal.

This couple were both working full-time as teachers and yet the sexual division of labour as far as food preparation and cooking was concerned was clearly unaffected by the woman's full-time employment outside the home. In fact, our findings suggest that women's employment does not have any effect on whether their partners cook or not, at least at this stage in the life cycle. Those who worked part time were just as likely to be responsible for all meal preparation as those who were full-time housewives. Even the few women who worked full-time did not receive any more help from their partners. They did, however, tend to have nannies who cooked for the children during the day or relied on their parents to look after their pre-school age children.

The nature of men's employment, on the other hand, seems to have some bearing on the extent of their involvement with cooking. The two men who shared cooking equally with their partners were both unemployed and in the other families with unemployed men it seemed that women were less likely to be solely responsible for the preparation of main meals than in other families. This finding needs to be treated with caution, however, as our sample of unemployed families was extremely small.

Social class seems to have more of an impact on men's participation in cooking than either the woman's or the man's employment: indeed, the gender division of labour seems to be mediated in interesting and significant ways (see Charles and Kerr, 1988, chapter 8). Here it is worth quoting an exchange on this topic between one of the women and the interviewer:

> I think men should be able to do some basic things like peel potatoes, fry an egg, fry bacon, but most men are absolutely useless aren't they? Really no idea, it's terrible. [I think some try, don't they?] Not in my walk of life. [My husband is not too bad.] Is he good? I wish mine would – you'll have to give my husband some lessons then. I think actually though if you're . . . 'cos you're quite middle class aren't you? I think middle-class men are more – they don't think it's sissy do they, whereas working-class men think it's real sissy even to be seen washing up. Say if on a Sunday if one of my brothers comes round for dinner well John won't wash up and if my sisters are there he won't, but if there's only us he'll wash up, whereas if there's anyone else there he won't. It's funny really. I think as I say – maybe middle-class mothers are more . . . I don't know but definitely I would say they're more adaptable I think, they're a lot less set in their ideas, you know, I think working-class . . . especially men are really stick in the mud, you know. [They tend

to be more traditional.] Traditional, the cloth-cap image. I think that's true, I mean not a lot of them wear the cloth caps – but even with young lads there doesn't seem to be much change from generation to generation – maybe a bit more now obviously but I think they're very traditionalist.

Despite these apparent class variations in the form taken by gender divisions it is still the case that the majority of women in all social classes are responsible for the preparation and cooking of the daily family meal. If men did cook without their wives' instructions it was often not a proper meal that they prepared:

If he said he was going to do a meal he would do something like fried egg, fried bread and fried potatoes which I wouldn't normally do.

Well he never cooks a dinner. He just does something simpler, something on toast. He could do more elaborate things but he thinks that's my job to cook, his is to make the money.

This last point is interesting because it underlines the significance of the way tasks are allocated within marriage. If men *were* to share cooking then it would clearly have implications for their undisputed status as the main breadwinner, it would indicate a willingness to discuss and even problematize the gender division of labour rather than accepting it as natural and immutable. However, most of the men ensured that this 'natural' division was not questioned by never, or only rarely, cooking run-of-the-mill, proper, family meals. If called upon to cook they usually relied on sausages and chips or other convenience foods:

Well, like me I can do Yorkshire puddings, roast potatoes and do a cheese pie and all he can seem to do is open a tin of beans or spaghetti. He'll get a few rashers of bacon and chips and a load of beans – ugh!

Clearly this type of food does not constitute a proper meal and men were not expected to be able to undertake this type of cooking. Most of the women felt that this was basically their job and any help they received was a demonstration of the generosity of their partner:

I do more than he does but I think that he does more than his fair share. When I compare him with my father and his father they do nothing, he does quite a lot...he'll get the meals a couple of times a week.

If men were involved in cooking proper meals it was usually a rather more special meal that they cooked, such as the Sunday roast or an elaborate meal for a dinner party. It was, however, only a small minority of the men who cooked in this way:

Alan does like to cook, he cooks quite often at weekends.... When we both worked Alan worked in a branch and he was home before me so he would cook most nights. It's just the convenience really that I'm here, that's the reason I cook. . . . He likes to bake, he likes baking and doing fancy stuff. He's not so keen on doing plain things, he finds that boring, he likes all the fancy stuff. . . . If we're having a dinner party then he'll cook that, he likes doing that sort of thing . . . he'll sort of go through the cookery books and pick out a main meal, he's quite good at that, he's quite good at organizing it all.

Most men in our sample only cooked as a standby or if they were particularly interested in cooking. They were able to choose to cook if and when the fancy took them, whereas women had to cook whether the fancy took them or not. But how do women feel about this? Is it accepted as natural and right – the way things ought to be? Is it rationalized as a purely individual response to specific circumstances? Or is it felt to be unfair and resented?

Should Men Cook?

To try to uncover women's attitudes towards these gender divisions we asked whether they thought it important for women to be able to cook. A majority of them (116) thought that it was important and only a minority (27) felt it equally important that men were able to; an even smaller minority (14) felt that the ability to cook was not important for women. Their responses to this question clearly revealed how intimately bound up with a woman's role as wife, and particularly mother, is the ability to cook: 'Very important really. *Especially* if she's a mother. I can't really envisage a woman not being able to cook. . . . You think it's the natural thing, it isn't I know, but you expect it to be'. It also reveals how much the division of labour which allocates the task of cooking to mothers is regarded as something that has to be:

> It depends what sort of a woman you are really. If you're going to go back to work after you've had children or if you're not going to have children at all then it's not really important. I think if your husband can cook and you're both working then that's fair enough, let him do it.

> But if you're going to have children and give up work you have to be able to cook really.

These two comments stress the importance of cooking to motherhood; the two below link its importance to being a 'proper' wife.

> I think it's very important really. I mean we enjoy our food – I don't know quite what Alan would do if I couldn't cook. I don't think we'd have quite married. I don't know how you manage if you can't cook really. . . . I suppose you buy it all, convenience type food.

> I think it's awful if she can't cook . . . I mean a fella can't do a proper day's work and not come home to a decent meal.

A few women, however, felt that *theoretically* it was no more important for women to be able to cook than for men, although it seemed that in practice they were the ones who *actually* cooked.

> Just as important as for a man. I think each relationship, whether married or not, finds its own level. I *don't believe* a woman's role is to be at home and cook and look after the children and her man. Having said that, that is what I *do*, but *purely* because it works out that way.

This type of explanation of gender divisions and their continuation, even when they are not seen as the only or even the most desirable alternative, assumes that women are free to choose their role within the family; it is worth noting that the choice made is actually in conformity with dominant gender roles.

Most women, however, saw this gender division of labour as something which was historically and socially determined. It was not something that could be wished away merely by individual women exercising free choice. When asked about the importance of being able to cook one woman replied:

> I'd say very important. [Why?] Well to me it's the basic history of the woman doing all that sort of thing and the man going out to work, you know, he's the breadwinner and the wives – I wouldn't say I agree with it that the wife should be at home to look after children, housekeep and cook, but I think it's just the way of the world isn't it really – that's the way it should be.

Several of the women explained the gender divisions within their own households in terms of the way their partners had been brought up:

> Well I don't think it's particularly important for a woman to be able to cook as long as one of you can cook. I think it's important for somebody to be able to cook 'cos then you can pass it on to whoever's coming up next. I mean I feel that my husband's lacking in interest and inability to cook is probably a direct result of the way he was brought up.

And another woman's comments suggest that she would probably repeat this process despite her criticisms of it:

> Well I've got a theory about this – it's women that bring men up and they bring them up to be bloody useless don't they? They do though don't they? I mean my mother annoys me – I've got two brothers and they're absolutely useless but, you know, we had to wash up and do everything but they never had to do anything and I think that's all wrong. But there again if I had sons of my own I'd probably be the same – I hope I wouldn't be.

There is, therefore, a feeling that it is women, as wives and mothers, who are to blame for men's ineptitude rather than the men themselves. Together with this view goes the opinion that cooking is so simple that anyone can do it, with the exception, it seems, of men:

> I couldn't cook, well I never did any cooking before I got married. I think anybody with a reasonable amount of intelligence can manage to knock something together you know... people say they can't cook, well it can only be because they haven't tried, I can't see anything very complicated about it you know... I think yes you should be able to cook, but there again I can't see why anybody shouldn't be able to cook.

It is common in our culture that women's skills are devalued and not regarded as skills at all. This also happens with cooking, traditionally a woman's skill, at least in the domestic sphere.

Alongside the view, shared by the majority of the women we spoke to, that cooking was an integral part of a woman's role as wife and mother went the view that men should be *able* to cook but should not be *required* to cook in the normal course of events: 'I think men should be able to as well.... There's always going to come that day when they're going to have to do something.' Women who felt that their own husbands deserved a meal on the table when they came home from work took a different view when they were considering the case of a couple where the man and woman were both working. One woman was asked if she thought that men should cook:

> I do – I mean if their wives are prepared to go all day if they're buying a house... if she's going to go out all day and he's going to go out all day why should *she* come home and set on and him sit in the chair and wait for it. He could be helping her, could peel potatoes and things like that.

However, even in this imagined set of circumstances it is clearly still regarded as the woman's responsibility to cook; the man is viewed as *helping* her. More usually women thought men should be able to cook in an emergency:

> I think they should, yeah, 'cos I mean if anything like crops up, y'know, if like you're in hospital or that. I mean, 'How do you cook mince?' I think there's a certain amount of stuff they should be able to do. I think they could do it if they put their minds to it but like most fellas they say, 'Well I've got a wife so she can get on with it'.

And other women thought it would be nice if their partners were able to cook just so they could sometimes relieve them of the chore:

> It's nice for a man to be able to cook, as well. I mean I would appreciate it if my husband said, 'Oh, I'll do a dinner', you know. He never would, but I know a lot of men that have lived on their own in flats and that have had to or are genuinely interested in cooking, you know. I think it's nice if they do take a turn in it. It's always much nicer to have a meal prepared for you than have to do it yourself – by the time you've fiddled around with it you're not really bothered whether you eat it or not anyway, are you?

A lot of the women's partners were not able to cook even in 'emergency' situations and certainly did not offer to relieve their wives of the chore. Women sometimes felt that they were aiding and abetting men in their helplessness. The two comments below illustrate this point. Usually women going into hospital to have their babies was the one and only occasion on which their partners were left to fend for themselves. Some managed admirably, others did not:

> On the Friday before I went in he made sausage, egg and chips but I had to give him instructions. I could see smoke coming out of the kitchen from the chip pan. And when I was in hospital having my daughter he set fire to the chip pan. He lived on Chinese and things like that – I wouldn't mind but I'd made him loads of individual pies and I'd frozen them and I'd said, 'Look, there they are', you know.

He had not even managed to open the freezer to get the pies out while she was away. Another woman's partner was slightly more adept at opening a freezer.

> He can warm things up. He can cook his own breakfast. But while I was having Jeremy in hospital for eight days I filled the freezer with meals which I wish I hadn't done, really. I think it's stupid. If I'd thought about it – I was just concerned that he would be eating properly but I think he could have fended for himself really, even down to the shopping.

Even though a lot of the women thought that men should be able to cook they did not necessarily apply it to their own situations, and most seemed happy with this state of affairs, or at least accepted it as just, given that men work outside the home:

> I mean a lot of men can cook, a lot of my friends say, 'My husband's doing the Sunday lunch today', or something. But it doesn't bother me that John can't. I mean he would try. But you see I'm quite happy if he's looking after the children to go and do the cooking.

> I think it's a woman's job, really – maybe you don't agree. I think it's good for them if they can because there's always the odd time when they might have to. I think when they're working and you're at home all day it's nice if you've got a meal ready for them to sit down to.

The ability to cook, and this implies the ability to provide proper meals for men and children, was viewed by most women as vital; it was a fundamental part of women's role as wife and mother. Because cooking is viewed in this way most of the women did not consider that men ought also to cook, they merely thought they should be able to in case a situation ever arose in which they might need to. This view is a long way from regarding cooking as a task to be shared between marriage partners and, as our sample shows, in families with young children a strict sexual division of labour usually operates so that women are the ones who cook. This is rationalized in terms of them being at home all day. But clearly familial ideology has deeper roots than this as even when women are out at work full time they still tend to be the ones who cook, at least in families with young children.

Although men's cooking activities were fairly minimal there were other ways in which they could be involved in 'helping' their partners at mealtimes. During the week, when men were out at work, women did not often expect much help, but at weekends it seemed that men might be expected to lend a hand – at least with the washing up. In fact, men were more likely to take on this task than any other connected with mealtimes; in 85 (43 per cent) of the families men helped with the washing up regularly and in a further 45 (23 per cent) of families men occasionally helped in this way, but this still meant that around a third of the women never received even this form of help. Very few men (7 per cent) helped regularly with actual food preparation, such as peeling potatoes for a meal; around a third (37 per cent) helped with this task from time to time, but half never did so. Even fewer men were involved in the laying and clearing of the table – almost 60 per cent never helped with these tasks: 'Wouldn't help with anything unless I was ill.... Come to Dave, he works and I do nowt all day so why should he?' Women mostly accept this lack of involvement on the part of men, again justifying it in terms of their work outside the home or their involvement in helping with the children or the garden:

> Well I usually say 'Do you want to go and bath the children or would you like to wash the dishes' and we take it in turns. Sometimes I'll say 'You go and pop them in the bath', say on an evening, and I'll start clearing the table and do the dishes... he's very good, he does help a lot.

There was always a feeling of gratitude if men 'helped'. They were doing more than their fair share, they were really 'good'. This again underlines how much it is accepted that these household tasks are women's responsibility and help with them is a bonus and not something that can reasonably be expected: 'He's very good, he'll do anything he's asked, he's not very good at spotting things that need to be done but if you ask him to do something he'll do it'. Some women, however, were not totally reconciled to their situation and resented their partner's lack of co-operation. One woman, when asked if her partner ever helped, told us:

> No; full stop... he doesn't sort of see the need for washing up pots and drying them, even when I ask him he's usually got some excuse. He won't thank me for telling you this but it's true. No, I always do the pots myself and cook myself so that's that.

She wasn't entirely happy with this state of affairs:

> I often have a grouse about who's going to do the pots afterwards 'cos I'm not one for getting up and doing them immediately, they quite often get left till the following morning which annoys me when I have to get up early. I know sort of if I've not done them it's my own fault but – I'm quite ashamed of it really. But I get so tired in the evenings sometimes I feel 'Oh I can't take that', you know.

If women worked in the evenings this made it more likely that their partners would do the washing up:

> Well I go to work you see at twenty past five and he always washes up afterwards which is quite good. He'll lay the table if I ask him.

This was not, however, always the case, as one woman described:

> Well what used to happen is I'd cook the meal and have it all ready and we'd sit down and eat it, I'd go to work and I'd come back and the pots would be left for me – which they are always left for me when I come home and I either do them when I come home or the next morning... I got quite fed up of this at one stage so I said 'Right you can cook the tea then'. I feel awful saying to cook the tea but when I'm working.... That's how I got it changed over you see 'cos I thought bugger it he can cook it and I'll wash it up after.

Obviously some men are prepared to change the gender division of labour to a certain extent if their partners make an issue of it, and it does seem that if women work outside the home men are more likely to help with mealtime tasks, although not, as we saw earlier, with cooking itself. Those women who were full-time housewives were much less likely to receive regular help from their partners than were women working outside the home, whether part-time or full-time. For example, over half the men married to women who were in paid employment helped with washing up on a regular basis (3 of the 4 men married to full-time and 54 per cent of those married to part-time workers) compared with a little over a third (38 per cent) of men married to women who were full-time housewives. However, apart from washing up, which appears to have become something most men do from time to time, it is a minority of men who are involved in these tasks. Meals, their preparation and all the work they involve, remain largely a woman's domain despite the impact of women's employment outside the home.

Work patterns are obviously crucial to this division of labour. Men being out all day was cited time and again as the main reason why women did all the cooking and why men could not be expected to take their share of these domestic tasks. This is emphasized by the changes that take place, although fairly minimal, when women are also working outside the home, and by the observations made by women about the increased involvement of their partners at weekends or during their holidays.

Clearly, in most of the families men were conspicuous by their absence from tasks connected with food preparation and clearing away after a meal. And when they were involved they were helping their wives. In other words, the chores were the women's responsibility and the amount of help they received with them depended on the good will and availability of their partners. Most of the women we spoke to accepted this division of labour with little criticism, particularly if they did not themselves have work outside the home. All the tasks associated with food and mealtimes were accepted as part of being a full-time wife and mother; a change in the gender division of labour might become part of the family agenda when women worked outside as well as inside the home.

Children and Cooking

Given women's views of the root cause of men's inability to cook and lack of interest in cooking, it is interesting to look at their attitudes towards the participation of their own children in cooking and food preparation. One of the women graphically described her own father's lack of cooking skills when she was asked if she thought men should cook:

> Oh I definitely think they should be able to do something because my dad is the most useless person at cooking. If anything happened to my mum my dad would live on cornflakes I think. He's awful, he can't – no I won't say he can't – he won't be bothered to do things for himself. When my mum goes to work she leaves him a sandwich for his lunch and if it's cold she does him soup, a packet soup. Well a packet soup you have to boil for five minutes or whatever – now she has to boil it for that five minutes so that he can just heat it up because he wouldn't be bothered to wait for five minutes. *I think boy children should be taught at school how to cook – I think it should be compulsory that they are taught how to look after themselves.* (Our emphasis.)

This sort of attitude seems to indicate that although men's participation in cooking and other mealtime tasks is minimal, that of their sons will be altogether different. However, our evidence suggests that although a number of women subscribe to these sorts of views, the majority are bringing up their children in conformity with the dominant gender division of labour. Socialization of children, at least as far as food is concerned, is differentiated along lines of gender.

We talked to the women about the ways in which their children helped in the kitchen and from these discussions it became clear that attitudes towards children's help depended very much on gender, even when a conscious attempt was being made to move away from these stereotypes.

Baking was the most likely form of food preparation for children to participate in and was often regarded as play. It was also seen as an appropriate occupation for boys and girls; after all, it is a game rather than the serious matter of feeding the family:

> When I bake he always lends a hand. He will always weigh the flour, he'll scoop it out of the big jars and things and put it onto my scales...and roll the pastry out...help me bake cakes and stir things. And whisking, he'll sometimes hold the handles of the mixer and mix things for me. It's just to keep him entertained as much as anything. (Son aged three years.)

> They help with baking – it's fun for them to cut out the shapes. (Sons five-and-a-half and three-and-a-half years.)

Some women noted differences between their boy and girl children in the amount they helped and often there is a clear attitude on their part that it is more appropriate for girls to help than boys:

> Stuart (four) shows more interest, *he should have been a girl*. I love to bake and he's the one that's in the kitchen wanting to do it . . . but Sarah (seven) keeps out of the kitchen, she keeps out of the way. (Our emphasis.)

> Emma sets the table ready for me and she'll – when I've done the vegetables she usually puts them in the pans for me. The boys don't do anything but Emma helps quite a lot.

Emma's brothers were positively discouraged by their father from helping in the kitchen:

> He doesn't mind them playing in the kitchen, he's a real chauvinist – he likes a man to be a man and he doesn't like anything like that particularly. . . . They play in the kitchen but they will never help like Emma does. (Boys one-and-a-half and four, girl seven.)

Several women mentioned that their daughters were more helpful than their sons. But in these cases it is difficult to assess whether this was due to their sex or their age, as in other families with two children of the same sex the younger one often seemed inclined to be more helpful. However, if the younger more helpful child was a girl women often gave their sex as the reason for their being more helpful:

> Sue's more interested. . . . If I start washing up she'll say, 'I'll dry for you mummy', and she'll pull the chair up and dry the pots for me so she's good, she's more into – well I suppose she's a little girl, she sees what I do. . . . But Martin won't, very rarely will he help me but I don't mind I just – sometimes I get mad with him, I'll say 'Look will you fold your clothes up?' (Girl four and a half, boy seven and a half.)

Some women consciously tried to ensure that their sons and daughters helped equally: 'As they get older I'll want them both to help, I had to help my mother and Gilbert had to help his mother' (girl three, boy one year eight months). Interestingly, even when women seemed to want their sons to learn to cook, differences emerged in the way that they spoke about girls and boys. One woman was asked whether she would teach the boys how to cook when they were older. This was in the context of her description of her partner's total inability to cook:

> Yes. Our Mark (nine years old) – they do a certain amount at school now when they get older and Mark will help. Say if there's something he wants to do then I'll do it with him but I think they should know how to look after themselves yes. [What about Rebecca (two years old), is it something you'll encourage her to do?] Oh yes. She sits on my work top and holds the mixer now and things like that

now. Oh yes I shall definitely teach her to cook properly – if she has a husband like mine she'll need to know.

This difference in treatment needs no comment, particularly when the ages of the children are taken into account. But it indicates the influence school can have on attitudes and practices regarding cooking. Another woman also mentioned this:

Yes they'll lay the table if I ask them to and they're quite good at clearing away. Julia occasionally likes to cook and Sam does cooking at school so he will experiment at home from time to time. (Boys aged fourteen and four years, girl eight years.)

The event of boys learning to cook at school was regarded positively by all the women whom it directly affected.

Women's attitudes towards their children helping varied. It seemed clear that most children, given the chance, enjoyed joining in tasks in the kitchen, but while some women let them help others found their help to be more of a hindrance than anything else:

She's just starting to take an interest. If I'm in the kitchen she's got to be in the kitchen. If I'm at the sink she's got her chair or stool at the sink – she loves it if I do any baking 'cos I let her slop it around a little bit or I give her some pastry to play with. She'll wash the dishes only I have to go and wash them again 'cos she's not done them properly, and she gets water all over the floor and down her sleeves and everywhere, but I don't stop her. They like to play with water so I let her do it. (Girls three and one).

They do try but, I know it's awful, I get impatient and I do tend to tell them to get away. I feel a bit rotten afterwards. I mean they've got to learn haven't they? (Girl three, boy one)

A number of women mentioned that the kitchen was a potentially dangerous place for toddlers, particularly as far as cooking was concerned, and very few children actually helped with meal preparation:

I try and keep him out of the way because he tends to reach over the cooker to see what's in the pans and I don't like that. The kitchen is only small so it could be dangerous (Boy four, girl seven).

Some women also didn't insist on their children helping because they felt that they would have enough to do when they were older:

I ask, they don't do it off their own bat. They will take their own plates out and put them in the kitchen and I'll say 'Who's going to do the washing up?' If I didn't say anything they wouldn't do it. It's a thing I've never pressed and I think it's because I'm not bothered. They like to go out and play so as far as I'm concerned they can go. They will do plenty when they get older so I don't stress it to them at all. (Daughters eleven, seven and one.)

This usually only applied to women's attitude towards daughters!

It seems clear from these comments that there are differences in the amounts that children helped in the kitchen, and that these differences relate to the age and sex of the children and the attitudes of the women themselves. Gender seems to be an important factor in determining whether women and men encourage or discourage their children from helping with cooking and other domestic tasks. It also seems that most very young children are enthusiastic about joining in with these tasks whether they are girls or boys; it is only gradually that they learn which tasks are appropriate to their gender.

Responsibility for Shopping

Shopping for food is another task which is defined as women's work within familial ideology and the vast majority of women we talked to did all or most of the food shopping. Of the women 92 (46 per cent) were wholly responsible for the food shopping – they shopped for food on their own. Only three of the men did the food shopping on their own. In 21 (10.5 per cent) of the families men and women shared the food shopping, either taking it in turns to shop or doing it together, and in 82 (41 per cent) of the families the women did most of the food shopping themselves with some help from their partners. This sort of help was usually driving women to the supermarket for the main shop, looking after the children in the supermarket aisles, or buying the odd item of food from time to time.

Given this sexual division of labour over food shopping, it is not surprising that the majority of the women – 170 (85 per cent) – said that it was they who decided what food was bought, while most of the others said that they made these decisions in consultation with their partners and children. It was not only the women who did all the food shopping on their own who decided on what food was bought, for even when men participated in food shopping their involvement tended to be tangential rather than central. Typically, they provided the transport and helped carry the shopping; they pushed the trolley or helped to look after the children; and occasionally they made individual forays down supermarket aisles for items already decided upon by their partners. One woman, whose husband took her in the car to the supermarket, described this typical pattern:

I think because we have three kids he's more or less keeping them in order and if I'm going to queue up at the cheese counter I'll say to him, 'Will you get the yoghurt?' or whatever. He's sufficiently in touch with what we are getting to know what I'm talking about. If he went by himself without a list I think it would be fairly chaotic – if I give him a list it's fine so long as I'm fairly precise. To him if I said 'Sugar', I would have to specify type and amounts. So mainly he's looking after the kids, pushing the trolley and occasionally we split up to get different lots of things.

Women, then, usually drew up the mental or literal list of what was to be bought and this was true even in those few cases where men did all of the food shopping. This is because shopping is, of course, intimately connected with cooking; the person who cooks knows what they require and what they have in stock: because men were rarely involved with cooking they were rarely aware of the range of foods required or of the various ways in which they might be prepared. This meant that items usually had to be specified in detail when men shopped for food:

> My husband will go, but you have to write down *everything*. He goes to the supermarket, you've even got to write down where they are – he's just not that way involved, I don't think, he's just not interested in it...if ever I've been ill and I write a list I've got to write down the *brand* of things that we get.

Understandably this led some women to feel that, as with cooking, they were better doing the job themselves. But, of course, women's expectation that men could not shop on their own initiative itself contributed to a situation in which men very rarely became efficient shoppers. Furthermore, there is some evidence that women preferred to do the shopping alone. In part, this was because shopping tended to be seen as one of the more pleasant household tasks; some women had few other opportunities either to get out of the home or indeed to spend money. As one woman whose husband never did any food shopping said:

> I don't really want him to either...I enjoy it, and I don't want him to take over. There's a certain amount of pleasure for me, shopping. I haven't lost the thrill of going into town to shop, y'know. Silly, really, isn't it? I like spending money, whatever I'm spending it on, I enjoy it.

Other women, however, felt that they could get the shopping done more quickly and efficiently if they went alone:

> If I go by myself I know what I want and get what I want, whereas if he's with me I tend to say 'Shall we have this?' or 'Shall we have that?' and I don't get a very good response from him. It doesn't work at all. I'm much, much better myself, I can think what I'm actually doing. Actually he quite enjoys going but as I say I prefer to go by myself.

And men were often reported as suggesting or picking up food which women did not consider necessary; indeed, husbands were often blamed by the women for buying food which they had not intended to purchase:

> He puts things in the basket that I wouldn't normally. You know, I can go to the supermarket and get just what I want, just what I need, but he can't, he has to buy all sorts, biscuits and cakes.

> We'll end up spending more than I would if I didn't have him with me. He goes 'Let's have some of this', 'Let's get some of that' but he does help, yes.

This sort of impulse buying created problems for women budgeting on a low income. In general, it must be emphasized that most men did not appear to be interested or keen food shoppers. Achieving a more egalitarian division of labour for food shopping appeared to some women to extract too high a cost in terms of both time and expense, while for others it was clear that men could not or should not be expected to share in shopping.

Although women were in the main the ones who decided on what food was to be bought, shopped for it and then cooked it, this responsibility is not necessarily accompanied by power and control. The social relations and gender divisions of labour within which these processes take place reveal that women's responsibilities are very circumscribed. It is, in fact, men who, both directly and indirectly, wield the power; women's own interests are subordinated to those of men. This subordination is explored in greater detail in Charles and Kerr (1988, chapter 4); here we wish to relate it to the gender division of labour within the families we spoke to as we think it is important to place women's responsibility for the purchase and provision of food in this wider context.

The Effect of Paid Employment

As we have already pointed out, the vast majority of women took daily decisions about the food that was to be bought and eaten by their families. But although women took these daily decisions, it was far more frequently men who decided on the amount of money that would be available for food expenditure. In fact, in fewer than half the families did women have the power to decide how much of the total family income would be spent on food. This was the case in forty-four families where women managed all the money and in forty families where money was managed jointly by both marriage partners. In the other families the men took out their own spending money, which was often an unknown amount (to the women), before handing over their wages (thirty-nine) or gave their wives a housekeeping allowance (fifty-two). In five families the men managed all the money, even going shopping with their partners in order to be able to sign the cheque, and in twenty households other arrangements which could not easily be classified were made. Clearly, however, the systems of money management adopted by the families we talked to meant that while women organized and carried out the food shopping, they had to work with a set amount of money decided on and handed out by their partners. In a large number of families it was therefore men who controlled food expenditure although women had the responsibility of carrying it out on a day-to-day basis. This, we would argue, is responsibility without control and is a very real demonstration of the unequal relations of power existing between men and women.

There is some support from our material for the conclusion that the power enjoyed by men results from, or is at least reinforced by, their participation in paid employment outside the home. At the time we spoke to the women most of them were at home looking after very young children. Those who did work in paid employment usually worked part-time or nights so that they could combine child-care with work outside the home. This picture contrasts strongly with the occupations of women before they had children when, almost without exception, they had been working full-time outside the home. (See Charles and Kerr (1988, table 1.1) for details of women's occupations prior to the birth of their first child.) However, most of them had had to give up work once they became mothers (it is important to note that this decision was often not made through choice) and if they managed to find work to fit in with the needs and demands of their children it was often of a lower occupational status than the work they had been doing previously. This is particularly true for women who had been doing secretarial or clerical work before they had children who often took jobs as cleaners or worked in a pub because the hours fitted in with their child-care responsibilities. With the exception of the four women in full-time employment, who were all professionals in the sphere of education, the women's work was characteristically low paid.

Most of the women's partners were, by contrast, in full-time employment, they were the ones who were bringing home the wherewithal to keep the family alive, they were, indeed, the breadwinners. In fact almost all the women (175 – 87.5 per cent) said that their partner was the main breadwinner while 7 (3.5 per cent) said they were joint breadwinners. Only two women regarded themselves as the main breadwinner, seven of the women lived alone and a further nine regarded themselves as having other sorts of arrangements. This situation clearly reflected the women's lack of status in occupational and financial terms and contrasted quite strongly with the situation that had existed prior to the birth of their first child. Even then 113 (56.5 per cent) of the women said that their partners had always been the main breadwinner. A typical response to this question was:

> It's difficult to say because we always knew that one day we'd want a family so we always lived off his income, his income always paid the bills, mine always paid the one-offs, 'cos at that time we were busy collecting our furniture and buying a car and things like that, so I suppose really we've always lived off him.

Women's wages are, realistically, regarded as impermanent if couples intend to have children; when that happens they will usually have to do without her income. But prior to this event there had been much more variety in the gender division of labour: 11 (5.5 per cent) of the women had been the main breadwinners, fairly often while their partners were students, 55 (27.5 per cent) of the women had regarded themselves and their partners as joint breadwinners, three women had lived alone and eighteen had either not lived as a nuclear family or had not responded to this question. Thus the arrival of children had pushed many couples into adopting a more sharply demarcated gender division of labour. Most of the women became financially dependent on men because they gave up their paid work to have children, and if men had previously shared some of the domestic tasks like cooking this also changed. Several of the women commented on this:

He used to do more when I worked full time . . . it's me being at home you see.

When I was working full time he finished work earlier than I and I usually left prepared what we were going to have and when I came home it was ready.

He used to cook a lot before we had Peter and I was working but now he doesn't seem to cook as much because I'm at home all day and it doesn't really bother me.

However, almost half of the men (93 – 46.5 per cent) had never cooked regularly even when their wives were working full time outside the home and only seven couples had shared cooking equally. Men's cooking was almost always sporadic and took place if their partners arrived home later than them or if they were ill. Even then it was not always the case that men cooked: 'I used to begrudge coming home, I used to get home later than him, and I didn't like going into the kitchen while he was sat down waiting for me'. Clearly, cooking, for most couples, had always been regarded as the responsibility of the women, and even those few couples who had shared cooking equally before the arrival of children adopted a much more rigid gender division of labour once they became parents. This did not always happen without resentment and regret, but even if women felt like this their partner's job outside the home was usually regarded as just cause for their not cooking or sharing other household tasks. One woman felt that because the woman is 'the one who gets lumbered [with cooking] . . . it helps if you are good at it and enjoy it'. She went on:

> At the moment I feel Graham's quite bogged down with his job and everything and I'm quite – I suppose I'm coming to terms with the fact that I'm at home all the time – whereas we used to share it and now I do it all and, I feel as though I *should*, but I do resent it a bit – that he can't help me so much. I don't expect him to because I think he's got enough to cope with just holding a job down really.

Often the type of food cooked also changed, partly because women had more time to spend on cooking and partly because they had less money. Instead of steaks or chops, which were quick and easy to cook on returning from work, stews and casseroles were made. As well as taking longer to cook they were usually cheaper. As one woman put it:

> I suppose with being working it was things for quickness like we'd buy chops to grill, steak to grill, rather than doing casseroles – more tinned vegetables, I buy more fresh vegetables now, tins of fruit for pudding and things like that.

So leaving paid work and having children has a profound effect on women and the gender division of labour within the family. It means that cooking and providing food assume much more importance for women, it takes more time and they have less money and more people to feed. Food provision moves to the centre of women's lives and, at least for the years while their children are at home, most of their waking hours are devoted to thinking about and preparing food. It is a constant preoccupation and it is clearly felt to be an important part of being a 'good' wife and mother.

REFERENCE

Charles, N. and Kerr, M. (1988), *Women, Food and Families*, Manchester: Manchester University Press.

The Household and the Labour Market

Lydia Morris

Throughout the last decade scholars in the UK from a variety of disciplines have become increasingly aware of the potential offered by the household as a focus for research, especially for the investigation of the effects of economic change. In the present chapter I would like to examine this development in two ways; first, to ask why it is that the household has risen to such prominence, from having been previously subsumed under the rather low-ranking concerns of 'family sociology'; second, I would like to examine the viability of the household approach and look more closely at precisely what is involved in attempts to understand the effects of economic change at the level of the household.

Why the Household?

Changes in the structure and availability of employment opportunities in the formal sector of the economy have begun to challenge certain taken-for-granted aspects of social life, both for the people most directly affected, who have seen the demise of the public commitment to full employment, and for sociologists, whose understanding and interpretation of social life has owed much to models of social structure based on employment relations. Over the last twenty years the UK has experienced dramatic economic decline and a major restructuring of industry and employment which has produced unprecedented levels of unemployment, changes in the nature of employment, and a marked shift in the composition of the work-force.

The number of female employees has grown by 2.5 million since 1948, much of the increase concentrated in part-time work and among married women. When set against the job loss from traditionally male-dominated heavy industry this development seemed to suggest a significant challenge to the basis of established gender relations within the household. The nuclear family household with a sole male breadwinner and 'dependent' wife seemed no longer to be viable as a basis for social organization. Thus the question of what was happening to domestic life became central for the understanding of change at a grander level, and the household as the setting in which the most fundamental aspects of gender relations are acted out was the obvious locus for research.

There are other factors which have contributed to the emergence of a household focus, one of which is a concern to understand the changing nature of work more broadly defined than paid employment in the formal sector of the economy. As rising unemployment has made paid work an increasingly unsatisfactory basis for conceptualizing social structure, interest in unpaid work has assumed correspondingly greater significance. The site of much of this work – domestic labour, self-provisioning and child care – is of course the household, and the combined interest in all these issues lead to the adoption in UK research of the 'household strategy' approach, pioneered by Ray Pahl.

In the event it proved that the creative variations thought possible in response to economic restructuring and decline (Pahl, 1980; Gershuny and Pahl, 1980) did not materialize. There was instead an emergent polarization between working and non-working households. It is the construction of a household strategy, and the constraints within which it occurs that I would like to discuss here.

Household Strategies

The notion of household strategies, often termed 'survival strategies', was first introduced in research into Third World or ghetto poverty, and the concern was simply to discover how people survived under severely constrained conditions. The idea was not well theorized and was used as a device to aid the accumulation of anthropological work revealing the details of everyday existence in the shanty town or ghetto (see Lomnitz, 1977; Peattie, 1968; Stack, 1974). Since the idea that Britain was itself becoming underdeveloped, and coming to share a number of the characteristics of Third World economies – notably high levels of unemployment and underemployment, and increasing dependence on foreign capital – Pahl's application of the strategy approach (Pahl, 1984) seemed timely and appropriate.

There are differences of emphasis between Pahl's work and the earlier survival strategy research in that the latter was adopted in circumstances under which the boundaries of the household were never rigidly defined, and often in flux, such that accounts have tended to highlight the flow of both people and resources in an ever changing situation. The household in our society, at least superficially, seems much easier to define and is assumed to have a much greater degree of stability. The strategy approach has therefore focused principally on different household outcomes in particular economic circumstances, or in Pahl's words, 'the best use of resources for getting by under given social and economic conditions', and 'how households allocated their collective effort to getting all the work they define has, or they feel needs, to be done' (ibid.: pp. 20, 113). The concern has therefore been with the division of labour between the sexes, and the apportionment of labour to different sectors of the economy – formal, hidden or underground and domestic/communal.

Whilst Pahl's work was certainly innovative, and provided a perspective through which to integrate the study of economic change at the macro level with concern about the detail of people's experience of that change at the micro level, there were certain limitations built into his endeavour. He was principally concerned to document variety in strategies, showing rather less concern for the factors constraining or facilitating different outcomes. To arrive at a fuller understanding of responses to economic change would require the examination of both the internal dynamic of the household, and its relation to the employment position or work prospects of various household members, as well as the links which connect these individuals to different kinds of work opportunities. In other words, we must examine the position of the household and its members in the labour market, and uncover the way in which that position relates to:

(a) relationships within the home, and their effects on availability or desire to seek paid work, and
(b) access to opportunities through networks of contact which may extend far beyond household boundaries.

This chapter considers these issues in the light of research in south Wales and the northeast of England; both regions which have in the past been dominated by the coal and steel industries, and which have experienced dramatic economic decline in the 1980s. Official male unemployment for the northern region at the end of 1987 stood at 13.8 per cent and in Wales at 11 per cent, as against a UK average of 8.8 per cent. By December 1989 these figures had fallen to 9.1 per cent for the north and 7.0 per cent for Wales, with the UK rate at 5.9 per cent. There are still areas within the north and Wales, however, where the figure rises to 15 per cent. Both the studies discussed here are based on intensive interviews with forty married couples, the Welsh sample being specific to men made redundant by British Steel in 1981, half of whom had found employment eighteen months on and half of whom had not. The northeast sample was more widely drawn but employed and unemployed men were equally represented.

Role Swap?

Despite predictions, role reversal did not commonly emerge as a response to male unemployment. Given rising employment for married women at a time of high male unemployment then we might expect to find women increasingly assuming the role of sole or principal breadwinner. The number of female employees rose from 33.6 per cent in 1948 to 41.7 per cent in 1980, and whilst married women made up 38 per cent of the 1951 female work-force, by 1971 the figure had risen to 63 per cent (Dex, 1986, p. 3) and was fairly stable thereafter, reaching 64 per cent in 1985 (General Household Survey, table 6.24). Conversely, male unemployment began to rise in 1966 and in March 1987 reached a peak of 13.3 per cent.

Neither the Welsh nor the northeast study showed any significant indication of role reversal. The cases that did occur were temporary, ending either because the woman left her own job or the man soon found employment himself, and were associated with both personal and marital strain. In both studies the association between male identity and paid work, and the argument that this was somehow natural, was very strong. Discussions on the viability of role reversal typically drew such comments as:

> Well it's not normal is it? We're brought up to believe in work. It's what the man does; the man's the breadwinner. (Unemployed man in Hartlepool (Morris, 1987b, p. 98))

and:

> A housewife means just that. She's supposed to stay at home.... While I was out of work I felt I wasn't playing a part in things, ashamed that I wasn't keeping my family. (Previously unemployed man, Port Talbot (Morris, 1985a, p. 231))

Such feelings in part account for the paucity of role reversals apparent in these two studies. Statistical confirmation is readily available from data compiled at national level.

The General Household Survey (GHS, 1986, table 6.18) shows that in 67 per cent of married couples where the man was employed the wife was also in paid work, whilst in homes experiencing male unemployment only 24 per cent had wives who were earning. This pattern reflects what Pahl (1984) has termed a process of social polarization, which produces a concentration of work in some homes and unemployment in others. The distinction seems to be on the increase nationally, for between 1973 and 1986 the number of two-earner couples rose by 12 per cent whilst non-earners also rose, by 10 per cent (GHS, 1986, table 6.18). Both the Port Talbot and Hartlepool studies found that any likelihood of a woman taking on the role of main wage-earner was reduced by the fact that it was judged to be financially unrewarding, the better part of their earnings being deducted from the couple's benefit claim.

A large-scale longitudinal study reported by Daniel and Stilgoe (1977), Daniel (1981) and Moylan, Miller and Davis (1984) suggested that once a married man moved from unemployment benefit with its higher disregards, to supplementary benefit (now Income Support), his wife was likely to withdraw from the labour force. Joshi (1984, p. 25) has noted additional reasons for an association of unemployment between husband and wife – an increased domestic load for the woman, a reluctance to usurp the breadwinner role, or a wish to spend time together. We should note, however, that from 1988 couples who had been unemployed for two years or more were granted a higher rate of disregard, and this could make the part-time employment of one of the partners a more attractive option – though which partner it should be may cause problems for the couple.

Married Women's Position in the Labour Market

The issue of disregards only arises because the majority of women are unlikely to command a wage which exceeds or even equals the amount claimed in benefit. The generally weak position of women in the labour market has been widely discussed (see Beechey, 1977, 1978; Dex, 1986), but of particular interest in the case of married women is their growing concentration in part-time work, and the corresponding growth in this form of employment. The proportion of female employees working part time in Britain has risen from 33.5 per cent in 1971 to 42 per cent in 1981, with the proportion of part-time employees who are female remaining stable at 83 per cent (Mallier and Rosser, 1986, p. 135). The growth in part-time work for women has continued in recent years and between 1981 and 1984 women's full-time jobs fell by 15,000, while women's part-time jobs rose by 77,000 (*Employment Gazette*, January, 1987).

Equally significant, however, is the concentration of part-time work among married women, accounting for 51 per cent of their employment in 1981, as against 15 per cent for single women, peaking for the 35–44 age group. Mallier and Rosser (1986, p. 139) offer the following explanation:

> Although the proportion of women with very young children is highest in the 25–34 age group, the percentage of this age group working part time is lower than the 35–44 age group. This is because between the ages of 25 and 34 those women without children will usually work full time, whereas those who have small children will often stop working completely.

At one level, explanation of the part-time phenomenon must be sought in the existence of a section of the potential work-force prepared to accept, or even actively seeking, part-time employment. The statistical coincidence of marital and child-care obligations has been demonstrated above. Research on a smaller scale, such as the Port Talbot and Hartlepool studies, provides some insight into the decisions made by married women seeking work, and their perceptions of the options available to them. This research reveals that given a well-established pattern of female responsibility for domestic and child-care tasks, a woman's paid work must either take account of her domestic obligations, or those obligations must accommodate her employment. For many married women then, entering paid work was found to be largely the result of exploiting informally acquired knowledge of 'suitable' work opportunities; suitability being defined as opportunities which did not interfere too severely with traditional patterns of domestic organization. Women explained their situation as follows:

I've always done part-time with these [the children] still little. I want to be here when they get in [from school], and there's the dinner to get for him. He likes it as soon as he's through the door, you know what they're like. (Married woman, Port Talbot (Morris, 1987a, p. 136))

or:

When you have children and they're only little it puts you off working 'cos you should be at home with them, and you try to manage without the money, then you start to look out for a little [i.e. part-time] job . . . it's a struggle but the money keeps you going. (Married woman, Hartlepool (Morris, 1987b, p. 96))

The constraints of women's domestic circumstances, and notably child-care needs, are clearly some part of the explanation for their concentration in part-time work, though we have also to explain the growth in employers' demand for part-time labour. Such jobs have always been more common in the service sector of the economy and this has been an area of recent employment expansion in the UK. Thus an increase in demand for part-time work may in part be a reflection of changes in the industrial structure. World recession and an emphasis on efficiency, flexibility and competitiveness have also favoured part-time workers who are less likely to be unionized or to oppose management decisions, and have commonly been denied a number of job-related benefits such as holidays, pension rights, sickness benefit, etc.

The final and perhaps conclusive influence on employers is the fact that part-time jobs are cheap jobs since below a specified earnings level (currently £41) no National Insurance contribution is required. Thus we have a configuration of circumstances whereby both married women and employers find part-time employment to their convenience, with the effect that married women are confirmed in their role as secondary rather than sole or principal earners.

Domestic Labour

Another aspect of role reversal does not concern responsibility for paid employment outside the home, but rather the distribution of responsibility for unpaid work inside the home, i.e. for domestic labour. Both the Port Talbot and the Hartlepool study found considerable resistance from men to the suggestion that they assume the 'housewife' role; indications of increased domestic responsibility for men, either in response to their wife's employment, or as a result of their own unemployment, were slight. Such adaptation was more likely, though never substantial, where both members of the couple were in employment than in cases of male unemployment. Job loss seems to constitute a threat to male gender identity, and this threat is heightened if the man assumes what are commonly regarded to be essentially female tasks.

The Port Talbot study looked in considerable detail at variety between couples, and found that despite differing degrees of flexibility or rigidity on the part of men there was an identifiable core division of labour termed 'traditional' (Morris, 1985a) which received normative support and was detectable in all homes. Although there was some evidence of a blurring of the boundaries between male and female responsibilities within the home this was in no way sufficient to constitute a threat to the established roles. Male defence of the traditional division was strong in both Hartlepool and south Wales, and expressed in statements such as:

> My job's earning and hers is the house. I wouldn't want to do it [housework] and she wouldn't want me to. It's her job.

> We discussed her going to work but I don't think I could handle it here. There's certain things they need their mothers for.

> No chance. I wouldn't mind the kids all day. (Hartlepool (Morris, 1987b, p. 94))

> He doesn't like housework anyway. I suppose he thinks it's not manly. He'd dust and tidy downstairs but he won't do upstairs because no one sees it, and he won't clean the front windows in case the neighbours see him.

> It wouldn't work and he wouldn't stand it and there'd be more quarrels than it's worth. I'd rather do the work myself. (Port Talbot (Morris, 1985a, pp. 230–1))

These findings are confirmed by a number of large-scale studies, notably Pahl (1984), Gershuny et al. (1986) and Laite and Halfpenny (1987), as well as recently published official statistics. *Social Trends 19* (HMSO, 1988) states that despite the rise in married women's employment, in 88 per cent of households women are responsible for washing and ironing, in 77 per cent they usually prepare the evening meal and in 72 per cent they do the household cleaning. The report concludes that:

> Greater acceptance of a woman's right to work outside the home does not (yet) appear to have translated itself into a sense of egalitarianism in the allocation of tasks within the home.

This distribution of domestic tasks and responsibilities has wider implications affecting the organization of household finance, the use of men's and women's personal resources, and the motivation of married women to seek employment.

Inside the Household

It is clear from discussion so far that an obvious starting point for the study of a 'household strategy' will be the division of responsibility for domestic labour. Rather more interesting, however, and certainly much less fully explored, is the question of the organization of household finance, and the relationship between individual access to funds, the allocation of spending responsibilities and the motivation to seek employment. An enquiry into these questions would necessarily challenge the assumption of consensuality implicit in the notion of a 'household' strategy, for as they imply, the household cannot be treated unproblematically as a unit.

Our attention must then be focused on the tension between individual and collective or household consumption, and the impact of this tension on labour market behaviour, attitudes and aspirations. Clearly the motivation to work will not be a major determinant of employment status where (a) job availability is low and (b) selective methods of channelling information and opportunities are decisive. There are, however, a number of ways in which the distribution of responsibilities within the household may influence the labour market behaviour of its members.

If we begin from a traditional sexual division of labour – as most married couples in Hartlepool and Port Talbot do – then this allocates to the man the responsibility for meeting household needs from the wage. As we have noted, however, the last thirty years have seen the viability of the nuclear family model with a sole male breadwinner undermined by high levels of unemployment for men, and increasing labour-force participation of married women. How do financial arrangements or 'strategies' *internal* to the household accommodate these changes, and how do these arrangements influence behaviour in the labour market?

The Woman's Wage

Female principal earners among married couples are rare and this has been attributed to the benefit ruling on additional earnings, the part-time nature of many employment opportunities for women, and women's preference for such employment because of domestic obligations. Thus most women who are employed have working husbands. A full understanding of their motivation to take up employment is dependent upon an appreciation of the workings of the household's financial system. Although I found little evidence of male resistance to a woman taking on employment when the man was working there was a general lack of awareness of the necessity for the woman's wage in many homes. This can be explained in a number of ways.

In a majority of households there was a rigid demarcation of financial responsibilities between men and women. Although the details of arrangements varied it was common to find the woman in charge of spending on food and often, though not in all cases, on rent and possibly the payment of bills. Amongst homes where the man was in employment this spending by the woman was accommodated by the payment of an 'allowance' from the man's wage. The size of the allowance was sometimes an area of contention, providing a means by which the man might endeavour to economize, either in favour of their personal spending or to accommodate other collective needs. Whatever the motive, data from Hartlepool suggest that many men were rigid in their allocation of the allowance:

It's not that I can't manage on what I bring home. It's just that I'm trying to get her to manage on what I give her. That way we might get a bit behind us like. (Employed husband, Hartlepool (Morris, 1987b, p. 92))

It was also usual for women in paid employment to use their wage to augment the allowance, whilst the necessity for doing so was not always acknowledged or perceived by the man. One man's remark on his wife's part-time employment was:

It's not that we needed the money. It's just that it helps her a bit with the house-keeping. (Employed husband, Hartlepool (ibid.: p. 93))

Similarly in Port Talbot, women's part-time work sometimes served to reduce the demands made on the husband's wage (Morris, 1984a, p. 509). The bread-winner image thus remains in art, although in fact the difficulty of covering all the necessary expenditures out of housekeeping money turned out to be a major motivation for women to seek work. This may in different homes be variously the result of a lost battle over the size of the allowance, an appreciation of the difficulties imposed by their husband's low wage, or a reluctance to confront the issue.

Unemployment and Household Finance

In cases of unemployment, relatively small amounts earned in the informal sector of the economy can be important additions to household or personal income, although the motivation for such earnings varies considerably, especially between the genders. Activity in the informal sector is fairly common amongst men though I would emphasize it is not highly remunerative. The common uses of the proceeds are as follows: (a) to finance minimal male social activity; (b) to meet unexpected demands on the household budget; (c) to maintain male contacts, work identity and gender identity. Informal earnings among women were much less common, and typically used for children's needs, and in the purchase of food.

The 'household' strategy in benefit-dependent homes, or where income is very low, is to place priority on items of collective expenditure commonly handled by the woman, and at least notionally to pass all control of income over to her, but this strategy has different implications for husband and wife. It places the burden of stretching inadequate income on her shoulders, as well as the need to economize, and to increase the value of that income by her labour. Added to this is the strain of making decisions about her husband's spending, and endeavouring to enforce them. If she holds the household income he will have to approach her for spending money, or forego any specifically personal expenditure, and with it the social contact it provides.

In these circumstances the husband's strategy may be to put pressure on his wife to meet his needs, to reduce his own spending requirements, or to seek alternative ways of funding his personal spending. This is the major motivation for a man to seek opportunities in the informal sector of the economy. The rigid demarcation of responsibilities, as well as a segregated social pattern, encourages a view which sees benefit money as 'her money', and any additional income the man can generate as 'his money'. Men's use of informal sector activity may be seen, like part-time employment for women, as a *personal* strategy for dealing with constraints which derive from internal household dynamics.

Gender Roles and Support Mechanisms

It is perhaps worth noting here that the social network can play a considerable part in shoring up traditional gender roles. A long-established line of argument in the sociology of the family derives from Elizabeth Bott's insight that the degree of jointness or segregation in a married couple's domestic and leisure activities is associated with the nature of their social network (for discussion see Morris, 1985b). Data from my own research suggests that rigidity in domestic roles is most likely to occur where there is a highly developed and interconnected social network, whilst flexibility in domestic roles will be more likely where social contact is individualistic, and hence exerts minimal consensual influence.

Material aid in money or goods which flows along these networks does, however, acknowledge the locally sanctioned gender responsibilities. Support passes between members of the same gender and facilitates the fulfilment of traditional roles. This is most noticeable in cases of male unemployment where male support is in the maintenance of some social activity through the pub or club, whilst women receive gifts of food or children's clothes, and help with domestic costs. Such exchange between households is not a well developed area of research in the UK, however.

We noted earlier that the idea of a survival strategy first appeared in a literature concerned with Third World or ghetto poverty, and studies in this mode seek to accomplish a detailed description of shanty town or slum life. Supportive exchanges between women have played a central role in such research. Whilst Pahl's appropriation of the concept of a strategy has proved fruitful, and has certainly stimulated a considerable amount of related research, his emphasis on sources of labour and his concern with household outcomes have meant an almost complete neglect of those areas which characterize the Third World studies – the regular flows of information and aid across household boundaries. Such flows may be significant in a number of ways, but notably in facilitating access to employment.

Access to Opportunities

In seeking some understanding of the employment mix in different households we must have some idea of the opportunities or alternatives available, and the varied means of access for members of different households. It has long been established that strength in the labour market varies with age, such that long-term unemployment tends to be concentrated at the beginning or end of working life. The old are more likely to have opted for redundancy, or having lost one job to have greater difficulty in gaining another, whilst the young will lack the skills and experience which would make them attractive to an employer. My research findings also reveal other factors which turn out to be age related, though not directly determined by age.

The importance of informal contacts in access to employment is apparent from statistics gathered at national level (GHS 1983, table 7.40). If we define informal access as the acquisition of employment either through friends and relatives, or direct approach by or to an employer, the proportion of male employees who found work through informal methods is 57 per cent, and of female employees, 58 per cent. Whilst this level has been relatively stable since 1973, over the same period formal advertising has fallen from 27 per cent to 16 per cent, though with the importance of job centres rising from 7.5 per cent to 17 per cent within this category.

In Hartlepool there is a long-established tradition of informal recruitment, with older members of families introducing the younger ones into employment, speaking for them to employers, guaranteeing the quality of their labour, and effectively providing an informal means of discipline. It is not possible from the scale of this study to say whether the proportion of jobs acquired through such means has risen, though we should note that of twenty employed men in the sample, fourteen (68 per cent) found their job through informal means. Informal recruitment will be used when there are large numbers of potential candidates and the employer wishes to reduce the labour of selection. It will also tend to be used to reduce the costs of recruitment, notably for temporary and/or low-paid jobs, to ensure acceptance of poor terms and conditions and avoid 'trouble makers', and also to secure particular sorts of skills (see Morris, 1984b). Informal contacts will thus exert a strong influence on the strategies *available* to particular households.

Although national figures show the formal/informal job access ratio to have changed little since 1973, what does seem likely is that the significance of informal access will have increased markedly as a sorting mechanism, and consequently as a determinant of individual employment prospects. Informal access will be a major means by which those successful in the labour market are distinguished from the unsuccessful. At least notionally any potential employee can respond to a publicly advertised vacancy; only those privileged with information can respond to an informally or 'selectively' advertised vacancy. Such recruitment is often through informal channels, dependent on previous experience, usually through work-based contacts – either approach by a previous employer or as a result of contact with a member of the existing work-force. It is interesting that at the national level the success of workers making an approach to employers has fallen off since recession (GHS 1983, table 7.40), whilst direct approach by employers has shown considerable increase.

Fitting Workers to Jobs

There may of course be significant variation in the nature of the market for labour between regions: the impact of the BSC steel redundancies on the structure of employment opportunities in Port Talbot is a good example of this. The redundancies were a result not simply of reduced production but a reorganization of the production process. Certain areas of work previously performed by BSC employees went out for tender by contracting firms. The nature of employment which resulted was short term and often skill specific. It certainly favoured those with previous experience, and informal networks of contact proved an effective means of identifying and recruiting men available for work and having the appropriate credentials, i.e. the old BSC employees (Morris, 1984a). This had an added advantage for the employer, allowing recruitment for a nominal wage, with workers claiming make-up pay from EEC funds for up to two years after the redundancy.

Such provisions, as well as the shift to contracting out work, changed the nature of the labour market. This is something of a contrast with Hartlepool where steel production, which was an important part of the town's economic history, had ceased completely by the late seventies. There is evidence of the increasing use of contract labour in other areas of employment in the town (Morris, 1986). One example is work at the BSC pipe mill, but more generally, transport and maintenance are the common areas of change. Contract work is, however, dependent on the *survival* of large-scale enterprise which the contracting firms would be called in to service. This is one way of holding down production costs in recession, and suggests limitations on the job creation potential of small-scale enterprise. It is certainly a development which affects the nature of jobs available, and possibly the distribution of employment opportunities by virtue of the informal channels used to identify appropriate workers.

One particularly significant use of informal recruitment has been to locate women seeking specifically part-time work. The low costs of the method and the certainty of acceptance of low pay and poor conditions of employment are important here from the point of view of the employer. Correspondingly, there are many married women who need a supplement to the income their husband's wage provides, but who cannot accommodate their domestic and child-care obligations if they enter full-time employment. They accordingly use friendship and kinship links to seek out part-time work.

What is clear so far is that the strategy adopted by any particular household is structured by more than a collective, calculative distribution of the labour of different household members according to perceived returns from different spheres of activity (e.g. Becker, 1981). The work pattern for any given household will be formed by some interaction between the particular characteristics of local employment opportunities, the nature of the social world in which the household is located, and the sorts of employment options available to or denied household members by virtue of that location.

The Social Segregation of the Long-term Unemployed

We have become familiar with arguments about the emergence of two Britains, the rift in our society between the 'haves' and 'have nots'. There is little evidence available, however, beyond a classification of household units, of how deep that rift may be. Data collected in the two studies under discussion throws some light on this issue when applied both to the question of mutual aid across household boundaries, and to employment prospects.

The first point of major importance is the residential clustering of the long-term unemployed. A weak position in the labour market has led to the concentration of the unemployed in large, local authority estates. The residential pattern to emerge is to some extent age related, with the middle aged who entered the labour market at a time of relative expansion having used their position to secure home ownership, whilst those more recently arrived in the labour market have been less able to do so. This section of the population will be housed together on the relatively new council estates, whilst the slum clearance of the fifties produced estates with now ageing populations.

The indications are that a coincidence of weakness in both the labour market and (as a result) the housing market, have led to spatial clusters of unemployment. This seems to have created circumstances amenable to flows of mutual aid, and it is notable that exchanges pass predominantly between those in like circumstances; aid is not typically from the employed to the unemployed. This is partly a result of a strategy of avoidance but more significant is the recurrence of unemployment in extended families. The concentration of unemployment in the family household has been noted in Payne's (1987) analysis of national statistics, but my own research found evidence that this tendency extends beyond the household to larger groups of kin. This, of course, will also affect the employment prospects of the unemployed.

It is informative to refer at this point to Third World studies (Lomnitz, 1977; Peattie, 1968; Arizpe, 1978; Perlman, 1976) which illustrate the role of kin networks in the provision of work opportunities, often in the context of rural/urban migration. A recent work by Grieco (1987) in the UK also focuses on the capture of opportunities by particular kin groups, and the importance of kin known to an employer in guaranteeing the performance and acceptability of a new recruit. All of these pointers suggest that the social segregation of the long-term unemployed may become self-perpetuating – the dependence on others in like situations for support, and the absence of contacts with the world of work which might lead to job opportunities.

These are also circumstances in which subcultural attitudes are likely to develop, especially where the clustering is of young households with little previous experience of employment. It is here that peer group reinforcement is most likely to develop, often revolving round mutual collaboration and/or competitiveness in informal economic activity. This argument should not, however, be seen as a revival of the 'Culture of Poverty' thesis (Lewis, 1965) or 'Cycles of Deprivation' (MacGregor, 1981). Such an orientation seeks to explain disadvantage at the level of the family and the individual through inadequate socialization. The present discussion has attempted to suggest what social mechanisms might be operating to place one household rather than another in the category of the 'have nots'.

Recent reports have drawn attention to improved economic growth and in the year to October 1987 the total claiming benefit fell by 169,000 nationally (*Independent*, 18 November 1987), representing a fall of 15 per cent nationally, and a fall of 12.6 per cent in long-term unemployment. This brought long-term unemployment to its lowest in four years, although it was reported in August 1987 that the long-term unemployed as a proportion of the total unemployed had risen from 41 per cent to 42.6 per cent over the previous year (*Independent*, 20 August 1987).The position of the long-term unemployed is highlighted by a report from the Institute of Manpower Studies (Meager and Metcalf, 1987) which states that the long-term unemployed are likely to be rejected in at least 50 per cent of jobs because they lack motivation, work habit, ability to do the job and flexibility. More recently (*Independent*, 27 November 1987) a government drive to help the long-term unemployed which involved calling in almost 1.2 million people to job centres for interviews resulted in only 0.5 per cent going into jobs. It seems that the long-term unemployed will be the last to benefit from recovery, and I have tried to suggest here that this may, at least in part, be accounted for by their segregation from the informal means by which to influence a prospective employer.

Conclusions

This chapter has attempted to expand the application of the concept of the 'household strategy' to place a greater emphasis on factors outside the control or even knowledge of household members; factors which are related to the nature and operation of the local market for labour. Of central importance are methods of recruitment and the structure of opportunities available for men and women respectively, as well as their interaction with benefit rulings. Without some attention to the social and economic environment of the household, what I have termed the position of the household in the labour market, the process by which different strategies emerge cannot be uncovered.

It has also been suggested that household work patterns would be influenced by the internal dynamic of the household, especially the allocation of financial responsibilities and resources. The nature of financial arrangements in many homes led us to suggest that the idea of a household strategy or collective household endeavour is not adequate for the analysis of homes in which individual interests may conflict. These conflicting interests can be crucial to an understanding of labour market behaviour.

An emphasis on labour, whether paid or unpaid, or in the formal or informal sector of the economy, has also served to distract attention away from other components in a household's survival, notably the exchange of information and influence, and the flow of mutual aid between households. These questions require that we examine groupings of households both in terms of spatial concentrations of unemployment, and employment status and social relations within extended families. With this broadened perspective we may arrive not only at an improved understanding of what goes on inside households, but also achieve a more precise idea of the ways in which, and means by which, individual households are located within local social structures.

REFERENCES

Arizpe, L. (1978), *Migracion, Etnicismo y Cambio Economic*, Mexico City: Colegio de Mexico.

Becker, G. (1981), *A Treatise on the Family*, Cambridge, MA: Harvard University Press.

Beechey, V. (1977), 'Some notes on female wage labour in capitalist production', *Capital and Class*, 3: 45–66.

Beechey, V. (1978), 'Women and production', in A. Kuhn and A. M. Wolpe (eds), *Feminism and Materialism*, London: Routledge and Kegan Paul.

Daniel, W. W. (1981;), *The Unemployed Flow: Interim Report*, London: PSI.

Daniel, W. W. and Stilgoe, S. (1977), *Where are They Now?*, London: Eyre and Spottiswoode.

Dex, S. (1986), *The Sexual Division of Work*, Brighton: Wheatsheaf.

Gershuny, J., Miles, I., Jones, S., Mullings, C., Thomas, G. and Wyatt, S. (1986), 'Preliminary analysis of the 1983/4 ESRC time budget data', *Quarterly Journal of Social Affairs*, 2: 13–39.

Gershuny, J. and Pahl, R. E. (1980), 'Britain in the decade of the three economies', *New Society*, 3, January, 7–9.

Grieco, M. (1987), *Keeping it in the Family*, London: Tavistock.

Joshi, H. (1984), *Women's Participation in Paid Work*, Research Paper No. 45, London: Department of Employment.

Laite, J. and Halfpenny, P. (1987), 'Employment, unemployment and the domestic division of labour', in D. Fryer and P. Ullah (eds), *Unemployed People*, Milton Keynes: Open University Press.

Lewis, O. (1965), 'The culture of poverty', in *La Vida*, Toronto: Random House.

Lomnitz, L. (1977), *Life in a Mexican Shanty Town*, London: Academic Press.

MacGregor, S. (1981), *The Politics of Poverty*, Essex: Longman.

Mallier, A. T. and Rosser, M. J. (1986), *Women and the Economy*, London: Macmillan.

Meager, N. and Metcalf, H. (1987), *Recruitment of the Long Term Unemployed*, Sussex University: IMS Report 138.

Morris, L. D. (1984a), 'Redundancy and patterns of household finance', *Sociological Review*, 32: 492–522.

Morris, L. D. (1984b), 'Patterns of social activity and post redundancy labour market experience', *Sociology*, 18: 339–52.

Morris, L. D. (1985a), 'Renegotiation of the domestic division of labour', in B. Roberts, R. Finnegan and D. Gailie (eds), *New Approaches to Economic Life*, Manchester: Manchester University Press.

Morris, L. D. (1985b), 'Local social networks and domestic organization', *Sociological Review*, 33: 327–42.

Morris, L. D. (1986), 'The changing social structure of Hartlepool', in P. Cooke (ed.), *Global Restructuring, Local Response*, 1 ESRC Imprint.

Morris, L. D. (1987a), chapters 6 and 7 in C. C. Harris (ed.), *Redundancy and Recession in South Wales*, Oxford: Blackwell Publishers.

Morris, L. D. (1987b), 'Constraints on gender', *Work, Employment and Society*, 1: 85–106.

Moylan, S., Miller, S. and Davis, R. (1984), *For Richer for Poorer*, DHSS cohort study of unemployed men, London: HMSO.

Pahl, R. E. (1980), 'Employment, work and the domestic division of labour', *International Journal of Urban and Regional Research*, 4: 1–20.

Pahl, R. E. (1984),. *Divisions of Labour*, Oxford: Blackwell Publishers.

Payne, J. (1987), 'Does unemployment run in families?', *Sociology*, 21: 199–214.

Peattie, L. R. (1968), *The View from the Barrio*, Ann Arbor: University of Michigan Press.

Perlman, J. (1976), *The Myth of Marginality*, Berkeley: University of California Press.

Stack, C. (1974), *All Our Kin*, New York: Harpers.

Part IV

Divorce and Lone-parenthood

As the title indicates, Part IV of this volume is concerned with the impact of divorce and lone-parenthood. A little over thirty years ago, it is unlikely that a book like this would have contained a section on these topics. At that time there were relatively few divorced people and relatively few lone-parent households. However, over the last two generations, patterns of family and household formation and dissolution have changed dramatically, as discussed in the introduction. For example, it is estimated that nearly half of those marrying in the late 1990s will eventually divorce. As importantly, fewer people are now choosing to marry, and those that do are marrying later. The numbers of children born outside marriage has increased dramatically, now standing at a third of all births, though roughly half of these are born to couples cohabiting at the time. However, there is no reason at all to believe that these unions will prove to be any more long-lasting than marriage; most indeed will be less permanent. Those who have children young are particularly likely to be single parents, with currently 17 out of every 20 teenage mothers being unmarried.

As a result of divorce and births outside marriage, there are now estimated to be approximately 1.4 million lone-parent families, with roughly 20 per cent of children living in such a family. Moreover, more children than this will experience living in a lone-parent family at some period in their lives; lone-parent families end not just as a result of children becoming adult but also as a result of their parents forming new partnerships. Some 90 per cent of all lone-parent families are mother-headed, and some four-fifths of these are dependent on state benefits or otherwise close to the poverty line. The implications of the increased number and disadvantaged material circumstances of lone-parent families have clearly been of concern to successive governments in the 1990s. At the time of writing – spring 1998 – the new Labour government is attempting to introduce policies that will encourage more lone mothers to become employed rather than relying on welfare payments, though there are numerous tensions in this, including issues over the provision of appropriate child-care facilities and the rights mothers have to choose whether or not to be full-time carers.

There are many commonalities in the circumstances of lone-parent families. In particular, the great majority are female-headed and in relative poverty compared to nearly all two-parent families. However, there is also much diversity in their experiences. The first chapter in Part IV, written by Graham Crow and Mike Hardey and first published in *Families and Households: Divisions and Change* edited by Cathie Marsh and Sara Arber, illustrates this point particularly well. One of its arguments is that there are numerous routes into lone-parenthood, and that these different routes affect the ways in which lone-parenthood is experienced. Richards (1982) has usefully written about the need to consider the 'natural histories' of divorces – the factors leading up to separation, the way the separation itself is managed, and the relationships which are sustained after separation – if we are to understand their different outcomes. So, too, it is helpful to think of lone-parent families as having their own distinct 'natural histories' or pathways, which influence how lone-parenthood is experienced. In turn, lone-parent families, like other families, develop different 'strategies' for coping with the constraints they face and the opportunities that arise. Indeed, what one lone parent experiences as a constraint – for example, living with children in a high-rise apartment block – may be experienced by another as an opportunity – giving them, for example, welcome control over personal space (Hardey, 1989). The key point here is that while many lone-parent families experience common material and, to some degree, social disadvantages, it is none the less important to recognize the level of diversity which there is in their experiences and responses.

The second chapter in Part IV, written by Jane Millar and originally published in *Feminist Review*, is also concerned with lone-parent families. Millar focuses on issues of social policy. As already noted, the growth in the number of lone-parent families, together with a high proportion being dependent on state benefits, has led successive governments to wrestle with the problems of finding appropriate policy measures. As Millar points out, in all such policy initiatives there is a continuing tension between the relative roles of individuals, families and the state in ensuring children's welfare. After providing details of the degree of hardship typically faced by lone mothers and their children, Millar examines the impact of the Child Support Act. Brought into force in 1993, this Act aimed to ensure that fathers continued to bear financial responsibility for their children, whether or not they were living with them. As such it was an attempt to change the balance of responsibility between the family and the state, in the process reducing the state's benefit expenditure. It is contentious whether lone mothers have been financially advantaged as a result, though potentially, in line with proposals being promoted by the Labour government in the later 1990s, it can do so when lone mothers are also in employment, even if this is poorly paid. However, as Millar points out, attempts at legislating for family responsibility in such ways run into difficulty precisely because of the problem with which it is grappling: the increasing diversity of family forms in the contemporary era. Thus the Act posits that natural parents should bear financial responsibility for their children, no matter what. But is this always appropriate? Many might agree in principle that parents have an absolute responsibility to meet their children's needs, but then also recognize that parental – like other kinship obligations (see Finch and Mason, chapter 15, this volume) – are situationally framed. So, for example, should financial responsibility continue even after new partnerships are formed, either by the father or the mother? Is a father's responsibility always the same, irrespective of the circumstances of conception and the nature of the relationship there was between the two parents? Moreover, do certain rights and benefits – for example, a right to regular contact with the child – attach to financial provision? Is it always in the child's interest that this is so? In examining questions like this, Millar illustrates the complexities of framing social policies about family affairs, especially in an era where increasing diversity renders ideas of the 'normal' family highly suspect. There is now a good deal of research literature on the experiences of lone-parent families. Bradshaw and Millar (1991), Burghes with Brown (1995), Chandler (1991), Haskey (1993, 1994) and Marsh, Ford and Finlayson (1997) all contain interesting material.

One of the key issues for social policies addressing divorce and lone parenthood concerns ways of protecting the interests of children. In America, especially, there has been a great deal of research conducted into the impact of marital separation and divorce on children, though the methodological difficulties of doing this well are immense. In particular, how is it possible to tell what the longer-term effects of divorce on a child's life have been, when there is no real basis for comparison – that is, when the outcomes there would have been had there been no divorce are themselves unknown? Even knowing the short-term consequences of marital separation is problematic because few studies are able to assess a child's well-being prior to the marital disharmony occurring. None the less, given the high levels of divorce occurring, it is important both in personal and policy terms that ways of managing separation and divorce are found which minimize the longer-term impacts of the experience for different children.

Martin Richards's chapter, first published in *Familles et Justice* edited by M. T. Meulders, focuses explicitly on this. In it he brings together a wide range of material from Britain and America to examine critically what we know – and do not know – about the ways in which parental divorce affects children's well-being. It is clear that in the short-term marital separation is traumatic, disruptive and painful for nearly all children. The middle- and longer-term consequences are less clear-cut, but depend quite heavily on the way that the divorce is managed by the parents as well as on the consequences the divorce has for the child's lifestyle. For example, such factors as continuing high levels of conflict between the parents, material hardship, loss of contact with the non-residential parent (and their kin network) and disruption to schooling and peer group relationships through geographical mobility, can all result from the divorce and be damaging to children's interests. Without these 'complications', the divorce will be experienced by the child differently and, in all likelihood, have different consequences for the child's longer-term welfare. Richards's chapter is extremely useful for teasing out these different processes and highlighting the error of assuming that divorce, *per se*, has a uniform impact on the children who are affected by it. Slowly social policy is recognizing this, for example, in the provision of mediation services that encourage divorcing couples to recognize the advantages of co-operation over their children's interests, even if conflict between them continues in other spheres. As noted, much of the research literature on the impact of marital separation and divorce on children is American. Amato (1993) provides a very useful review of much of this research. The papers included in Hetherington and Arasteh's (1988) volume will also be of interest.

A final issue to raise here concerns step-families, a family form which has been increasing significantly as a direct result of the changes there have been in the numbers of divorces and births to unmarried mothers. In the late 1990s one in every fourteen children was living in a step-family, with many others being involved in step-families through their non-residential parent forming new partnerships. The numbers of people with direct experience of living in a step-family are certain to increase with the trends discussed above; furthermore, many of those without direct experience will have indirect experience through close family or friends being part of a step-family. Unfortunately, it has not proved possible to include a chapter in this volume on step-families. In part, this reflects the shortage of recent sociological research there has been in Britain on this family form. The classic study is Burgoyne and Clark's *Making a Go of It*, though the research for this took place nearly twenty years ago. There are currently a number of studies in progress that will add significantly to our knowledge of step-family patterns, but these have not yet reached publication stage. In the meantime Burgoyne and Clark's work remains an important reference, while Smith (1990) and Robinson and Smith (1991) also provide very useful analyses of many of the issues step-families face. Simpson's (1994) paper on the '*unc*lear family' (as distinct from the '*nuc*lear family') is also very insightful.

REFERENCES

Amato, P. (1993), 'Children's adjustment to divorce; theories, hypotheses and empirical support', *Journal of Marriage and the Family*, 55: 23–38.

Bradshaw J. and Millar, J. (1991), *Lone-parent Families in the UK*, London: HMSO.

Burghes, L. with Brown, M. (1995), *Single Lone Mothers: Problems, Prospects and Policies*, London: Family Policy Studies Centre.

Burgoyne, J. and Clark, D. (1984), *Making A Go of It*, London: Routledge and Kegan Paul.

Chandler, J. (1991), *Women Without Husbands*, London: Macmillan.

Hardey, M. (1989), 'Lone parents and the home', in G. Allan and G. Crow (eds), *Home and Family*, London: Macmillan.

Haskey, J. (1993), 'Trends in the number of one-parent families in Britain', *Population Trends*, 71: 26–33.

Haskey, J. (1994), 'Estimated numbers of one-parent families and their prevalence in Great Britain in 1991', *Population Trends*, 78: 5–19.

Hetherington, E. and Arasteh, J. (1988), *Impact of Divorce, Single Parenting and Stepparenting on Children*, Hillsdale, NJ: Lawrence Erlbaum.

Marsh, A., Ford, R. and Finlayson, L. (1997), *Lone Parents: Work and Benefits*, London: The Stationery Office.

Marsh, C. and Arber S. (eds) (1992), *Families and Households: Divisions and Change*, London: Macmillan.

Meulders, M. T. (1997), *Familles et Justice*, Brussels: Bruylant/Paris: Librairie général de droit et jurisprudence.

Richards, M. (1982), 'Do broken marriages affect children?', *Health Visitor*, 55: 152–3.

Robinson, M. and Smith, D. (1993), *Step By Step: Focus on Stepfamilies*, Hemel Hempstead: Harvester Wheatsheaf.

Simpson, B. (1994), 'Bringing the unclear family into focus: divorce and remarriage in contemporary Britain', *Man*, 29: 831–51.

Smith, D. (1990), *Stepmothering*, Hemel Hempstead: Harvester Wheatsheaf.

11

Diversity and Ambiguity Among Lone-parent Households in Modern Britain

Graham Crow and Michael Hardey

Lone-parent households constitute an increasingly important group in British society. Although precise estimates of their number vary, there are certainly well over a million such households, and the number is rising. One in eight dependent children currently live in one-parent families, and these family types make up one in six of all families with dependent children – a proportion which has doubled in the space of less than two decades. Of all households, 8 per cent are headed by a lone parent (over 90 per cent of whom are lone mothers) and 9 per cent of the general population live in lone-parent households (Haskey, 1989; OPCS, 1989). The number of people who live in a lone-parent household at some stage can only be guessed at on the basis of existing data, but the figure is undoubtedly high (Rimmer, 1983).

In addition to their growing numerical significance, lone-parent households are important because of certain structural characteristics of the group. For example, their poverty represents a major challenge to social policy (Millar, 1989). Unlike childless single-person householders (Bien, Marbach and Templeton, 1992), their aloneness works to exclude them from much conventional, couple-centred social life (Elliot, 1986). On the basis of this adverse economic and social situation, Field (1989) has argued that single-parent families, together with the long-term unemployed and pensioners, are among the most deprived sections of society.

The continued clustering of lone-parent households at the disadvantaged end of the social structure has confounded earlier optimism regarding their status. Chester (1977) based his claim that the situation of one-parent families was improving on their growing visibility, on greater tolerance in society, on wider economic opportunities, and on more favourable treatment in public policy. Such assessments have proved at best premature. Social changes such as the growth of separation and divorce as routes into lone parenthood have undoubtedly worked to undermine old stereotypes of 'unmarried mothers', but the material divisions between lone-parent households and other household types (in particular two-parent households) remain pronounced. Lone-parent households are still subject to a degree of social and economic marginalization which policy measures have done little to alleviate, and may even have exacerbated.

This chapter is concerned to investigate why a group as significant as lone-parent households has not secured the improvement in its situation which the growth in its numbers led commentators to expect. We suggest that part of the answer reflects the diversity of lone-parent households which limits their collective strength, while the blurred boundary surrounding lone parenthood creates ambiguities relating to identity and action as lone parents. This diversity and ambiguity found amongst lone parents also presents difficulties for social policy which have as yet been unresolved, and the chapter concludes by considering these issues.

The Evolving Category of 'Lone-parent Households'

For a long time the common situation of lone parents went unrecognized, not least in official thinking, and it is only in the last three decades that the categories 'lone-parent households' and 'one-parent families' have come into common usage. Townsend (1979, p. 754) notes that, as late as the 1960s, 'there was, significantly, no collective name for, and no official estimate of the numbers of, one-parent families', and that establishing the case for common treatment of one-parent families was a long struggle. Thus, while the Finer Report (DHSS, 1974) stands as something of a watershed by recommending the introduction of a new, non-contributory benefit that was to be available to all lone parents (the Guaranteed Maintenance Allowance), it had to be preceded by extensive argument over the unfairness and unworkability of previous classifications (Smart, 1984). The report acknowledged the force of the case against the highly generalized, imprecise and emotive term 'broken homes', and recognized as illogical the different treatment of widows and other single parents.

The term 'one-parent family' promised in addition to avoid the stigma attached to alternatives (such as 'unmarried mother' and 'unsupported mother') which conveyed a sense of deviance from a two-parent norm. This factor also contributed to the decision of the National Council for the Unmarried Mother and her Child to change its name in 1973 to the National Council for One Parent Families (MacIntyre, 1977). More recently 'lone-parent family' has come to be preferred to 'one-parent family' by some writers (Millar, 1989), although 'lone-parent household' is arguably a more precise term sociologically speaking, since many lone-parent families involve a parent who is absent from the household, not living under the same roof, but who is involved in 'family' relationships to some extent (Harris, 1983; Rimmer, 1983). Illustrating this point, O'Brien (1987, p. 225) identifies the lone fathers of her study as single parents by virtue of the fact that although their children's mothers may be involved in some way as a non-custodial parent, it is they who have 'major responsibility for care of the children'. Similarly, Hipgrave (1982, p. 173) describes lone fathers as 'the sole major parent'.

Further alternatives include 'the sole supporter' (Yudkin and Holme, 1963, p. 68), 'single-handed parents' (Blaxter, 1990, p. 228), 'solo parenthood' (Elliott, 1986, p. 152), and 'the "one-parent family" type household' (Close, 1985, p. 16), each with its own nuances, and all adding to the general uncertainty over terminology. What matters most, however, is that lone parents head a separate 'income unit' (Townsend, 1979, p. 756); single-parent families are functioning households whose organization rests on a different pattern of work to that found in two-parent families (Graham, 1984). Single parents are, as a category, 'obliged to adopt a distinctive household work strategy' (R. Pahl, 1984, p. 225).

The evolving category of single-parent families reflected a growing awareness of the disadvantaged position and particular needs common to such families, a development which challenged established conceptions. Negative stereotypes of lone parents can be traced back several centuries (Page, 1984). The general treatment of lone mothers under the Poor Law was notably punitive (Wilson, 1977), although over time the distinctions drawn between them were liable to change, altering the relative positions of widows and others, for example. Unmarried mothers were at one stage divided into two broad types, 'the young innocent who needed sensitive help and the depraved or mentally defective who required punishment or incarceration' (Ginsburg, 1979, p. 82), with such classifications being open to further subdivision (Page, 1984).

Essentially these distinctions were variations on the deserving vs undeserving poor theme. Those lone mothers falling into the latter category were seen as having more in common with other members of 'the social problem group' (where social dependency was rolled together with characteristics such as insanity and inebriety) than they did with their more sympathetically treated deserving fellows (Lewis, 1986). Even the liberal Beveridge proposals of the 1940s retained an element of this distinction by discriminating between those lone parents 'at fault' in creating their situation and those not (Millar, 1989). Unmarried mothers were still seen as essentially 'pathological'.

These moralistic distinctions between different types of lone parents broke down in the 1960s under the weight of social change, with increasing numbers of lone-parent households, and growing criticism of existing policy arrangements by both pressure groups (such as the campaigning group Gingerbread) and social researchers (such as Wynn, 1964). Typical of the latter is the following passage from a study of working mothers:

> The difficulties and distresses facing the widowed, divorced or deserted wife, or the unmarried mother, will vary enormously, but in the long run, unless they are fortunate enough to possess a private income or to have the financial support of their families, or to make or complete a family by marriage or remarriage, they will all be faced with the common problem of making ends meet on inadequate or no statutory allowances. (Yudkin and Holme, 1963, p. 69)

The presence of common problems amongst lone parents meant that it made little sense to discriminate between them for welfare purposes. Wynn's (1972, p. 237) policy conclusion was to 'raise the standards of all lone mothers and their children at least to the modest level of the widows'. Ideally, social security schemes would treat fatherless families 'simply and equitably' (Marsden, 1973, p. 4).

Yet lone-parent households are not a homogeneous or unified group, and it is an oversimplification to treat them as such. As Rimmer (1983, p. 12) notes, 'In many ways the term "one parent family" is a convenient but misleading short-hand for a complex variety of family situations', between which important lines of division exist. Earlier and more judgemental terms such as 'deserted wives', 'fatherless families', 'incomplete families' and 'broken homes' may have given way to less value-laden language, but even apparently neutral distinctions between different types of lone parent have significant implications.

The contrasting assumptions made about lone fathers and lone mothers, with the former being seen as less capable carers and the latter placing a lower priority on taking paid work, are well documented (George and Wilding, 1972; O'Brien, 1987). Further, Ginsburg (1979) has argued that the old distinction between deserving and undeserving poor continues to apply to widows and other lone parents respectively. Rightly or wrongly, certain groups of lone parents are more likely than others to be seen as having chosen lone parenthood, as being responsible for their situation, and this has a bearing on both their treatment in the formal welfare system and the extent of informal aid and assistance sought and forthcoming from kin.

A clearer sense of the common needs of lone-parent households has not produced a 'simple and equitable' scheme through which welfare support is organized. There are marked differences in lone-parent households' housing situations, for example, with over half of all widowed mothers being owner occupiers, while 93 per cent of never-married lone mothers are tenants (Haskey, 1989). More generally, Field (1989) argues that one of the main divisions currently emerging is that between lone mothers locked into long-term dependency on welfare benefits and others who pass through lone parenthood for briefer periods.

In part these divisions reflect the difficulties of defining lone-parent households for the purposes of formulating social policy. The Finer Report adopted as its working definition of a single-parent family 'a family in which there is an adult and dependent child or children, one parent or partner is absent (for whatever reason), there is no reasonable prospect of his or her return within a fairly short period and there is no effective parent substitute' (DHSS, 1974, p. 39). Graham (1984) has argued that such definitions may lose sight of several important groups of lone parents, including those with sharing arrangements which disguise their situation (such as those living with parents), and those whose children are taken into care, about whom insufficient is known.

In addition, there are definitional problems raised by the fact that lone parenthood is 'a shifting experience' (Jackson, 1982, p. 163) which needs to be understood dynamically. The boundary line around lone parenthood is in practice far from clear-cut, and definitions may fail to convey the often con-fused nature of the transitions into and out of lone parenthood at certain points, such as where lone parenthood blurs into cohabitation and the point at which children cease being dependent. The problematic nature of the boundary around the category of lone-parent households has thrown up awkward cases fairly consistently. These include the situation where women seeking protection from violent husbands experience difficulty in establishing their claim to hous-ing assistance (Brailey, 1985) or financial support (J. Pahl, 1984), and that where a mother's cohabitation with a new partner does not necessarily imply his economic support of her (Popay, Rimmer and Rossiter, 1983).

More routinely (in a bureaucratic sense), there is a genuine problem in answering Jackson's question about single-parent families, 'How long or form-ally does a family have to be split up in order to qualify?' (Jackson, 1982, p. 175) and the related issue of how long a new parent needs to be around before the label no longer applies. There have long been suspicions on the part of officials that some 'deserted' wives may be in collusion with their absent husbands, as a means of improving their eligibility for benefits – the practice of 'collusive desertion' (Ginsburg, 1979) – raising doubts about their status as lone parents. More generally the Finer Report observed that 'it is often very difficult to distinguish between temporary separations and marriages that have finally broken down' (DHSS, 1974, p. 1).

Similarly, the point of exit from lone parenthood is often hard to specify precisely. Donnison (1982), for example, notes that three-quarters of the 8,000 cases of benefits being withdrawn on grounds of cohabitation which came before the Supplementary Benefits Commission in the 1970s related to women with dependent children. He found that the procedures inevitably involved arbitrary decisions on where to draw the line concerning what counted as 'lone parenthood', confirming the view that the single-parent family's social situation is 'full of ambiguities' (Oakley, 1976, p. 70).

Having outlined the evolution of the category of lone-parent households, we now turn to consider evidence relating to the experience of lone parenthood. The argument is supported by quotations derived from in-depth interviews conducted by one of the authors, Michael Hardey, among a sample of sixty lone parents from Birmingham, London and the Home Counties. The inter-views were conducted in 1988 with lone parents who had been living on their own for at least a year. Although not formally representative, the sample included individuals from across the range of circumstances to be found amongst lone parents.

The Blurred Boundary Around the Category of 'Lone-parent Households'

Following Leete (1978) and Haskey (1986) it is possible to portray diagram-matically the various routes 'into and out of lone parenthood' (figure 11.1). Of the routes into lone parenthood, the death of a partner and births to single

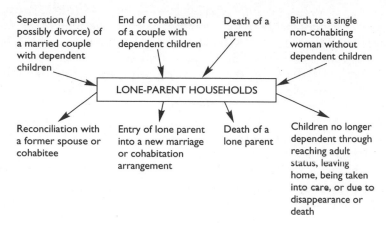

Figure 11.1   Routes into and out of lone parenthood

mothers are more or less clear-cut changes, but the ending of marriage through separation (and possibly divorce) and the ending of cohabitation are much more ambiguous processes. Similarly, the routes out of lone parenthood (marriage or remarriage, reconciliation, cohabitation, children growing up and leaving home, children being taken into care, and the death of the lone parent or child) embody a range of transitions, some sudden and simple, others prolonged and complicated.

The blurred nature of some routes into lone parenthood is not a new discovery. For example, Illsley and Thompson's study of 'broken homes' noted that 'Parental death produces a clear-cut situation and the date of the break can easily be specified. Separation and divorce, on the other hand, are usually only the final stages of a long drawn-out process' (Illsley and Thompson, 1961, p. 36). Given that most lone-parent households are created by separation and/ or divorce, with 60 per cent of lone mothers falling into this category (OPCS, 1989), closer consideration of these blurred transitions promises to illuminate the problems faced in estimating the number of lone-parent households and also to aid understanding of the diversity of lone parents' experiences and identities.

Difficulties of classifying cases were thrown up regularly in Illsley and Thompson's research by the irregularity of people's behaviour as they moved towards divorce. Sometimes the couple 'continued to live together until the formal break occurred, sometimes one or other partner left the home several times' (Illsley and Thompson, 1961, p. 36). In such circumstances, precise definitions may be inapplicable; a terminating relationship is often better understood as a process rather than an event (Maclean, 1987). The reality of becoming a lone parent, with all its confusion and ambiguity, resists attempts to impose onto it tidy classification (J. Pahl, 1984).

It is certainly the case that many individuals experience the move into lone parenthood as a lengthy transition. Hart (1976) has described the process of marital breakdown as a status passage, and suggests that 'the precise point at which a person recognizes complete dissociation from his [or her] partner in life is often hard to define. "Being divorced" is better thought of as *becoming* something than as occupying a fixed social position with well demarcated boundaries in time' (ibid.: p. 103; original emphasis). The question of when a marriage ends may have several answers, with those of the individuals involved quite possibly identifying times or periods long before official recognition is granted. The difference between the 'objective' and 'subjective' definitions of the situation came out in Hart's respondents who 'said that they had "felt divorced" months before a judge ratified their feelings' (ibid.: p. 106). Other research has found it more accurate to think of a terminating marriage's 'dead period' in terms of years (Ambrose, Harper and Pemberton, 1983).

There is in addition nothing to prevent the wishes and perceptions of two people separating being quite at variance as they renegotiate their relationship. Vaughan's (1988, p. 6) account of relationships coming apart treats it as typical that 'uncoupling' is 'a tale of two transitions: one that begins before the other'. Within these transitions there may be particular 'turning points' (Burgoyne, 1984, p. 12) that stand out, but they follow the build up of difficulties over a considerable period. For the non-initiator, the transition may not be complete at the point of divorce, and the subjective feeling of being married may continue for some time after.

As one lone mother in Hardey's research who had been divorced for two years said,

> I think it takes a time to come to terms with being a single mother. In my case I've only accepted that's what I am in the past year. I suppose before I always thought we might get back together but when he got married I had to give that up. I felt very bad at the time, but now I think it was the best thing that could happen because it made me come to terms with my life.

Another divorced lone mother spoke of it taking the greater part of two years before she 'started to surface. I had to come to terms with being a lone parent, you know, accept it as a positive thing'. This ties in with Ebaugh's (1988, p. 144) comments on divorce as an example of 'the process of role exit', where she describes the intermediate stage between being married and being divorced as a type of 'vacuum' in which the individual is neither married nor divorced.

Other routes into lone parenthood can also contain an intermediate stage of indeterminacy, even when they appear clear-cut at first sight. One single mother experienced the disadvantages of lone parenthood early when she was told by her landlord to leave her flat before her child was born: 'I had this nice little place but someone must have told the landlord I was expecting … I was a good tenant but it was made very clear to me that I would have to go'. In another way, a widower from Birmingham had experienced some of the practical aspects of lone fatherhood before his wife had died, as her illness made her incapable of contributing to the running of the household:·

My wife had got problems and it was the sort of problem where most of the time she was all right, but then the illness or whatever you want to call it would start and she'd be absolutely hopeless ... I began being a single father from almost the start. ... So when she passed on it was nothing new to me to be on my own with a young child.

Becoming a lone parent is also likely to have an impact on the income available to the household. The dealings which individuals have with official-dom may have an important part to play in shaping their new identity. One respondent's story of her interaction with the Department of Social Security brings out this point well:

I explained about myself to the woman and she said, 'Oh, you're a single parent then?' I hadn't really thought of myself like that before. ... She kept on about 'people like you', you know, single parents. I think that changed my outlook because it was like having an official stamp say that you were not an ordinary person but a single parent.

This lone parent's negative experiences of official treatment echoes other research findings (see, for example, Collins, 1992). In general, lone parents are 'singled out for more grudging and inferior assistance, and subject to more official controls over their credentials and honesty' (Lawson, 1987, pp. 93–4).

With the passage of time other interactions could generate more positive images of single parenthood, as was the case for the divorced woman who joined Gingerbread and found it 'very good because I've got lots of friends who are also in my situation and you can see that it's quite OK to be a single mum'. Another respondent spoke of reorganizing her life so that she could get herself 'established as lone parent', wanting to see how she and her child managed in the absence of her ex-husband. As time goes on, lone parents learn to develop a range of coping strategies through which they can come to be 'better off poorer' (Graham, 1987, p. 235). Even though the level of household income is almost certain to drop following separation or divorce, single mothers may have greater access to and control over household income than they had when married/cohabiting, and this may make them wary of the idea of entering a new relationship.

Further ways exist in which lone parenthood may come to be compared favourably with marriage. It may, for example, bring greater independence in the organization of home life and leisure time, at least for lone mothers (Sharpe, 1984), although the difference is not always obvious to outsiders:

It's what makes single parents different. We have to explain ourselves whereas couples are just seen as normal. You know the reaction: 'Oh dear, I'm sure you will find a nice partner soon', that kind of thing, as if you can't manage without one. I'll tell you, I'm a bloody sight better off than many women who are married and have to run around after the husband as well as the kids.

Nor is it an immediate change for people coming to terms with lone parent-hood; one of Green and Hebron's (1988) respondents spoke of it taking over four years to build up a new social life as a lone parent. The general point to draw out here is that lone parenthood is not an easy status to adapt to. In the transitional period there is no automatic association or identification with other lone parents, social isolation being the more likely outcome.

Less is known about the processes involved in the movement out of lone parenthood than is known about becoming a lone parent, but similar points apply about the boundary around the category of lone parents being blurred. In Burgoyne and Clark's study of step-families, in some instances 'the end of one relationship overlapped with the beginning of another', while others who had not initiated the ending of their first marriage went through 'a distinct stage of demarriage' (Burgoyne and Clark, 1984, pp. 70, 67). The 'ambiguities of the state of demarriage' (ibid.: p. 81) contributed to the pressures to remarry, but most of the couples in the study cohabited before getting married again, and in some of these cases it was difficult to identify a precise moment at which cohabitation began.

It is also worth noting that moving out of lone parenthood does not necessarily improve people's positions. It is quite common to find arrangements made whereby a divorced mother and children stay on in what was formerly the marital home until the children become adults, although such agreements came more grudgingly in some cases than in others. Two contrasting situations illustrate the point. One lone mother felt that her ex-husband had 'been very good. He wanted us to stay in the house even though it is really too big for the three of us. He felt that it was important that the children should keep the home and environment they were used to.'

She was under much less pressure than the lone mother who said, 'Technically we can live here until the children leave home after which the house has to be sold. My ex resents us staying here and now that he has remarried and is living abroad he can be very awkward when it comes to maintenance and things.'

Either way, however, lone parents in this situation face downward mobility in the housing market following their exit from lone parenthood. The same is true for tenants of local authorities, which place single-person households further down their list of priorities than single-parent families, although both groups are vulnerable to homelessness (Watson with Austerberry, 1986).

Opportunities, Constraints and Strategies within Lone Parenthood

In terms of their material situation and their subjective experiences, lone-parent households are neither a homogeneous social group nor, given the blurred boundary that surrounds them, a type of people easily distinguished from others. Striving to establish a unitary category of one-parent families rather than distinguishing between widows, separated and divorced mothers, single mothers, and lone fathers, served the important purpose of highlighting the existence of common problems amongst lone parents, whatever their route into lone parenthood, but it has not solved those problems. In Jackson's (1982, p. 175) view, 'the naming of it [the one-parent family] as a social phenomenon has enlarged our knowledge, mildly increased our action and generally created a characteristically misleading stereotype'.

That a negative stereotype of lone-parent households exists is evident in a whole range of fields, including the criminal justice system (Carlen, 1988) and public housing allocation, where single mothers and their children (particularly those from ethnic minorities) are 'frequently described as "problem families"' (Karn and Henderson, 1983, p. 78). Yet lone-parent households are too sizeable a section of the population to be ignored, and too complex a group to have their situation explained in simple terms of either individual responsibility and choice or personal misfortune, although analysis is frequently conducted on this level. There is, for example, an extensive debate about whether young single women in disadvantaged situations may use motherhood as a way of improving their housing prospects by increasing their eligibility for local authority tenancy. The evidence on this is at best inconclusive, however (Holme, 1985; Clark, 1989). More generally, while it is clear that the description 'single mothers by choice' fits some lone parents well (Renvoize, 1985), it is 'unlikely that very many one-parent households will be created out of choice or preference' (Close, 1985, p. 16). Collins (1992) shows that the rate of births outside of marriage correlates highly with various indicators of poverty and social distress in Britain.

There is, of course, no clear-cut dividing line between those cases where lone parenthood is 'an active choice' (Jackson, 1982, p. 176), such as those women leaving violent husbands, and those where it is involuntary, for example through bereavement. R. Pahl (1984, p. 329) argues that 'It is surely wrong to assume that all young unmarried mothers are in that position by mistake', while Cashmore (1985, p. 199) takes the discussion further by noting that although some 15 per cent of lone parents may be considered to have entered their situation freely, 'the voluntary one parent family is rarely a planned phenomenon. People don't assess their futures and weigh up the strengths and weaknesses of having children and rearing them alone'. The debate about choice, in other words, needs to be set in the broader context of the structures of opportunity and constraint within which choices take place, and the ways in which those structures shift over time.

The nature of the choice about becoming a lone parent has undoubtedly changed significantly since the nineteenth century when 'the options for the single, pregnant woman were few' (Lewis 1984, p. 64), as is indicated by the widespread practices of infanticide and informal adoption. More recently, the issue of choice was raised in the Finer Report in relation to the discussion of lone mothers becoming more independent through taking up paid work. The view expressed was in the tradition of laudably liberal sentiment, if rather superficial in its sociological analysis: 'lone parents should have a free and effective choice whether or not to take up paid employment. The decision is one which lone parents must make for themselves. ... Our concern is to see that the choice is a real one' (DHSS, 1974, p. 17).

Deacon and Bradshaw (1983) have pointed out that the great obstacles to implementing the Finer Report's proposals, through which it was hoped greater choice could be introduced for lone parents, were essentially two: the cost of the measures, and 'the problem of equity with married people. ... These problems of cost and equity have effectively blocked any substantial development of non means-tested benefits for single parents' (ibid.: p. 179). The means-testing of the one-parent benefit available on top of child benefit resulted in a situation whereby 'in the mid 1980s it was only claimed by around a half of those entitled' (Alcock, 1987, p. 101). Similar arguments applied earlier this century, at the end of the First World War, when attempts to take one-parent families out of the ambit of the Poor Law failed on grounds of cost and fear of increased illegitimacy (Lewis, 1984). The conventional wisdom is that welfare provision should not be seen to favour alternative household types to the two-parent married family, compared to which one-parent families are treated as somehow deviant, special cases (Oakley, 1976; Smart, 1984).

However, there are limits to how far people behave in a calculating way about something as emotionally significant as their marital status. For most of Burgoyne and Clark's (1984) respondents,

> The passage from first marriage to demarriage to remarriage, whilst punctuated in some cases by numerous contacts with the public structures of the law and welfare agencies, was typically seen as a private trauma, something to be negotiated personally and to be come to terms with individually. (Ibid.: p. 75)

Similarly, the calculations which lone parents make about taking up paid employment are not narrowly economic. In addition to the system of benefits being so complex, it is very difficult to work out precisely the costs and rewards of working (Beechey and Perkins, 1987). In general, paid work represents independence and offers a potential route out of poverty for single mothers (Sharpe, 1984; Gordon, 1990).

Further, it is not at all clear on what basis the comparison between lone-parent households and two-parent households is most appropriately conducted. The comparison which separated or divorced lone parents make with their former married state is not a narrowly economic one, but also refers to issues such as autonomy (Hardey, 1989). The single mothers in Sharpe's (1984) study are portrayed as being 'happier alone' (p. 205), while lone motherhood does not necessarily lead to greater social isolation than that of married women, at least in the longer term (Green and Hebron, 1988). And, provided that material circumstances are held constant in comparisons between lone- and two-parent households, expectations of children's welfare being unfavourable in lone-parent households are not necessarily borne out (Kruk and Wolkind, 1983; see also Illsley and Thompson, 1961). Put another way, it is the poverty of the lone-parent household which is primarily responsible for the difficulties and restrictions on choices encountered, and poverty is not unique to lone-parent households. It is this poverty which is the central question for social policy relating to lone-parent households to address.

It is, of course, correct to observe that social policy-makers are rarely ahead of their times, but it does not follow from this that lone-parent households will necessarily see an improvement in their situation in the future, even with continued growth in their numbers. Similarly, lone-parent households do not necessarily stand to benefit from the fact that several of the points of entry into and exit from lone parenthood are blurred. Goodin and Le Grand (1987) have argued that where boundary problems exist, selective benefits will have a tendency to become more widely available because in difficult, marginal cases there is a 'bias towards generosity' (ibid.: pp. 109–10). While it is undeniable that marginal cases inevitably throw up problems for systems of welfare admin- istration, it is far from clear that benefits always become more widely available. In the case of lone parents, there has not been a levelling up of their conditions, either within the broad category of lone-parent households or between lone-parent households and adjacent household types which they blur into. Instead, lone-parent households are confronted by a system of support which has been described as 'fragmented' and 'woefully inadequate' (Rimmer and Wicks, 1984, p. 39).

Conclusion

It is becoming increasingly clear that a key aspect of improving the situation of lone parents lies in the promotion of measures to facilitate their participation in the labour market (Millar, 1989). Already, significant numbers of lone parents manage to combine bringing up children with employment, but the majority experience the absence of adequate and affordable child-care facilities as a serious obstacle to this route to greater independence and would benefit from more extensive nursery provision, after-school care and parental leave. Such difficulties are not unique to lone parents, but they are problems to which lone parents are particularly prone.

The evolution of the broad category of lone-parent household has served to draw attention to the presence of common problems faced by lone parents which arise out of their structurally disadvantaged position in the housing and labour markets. The diversity of routes into lone parenthood and the blurred nature of the boundary around the category of lone parent households have proved to be obstacles to social policy-makers in the past, but it does not follow that common problems necessitate common solutions, particularly if the Finer Report's point about choice is to be taken seriously. Just as two-parent house-holds have devised a range of strategies for coping with the competing demands of child-care and work, so too have lone-parent households, and extending choice requires that such options are increased, not foreclosed. To the extent that this is achieved, lone-parent households are set to become more hetero-geneous yet.

REFERENCES

Alcock, P. (1987), *Poverty and State Support*, London: Longman.

Ambrose, P., Harper, J. and Pemberton, R. (1983), *Surviving Divorce*, Brighton: Wheatsheaf.

Beechey, V. and Perkins, T. (1987), *A Matter of Hours*, Cambridge: Polity Press.

Bien, W., Marbach, J. and Templeton, R. (1992), 'Social networks of single-person households', in C. Marsh and S. Arber (eds), *Families and Households: Divisions and Change*, Basingstoke: Macmillan.

Blaxter, M. (1990), *Health and Lifestyles*, London: Routledge.

Brailey, M. (1985), 'Making the break', in N. Johnson (ed.), *Marital Violence*, London: Routledge and Kegan Paul.

Braithwaite, V. A. (1990), *Bound to Care*, Sydney: Allen & Unwin.

Burgoyne, J. (1984), *Breaking Even*, Harmondsworth: Penguin.

Burgoyne, J. and Clark, D. (1984), *Making A Go of It*, London: Routledge & Kegan Paul.

Carlen, P. (1988), *Women, Crime and Poverty*, Milton Keynes: Open University Press.

Cashmore, E. E. (1985), *Having To*, London: Unwin.

Chester, R. (1977), 'The one-parent family', in R. Chester and J. Peel (eds), *Equalities and Inequalities in Family Life*, London: Academic Press.

Clark, E. (1989), *Young Single Mothers Today*, London: National Council for One Parent Families.

Close, P. (1985), 'Family form and economic production', in P. Close and R. Collins (eds), *Family and Economy in Modern Society*, Basingstoke: Macmillan.

Collins, R. (1992), 'Upholding the nuclear family: a study of unmarried parents and domestic courts', in C. Marsh and S. Arber (eds), *Families and Households: Divisions and Change*, Basingstoke: Macmillan.

Deacon, A. and Bradshaw, J. (1983), *Reserved for the Poor*, Oxford: Martin Robertson.

Department of Health and Social Security (1974), *Report of the Committee on One-Parent Families*, London: HMSO.

Donnison, D. (1982), *The Politics of Poverty*, Oxford: Martin Robertson.

Ebaugh, H. (1988), *Becoming an Ex.*, Chicago: University of Chicago Press.

Elliot, F. R. (1986), *The Family*, Basingstoke: Macmillan.

Field, F. (1989), *Losing Out*, Oxford: Blackwell Publishers.

George, V. and Wilding, P. (1972), *Motherless Families*, London: Routledge & Kegan Paul.

Ginsburg, N. (1979), *Class, Capital and Social Policy*, London: Macmillan.

Goodin, R. and Le Grand, J. (1987), *Not Only The Poor*, London: Allen & Unwin.

Gordon, T. (1990), *Feminist Mothers*, Basingstoke: Macmillan.

Graham, H. (1984), *Women, Health and the Family*, Brighton: Wheatsheaf.

Graham, H. (1987), 'Women's poverty and caring', in C. Glendinning and J. Millar (eds), *Women and Poverty in Britain*, Brighton: Wheatsheaf.

Green, E. and Hebron, S. (1988), 'Leisure and male partners', in E. Wimbush and M. Talbot (eds), *Relative Freedoms*, Milton Keynes: Open University Press.

Hardey, M. (1989), 'Lone parents and the home', in G. Allan and G. Crow (eds), *Home and Family*, Basingstoke: Macmillan.

Harris, C. C. (1983), *The Family and Industrial Society*, London: George Allen & Unwin.

Hart, N. (1976), *When Marriage Ends*, London: Tavistock.

Haskey, J. (1986), 'One-parent families in Great Britain', *Population Trends*, 45: 5–13.

Haskey, J. (1989), 'One-parent families and their children in Great Britain', *Population Trends*, 55: 27–33.

Hipgrave, T. (1982), 'Lone fatherhood', in L. McKee and M. O'Brien (eds), *The Father Figure*, London: Tavistock.

Holme, A. (1985), *Housing and Young Families*, London: Routledge & Kegan Paul.

Illsley, R. and Thompson, B. (1961), 'Women from broken homes', *Sociological Review*, 9: 27–54.

Jackson, B. (1982), 'Single-parent families', in R. N. Rapoport, M. P. Fogarty and R. Rapoport (eds), *Families in Britain*, London: Routledge & Kegan Paul.

Karn, V. and Henderson, J. (1983), 'Housing atypical households', in A. W. Franklin (ed.), *Family Matters*, Oxford: Pergamon Press.

Kruk, S. and Wolkind, S. (1983), 'Single mothers and their children', in N. Madge (ed.), *Families at Risk*, London: Heinemann.

Lawson, R. (1987) 'Social security and the division of welfare', in G. Causer (ed.), *Inside British Society*, Brighton: Wheatsheaf.

Leete, R. (1978), 'One-parent families', *Population Trends*, 13, 4–9.

Lewis, J. (1984), *Women in England 1870–1950*, Brighton: Wheatsheaf.

Lewis, J. (1986) 'Anxieties about the family', in M. Richards and P. Light (eds), *Children of Social Worlds*, Cambridge: Polity Press.

MacIntyre, S. (1977), *Single and Pregnant*, London: Croom Helm.

Maclean, M. (1987), 'Households after divorce', in J. Brannen and G. Wilson (eds), *Give and Take in Families*, London: Allen & Unwin.

Marsden, D. (1973), *Mothers Alone*, Harmondsworth: Penguin.

Millar, J. (1989), *Poverty and the Lone-parent Family*, Aldershot: Avebury.

Oakley, A. (1976), *Housewife*, Harmondsworth: Penguin.

O'Brien, M. (1987), 'Patterns of kinship and friendship among lone fathers', in C. Lewis and M. O'Brien (eds), *Reassessing Fatherhood*, London: Sage.

Office of Population Censuses and Surveys (1989), *OPCS Monitor*, SS 89/1, London: Government Statistical Service.

Page, R. (1984), *Stigma*, London: Routledge & Kegan Paul.

Pahl, J. (1984), 'The allocation of money within the household', in M. Freeman (ed.), *State, Law and the Family*, London: Tavistock.

Pahl, R. E. (1984), *Divisions of Labour*, Oxford: Blackwell Publishers.

Popay, J., Rimmer, L. and Rossiter, C. (1983), *One Parent Families: Parents, Children And Public Policy*, London: Study Commission on the Family.

Renvoize, J. (1985), *Going Solo*, London: Routledge & Kegan Paul.

Rimmer, L. (1983), 'Changing family patterns', in A. W. Franklin (ed.), *Family Matters*, Oxford: Pergamon Press.

Rimmer, L. and Wicks, M. (1984), 'The family today', in E. Butterworth and D. Weir (eds), *The New Sociology of Modern Britain*, Glasgow: Fontana.

Sharpe, S. (1984), *Double Identity*, Harmondsworth: Penguin.

Smart, C. (1984), *The Ties That Bind: Law in Marriage and the Reproduction of Patriarchal Relations*, London: Routledge & Kegan Paul.

Townsend, P. (1979), *Poverty in the United Kingdom*, London: Allen Lane.

Vaughan, D. (1988), *Uncoupling*, London: Methuen.

Watson, S. with Austerberry, H. (1986), *Housing and Homelessness*, London: Routledge & Kegan Paul.

Wilson, E. (1977), *Women and the Welfare State*, London: Tavistock.

Wynn, M. (1964), *Fatherless Families*, London: Michael Joseph.
Wynn, M. (1972), *Family Policy*, Harmondsworth: Penguin.
Yudkin, S. and Holme, A. (1963), *Working Mothers and their Children*, London: Michael Joseph.

12

State, Family and Personal Responsibility: The Changing Balance for Lone Mothers in the United Kingdom

Jane Millar

Introduction

In the UK there are about one and a quarter million lone-parent families, making up 19 per cent of all families with children. The numbers of lone parents have almost doubled since the early 1970s and this increase is part of wider patterns of change in family structure. These are the result, for example, of the rise in extramarital births (now accounting for over a quarter of all births), the increase in cohabitation (half of women have cohabited prior to marriage), the rise in divorce (one in three marriages currently contracted will end in divorce), and the extent of remarriage and cohabitation after divorce (about a quarter of all marriages are second marriages for one or both partners). Kiernan and Wicks (1990) suggest that by the year 2000 it may be that as few as half of all children in Britain will have spent all their lives in a conventional two-parent family with both their natural parents.

These changing family structures present something of a challenge for social policy, especially in relation to the issue of state financial support for families. The British postwar social security system was founded on three important assumptions: full employment, male breadwinners and stable families. Thus the main form of family support is male wages, which the state will replace under certain conditions (for example, in the case of involuntary unemployment, sickness, disability and death). The state will also supplement male wages with child benefit for all families, and more recently with means-tested benefits for families with low wages. Otherwise the financial arrangements of families are considered to be essentially private. This has two particular consequences. First, decisions about how families allocate and spend their money are seen as the responsibility of the family and not the business of the state. Second, because male wages are perceived as the main element of family support, decisions about whether or not the woman should work outside the home are also seen as private family decisions.

But separation and divorce, and unmarried motherhood, do not fit easily into this model. The financial arrangements of the 'family' are not private because the state becomes involved in deciding the allocation of resources between the two new households: the lone parent and the children on the one side; and the absent parent, usually the father, on the other side. The state must also take responsibility for enforcing the financial arrangements made and, if the absent parent is unwilling or unable to pay, must either replace his contribution or expect the lone mother to support herself and her children through employment. Thus the mother's decisions about employment are no longer simply private, but are influenced, or even determined, by state policy.

The rising numbers of lone-parent families therefore raise fundamental issues about the balance between family, state and individual financial responsibilities; and about the roles of men and women as parents and as workers. The 1991 Child Support Act, implemented from 1993, represents an attempt to change this balance by introducing new mechanisms for setting and enforcing maintenance payments for children. It is similar to the 'child support' schemes recently introduced in some other countries, notably parts of the USA (Kahn and Kamerman, 1988; Garfinkel and Wong, 1990) and Australia (Harrison, Snider and Merlo, 1990; Harrison et al., 1991). This article examines these policy developments in the UK and their implications for separated couples and their children. The first section provides the background, describing recent trends in lone parenthood and the financial circumstances of lone parents in the UK. The second section looks at the context in which recent policy has been developed. The third section looks at the provisions of the Child Support Act in more detail, and the final section concludes by considering some of the wider implications for family and gender roles.

Background

In 1974 the Finer Committee on One-parent Families (Finer, 1974) reported, in two large volumes, on the circumstances of lone parents in the UK. The committee had been set up in response to concerns about the increasing numbers of lone parents, who were very often reliant upon state benefits and at risk of poverty. In the early 1970s there were about half a million lone-parent families. Today that number has more than doubled and lone parents are once again the subject of policy concern. The reasons are similar.

First, there has been a significant rise in the numbers of lone-parent families. Table 12.1 shows the increase in the numbers of lone-parent families since the early 1970s, when the 1969 Divorce Reform Act came into operation. This made divorce much more widely available and led to a substantial increase in the number of divorcing couples. Between 1971 and 1990 the number of divorced and separated women with children rose from 290,000 to 650,000; the number of single mothers rose from 90,000 to 390,000. The numbers of lone fathers have also increased (from 70,000 to 110,000) but they remain very much in the minority, at about 10 per cent of all lone parents. Thus most lone

Table 12.1   Numbers of lone-parent families, Great Britain 1971 and 1990

	1971	1990
Single mothers	90,000	390,000
Divorced/separated	290,000	650,000
Widowed mothers	120,000	75,000
All mothers	500,000	1,115,000
Lone fathers	70,000	110,000
Lone parents	570,000	1,225,000
As a proportion of all families with children	8%	19%

Source: Haskey (1993), figure 2.

parents are women and just over half are women who are divorced or separated from their former husbands. Black families are slightly more likely than white families to be headed by a lone parent (18 per cent and 15 per cent respectively in 1988) with particularly high rates of lone parenthood (about half of all families) among West Indian families (Haskey, 1991).

Many other countries have also seen significant increases in the number and proportion of lone-parent families, again mainly as a consequence of marital breakdown (Ermisch, 1990). It is difficult to get estimates for the number of lone-parent families which compare different countries on exactly the same basis because different countries define and count lone parents in different ways (Roll, 1992). However, table 12.2 shows some recent estimates for the proportion of lone-parent families in other countries. The UK has a relatively high proportion of families headed by a lone parent in relation to the rest of the EC (at about 17 per cent compared with an EC average of about 10 per cent), but many other countries have at least as many, or more, lone-parent families as the UK.

The increase in the numbers of lone parents would not, by itself, necessarily give rise to policy concern. However, alongside the increase in overall numbers there has been a substantial rise in both the number and proportion of lone parents in receipt of state benefits, especially social assistance benefits (supple-

Table 12.2   Proportion of families headed by a lone parent, various countries, late 1980s

European Community countries	%	OECD countries	%
UK	17	USA	21
Denmark	15	Sweden	15
France, Germany	11–13	Australia, Austria, Canada, Finland	13
Belgium Luxembourg, Ireland, Portugal, The Netherlands	9–11		
Greece, Spain, Italy	5–6		

Sources: European Community from Roll (1992); OECD from OECD (1993).
Note: refers to families with children aged under 18.

mentary benefit, or as it is now known, income support). In 1979 there were about 310,000 lone mothers on supplementary benefit, equivalent to about 45 per cent of all lone mothers. By 1989 this had risen to about 740,000 lone mothers on income support, or about 72 per cent of the total (DSS, 1991). In all about 30 per cent of people of working age receiving income support are lone parents, and over 60 per cent of the children living in families on income support live in lone-parent families.

The main reason for the increased reliance on state benefits has been a fall in employment rates, especially in full-time employment. In the late 1970s just about half (47 per cent) of lone mothers were employed, 22 per cent full time and 24 per cent part time. By the late 1980s less than two-fifths (39 per cent) of lone mothers were employed, 17 per cent full time and 22 per cent part time (OPCS, 1990). Lone mothers are now less likely to be employed than married mothers, of whom 56 per cent are employed (18 per cent full time and 38 per cent part time).

Falling employment and increased reliance on state benefits have in turn meant that the incomes of lone mothers have fallen, both relatively (compared with other families) and absolutely (compared with prices). In 1979 lone parents had incomes which were on average equivalent to about 57 per cent of the incomes of couples with two children, but by 1989 this had fallen to about 40 per cent. Over the same period the average incomes of lone parents rose by less than the Retail Price Index (DE, 1980, 1990; see also Roll, 1988). Thus lone mothers are increasingly at risk of poverty, as shown in both official statistics (DSS, 1993) and independent research studies (Frayman, 1991; Bradshaw and Millar, 1991). According to the official statistics, the proportion of lone parents with disposable incomes of less than half of the average (taking into account family size) rose from 19 to 60 per cent between 1979 and 1990/91.

In recent years, therefore, the number of lone parents in the UK has been increasing, their reliance on state benefits has been rising and their employment rates have been falling. Poverty has increased and most lone parents live on incomes substantially lower than the average for other families with children. However, during this time policy for lone parents has been, as Bradshaw (1989) puts it, 'in the doldrums'. The Finer Committee recommendations were not taken up and such policy developments as there have been have consisted of fairly minor modifications to existing benefits rather than any fundamental review (Millar, 1989).

Changing Policy

In the late 1980s, however, lone parents came under more detailed scrutiny from the government. The social security system as a whole had been reviewed in the mid 1980s and legislation introduced in 1986. Lone parents were not particularly targeted in that review although they were, of course, affected by the changes introduced (Millar, 1992). However, after that review was completed, policy attention turned specifically towards lone parents. One of the most important reasons for this was financial. As described above, the number of lone parents on income support had been rising rapidly throughout the 1980s and so therefore had the costs – in real terms social security spending on lone parents increased threefold between 1981 and 1988 (DSS, 1990). The control of public expenditure was a key economic objective for conservative governments in the 1980s and so these rising costs were bound to cause concern.

However, although the pressure for policy change may have been primarily financial, it was ideological factors which largely determined the direction of the policy response. These ideological factors included a number of related threads, tied in various ways to ideas and ideals about the 'family' and family obligations. First, there was the long-standing and generalized concern that lone parenthood *per se* is bad for both the families themselves and for society in general and the state, therefore, should seek to discourage the formation of such families, or at the very least, not encourage them. This is a view which, despite the lack of evidence to support it, has gained even more ground recently with a series of speeches from government ministers – including Peter Lilley as Secretary of State at the Department of Social Security – critical of lone parents. Dennis and Erdos (1992) and Dennis (1993) have gained significant publicity for their argument that 'families without fatherhood' are destroying communities and society.

Second, one of the central tenets of Conservative social policy in the 1980s was that the state had become too supportive, providing too much welfare, and this meant that individuals and families were no longer taking responsibility for themselves. This, it was argued, meant that a 'culture of dependency' had grown up in which people had lost the motivation to help themselves and instead relied on the state to meet all their needs. Separated, or unmarried, parents provided two prime examples of this abdication of personal responsibility. On the one hand there is the father, walking away from his family responsibilities and expecting the state to carry the cost. On the other hand there is the lone mother, increasingly relying on the state to provide an income. Receipt of benefits, or 'dependency' as such receipt was pejoratively termed, was thus increasingly defined as a matter of personal choice rather than external constraint.

These ideas are linked in the concept of the 'underclass' as it was developed in the US (most influentially for British social policy by Murray, 1984, 1990). According to these accounts the underclass is mainly composed of unemployed men and single mothers, who have no incentive to work or to marry, and no motivation either to support their families or to help themselves out of dependency on the state. They are thus excluded from the labour market and excluded from the values of society as a whole (Smith, 1992). The US debate has had very strong racial overtones that are largely lacking in the UK context (Morris, 1994) but, that aside, these sorts of ideas have been influential in policy, especially towards unemployed people. Unemployment has been increasingly defined as a problem of unemployed people not wanting to work rather than a problem of lack of jobs, and this has led to a very harsh benefit regime for unemployed people in the 1980s, with cuts in benefit and restrictions on benefit entitlement (Atkinson and Mickelwright, 1989; McLaughlin, 1992).

However, for lone parents – especially lone mothers – the solution to the 'culture of dependency' is not so straightforward. This is because there is considerable ambiguity over the way in which the 'personal obligations and duties' of lone mothers should be defined. On the one hand, because they are mothers, their primary role and responsibility is defined as being the care of their children. This means that they should not necessarily be expected to work outside the home and indeed current policy does not require lone parents to work if they have dependent children under sixteen years of age. On the other hand, however, many mothers are now employed and nearly all the recent, and predicted future, employment growth has been among women (NEDO, 1989). The question of mothers and employment thus raises some difficult issues for Conservative values and the situation of lone mothers brings these very clearly into focus (Brown, 1989). Should lone mothers be expected, or even compelled, to reduce their 'benefit dependency' through employment? Or should they, as mothers, be expected to stay at home and care for their children? Are they, as Lewis (1988) has put it, mothers or workers?

Directly confronting the issue of whether lone mothers should or should not be expected to take paid work therefore raises much wider issues about the state's role in relation to women's employment. If lone mothers were to be required to work outside the home the state would almost certainly have to make much more provision for child care, or accept that children might not be properly cared for while their mothers were at work. Providing, or subsidizing, such child care would not only be expensive but would also raise the issue of the child-care demands of married mothers. In comparison with other EC countries the UK has very low levels of child-care provision (Moss, 1990) and, as employment rates of married mothers have risen, there has been increasing pressure on the government to reconsider child-care policy (Cohen and Fraser, 1992). This has so far largely been resisted but if child care were to be provided for lone mothers this would undoubtedly raise the pressure from employed married mothers for more help with their pressing child-care problems. Thus the current policy – that the state is neutral with regard to employment among lone mothers, neither encouraging nor discouraging paid work (NAO, 1990) – is important in maintaining the notion that for mothers paid employment is a private choice and the needs that arise out of it, such as the need for child care, are not the responsibility of the state.

But if lone mothers cannot be rescued from benefit dependency by their own employment, then what other alternatives are there? Fortunately for the government a potential solution to this dilemma can be found by turning to the 'personal obligations and duties' of the absent parent, which is usually the father. Here the obligations and duties can apparently be much more easily and unambiguously defined: 'parenthood is for life.... Legislation cannot make irresponsible parents responsible. But it can and must ensure that absent fathers pay maintenance for their children' (Margaret Thatcher, reported in *The*

Independent 19 July 1990). The role of fathers is to financially support their families through employment and so enforcing this obligation for separated couples would seem to provide the required alternative to either open-ended state financial support or to a positive employment policy for lone mothers. Enforcing maintenance obligations thus has the potential to kill as many as three birds with one stone – it increases the 'responsibility' of the absent father (who would no longer simply be able to walk away from his financial obligations to his family); it reduces the 'dependency' of the lone mother on the state (if child support can replace income support); and it saves the state money. Policy-makers therefore started to look towards the issue of maintenance and this led to the 1991 Child Support Act.

The 1991 Child Support Act

In theory children are already entitled to financial support from both parents following family breakdown. In practice many children in lone-parent families receive little or no financial support from their absent parent. Table 12.3, drawn from a recent national survey of lone-parent families, shows that only about three in ten of the families were receiving maintenance. Separated and divorced families were more likely to receive maintenance than those who had never been married. For those receiving maintenance the payments contributed, on average, about a fifth of net income. For all lone parents maintenance contributed only about 7 per cent of total net income.

Prior to the introduction of the Child Support Act the courts had responsibility for setting and enforcing maintenance obligations. The White Paper introducing the Child Support proposals (DSS, 1990; para. 1.5) identified a number of problems with these existing procedures:

- discretionary decisions and hence inconsistent and inequitable treatment;
- the levels of maintenance awarded are often low;
- there is no automatic review of awards;
- many awards are not paid or not paid regularly;
- the system takes too long; and
- requires considerable effort on the part of the lone parent to pursue maintenance.

Table 12.3 Receipt of maintenance among lone mothers, UK 1989

	% in receipt	(base)
All lone parents	29	(1420)
Divorced	40	(622)
Separated	32	(279)
Single	14	(519)

Source: Bradshaw and Millar (1991), table 7.1.

The Child Support Act aims to solve these problems by establishing an agency to take responsibility for setting and enforcing maintenance payments for children; and by determining levels of maintenance according to a fixed formula. Thus the Act has shifted child maintenance away from a system of judicial discretion to a system of administrative procedures, with the aim of producing 'consistent and predictable results' and enabling 'maintenance to be decided in a fair and reasonable way' (ibid.: para. 2.1). However, it should be noted that only child maintenance is included in this, all other financial matters (e.g. property settlements) are left to the courts; as are all issues of child custody and access.

Alongside the agency and the formula the Act also introduces a major change to the eligibility criteria for claiming income support and family credit. This relates to the hours of paid work that are allowed for each benefit. Prior to 1992 the dividing line between these two benefits was set at 24 hours – only those working for less than 24 hours could claim income support, while those working 24 hours or more (and with low wages) could claim family credit. Now the cross-over point comes at 16 hours so anyone working 16 hours or more per week cannot claim income support but may be able to claim family credit. At first sight this might seem a little out of place in this legislation, given that the main concern is with child maintenance. In fact it is an integral part of the philosophy behind the Act because the aim of these rules is to encourage more part-time work among lone mothers. As we have seen, part-time work is relatively uncommon among lone mothers, although for married mothers it is more common than full-time work. Part-time work is expanding and has the advantage of reducing the need for child care but, for lone mothers, it has the serious disadvantage of not providing an adequate income. Part-time earnings tend to be low and cannot provide lone mothers with enough money to support themselves and their children (Bradshaw and Millar, 1991). The Child Support Act aims to get round this by encouraging lone mothers to work part-time to supplement their earnings with child support and with in-work benefits such as family credit. So, instead of relying on one source of income (earnings or benefits or maintenance), total income can be made up as a 'package' of all three. The rules are intended to encourage this – any child support received by lone mothers on income support will be deducted from their benefit, so there will be no financial gain from child support for those receiving income support. But, for those who take jobs and claim family credit, the first £15 of any child support received is ignored. (The subsequent announcement in the 1993 budget of a 'child-care disregard' for family credit also relates to this policy objective.) The three parts of the Act – the agency, the formula and the changed benefit rules – all act together to encourage more *private* as opposed to *public* financial support for lone parents.

When the Act went through parliament there were two issues in particular that caused the most controversy. The first concerns the point mentioned above that lone mothers on income support will gain nothing financially from any child maintenance collected. About three-quarters of lone parents are on income support, so unless they can get off income support benefits and into employment they will be no better off financially, no matter how much child support is collected. Thus it was argued that these proposals would increase rather than reduce family poverty, because second families could be struggling to make child support payments which do not even financially benefit the first families (Millar, 1992). Second, the Act requires all lone parents who claim means-tested benefits (income support, family credit, housing benefits) to register with the agency and to comply by giving details of the absent parent. Those who refuse to do so will in effect be fined by having their income support personal allowance reduced unless they have 'good cause' not to name the absent parent. The government has been reluctant to define 'good cause' but has indicated that this includes rape, incest and fear of violence. Critics have argued that this measure penalizes lone mothers and allows violent partners to escape making payments.

These two features of the legislation lead some commentators to suggest that the White Paper that introduced these changes should have been called 'Treasury Comes First' rather than 'Children Come First', since it seems that saving money was the main policy objective. This view is strongly reinforced by the fact that registration with the Child Support Agency will be compulsory for benefit recipients but only voluntary for other separating couples. But alongside this drive to reduce public expenditure the Child Support Act also reflects a particular response to changing family structures and gender roles.

Family Structure and Gender Roles

The UK is not alone in either the problems with the 'old' maintenance system or in the proposed solutions. Studies in other countries (for example USA, Australia, Canada, Ireland, France) find the same sorts of difficulties – low and variable awards, irregular or non-existent payments – and so maintenance rarely contributes much to the incomes of lone-parent families (Griffiths, Cooper and McVicar, 1986; Millar, 1989; Maclean, 1990; Millar, Leeper and Davies, 1992). In a recent review of child support measures in the OECD countries, Garfinkel and Wong (1990, p. 112) conclude that there has been a movement towards 'standardization and administrative enforcement across countries' and that many countries are looking at ways to strengthen and enforce the financial obligations of non-custodial parents. Thus Britain is far from alone in responding to the increasing numbers of lone-parent families by trying to ensure more private as opposed to public support. However, as a response to changing family structures, the measures introduced in the UK seem to be aimed at *containing* change rather than *adapting* to it. There are several aspects to this.

First, what these proposals do is to try and reproduce traditional family and gender relationships after couples have separated. The separated family is treated almost as if the relationship had not broken down at all. Thus the men are to fulfil their traditional role as financial provider and the women are to fulfil their traditional role as mother. These days the acceptable role for mothers includes some part-time work, so lone mothers are also to have improved access to part-time employment. In a way the government is trying to 'turn back the clock' and make policy on the assumption that the traditional gender division of labour within the family can continue even when other aspects of the family, such as marriage, have begun to disappear.

For lone mothers there are likely to be a number of negative consequences of this fixation on traditional gender roles. In the first place the women's ability to improve their incomes much above basic levels will be very limited. The income 'package' of part-time (low-paid) work, child support and means-tested benefits creates a very long 'poverty trap', since increases in either earnings or child support will simply mean reductions in benefit so that total income changes very little. Furthermore, if lone mothers do try to achieve this package they will continue to be financially dependent on their former partners, and their incomes will to some extent depend on the circumstances and choices that he makes. The child maintenance is not guaranteed by the state (as it is in some countries) and so the women will continue to be dependent on the willingness and ability of the men to pay. Finally, the focus on part-time work means that the question of state responsibility for child care can continue to be sidestepped. Lack of child care is the largest single barrier to employment for lone mothers and nothing in these proposals is going to increase child-care provision. Thus it could be argued that lone mothers will suffer the disadvantages of marriage – the double burden of paid and unpaid work, the financial dependency on men, the responsibility for arranging child care – but with none of the advantages.

Second, the child support proposals centre on reinforcing the financial obligation of the 'natural' or 'biological' parents. Fathers (and mothers) remain responsible for 'their' children, no matter what happens. So, for example, if a man remarries his maintenance bill will be reassessed if he has children with his second wife but not if she already has children for whom he becomes a stepfather. About a million children live in step-families (Kiernan and Wicks, 1990), but these measures imply that step-parents are not financially responsible for their step-children, who always remain the financial responsibility of their 'natural' parents. Given current patterns of marriage and remarriage the outcome of the strict application of this principle would be that money would have to pass between and through several households. Even a fairly simple example – two divorced people each with children who marry and have more children – produces quite a complicated set of financial obligations across a number of households.

In addition, all children do not have two 'natural' parents – 'family formation can be as diverse as assisted reproduction, surrogacy, substitute parents, serial marriage or cohabitation and single parenthood, as well as the normal (*sic*) situation of blood parents married to each other' (Craven-Griffiths, 1991, p. 326). Such families are difficult to fit into the current provisions and will tend to remain so in the future.

Third, the provisions are based on the principle that the obligations of natural parents are absolutely unconditional. As the opening words of the White Paper setting out the changes put it:

> Every child has a right to care from his or her parents. Parents generally have a legal and moral obligation to care for their children until the children are old enough to look after themselves. The parents of a child may separate. In some instances the parents may not have lived together as a family at all. Although events may change the relationship between the parents – for example, when they divorce – those events *cannot in any way* change their responsibilities towards their children. (DSS, 1990, foreword; emphasis added)

But, as the response to this legislation has shown, not everyone agrees that there is such an unconditional responsibility. Clearly many men do not think so and have been very active in their opposition to the Act and indeed instrumental in having changes made to the formula since the Act was introduced (Social Security Committee, 1993). Criticisms of the Act from pressure groups such as Families Need Fathers (and the many other groups that have been formed to oppose the legislation) have focused on issues such as the retrospective nature of the Act (such as that previous 'clean break' arrangements can be overturned); the failure to adequately recognize the needs of second families; the failure to take into account the costs of being an absent parent (costs to visit children, etc.); the introduction of higher payments without any phasing-in period; the way in which the formula includes an amount for money for the lone parent (intended to reflect her role as carer of the child but perceived by many as spouse maintenance). In addition, the way in which the Act was implemented – apparently focusing on extracting higher payments from those already paying rather than on enforcing payments among non-payers – has lead to criticisms of inequity and injustice (ibid.).

The groups representing absent parents have given much less attention to the issues of principle raised by the Act, which is not surprising given that they have sought to stress their 'responsibility' towards their children. However, the issue of contact with children has been stressed and it has been argued that, if fathers are not allowed access to their children, they should not have to pay child maintenance. Burgoyne and Millar (1994), on the basis of in-depth interviews with a small group of absent fathers, argue that the obligation to maintain children is not seen as an unconditional obligation but rather depends on a number of factors including the men's view of their own, and their former partner's, situations. If former partners had remarried then very often the view was taken that maintenance obligations should be reduced or even cancelled, and evidence from the 1990 *British Social Attitudes Survey* found the population in general ambivalent about this. Half (51 per cent) of the respondents said that maintenance payments should continue if the woman remarried, 13 per cent said that they should stop, and 33 per cent that it would depend on the new husband's income (Kiernan, 1992). The absolutely unconditional obligation that underpins the White Paper does not seem to command widespread support.

From the point of view of the women there are also many reasons why some will be reluctant to receive maintenance. For some there is a fear of violence and Bradshaw and Millar (1991) found that violence was reported by 20 per cent of the lone mothers as a factor in the breakdown of their relationship. Others might have had no substantive relationship with the child's father. Others might want the relationship to end completely and not want to be financially dependent on their former partners. Others might be trying to maintain a relationship between the father and the children and fear that this would be more difficult if financial matters were introduced. Among lone mothers on income support both the women and the men might consider that there is little point in the man having to make payments which reduce his income quite substantially while doing nothing to increase hers or that of the children. The lone mothers interviewed in depth by Clarke, Craig and Glendinning (1993) were thus rather uncertain about the value of the Act to them in practice:

> There was a marked contrast between the lone mothers' beliefs about the principles underpinning fathers' continuing financial obligations to their families, and the realities surrounding such payments...[there was] a profound ambivalence surrounding the receipt of maintenance by these lone mothers. On the one hand they felt that fathers did have a continuing obligation to make a financial contribution to their children. But on the other hand, the giving of that support enmeshed them in the very same patterns of obligation and control from which they had tried to escape in the course of rebuilding their lives as single parents.

The response of the government to these sorts of points has been that it is right to enforce child support because the obligation to support children *is* unconditional and that neither the mother nor the father has the right to abrogate this responsibility, either for themselves or for the other person. Thus the mother cannot refuse to co-operate in finding the father and the father cannot refuse to pay. But in practice enforcing a particular definition of family responsibilities requires at least some degree of acceptance that the definition is fair or just (Finch, 1990), and it is by no means clear that these child support provisions will be seen in this way – indeed quite the reverse seems to be the case.

Finally, these measures do little or nothing to tackle the underlying issues of gender inequality that are apparent in the breakdown of marriage. When couples separate the extent to which the costs of caring for children fall on women and not on men becomes very clear. The women's access to employment is limited and so current income tends to be low, making it difficult for them to support themselves. Their future income security is reduced because they lose access to the pension entitlements derived from their partners. The distribution of property, including pension rights, after divorce does not fully take into account the unpaid contribution of women's work to the marriage. The child support scheme focuses mainly on the direct costs of children, attempting to share these more equally between the mother and the father. The indirect costs are partially recognized in that the maintenance bill includes an assessment for the 'mother as carer' but this relates to the caring costs incurred after separation and does not compensate for the costs incurred during marriage.

Allocating the direct and indirect costs of children between the mother, the father and the state raises many difficult issues. The child support approach analysed here for the UK and also adopted, in broadly similar ways, by several other countries in what have been called the 'liberal' welfare state regimes (Esping-Anderson, 1990), provides one response to these issues. An alternative approach can be seen in the 'advanced maintenance schemes' adopted in many of the 'social democratic' welfare regimes, notably Sweden. The key features of this approach are that it provides an assured child-support benefit, payable to all lone parents regardless of income or employment status, and recouped by the state from the absent parent. In Sweden the children receive a payment set at 40 per cent of the officially determined basic needs of a child and the absent parents pay a standardized amount (Garfinkel and Wong, 1990; Kamerman and Kahn, 1983). Thus advanced maintenance payments seem to 'provide something of a bridge between the private and the public systems of income support, providing the custodial parent with guaranteed support without entirely undermining the obligation of the absent parent to provide support' (Millar, 1989, p. 150). As Joshi (1987, p. 131) has written:

> The price a man pays for parenthood is generally being expected to support his children and their mother. The price a woman pays is that of continuing economic handicap and an increased risk of poverty. One of the many advantages of being male is that it is easier to opt out of the obligation to maintain than it is to opt out of the unwritten obligation to care.

Whether measures such as these are enough to prevent men from 'opting out' remains to be seen. But also legislation such as this arguably starts in the wrong place – in order to reduce inequalities *after* marriage (or relationship) breakdown we also need to find ways to reduce inequalities between women and men *within* marriage. Women and children will continue to be poor as lone-parent families until women in general are able to achieve a more substantial degree of equality and independence.

NOTE

An earlier version of this article was given at a seminar on 'Gender and Family Change in Industrialized Countries' organized by the International Union for the Scientific Study of Population in Rome, January 1992.

REFERENCES

Atkinson, A. B. and Mickelwright, J. (1989), 'Turning the screw: benefits for the unemployed 1978–1988', in A. B. Atkinson (ed.), *Poverty and Social Security*, Brighton: Harvester Wheatsheaf.

Bradshaw, J. (1989), *Policy in the Doldrums*, London: Family Policy Studies Centre.

Bradshaw, J. and Millar, J. (1991), *Lone-parent Families in the UK*, London: HMSO.

Brown, J. (1989), *Why Don't They go to Work?*, London: HMSO.

Burgoyne, C. and Millar, J. (1994) 'Child support: the views of separated fathers', *Policy and Politics*, 22: 95–104.

Clarke, K., Craig, G. and Glendinning, C. (1993), *Children Come First? The Child Support Act and Lone Parent Families*, London: The Children's Society/NSPCC/NCH/Save the Children/Barnados.

Craven-Griffiths, J. (1991), 'New families for old: have the statutes caught up with reality?', *Family Law*, 21: 326–30.

Cohen, B. and Fraser, N. (1992), *Childcare in a Modern Welfare State*, London: Institute for Public Policy Research.

Dennis, N. (1993), *Rising Crime and the Dismembered Family*, London: Institute of Economic Affairs.

Dennis, N. and Erdos, G. (1992), *Families without Fatherhood*, London: Institute of Economic Affairs.

Department of Employment (1980), *Family Expenditure Survey 1979*, London: HMSO.

Department of Employment (1990), *Family Expenditure Survey 1989*, London: HMSO.

Department of Social Security (1990), *Children Come First*, Cm. 1263, London: HMSO.

Department of Social Security (1991), *Social Security Statistics 1990*, London: HMSO.

Department of Social Security (1993), *Households Below Average Income: 1979–1990/91*, London: HMSO.

Duskin, E. (ed.) (1990), *Lone-parent Families: The Economic Challenge*, Paris: OECD.

Ermisch, J. (1990), 'Demographic aspects of the growing number of lone-parent families', in E. Duskin (ed.), *Lone-parent Families: The Economic Challenge*, Paris: OECD.

Esping-Anderson, G. (1990), *The Three Worlds of Welfare Capitalism*, Cambridge: Polity Press.

Finch, J. (1990), *Family Obligations and Social Change*, Cambridge: Polity Press.

Finer, M. (1974), *Report of the Committee on One-parent Families*, London: HMSO.

Frayman, H. (1991), *Breadline Britain in the 1990s*, London: Domino Films/LWT.

Garfinkel, I. and Wong, P. (1990), 'Child support and public policy', in E. Duskin (ed.), *Lone-parent Families: The Economic Challenge*, Paris: OECD.

Glendinning, C. and Millar, J. (eds) (1992), *Women and Poverty in Britain: The 1990s*, Hemel Hempstead: Harvester Wheatsheaf.

Griffiths, B., Cooper, S. and McVicar, N. (1986), *Overseas Countries Maintenance Provisions*, Canberra: Department of Social Security.

Harrison, M., Snider, G. and Merlo, R. (1990), *Who Pays for the Children?*, Melbourne: Australian Institute of Family Studies.

Harrison, M., Snider, G., Merlo, R. and Lucchesi, V. (1991), *Paying for the Children*, Melbourne: Australian Institute of Family Studies.

Haskey, J. (1991), 'Estimated numbers and demographic characteristics of one-parent families in the UK', *Population Trends*, 65: 35–48.

Haskey, J. (1993), 'Trends in the number of one-parent families in Britain', *Population Trends*, 67: 26–33.

Joshi, H. (1987), 'The cost of caring', in C. Glendinning and J. Millar (eds), *Women and Poverty in Britain*, Brighton: Harvester Wheatsheaf.

Kahn, A. J. and Kamerman, S. B. (1988), *Child Support*, Beverly Hills: Sage.

Kamerman, S. B. and Kahn, A. J. (1983), 'Income transfers and mother-only families in eight countries', *Social Service Review*, 57: 448–64.

Kiernan, K. (1992), 'Men and women at work and in the home', in R. Jowell (ed.), *British Social Attitudes: The Ninth Report*, London: Social and Community Planning Research.

Kiernan, K. and Wicks, M. (1990), *Family Change and Future Policy*, London: Family Policy Studies Centre.

Lewis, J. (1988), 'Lone-parent families: politics and economics', *Journal of Social Policy*, 17, 5'5 600.

McLaughlin, E. (1992) *Understanding Unemployment*, London: Routledge.

Maclean, M. (1990), 'Lone-parent families: family law and income transfers', in E. Duskin (ed.), *Lone-parent Families: The Economic Challenge*, Paris: OECD.

Millar, J. (1989), *Poverty and the Lone-parent Family: The Challenge to Social Policy*, Avebury: Gower.

Millar, J. (1992), 'Lone mothers and poverty', in C. Glendinning and J. Millar (eds), *Women and Poverty: The 1990s*, Hemel Hempstead: Harvester Wheatsheaf.

Millar, J. and Whiteford, P. (1992), *Child Support and Lone-parent Families: Policies in Australia and the UK*, Bath: University of Bath.

Millar, J., Leeper, S. and Davies, C. (1992), *Lone Parents, Poverty and Public Policy in Ireland: A Comparative Study*, Ulster: Centre for Research on Women, University of Ulster.

Morris, L. (1994), *Dangerous Classes: The Underclass and Social Citizenship*, London: Routledge.

Moss, P. (1990), *Childcare in the European Community*, Brussels: European Commission Child Care Network.

Murray C. (1984), *Losing Ground*, New York: Basic Books.

Murray C. (1990), *The Emerging British Underclass*, London: Institute for Economic Affairs.

National Audit Office (1990), *Department of Social Security: Support for Lone-Parent Families*, London: HMSO.

National Economic Development Office (1989), *Defusing the Demographic Time-Bomb*, London: NEDO/TA.

Office of Population Censuses and Surveys (1990), *General Household Survey 1988*, London: HMSO.

Organization for Economic Cooperation and Development (1993), *Breadwinners or Carers? Lone Mothers and Employment*, Paris: OECD.

Roll, J. (1988), *Family Fortunes: Parents' Incomes in the 1980s*, London: Family Policy Studies Centre.

Roll, J. (1992), *Lone-parent Families in the European Community: The 1992 Report*, London: Family Policy Studies Centre.

Smith, D. (ed.) (1992), *Understanding the Underclass*, London: Policy Studies Institute.

Social Security Committee (1993), *The Operation of the Child Support Act*, London: HMSO.

13

The Interests of Children at Divorce

M. P. M. Richards

Introduction

As divorce rates have risen in industrialized countries (Goode, 1993) concern about the consequences for children has increased. This concern has led to a considerable body of research from Britain, the USA, Australia, New Zealand and elsewhere which examines the associations between the development of children and young adults and parental separation or divorce. This body of research has been reviewed many times and despite weaknesses in the methodology of some research the overall patterns are now well established (e.g. Rutter, 1981; Hetherington, Cox and Cox, 1982; Richards and Dyson, 1982; Burgoyne, Ormrod and Richards, 1987; Demo and Acock, 1988; Emery, 1988; Hetherington and Aresteh, 1988; Amato and Keith, 1991a, 1991b; Hetherington and Clingempeel, 1992; Amato, 1993a).

Compared with those of similar social backgrounds whose parents remain married, children whose parents divorce show consistent but small differences in their behaviour throughout childhood and adolescence and somewhat different life courses as they move into adulthood. More specifically, the research indicates on average lower levels of academic achievement and self-esteem and a higher incidence of conduct and other problems of psychological adjustment during childhood. Also during childhood a somewhat earlier social maturity has been recorded. A number of the transitions to adulthood are typically reached at earlier ages; these include leaving home, beginning heterosexual relationships and entering cohabitation, marriage and childbearing. In young adulthood there is a tendency toward more changes of job, lower socio-economic status, a greater propensity to divorce and there are some indications of a higher frequency of depression and lower measures of psychological well-being. The relationships (in adulthood) with parents and other kin relationships may be more distant.

These broad conclusions require a number of qualifications. There is a wide range of response amongst children and adults. The statements I have made are based on differences in means in particular assessment measures between groups of those whose parents divorce and those who stay together. Such averages conceal wide ranges. Some children whose parents divorce will do very well at school with excellent psychological well-being, while others whose parents remain together will have unhappy or traumatic childhoods and do poorly at school. Clearly, children's problems are by no means confined to those whose parents divorce; however, they are slightly more common for such children and young people. Marital separation happens in many different ways and at different points in childhoods. Parents' ways of coping themselves and their style of caring for their children, the arrangements made after the separation and many other aspects of family life will differ and these, together with the differences in reactions of individual children, will all contribute to the wide variety of outcomes. Both social class and the gender of children are likely to play a role. Overall, the research suggests that young adult women from middle-class families show the greatest differences. This is largely because the socio-economic costs of leaving education and embarking on early childbearing are likely to differentiate these young women from their peers most sharply (e.g. Maclean and Wadsworth, 1988; Kuh and Maclean, 1990; Elliott and Richards, 1991).

We should also be aware of historical and cultural effects. By their nature, long-term follow-up studies refer to the past and, particularly at times of rapid social and economic change, we cannot assume that divorce will bear equally on each generation. Matters such as welfare provision, housing policies, availability of child care, minimum wage legislation, as well as general attitudes to divorce and marriage, may all have very significant effects. It is for these kinds of reasons that it is widely believed that parental divorce has less damaging effects on children in Scandinavia than in Britain. Unfortunately, we do not have good evidence to examine this suggestion.

Finally we should note that in this field, as in others concerning family matters, writing and research may be strongly driven by prior beliefs, and several researchers have pointed out (e.g. Demo, 1993) that there are biases in some of the research literature toward an exaggeration of negative effects of parental divorce.

In this chapter I will first discuss the developmental processes that may link the process of parental divorce to the aspects of the behaviour of children and young people. Then in the light of these I will consider possible aims for public policy related to divorce. In the final part of the chapter I will discuss some recent changes in divorce procedures in Britain.

Developmental Processes

The research I have described so far concerns *associations* between a particular change in family structure and a wide range of measures in the children. As such, it does not tell us why these should be linked. In order to consider ways in which we might attempt to alleviate some of the negative effects of divorce for children, we need to understand the developmental processes that lie behind these associations. Here, we are on much weaker ground. While it is relatively easy to establish associations, it is a great deal more difficult to unravel the processes that may produce them. I shall next outline some of the most commonly cited hypotheses about these processes. These are not mutually exclusive, indeed it is most likely that all of these (and perhaps others yet to be described) play a role, but their importance in particular cases and situations may well vary.

Divorce-prone couples

It has been suggested that separation and divorce, in themselves, may be of little consequence for children but that couples who are likely to divorce may have rather different styles of childrearing which account for what are often regarded as the consequences of divorce. It is well established that overt conflict within a marriage is associated with negative effects for children (e.g. Emery, 1988; Smith and Jenkins, 1991). Furthermore, some (but not all) of the attributes in children which have been associated with divorce can be seen *before* a couple separate (e.g. Elliott and Richards, 1991). However, while we cannot completely rule out an effect of divorce-prone couples producing specific effects on their children, nobody has specified exactly what might characterize such marriages. Furthermore, pre-divorce effects cannot account for all the differences which have been described after divorce (Booth and Amato, 1994).

However, these considerations are important in showing that simple cause and effect models of divorce are not very helpful. There are clearly some continuities between difficulties children may experience within some marriages, whether or not these end in divorce, and after marital separation. From a child's point of view, difficulties are likely to begin before a separation. Indeed, a separation may simply be one step in a long process that may begin much earlier and continues throughout their lives long after the separation.

Relationships with mothers and fathers

In most cases at separation, the children remain with the mother while the father becomes, at best, a visitor in their lives. Relationships with both parents are likely to change. Initially at least, with all the upheavals and emotional turmoil that usually accompany separation, relationships often deteriorate while parents are likely to be particularly preoccupied with their own lives (e.g. Cummings and Davies, 1994). Later, as new household patterns become established, there may well be a redrawing of the inter-generational boundary, especially with older children living with a lone parent. The arrival of new partners may create further periods of upheaval and times when parents' attention may become focused away from children. It is also important to note that following a parental divorce children may leave home earlier (Kiernan, 1992) and so be removed from the direct influence of a parent at an earlier age than for some other children.

Research has clearly demonstrated that it is not simply a matter of the presence or absence of a parent in a child's life which is significant, but the style and pattern of parenting (Amato, 1993a). Children who experience what researchers have described as an authoritative (not authoritarian) style with warmth, but also a monitoring and sensitivity to their needs, seem to do best. However, it may be very difficult to maintain such a style through the turmoil of a divorce (e.g. Hetherington and Clingempeel, 1992).

Contrary to widespread belief, children do not seem to do particularly well (or badly) if reared in a single-parent household with a parent of the same sex (Downey and Powell, 1993). What is obvious is that post divorce, as within marriage, the great bulk of child care is provided by women. Female-headed single-parent households tend to be poorer than those headed by men.

Research suggests that growing up in a single-parent household, in itself, may not be a great disadvantage to children. It is the *change* from two parents to a single residential parent, especially when this is brought about by divorce (rather than the death of a parent) that is significant (Richards, 1987), coupled with the usual, but not inevitable, low income of households of lone mothers. It is widely assumed that, post divorce, children do best if they maintain a good relationship with both parents. Unfortunately, there is little evidence that supports or refutes this notion as the required research is yet to be done. On general developmental grounds, it certainly seems likely that children will do better if a break in the relationship with either parent is avoided; however, in some situations there may be a trade-off between continued contact and continued involvement of a child in conflict between parents. Given the likelihood of a continuing relationship with the mother rather than the father, the quality of the mother–child relationship may have most salience for most children. However, the father–child relationship has been shown to be of significance (Amato, 1994).

Finally, the point needs to be made that post-divorce arrangements often change. A visiting father may gradually fade from the children's lives or a remarriage (of either parent) may bring a sudden end to a relationship. Conversely, a relationship may be re-established with a non-resident parent after a break. We know little about the effects of such changes. It has been suggested that in young adulthood it is more common for men than women to re-establish a relationship with a father which was broken earlier.

Conflict

As has been said already, conflict between parents who live together can have negative effects on children (Slater and Haber, 1984). Some have argued that this is the major source of difficulties for children of separated parents and, in particular, is associated with low self-esteem (Amato, 1993b; but see Clark and

Barber, 1994, for a contrary view). Low self-esteem may then be the root of a whole range of subsequent difficulties including poor performance at school, poor relationships with peers, premature entry into romantic and sexual relationships and poorer employment prospects.

Marital conflict is likely to have very important consequences but it must be recognized that it can be acted out in a variety of ways which may have differential effects on children (Katz and Gottman, 1993). Often the conflict will persist after the separation, but the ways it may affect children at that time may be rather different than while the two parents were living together. While parents are together it may be important whether or not they involve the children in their quarrels, either directly by using them as the subject of conflicts or more indirectly by conducting their rows in the presence of children. Indications are that direct or indirect involvement in conflict by children is what may be crucial rather than the presence or absence of conflict itself. After separation a major effect of continued conflict is that it may reduce or end contact with the non-residential parent. This may be through the denial of contact or more indirectly by creating a situation in which a child feels that it is too emotionally dangerous and disloyal to the resident parent to visit the non-resident parent. Hearing one parent denigrating the other, to whom the child will usually feel attachment, is likely to be particularly damaging to the child's self-esteem.

Economic factors

Divorce almost always brings a sharp decline in income for households headed by women (e.g. Maclean, 1991; Everett, 1991; Jackson, Wasoff, Maclean and Dobash, 1993). For many women it will be the first experience of living on state benefits. Poverty and low incomes damage the life-chances of children (see Oppenheim, 1993). Research suggests that some of the differences between children associated with separation are mediated by the fall in income, though this cannot account for all the associations. This is perhaps most obvious in cases where there is a remarriage (see Elliott and Richards, 1991). In general, remarriage restores incomes to something approaching the pre-divorce situation. However, outcomes for children are no better, and sometimes worse, than where mothers with children remain on their own. Presumably the advantages that an increased income may bring are offset by the upheaval and complex dynamics for children of the advent of a new partner for their mother.

The economic disadvantages of parental divorce may continue into adulthood, not only because of the accumulated effects of deprivation in childhood, but also because inter-generational transfers which might benefit adults may be disrupted by parental divorce and remarriage (White, 1992).

In recent years a number of jurisdictions have introduced child support schemes which are intended to increase the support provided for children by non-resident parents, usually, of course, fathers (Maclean, 1994). Typically such schemes prioritize children in first relationships, while the previous practice as in England and Wales, which has been supported by the courts and the tax and benefit systems, has been for men to give priority to the children of their current relationship. While studies of the scheme in Britain suggest it makes little difference to the income of households of divorced and separated women and their children (Garnham and Knights, 1994; Clarke, Glendinning and Craig, 1994), the importance of these schemes in the longer term may be the way in which they aim to uphold the interests of the children of earlier relationships and their carers. In time, if these aims are achieved, there may be significant effects in reducing the economic effects of parental divorce for children.

Life changes

Parental divorce often brings life changes for children. For example, there may be a move to a new house or change of school. Such changes may be upsetting in themselves, as well as leading to a loss of friendships and familiar environments (see Sandler, Tein and West, 1994). As with other aspects of the divorce, moves may cause children to feel very powerless and victims of circumstances brought about by the very people – their parents – who they look to for support and protection. In this connection we should note that parents often do not give children a clear account of what is happening and what they may expect in the future. It is not uncommon for children to discover that their parents are going to separate, or have separated, from a third party. A lack of direct communication and information not only erodes parent–child relationships but may further add to a child's sense of powerlessness and lack of self-esteem.

Relationships with wider kin

A divorce may not only lead to changes in the relationship between a child and their parents but also to those with members of the wider kin network. It is not uncommon for a child to lose contact with all relatives on the non-residential parent's side of the family. In other cases kin may be able to offer help and support to children and provide a safe haven during times of particular stress. The quality of relationships with kin, particularly grandparents, is not only important around the time of a separation in terms of the support they may, or may not, offer, but can have significant effects later in life. It has been suggested that some of the poorer economic status seen in young adults who have experienced a parental divorce are the consequence of a lack of flow of resources from kin which might have taken place had the divorce not happened. Divorce and remarriage may have important influences on family solidarity and relationships in the long term (e.g. White, 1992, 1994). We should also note that divorce after children have reached adulthood may have significant consequences for family relationships (Aquilino, 1994).

Relationship patterns

There is research evidence that the patterns of heterosexual relationships for those who have experienced parental divorce are rather different. Young people may begin such relationships and enter long-term commitments at earlier ages. Their own divorce rate is higher, perhaps as a consequence of marriage and childbearing at relatively early ages. However, there is an apparent contradiction in the evidence, as studies of the attitudes toward marriage of young people show that those who have experienced a parental divorce tend to be more cautious (Tasker and Richards, 1994). It seems that while they are particularly well aware of the potential difficulties in long-term relationships and express the need to be careful before entering into commitments, when they meet a potential partner they tend to move through the earlier stages of a relationship more quickly, so that the interval between meeting and cohabitation or marriage is, on average, shorter. At present this conclusion must remain rather speculative and is a topic that deserves more study. However, it is tempting to link this to the evidence of reduced self-esteem and more distant kin relationships. But these are complex issues and it is important not to ignore the strong links between educational and occupational achievement and marriage and fertility patterns. There are also gender differences that may be very significant in the ways these are interrelated (see Maclean and Kuh, 1991; Kiernan, 1986). These considerations mean that it might be misleading to attempt to explain the links between divorce over generations as a reduction in a psychological capacity to sustain relationships, as some have done (Kalter, 1987; Wallerstein and Corbin, 1989). We should also note the interesting findings of Rodgers (1994). He found that for women, but not men, there was a link between depression and anxiety amongst those whose parents have divorced, who, themselves, in their forties were divorced, never married or remarried. This association was not present for those who at that age remained in their first marriage.

Aims of Policy

Having sketched out some of the processes that may link a child's experience of parental divorce and the social and psychological factors that were discussed in the first part of this chapter, I will now turn to issues of social policy. What might be the aims of policy in this area if we are concerned to reduce ill effects for children of parental divorce? Most obviously, of course, we might aim to reduce the divorce rate itself. Whether or not such a reduction is a feasible policy goal, making divorce more 'difficult' as is often suggested, probably misses the point from the children's point of view. It may do nothing for the well-being of children in those conflicted marriages that would otherwise move on to a divorce. In making this point it is not being claimed that divorce is better than a bad marriage – or vice versa – but simply that the issue is the quality of the relationship between the parents, and parents and children, rather than parents' marital status. Realistically, we have to accept that some divorce will occur. Social policy should aim to produce a context in which marital and parental relationships may thrive, to provide help and support when these run into difficulties, but also to allow couples to end their relationship if they reach the point when it is not sensible to continue. Assuming this latter point has been reached, what then might be the aims of a policy designed to protect the interests of children? In addressing this question it is important to acknowledge that the interests of parents and children (and not just those between the parents) may diverge at divorce. While there is much mention of the needs of children, policy at present seems largely preoccupied with adult issues and attempting to settle disputes between spouses (see Hassell and Maxwell (1992) for an unusual view which emphasizes children's interests).

Relationship with parents

A major aim of policy should be to support and protect relationships between parents and children, at divorce – as at other times (e.g. Family Law Council, 1992). Most concern has centred on the resolution of disputes or potential disputes – decisions about where children should live, arrangements for seeing the non-residential parent and financial support. Clearly, for relationships to prosper there must be the possibility of parents and children spending time together and for other means of contact, but concern needs to move beyond this to address issues of the quality of relationships between parents and children.

There has been an enormous amount of debate about which post-divorce arrangements are most appropriate for children. I do not intend to review all the issues here but simply to say that we should aim to support a child's relationship with both their mother and father and wider kin network. This might be best achieved by the adoption of a principle of continuity of relationships with the primary caretaker becoming the residential parent (see Crippen, 1990) and strong support for the relationship with the non-residential parent. Such a principle might be tempered by a bias toward the residential parent being the one most likely to foster the child's relationship with the non-residential parent. We should also note that circumstances and the needs of children change with age, and, particularly at adolescence, there is a significant movement of children's main home. Arrangements should allow for such flexibility.

As already noted, a key research finding is that the *quality* of parental relationships is what is most significant for children. We also know that in many cases the quality of these relationships deteriorates around the time of separation. But in our concerns about where children should be living and in trying to resolve disputes between parents, this is an issue that is seldom addressed directly. We need to think clearly about how we might best support and encourage effective parenting at and after divorce by mothers and fathers, whether residential or non-residential, over the period of time when there is likely to be a great deal of upheaval and emotional stress in their lives (see Wolcott (1989) and Crisp (1994) for reviews of family support services).

Conflict between parents

Conflict is near universal at divorce and its reduction is already a key policy aim in mediation and, increasingly, in the legal system. The complex psychology of the uncoupling process (Vaughan, 1987) will usually engender conflict even where it has not been prominent in the decay of a marriage or cohabitation. Sometimes in our concern to move couples on and to get them to agree post-divorce arrangements, insufficient attention is paid to the psychology of uncoupling. This may leave unaddressed dynamics which may in time upset any future plans, especially those concerning matters as central and significant as the children of the relationship. It may be hard to achieve, but for effective post-divorce parenthood it is usually necessary to separate out issues of conflict between ex-spouses and those concerning children and for both parties to feel that disputes have been settled with a reasonable measure of justice. There is much work yet to be done in assessing different styles of mediation and their effectiveness in helping couples to manage conflict.

Material support

All households where children live need a reasonable provision of material resources. This need is frequently unmet after a parental divorce. Many aspects of public policy are concerned here – welfare provision, provision of child care, employment policies, child support arrangements and so on. Co-ordination between the different policy areas is often poor and policies do not always take account of the specific problems that can arise at divorce, particularly from the perspective of children. It would be helpful if the range of policies that impinge on households with children were reviewed from the perspective of the post-divorce household.

Psychological needs of children

A reduction in a child's self-esteem is a common accompaniment of parental divorce which may have far-reaching consequences for their life chances. Policies are required which directly address this and other psychological issues for children. Policy in this area is almost always indirect, following the trickle-down principle, operating via interventions aimed at parents rather than directly at children. We need to pay greater attention to such direct services as child counselling and other activities aimed at boosting children's self-esteem and addressing their other psychological needs. Work with parents should aim to draw attention to ways in which they might better meet their children's needs and these should be supplemented with support for others who have a lot of contact with children, especially teachers.

The four areas I have drawn attention to are, of course, very broad and each deserves detailed discussion. However, this is beyond the scope of this brief chapter. Instead, in the final section, I want to concentrate on recent changes in the law in England and Wales and the issue of mediation and how this deals with children's issues.

Recent Legal Changes in England and Wales

In England and Wales, in common with some other European countries and the United States, there have been recent changes in the law which affect the position of children at divorce (see Fine and Fine (1994) for an account of the changes).

The Children Act 1989 shifts the emphasis at divorce from a notion of parental rights to one of parental duties toward children. It was argued that the changes would reduce conflict between parents, facilitate co-operative joint parenting after divorce and reduce divorce litigation (Law Commission, 1988). Under the previous legislation, even where there was no dispute between the parents, the court required a statement of the proposed arrangements for the children. A hearing would be held (so-called Section 41 hearing) at which this would be scrutinized by the court. Subsequently the court would make such orders relating to the custody of the children (joint or sole) and access by the non-custodial parent. While it was often pointed out that the Section 41 hearings were brief and perfunctory, the court had a clear role to review proposed child-care arrangements in all cases and did not simply serve to adjudicate in disputes. It was argued by some that this reviewing of arrangements seemed an important symbolic function indicating to divorcing couples that there was a public concern with their child-care arrangements. Under the Children Act 1989 these hearings disappear. There is no requirement for parents to seek orders relating to their children at divorce or for courts to make them. Only where there is a dispute will the court make an order (now termed residence and contact orders). We await research which might show that the stated intentions of the legislators have been borne out and that there is no less conflict between parents and co-operative joint parenting after a divorce has been facilitated. Others suggest that the lack of orders in the great majority of cases may simply serve to encourage mothers to become the sole caretaker of children after divorce.

There has also been concern expressed about what appears to be a growing discrepancy between public and private law in the way in which a child's contact with both parents may be safeguarded. For several decades it appears to be clear from case law that the contact with both parents was a right of a child. For example, in a judgement in 1994 the President of Family Division stated in the Court of Appeal that 'contact with a parent was a fundamental right of a child, save in wholly exceptional circumstances' (ReW (a minor) (contact) [1994] 2FLR 441). It has been argued that a more recent case has changed this position (ReM (contact: Welfare Test) [1995] IFLR 274 CA). In this case it is suggested that a new test for maintaining the relationship of a parent and a child appears to have been set up. This is whether the emotional need of a child to have an enduring relationship with both parents is outweighed by the depth of harm which in the light of a child's wishes and feeling, a child would be at risk of suffering by virtue of a contact order. Commentators on this case (e.g. Willbourne and Geddes, 1995) argue that this position stands in contrast to that in public law which establishes a clear presumption of contact with parents for children who are in the care of the state. The Children Act 1989 does not contain statutory reference to a presumption of contact in private law and so it may be that the burden has been shifted to a parent who has to prove that contact is in the best interests of the child. Willbourne and Geddes (1995) comment, 'this decision represents a serious setback to efforts by the courts and practitioners to promote normal contact between parents and children after acrimonious marriage breakdown'.

It is widely acknowledged that The Children Act 1989 achieved a simplification of law. All would support the expressed intentions of reducing conflict between parents and encouraging co-operation in child care after divorce. However, it is not clear whether the new Act has in fact served to improve matters for the children of divorcing parents. Of course, the law can only have limited influence on patterns of parenting, but it is not clear whether that limited influence is being effectively applied. In particular, there seems no justification for what appears to be a double standard between public and private law.

Children and Mediation

One of the most striking shifts in the divorce process in recent years in Britain and elsewhere has been the rise in divorce mediation, though we should not forget that at present only a tiny percentage of divorcing or separating couples use mediation services. There is a movement from public ordering by the courts (and in their shadow by solicitors) to the more private system of negotiation within the context of mediation. Mediation is a form of dispute resolution which, in Britain at least, is said to focus on the needs of children. Indeed, most mediation is confined to children's issues and only recently has 'comprehensive' (concerned with all issues, including finance and property) mediation developed (see Walker, McCarthy, and Timms, 1994). While it is the policy of most mediation services in Britain to focus on issues related to children, it is unclear how mediation, as currently practised, does this. The process is one in which parents are assisted in reaching decisions about children (and other matters). In a reasonable number of cases agreement is reached and research indicates that the process may improve communication between the couple. But how well does the process serve the interests of children rather than those of the adults? The short answer is, I would suggest, that we do not know. While an agreement and better communication may well improve things for children, this has not been established by the research carried out so far. Indeed, it is striking that in the largest piece of research carried out so far on mediation in Britain there was no attempt to directly assess effects for children (Ogus, Walker, and Jones-Lee, 1989). We have no evidence about the well-being of children of parents who have chosen to use mediation to resolve their disputes and how this might compare with that of children of parents whose disputes have been dealt with in other ways. We do not even know whether the range of post-divorce arrangements for children is any different for those opting for mediation.

Mediation practice varies widely. In most cases children play no direct part in the process. It is assumed they will benefit indirectly from whatever agreements their parents may be able to make and from the attention that the mediation processes may have focused on their needs. Improving communication between parents and children is often a stated aim of mediators. This is sometimes done by including children in a final mediation session during which the decisions reached are reviewed and children have a chance of hearing what has been decided at first hand. While it seems plausible that such a process is helpful for children, the practice is rare and has never been evaluated.

Recently a few mediators have placed more emphasis on obtaining a view from children as part of the mediation process. This is usually done by seeing the children in separate sessions as an adjunct to the mediation itself (National Family Mediation, 1994). However, it is unclear how such views are incorporated into the mediation process or how they might influence the outcome. Again, this approach is rare and unevaluated.

The whole issue of how children's views may be determined and how best these might be fed into the mediation process is complex (see Garwood, 1988). In court-based decision-making it is generally agreed that children's views should be known, but not necessarily followed directly, in a judgement (see Eekelaar, 1994). For both psychological reasons and those of practicality, children's views cannot simply be used to determine an outcome. Children may simply want to maintain the familiar past and remain with both parents and so find any choice between them in terms of where they will live impossible. Putting children in the position of having to make choices may serve to tie them more firmly into the conflicts between their parents and can be very damaging for them. But while children (except perhaps the older age groups) cannot decide their own best outcome, they may have important considerations that a court needs to take into account when making a decision. Ideally at least, the system allows for this through a Court Welfare Officer's report which should embody the children's views. How can this work in mediation? If the children express views to a mediator which are contrary to the arrangement the parents agree to, is the mediator to intervene? It is unclear who represents the children in mediation or how mediators deal with conflicts of interest between children and parents. Clearly, if mediators are to maintain their own professed neutral position they cannot become advocates for children. Mediation agreements are subject to legal scrutiny. But, especially given a desire not to upset agreements already made, it seems unlikely that this process can ensure that the interests of children are safeguarded, although it could be some kind of crude long-stop.

Leaving aside the issue of decision-making, it is clear that mediation can only address children's emotional needs indirectly – by setting up residence and visiting arrangements, improving communication, reducing conflict between parents, etc. It cannot, and does not, set out to address children's emotional conflicts and needs directly. Because of the difference of interest at divorce and the dynamics of parent–child relationships, parents themselves cannot always do this effectively. It may be precisely the relationship with a parent that a child needs to talk about. Child counselling has been developed to respond to this need, either to work independently, but alongside, mediation, or quite separately for children whose parents may not be involved in mediation. Both individual work with children and that with small groups, perhaps in a school, have been offered (see also Bolen, 1993). Like mediation itself, child counselling needs to be evaluated. But at least it is an attempt to directly address emotional needs of children which otherwise may be ignored.

A further intervention, but one that at present is hardly ever being offered, is to concentrate directly on parenting, rather than decision-making about children. Given what we know of the disruption in parenting that separation and divorce often brings, interventions designed to offer support to parents at this time might be a very effective short-term intervention (see Wolcott, 1989; Crisp, 1994). We need to try and see what works, drawing what we can from support schemes offered to parents, in other situations. Rather different kinds of support may be required for mothers and fathers. Some access centres already offer support to fathers; these are initiatives we could build on.

So is this likely to be the future: mediation, supplemented by child counselling and schemes offering support to mothers and fathers? I would argue that we must always retain the court system itself and the necessary legal aid to provide access to it for all. Mediation is a form of bargaining in the shadow of the law. While it may be right that the courts remain a last resort which, hopefully, is seldom used, it is, I would argue, essential that it should remain, especially to protect children. Assuming that we agree that there should be some attempt to safeguard children's interests at divorce (over and above those provided by child protection procedures) it is very hard to see how any system of private ordering alone can do this. Such systems need a public review, which, in theory at least, the courts could provide. But for it to do this most effectively for the child, we should ensure independent representation of children in proceedings.

ACKNOWLEDGEMENTS

I thank Jill Brown for her technical help in the preparation of this chapter, Shelly Day Sclater and Ros Pickford for comments on an earlier draft, and Bill Clifton, Chris Ledonox and Jimmy Martin for their support. I am grateful to the Joseph Rowntree Foundation for a grant to support our Transitions to Adulthood project.

REFERENCES

Amato, P. R. (1993a), 'Children's adjustment to divorce: theories, hypotheses, and empirical support', *Journal of Marriage and the Family*, 55: 23–38.

Amato, P. R. (1993b), 'Contact with non-custodial fathers and children's well-being', *Family Matters*, 36: 32–4.

Amato, P. R. (1994), 'Father–child relations, mother–child relations, and offspring psychological well-being in early adulthood', *Journal of Marriage and the Family*, 56: 1031–42.

Amato, P. R. and Keith, B. (1991a), 'Parental divorce and the well-being of children: a meta-analysis', *Psychological Bulletin*, 110: 26–46.

Amato, P. R. and Keith, B. (1991b), 'Parental divorce and adult well-being: a meta-analysis', *Journal of Marriage and the Family*, 53: 59–69.

Aquilino, W. S. (1994), 'Later-life parental divorce and widowhood: impact on young adults' assessment of parent–child relations', *Journal of Marriage and the Family*, 56: 908–22.

Bolen, R. (1993), 'Kids' turn: helping kids cope with divorce', *Family and Conciliation Review*, 31: 249–54.

Booth, A. and Amato, P. (1994), 'Parental marital quality, parental divorce and relations with parents', *Journal of Marriage and the Family*, 56: 21–34.

Burgoyne, J., Ormrod, R. and Richards, M. (1987), *Divorce Matters*, Harmondsworth: Penguin.

Clark, J. and Barber, B. L. (1994), 'Adolescents in post-divorce and always-married families: self-esteem and perceptions of father's interest', *Journal of Marriage and the Family*, 56: 608–14.

Clarke, K, Glendinning, L. and Craig, G. (1994), *Losing Support: Children and the Child Support Act*, London: The Children's Society.

Crippen, G. (1990), 'Stumbling beyond best interests of the child: reexamining child custody standard setting in the wake of Minnesota's four year experiment with the primary caretaker preference', *Minnesota Law Review*, 75: 427–503.

Crisp, S. (1994), *Counting on Families: Social Audit Report on the Provision of Family Support Services*, London: Exploring Parenthood.

Cummings, E . M. and Davies, P. T. (1994), 'Maternal depression and child development', *Journal of Child Psychology and Psychiatry and Allied Disciplines*, 35: 73–112.

Demo, D. E. (1993), 'The relentless search for effects of divorce: forging new trails or tumbling down the beaten path', *Journal of Marriage and the Family*, 55: 42–5.

Demo, D. K. and Acock, A. C. (1988), 'The impact of divorce on children', *Journal of Marriage and the Family*, 50: 619–48.

Downey, D. B. and Powell, B. (1993), 'Do children in single-parent households fare better living with same-sex parents?', *Journal of Marriage and the Family*, 55: 65–71.

Eekelaar, J. (1994), 'The interests of the child and the child's wishes: the role of dynamic self-determinism', *International Journal of Law and the Family*, 8: 42–61.

Elliott, B. J. and Richards, M. P. M. (1991), 'Children and divorce: educational performance and behaviour, before and after parental separation', *International Journal of Law and the Family*, 5: 258–78.

Emery, R. F. (1988), *Marriage, Divorce and Children's Adjustment*, Beverly Hills, CA: Sage.

Everett, C. A. (ed.) (1991),*The Consequences of Divorce: Economic and Custodial Impact on Children and Adults*, New York: Haworth Press.

Family Law Council (1992), *Patterns of Parenting after Separation*, Canberra: Australian Government Printing Service.

Fine, M. A. and Fine, D. R. (1994), 'An examination and evaluation of recent changes in divorce laws in five western countries: the critical role of values', *Journal of Marriage and the Family*, 56: 249–63.

Garnham, A. and Knights, E. (1994), *Putting the Treasury First: The Truth about Child Support*, London: Child Poverty Action Group.

Garwood, F. (1988), *Research Project on Children in Conciliation in the Lothian Family Conciliation Service*, Edinburgh: Report to the Scottish Home and Health Department.

Goode, W. J. (1993), *World Changes in Divorce Patterns*, New Haven, CN: Yale University Press.

Hassell, I. and Maxwell, G. (1992), *A Children's Rights Approach to Custody and Access*, Wellington, New Zealand: Office of the Commissioner for Children.

Hetherington, E. M. and Arasteh, J. D. (eds) (1988), *Impact of Divorce, Single Parenting, and Stepparenting on Children*. Hillsdale, NJ: Lawrence Erlbaum.

Hetherington, E. M. and Clingempeel, W. G. (1992), 'Coping with marital transitions', Monographs of the Society for Research in Child Development, 57: nos 2–3.

Hetherington, E. M., Cox, M. and Cox, R. (1982), 'Effects of divorce on parents and children', in M. E. Lamb (ed.), *Non-Traditional Families: Parenting and Child Development*, Hillsdale, NJ: Lawrence Erlbaum.

Jackson, E., Wasoff, F., Maclean, M. and Dobash, R. E. (1993), 'Financial support on divorce: the right mixture of rules and discretion', *International Journal of Law and the Family*, 7: 230–54.

Kalter, N. (1987), 'Long-term effects of divorce on children: a developmental vulnerability model', *American Journal of Orthopsychiatry*, 59: 587–600.

Katz, L. F. and Gottman, J. M. (1993), 'Patterns of marital conflict predict children's internalizing and externalizing behaviors', *Developmental Psychology*, 29: 940–50.

Kiernan, K. (1986), 'Teenage marriage and marital breakdown', *Population Studies*, 37: 368–80.

Kiernan, K. (1992), 'The impact of family disruption in childhood on transitions in young adulthood', *Population Studies*, 46: 213–21.

Kuh, D. and Maclean, M. (1990), 'Women's childhood experience of parental separation and their subsequent health and socio-economic status in adulthood', *Journal of Biosocial Science*, 22: 1–15.

Law Commission (1988), (Law Comm. N.172) *Family Law, Review of Child Law, Guardianship and Custody*, London: HMSO.

Lord Chancellor's Department (1994), *Looking to the Future: Mediation and the Grounds for Divorce. A Consultation Paper*, Cmd. 2424, London: HMSO.

Maclean, M. (1991), *Surviving Divorce: Women's Resources after Separation*, London: Macmillan.

Maclean, M. (1994), 'Delegalizing child support', in M. Maclean and J. Kurczewski (eds), *Families, Politics and the Law*, Oxford: Clarendon Press.

Maclean, M. and Kuh, D. (1991), 'The long-term effects for girls of parental divorce', in M. Maclean and D. Groves (eds), *Women's Issues in Social Policy*, London: Routledge.

Maclean, M. and Wadsworth, M. E. J. (1988), 'The interests of children after parental divorce: a long-term perspective', *International Journal of Law and the Family*, 2: 155–66.

National Family Mediation (1994), *Giving Children a Voice in Mediation*, London: National Family Mediation.

Ogus, A., Walker, J. and Jones-Lee, M. (1989), *The Cost and Effectiveness of Conciliation in England and Wales*, Newcastle-upon-Tyne: unpublished report, Conciliation Project Unit, University of Newcastle-upon-Tyne.

Oppenheim, C. (1993), *Poverty: The Facts*, London: Child Poverty Action Group.

Richards, M. P. M. and Dyson, M. (1982), *Separation, Divorce and the Development of Children: A Review*, London: Department of Health and Social Security.

Richards, M. P. M. (1987), 'Children, parents and families: developmental psychology and the re-ordering of relationships at divorce', *International Journal of Law and the Family*, 1: 295–317.

Rodgers, B. (1994), 'Pathways towards parental divorce and adult depression', *Journal of Child Psychology and Psychiatry and Allied Disciplines*, 35: 1289–308.

Rutter, M. (1981), *Maternal Deprivation Reassessed*, 2nd edn, Harmondsworth: Penguin.

Sandler, I. N., Tein, J. Y. and West, S. G. (1994), 'Coping, stress, and the psychological symptoms of children of divorce: a cross-sectional and longitudinal study', *Child Development*, 65: 1744–63.

Slater, E. J. and Haber, J. D. (1984), 'Adolescent adjustment following divorce as a function of familial conflict', *Journal of Consulting and Clinical Psychology*, 52: 920–1.

Smith, M. A. and Jenkins, J. M. (1991), 'The effects of marital disharmony on pre-pubertal children', *Journal of Abnormal Child Psychology*, 19: 625–44.

Tasker, F. L. and Richards, M. P. M. (1994), 'Adolescents' attitude toward marriage and marital prospects after parental divorce: a review', *Journal of Adolescence Research*, 9: 340–62.

Vaughan, D. (1987), *Uncoupling: Turning Points in Intimate Relationships*, London: Methuen.

Walker, J., McCarthy, P. and Timms, N. (1994), *Mediation: The Making and Remaking of Co-operative Relationships. An Evaluation of the Effectiveness of Comprehensive Mediation*, Newcastle: Relate Centre for Family Studies.

Wallerstein, J. S. and Corbin, S. B. (1989), 'Daughters of divorce: report from a ten year follow up', *American Journal of Orthopsychiatry*, 59: 593–604.

White, L. (1992), 'The effect of parental divorce and remarriage on parental support for adult children', *Journal of Family Issues*, 13: 234–50.

White, L. (1994), 'Growing up with single parents and stepparents: long-term effects on family solidarity', *Journal of Marriage and the Family*, 56: 935–48.

Wilbourne, C. and Geddes, J. (1995), 'Presumption of contact – what presumption?', *Family Law*, 25: 87–9.

Wolcott, I. (1989), *Family Support Services: A Review of the Literature and Selected Annotated Bibliography*, Melbourne: Australian Institute of Family Studies.

Part V

Family, Kinship and Care

Part V is somewhat more diverse than previous parts, but shares the social policy focus of Part IV. In particular, it contains chapters which address different aspects of care provision. Clearly, in all societies family relationships – however these are defined – provide much informal care and support. With industrialization, there have been arguments that such care functions are no longer the province of the family, having been taken over by specialist organizations which have developed over the last century and more. Certainly the growth of state bureaucracies in the second half of the twentieth century, in particular those associated with health, education and social services, has been pronounced. However, as is now better appreciated than a generation ago, these state and other agencies have not replaced family support; instead, they have augmented such support. Health care is the classic example. New medical and health care developments have ensured better treatment for many conditions. Hospitals, health centres and the like see more patients than ever before. Yet still most of the active care that people receive when they are ill, infirm or otherwise in need of support comes from informal sources; principally from family and others living in the same household. Some of the tasks involved in caring are now different, shaped in part by the changed demands of technological innovation and formal agencies, but families – and especially women – continue to have responsibility for meeting care needs.

In chapter 14, first published in *Social Science and Medicine*, Hilary Graham discusses the idea of informal caring in its different guises. Importantly she points out how in policy and academic debates informal care is often defined in quite a narrow fashion – as care for those with disabilities. Yet the provision of such care is very much linked to other forms of informal caring, in particular the range of unpaid work that women do within the home for their immediate families (see Part III of this volume). Writing in the early 1990s when the New Right had been in government for over a decade, Graham argues that the care policies which were being developed in the late 1980s and early 1990s were premised on an uncritical – and largely unstated

– acceptance of a domestic division of labour in which women held responsibility for care provision. Because women are involved in what she terms a 'cycle of caring' over the life course, the conditions of their lives are usually such as to make it reasonable that they should continue to act as carers when new care needs – in particular, increasing infirmity of elderly parents – arise. Yet, as we have seen, responsibility for providing care within the household inevitably shapes women's lives, often leaving them significantly disadvantaged. Likewise those providing informal care to others in the kin network frequently pay a high price, both socially and economically, especially when the amount of care required is extensive. Thus, while from the state's perspective such caring may appear 'cost free', for those involved it perpetuates systems of inequality and disadvantage rooted more widely in the economic and social structure, inequalities which themselves have a direct link with health outcomes.

Chapter 15, by Janet Finch and Jennifer Mason, is concerned with the nature of kinship obligations in contemporary Britain, and was originally published in the *British Journal of Sociology*. Part of a much larger study – see, in particular, Finch (1989) and Finch and Mason (1993) – it focuses on the degree to which ideas about kinship obligations and responsibilities inherent in current policy initiatives correspond to the beliefs and values which people actually hold. The chapter draws on data from interviews with over 900 respondents about appropriate kinship behaviour in different circumstances. The authors used a 'vignette technique' in which those interviewed were asked how they thought people should respond to a varied set of kin 'dilemmas'. Overall they found there was relatively little consensus over what people regarded as the 'right' or 'proper' action to take in different circumstances, though there was more agreement about the types of issue that needed to be considered in making such decisions. The main conclusion of the research is that kinship obligations and behaviour are 'situationally specific'. That is, while people recognize a general sense of obligation to genealogically close kin – essentially parents, children, siblings, grandparents and grandchildren – the way those obligations are enacted depends very much on the circumstances of both those giving and requiring help or support. In other words, kinship behaviour does not follow set cultural 'rules' in any simple fashion. Instead, people interpret what is most appropriate contextually in the light of their own (and others') overall situation and commitments. These arguments are developed further by Finch and Mason in their book *Negotiating Family Responsibilities*, in which they also draw on extensive qualitative interviews. A summary of some of the arguments is provided in Allan (1996).

Finch and Mason are interested in a wide range of kinship obligations, some of which entail providing care for elderly parents or other relatives in need of what Parker (1981) usefully termed 'tending' – that is, actively providing care for someone rather than just caring about them. Over the last twenty years a great deal of attention has been paid by researchers to the ways in which 'tending' care is socially organized, and the costs and rewards which attach to it. While much rhetoric has been produced by politicians and others about 'community care', it is now widely accepted that the enormous majority of significant 'tending' occurs within 'the family', often falling disproportionately on women. However, as Arber and Ginn discuss in chapter 16, in some circumstances men are also involved in providing high levels of support. Their chapter analyses data collected in the General Household Survey – a large nationally representative survey of private households – on people who report providing care for someone who is 'sick, handicapped or elderly'. From this data they demonstrate that 'family care' does not always equal 'female care', in part because in the first instance 'family care' should be understood as 'household care'. That is, when an individual needs practical support and personal care in daily living tasks, it usually falls first on someone living in the household (see Qureshi and Walker, 1989). If a female is available within the household, responsibility for providing the care needed generally falls on her. However, if there is only a male available, he is frequently the one who does the necessary tending. So, for example, married men with a disabled child rarely carry main responsibility for the day-to-day care of the child; this is typically defined as their wives' role. But among older couples especially, where a wife becomes infirm and in need of support, it is frequently her husband who provides much of it, albeit sometimes supported by daughters (or daughters-in-law) living nearby. While Arber and Ginn are certainly not arguing that men and women play an equal part in providing informal care, their analysis does highlight the dangers of assuming too readily that the burdens of caring are only experienced by women. In this their work echoes that of Finch and Mason in recognizing that kinship responsibilities are contextually framed.

The final chapter of the book, taken from *Social Support for Disabled Children and Their Families: A Review of the Literature* by Sally Baldwin and Jane Carlisle, is concerned with the impact which a child's disability has on family life. In it, Baldwin and Carlisle provide a very thorough review of a wide range of research examining the different consequences which having a child with significant disabilities has on the household. Importantly, though they examined research concerned with diverse disabilities and conditions, they found many commonalities in the experiences of both parents and the children. Certainly the majority of families in which there was a child with disabilities experienced a degree of financial hardship, often quite severe. Principally this was because the mother's involvement in providing care restricted her opportunities for employment, resulting in the household being dependent on one income at a time when family economies are increasingly built upon two incomes (Pahl, 1984). Even though wives generally earn significantly less than their husbands, the additional income they earn typically ensures a standard of living well above the poverty line. Moreover, there are the additional costs often associated with providing for a child with disabilities, be these the need for special equipment or the additional expense of, say, heating, laundry or hospital visits. Equally, as much other research has demonstrated, providing extensive care often has a significant impact on sociability and other aspects of personal life, for both the carer and the recipient of the care. Siblings, too, will be affected by the demands of caring, if not directly – and often parents seek to 'protect' them from any significant involvement in caring tasks – then indirectly, through poverty, reduced parental time, or embarrassment over household conditions. Of course, different families develop different ways of coping with the additional pressures that having a child with disabilities generates. Some manage extremely successfully; others struggle to maintain any sort of equilibrium. As Baldwin and Carlisle point out, we need to know far more than we do about successful strategies for coping, so that these experiences can inform policy initiatives.

Being a research review, Baldwin and Carlisle's chapter contains numerous references on aspects of caring; readers interested in exploring the topics covered in this chapter – or, indeed, in many of the other issues raised in Part V – will find much relevant material in the sources they cite. Indeed, generally, the topic of 'caring' is one which has generated many excellent – and accessible – analyses in recent years. These include Finch and Groves (1983), Glendinning (1983), Baldwin (1985), Ungerson (1987), Qureshi and Walker (1989), Parker (1990), Allen and Perkins (1995) and Dalley (1996).

REFERENCES

Allan, G. (1996), *Kinship and Friendship in Modern Britain*, Oxford: Oxford University Press.

Allen, I. and Perkins, E. (1995) *The Future of Family Care for Older People*, London: HMSO.

Baldwin, S. (1985), *The Costs of Caring: Families with Disabled Children*, London: Routledge & Kegan Paul.

Dalley, G. (1996), *Ideologies of Caring*, London: Macmillan.

Finch, J. (1989), *Family Obligations and Social Change*, Cambridge: Polity Press.

Finch, J. and Groves, D. (1983), *A Labour of Love: Women, Work and Caring*, London: Routledge & Kegan Paul.

Finch, J. and Mason, J. (1993), *Negotiating Family Responsibilities*, London: Routledge.

Glendinning, C. (1983), *Unshared Care: Parents and their Disabled Children*, London: Routledge & Kegan Paul.

Pahl, R. (1984), *Divisions of Labour*, Oxford: Blackwell Publishers.

Parker, G. (1990), *With Due Care and Attention*, London: Family Policy Studies Centre.

Parker, R. (1981), 'Tending and social policy', in E. Goldberg and S. Hatch (eds), *A New Look at the Personal Social Services*, London: Policy Studies Institute.

Qureshi, H. and Walker, A. (1989), *The Caring Relationship: Elderly People and their Families*, London: Macmillan.

Ungerson, C. (1987), *Policy is Personal: Sex, Gender and Informal Care*, London: Tavistock.

14

The Informal Sector of Welfare: A Crisis in Caring?

Hilary Graham

Introduction

Since the mid 1970s, policy documents in the health and welfare fields have increasingly emphasized the fact that care in Britain is not a state monopoly (DHSS, 1981, 1983; Social Services Committee, 1985; Griffiths Report, 1988; Wagner Report, 1988; *Caring for People*, 1989). Government proposals for the care of dependent groups explicitly acknowledge that care comes from a variety of sources: the state, the private market, volunteers and family and friends (DHSS, 1981; Griffiths Report, 1988; Wagner Report, 1988; *Caring for People*, 1989). Of these sources, the informal sector of family and friends is – and is recognized to be – the most fundamental.

While providing the material base on which the other sectors of care are built, the debate about care in Britain has been more narrowly drawn around the formal sectors of the state and the market. It is in this arena that the 'crisis in care' has been located. The informal sector features as a resource: a care-providing network which, with an expanded role, could help solve the problems identified in the formal health and social care systems. Locating informal care within the wider patterns of everyday care within families, this chapter seeks to develop a more critical perspective on the informal sector.

The chapter develops its arguments in four sections. The first section considers the concept of informal care as it has been defined within British policy and research. Noting that the concept of informal care has been restricted to the care of people with long-term dependencies, the section argues for a perspective that locates these patterns of care within the wider organization of everyday social reproduction. The second section considers the way in which policies for the care of those with long-term dependencies have developed over the last decade. Highlighting the pivotal role identified for the informal sector in these policies, the section again underlines the need for a broader understanding of care within families. Adopting this broader perspective, the third and fourth sections of the chapter argue that features identified as strengths of care within families can also be experienced as deeply problematic by those seeking and providing such care. The fourth section focuses on the experiences of mothers caring for children in disadvantaged circumstances. As a case study, these experiences highlight some of the contradictory dimensions of caring informally for health.

In focusing on the experiences of one group of carers, it should be recognized that the chapter will illuminate only some aspects of the caring process. In particular, the chapter provides a limited insight into the experiences of people who receive more care than they give. While we know little about the giving of care, we know less about the position of those living in the community who are dependent on such care, and the wider provision of voluntary and statutory care in which it is embedded.

What is Informal Care?

Over the last two decades a vocabulary of care has become incorporated into British welfare policy. A new set of terms – carer, informal care, caring networks – have been employed in research reports and policy documents to describe the everyday arrangements that people develop to look after each other (DHSS, 1981; Social Services Committee, 1985; Griffiths Report, 1988; *Caring for People*, 1989; Finch and Groves, 1983; Parker, 1985; Allen et al., 1987; Green, 1988). At first glance, these concepts could be taken as signalling a broad concern with the day-to-day roles and relationships that are constructed through the process of keeping people alive and healthy. However, within the British context, the concept of informal care, and the related concept of carer, have both a more specific and more complex meaning. While the different dimensions of care captured in the concept of informal care tend to be fused in the experience of those working in the informal sector, it is important to recognize that it is a term which condenses a number of analytically distinct dimensions of the giving of everyday care. This section identifies five specific aspects which define the informality of informal care.

First, informal care is care provided for others. In contrast to the debate within Sweden, care within the community is defined more in terms of care-for-others than care-for-self. The informal sector is seen primarily as a resource through which an individual's care-needs can be met by relatives and friends. While the extent of self-care is recognized, the policy emphasis is on those who depend on others for help with the tasks of daily living. There is an implicit division between those who give care (carers or the informal sector more generally) and those who receive it. In such a division, the extent to which care-receivers are also engaged in giving care can be overlooked (Wenger, 1984). The importance of self-care among those in receipt of care, too, can be obscured. As Stacey (1988) reminds us, patients are also health workers, actively engaged in their own care and the promotion of their own health.

Second, informal care is non-institutional care. Within both the policy and research literature, there is a broad consensus that informal care refers to care outside institutions. However informal the atmosphere and however caring the relationships, care within hospitals or within residential homes is not defined as informal care. Instead, the term is restricted to care within the 'informal sector', differentiated from the state, market and voluntary sectors by its base within the social relations of family and community.

Third, informal care is unpaid care. In Britain, as in Sweden, many aspects of social reproduction (aspects of child socialization, domestic labour and health care, for example) have been absorbed within the capitalist economy (in the form of nursery and school education, the personal service industries and the health service). In contrast, the basic routines of caring for others have not become market commodities: they are typically performed on an unpaid basis in the home. Provided on this basis, the economic costs of caring tend to be high. In addition to the direct costs of caring – the additional expenditure on fuel, food, laundry, transport – there are the costs of lost opportunities for earning. For mothers, for example, the costs of caring for children include earnings foregone while out of employment and as a result of the lower-paid and part-time work to which women typically return. Joshi (1987) has estimated the opportunity costs of motherhood (at mid-1980 prices) to be around £135,000 for each mother in Britain.

Fourth, informal care is provided through the bonds of kinship. In contrast to the formal sectors of care, the ties that bind carer and cared-for do not come from a formal contract of employment or a code of professional ethics. They arise, instead, from the normative obligations of kinship and friendship. It is in these terms that the informal sector is usually distinguished from the voluntary sector, where care is provided through the intermediary of a voluntary group or organization, by those who are not bound by kin and friendship obligations. Reflecting the kinship-base of caring, carers are typically the relatives of those they care for. The recent OPCS survey indicates that four out of five carers looking after disabled, sick and elderly people are related to them (Green, 1988). In interpreting these figures, it is important to note that the survey relied on respondents' assessments of whether they were engaged in providing 'special care' to others and of how much time was spent in these care activities. For those for whom 'special care' was a routine feature of their lives, such assessments may underestimate the extent of their caring responsibilities.

Because of its kinship-base, the relationships between carer and cared-for constitute a 'sector' rather than a 'system' of care. Unlike other sources of health care – the private market, the state and the voluntary sector – caring in the informal sector does not integrate the carer into an organizational structure of carers. While often described in system-like terms ('the informal *system*', '*community* care,' 'caring *networks*', '*army* of carers'), the informal sector is characterized by literally millions of separate carer-dependent relationships where individual family members work on their own for their kin. Here, the giving of care reflects the familial obligations of carers rather than the statutory rights of dependents. As a result, those with fractured family networks can find themselves denied access to informal care. The informal sector, Walker (1987) suggests, is 'unable to establish rights to support; it is only the public sector that can implement and secure rights'.

The four features so far identified suggest that informal care is a concept with a wide frame of reference. 'Informal care' appears to embrace a broad category of care which is unpaid and home-based and governed by the moral and emotional ties of kinship. It is a concept which, at first glance at least, alerts us to the social and material processes through which both individual and family life are sustained.

However, there is a fifth dimension to the concept of informal care which restricts this wide-ranging concern with everyday social reproduction. Informal care is a term which is typically restricted to the care of individuals with a long-term need for help and support. Thus, while suggesting a general interest in the ways in which families work to promote the health of individuals, research and policy on informal care has focused on the care of people who might otherwise require institutional care. As a result, the concept has typically been defined in terms of the care of physically disabled children and adults, older people, those with learning difficulties and the long-term sick (Social Services Committee, 1985; Griffiths Report, 1988; Parker, 1985; Allen et al., 1987; Johnson, 1988). As the recent OPCS study of *Informal Carers* (Green, 1988) succinctly puts it, informal carers are 'people caring for a sick, handicapped or elderly person'. On the basis of this definition, it estimates that there are 1.4 million carers spending at least twenty hours a week on caring for a sick, disabled or older person living with them. While this figure may underestimate the scale and volume of unpaid care which routinely goes on in Britain's homes, it points to a caring labour force which is at least twice that of Britain's largest employer, the National Health Service.

Restricted to the care of those with long-term dependencies, the concept of informal care none the less remains a broad one. Its inclusion of a range of client groups means that it encompasses a complex of caring experiences. Studies have highlighted the diversity of needs and obligations faced by those caring for sick, older and physically disabled adults and children and adults and children with learning difficulties (Lewis and Meredith, 1988; Ungerson, 1987; Glendinning, 1983; Hicks, 1988). Such studies point to the way in which the shared identity of 'being an informal carer' can mask a diverse and changing set of experiences.

Recognizing the breadth of the concept is clearly important. Important, too, is an awareness of what the concept excludes. Limited to the care of those with long-term needs, it is a concept which restricts the boundaries of caring inform-ally to particular kinds of caring relationship. Focusing attention on what is distinct (and difficult) about caring for disabled and sick adults and children is clearly important. But defining informal care in these terms can obscure other forms of care carried out on an unpaid and informal basis within households. Specifically, it can obscure the ways in which informal care is embedded within the organization of care for able-bodied partners and children.

Studies suggest that informal carers tend to be relatives who are caring for, or have cared for, able-bodied members of their households. The process of becoming an informal carer, it seems, is one that has its roots in everyday family care (Ungerson, 1987; Glendinning, 1983; Hicks, 1988; Ungerson, 1983). It is feminist research which has highlighted the interconnected nature of informal and everyday caring responsibilities (Ungerson, 1983; Land, 1978; Graham, 1985; Waerness, 1984). This important body of literature has pointed to the way in which kinship obligations are 'gendered', with informal care defined as part of the kinship obligations of close female relatives (Finch and Groves, 1983; Ungerson, 1987; Dalley, 1988). While the OPCS survey may underestimate the extent of care by women, it none the less confirms that the majority (two thirds) of those caring for at least twenty hours a week are women (Green, 1988). The basis for the gender differences in caring is seen to lie in women's responsibilities for the care of able-bodied partners and children. In other words, women find themselves engaged in the care of other kin because they are engaged in the care of their immediate family: the patterns of informal care in its restricted sense are shaped and supported by the patterns of informal care viewed in a broader perspective.

Engaged in caring for the family across the life-cycle, it is women rather than men who are likely to find themselves working as principal carers through a 'cycle of caring'. Two in three households in Britain are households of married couples (CSO, 1989). In the majority of these households, it is the woman who takes responsibility for the care of both partners, doing the housework, the washing and ironing and the shopping and cooking on behalf of the household (Jowell, Witherspoon and Brook, 1988). Data from the General Household Survey indicate that three out of every four women in households with pre-school children are full-time carers (OPCS, 1989). This suggests that there are over 3 million women in Great Britain working in the informal sector as the principal carers of children under five years of age (OPCS, 1984). If those caring for children aged 5–15 are included, the figure rises by over 4 million, to nearly 8 million. Among parents caring for children alone, women outnumber men nine to one (OPCS, 1989).

Set against this backdrop, it is clear that informal care is only one part of the spectrum of care provided within households. While a significant part, informal care none the less constitutes only one aspect of the unpaid reproductive work that makes up the informal sector of welfare. In other words, informal care is not coterminous with the informal sector: it represents one segment of a larger and more complex whole. It is clear, too, that informal care rests on the wider patterns of care which make up this sector. The informal arrangements made for the care of dependent people emerge out of, and are embedded within, the routines through which families are reconstituted both day by day and generation by generation. To understand more about the experience of informal care, we therefore need to understand more about its structural location as part of the reproductive work that defines and marks out home and family life.

Before turning to examine some of the routine experiences of keeping individuals and families going, the next section reviews the place accorded to informal care, and to the informal sector more generally, in welfare policies over the last decade. Over this period, an enhanced role for the informal sector has come to be seen as a solution to the crises identified in formal systems of care.

Informal Caring in a Pluralist Welfare System

Most commentators on British social policy depict the thirty years from 1945 as a period of consensus about, and of growth in, state welfare (Offe, 1984; Mishra, 1984; Seldon, 1981). A similar consensus has been identified in Western Europe as a whole (Johnson, 1988; Jallade, 1989). Until the mid 1970s the principle of a welfare state was one which – at least in public – all the major political parties in Britain supported. From the mid 1970s the economic prosperity which had been associated with the postwar growth of state welfare gave way to recession. No longer bedded into an expanding economy, the welfare state has increasingly faced both economic crisis and ideological conflict.

In 1979 a Conservative government was elected which was committed to reducing state intervention in the economy and welfare. This 'New Right' government (the prefix 'New' distinguishing it from its postwar Conservative predecessors) has now been in office for over a decade. Challenging the principle of a universal and collectively provided system of welfare, it has argued instead for a more residual role for the state (Harris, 1988; Harris and Seldon, 1987). In its place, policy statements have emphasized the potential for a larger and stronger private market, an expanded role for the voluntary sector and the greater involvement of families and communities in the care of dependent groups.

This mixed approach to welfare has provided the major framework for policy-making since the late 1970s (Webb and Wistow, 1982). It is referred to as the 'mixed economy of welfare' or, increasingly, as 'welfare pluralism'. Used descriptively, the concept of pluralism reminds us that care comes from a plurality of sources – the state sector, the private sector, the voluntary sector and the informal sector. Charting the patterns of care 'on the ground', it draws particular attention to the contribution that the informal sector makes to health and social care in Britain (Parker, 1985).

The pluralism embedded in current welfare policy in Britain goes beyond describing what is. It is a prescriptive concept. It is part of an argument for greater diversity in welfare provision, with a less dominant role for the state in the care of dependent groups (Hatch and Mocroft, 1983). This prescriptive pluralism has been strongly in evidence in government policy statements about health and social care. For example, the 1981 White Paper, *Growing Older* (DHSS, 1981, p. 3), argues that, in the care of older people: 'Everyone has a contribution to make. Individuals can offer their services as volunteers. Voluntary and religious groups...can increase their effectiveness. ...Commercial organizations can help. ... And employers have an increasingly important part to play.'

More recently, the 1988 Griffiths Report has argued in similar terms for community care policies, not simply for older people, but across the range of adult dependencies. While its emphasis on the co-ordinating role of local authorities in the mixed economy of welfare initially met with a cool reception from government, its basic philosophy is in line with government priorities. *Community Care: Agenda for Action* (Griffiths Report, 1988, p. 5) affirms the current pluralist structure of provision and argues for greater pluralism in future:

> Care and support can be provided from a variety of sources. There is value in a multiplicity of provision, not least from the consumer's point of view, because of the widening of choice, flexibility, innovation and competition it should stimulate. The proposals are therefore aimed at stimulating further the 'mixed economy' of care.

These themes have been reiterated in the 1989 White Paper, *Caring for People*, and have taken a legislative form in the NHS and Community Care Act. As these documents make clear, a mixed economy of care means a reduced role for local authorities. The public sector is encouraged to retreat from the direct provision of welfare services and concentrate instead on developing and co-ordinating the pluralist system in general and the informal sector in particular. Policy documents put it like this:

> The Government sees the primary role of the public services as an enabling one, helping people to care for themselves and their families by providing a framework of support. ... It is essential that scarce professional skills should be reserved for the circumstances in which they can provide care and treatment not otherwise available. (DHSS, 1981, p. 3)

> The first task of publically provided services is to support and where possible strengthen these networks of carers. ... It is vital that social service authorities should see themselves as the arrangers and purchasers of care services – not as monopolistic providers. (Griffiths Report, 1988, p. 5)

As these statements indicate, the informal sector is central to the reshaping of the state's role within a mixed economy of care. It is care by and within families which provides both the structure and the resource for welfare pluralism. The following comments, drawn from White Papers and government reports published in the 1980s, illustrate the place accorded to unpaid care in the emerging pluralist policies of the period:

> The primary sources of support for the elderly are informal and voluntary. These spring from the personal ties of kinship, friendship and neighbourhood. They are irreplaceable. It is the role of public authorities to sustain and, where necessary, develop – but never to displace – such care and support. Care *in* the community must increasingly mean care *by* the community. (DHSS, 1981, p. 3; original emphasis)

Families, friends and other local people provide the majority of care in response to needs that they are uniquely well placed to identify and respond to. This will continue to be the primary means by which people are enabled to live normal lives in community settings. The proposals take as their starting point that this is how it should be. (Griffiths Report, 1988, p. 5)

The greater part of care has been, is and always will be provided by families and friends. (*Caring for People*, 1989, foreword)

As such statements suggest, government policies acknowledge, and seek to build on, the routine and unpaid care that goes on in households. They recognize, if only implicitly, that informal care rests on a larger informal sector of welfare sustained through the everyday reproductive work that keeps individuals and families going. Thus, while seen as a radical departure from previous postwar approaches, this policy appears to rest on a deeper ideological consensus about the role of families in welfare. In advocating change in the formal and voluntary sectors of welfare, government policy emphasizes continuity in the informal sector. New roles for local and health authorities, and for private and voluntary agencies, are to be achieved through an emphasis on a traditional role for families. In confirming this role, current government policy draws heavily on the welfare orthodoxy of the 1970s: that informal care provides a better solution to the problems of dependency than institutional care (Walker, 1987). Specifically, informal care is seen to help dependent people become more independent, a goal which, as Waerness (1984, p. 85) has pointed out, lies 'at the very foundation of the "helping people to help themselves" or the "self-care" ideology upon which public care system of the welfare state is based'.

The informal sector, it seems, provides both the ideological and material base for a mixed economy of care, an economy which, according to the 1989 White Paper, is set to shape Britain's 'caring services for the 1990s and beyond' (*Caring for People*, 1989, p. 2). Yet, while an integral part of Britain's care system, it is the formal sectors of welfare that have been subject to governmental review – in the Griffiths Report (1988) on community care and the Wagner Report (1988) on residential care. In contrast, there has been no Wagner or Griffiths Report on informal care or on the informal sector of which it is part. Similarly, the process of legislation assumes rather than explores the organization of care within the home. As the government acknowledges in *Caring for People* (1989, p. 9), 'while this White Paper focuses largely on the role of statutory and independent bodies in the provision of community care services, the reality is that most care is provided by family, friends and neighbours'.

The next two sections of the chapter turn to consider the reality of care within families. Featured in government policies as part of the solution to the crises besetting the formal sectors of welfare, the sections explore some of the problems facing those who work for health at home.

The Welfare of the Informal Sector

The policy debate about informal care recognizes that there are limits to the sector's capacity to care. However, these tend to be seen in aggregate terms, as problems of supply and demand. Thus, for example, research has pointed to a 'care gap', with current demographic trends, patterns of household formation and women's employment pointing to a future excess of dependents relative to carers (Wicks, 1987). The rate of discharge of people from residential care is causing more immediate difficulties. As the Social Services Committee report on Community Care (1985, pp. xviii, xvi) put it, 'the pace of removal of hospital facilities for mental illness has far outnumbered the provision of services in the community'. In the light of evidence presented to them, they concluded that 'there may be an approaching crisis in the community'.

While the number of carers and the level of professional support clearly sets limits on the informal sector's capacity to care, there is evidence of other, and more fundamental, sources of crisis. These appear to be endemic, springing from the features which define care in the informal sector. As the first section suggested, key features include the provision of care on an unpaid basis through the social relations of family and kinship. These features of informal sector care, common to both informal care and the care of able-bodied adults and children, are depicted as its strengths in policy debates. Yet these dimensions of caring can prove problematic for those seeking and providing unpaid care at home. As a result, experiences can be confusing and contradictory. This section focuses on two structural features of care within the informal sector – as kin care and as unpaid care – to gain a sense of the contradictions of caring.

With care mediated through kinship obligations, access to care within the informal sector is determined not so much by the dependant's needs (and rights) as by their access to kinship networks. As a result, those whose kinship networks have been fractured, for example by marital separation or by the experience of being a principal carer, can find themselves outside the informal care sector (Wicks, 1987; Lewis and Meredith, 1988). The position of black elders in Britain highlights the problems of growing old without access to the informal relationships which policy documents identify as 'primary' and 'irreplaceable'. Fenton's (1988) study of growing old in Bristol, for example, points to the way in which immigration policies and the low-waged, racially segregated labour market combine to make the unification of family and kin an impossible dream for many of those who are now growing old in Britain. While over half (56 per cent) of the white respondents in Fenton's study felt that 'their families had mostly been able to stay together', only one third of the South Asian and Afro-Caribbean respondents gave this response. Reflecting their differing assessments, one third of Asian respondents and one fifth of the Afro-Caribbean respondents reported that members of their wider family (brothers, sisters and their children) lived in Bristol. The black elders who participated in the survey spoke of their struggle to construct and sustain a nuclear family in Britain in the face of increasingly restrictive immigration regulations and increasing poverty.

Many found themselves growing old outside both the formal and informal sectors of care: as two black respondents summed up, 'I pray to God I don't die in this country...I have found myself trapped in a country that does not like me except for my work' (ibid.).

The kinship-base of care within the informal sector can prove problematic for those providing as well as those seeking informal care. While informal care is seen to stem from the sense of collective responsibility that exists within families, care typically comes from relatives, working alone, rather than networks, caring together. Once a carer is identified, and particularly once co-residence is established, s/he tends to become the principal carer, with other members of the family network withdrawing (Lewis and Meredith, 1988). As the dependant's needs increase and the carer's emotional and physical energy declines, carers find they have to sacrifice outside activities and contacts in order to maintain their caring role. Their enforced withdrawal both increases the isolation of caring, and, paradoxically, can leave them without the kinship and friendship networks they will need for their own old age (ibid.). Informal care, it seems, can threaten the social relations on which it is built.

With Britain's social security system geared to the needs of those who work in the paid rather than unpaid sectors of the economy, informal care can bring economic as well as social difficulties. Because caring is unpaid, carers are typically economically dependent on others for their income. In contrast to Sweden, where the insurance system serves to protect the financial position of those giving and receiving informal care, economic dependency tends in Britain to be a condition which is shared both by those who receive, and those who give, informal care (Baldwin, Parker and Walker, 1988). Unable to support themselves financially, care-givers and care-receivers are heavily over-represented among Britain's poor.

Government figures suggest that, in 1985, one in eight of two-parent households with children in Britain were living at or below the supplementary benefit line (DHSS, 1988). Among female-headed households with children (where Afro-Caribbean women are over-represented), 65 per cent were living at or below the poverty line. Where these households combine caring for those in health with caring for sick and disabled people, the risks of poverty can be greater still. Baldwin's study of the economic circumstances of families with severely disabled children suggested that household incomes were significantly lower than the average incomes of other families with children, even when benefits intended to help with the costs of disablement were taken into account. These income differences stemmed from the fact that mothers of disabled children, as the primary carers, were much less likely to go out to work than other mothers, and when they did work, to work fewer hours for lower rates of pay. In addition, the families faced extra expenses associated with caring for disabled children (Baldwin, 1985).

In households vulnerable to poverty, there is pressure on carers to extend their economic role to include paid as well as unpaid work. In other words, while full-time and unpaid caring may be both prescribed and preferred, it is the poverty that results that makes paid work a necessity. For many women, and particularly for Afro-Caribbean and Asian women, unpaid caring is supplemented by low-paid service work in the 'feminized' sector of the economy (Westwood and Bhachu, 1988). In seeking paid work, female carers – particularly lone mothers and mothers from minority ethnic groups – can find both jobs and alternative sources of child care hard to find (Warrier, 1988; Brown, 1984). Reflecting these problems, the proportion of lone mothers working full time, whose youngest child is under five, fell by 50 per cent between 1978 and 1984. At the same time, the proportion of women in two-parent households working part time rose sharply to 22 per cent (Equal Opportunities Commission, 1988).

The Poverty of Caring

Identifying tensions in the structure of care within the informal sector helps us understand the problems that can arise for those giving (and receiving) informal care. While structurally determined, such problems tend to be experienced as individual. In understanding the nature of 'crisis' in the informal sector, we must therefore focus on the position of those who see crisis as an endemic feature of their lives. In this section, we look more closely at the experience of caring in poverty. Our understanding is hampered by the fact that most research on poverty – whether based on an absolute or relative definition – takes the household as the unit of analysis (DHSS, 1988; Townsend, 1979). Household measures of poverty (usually based on income) present particular problems for those concerned with the economic position of those on the giving and receiving end of care.

First, household-based measures can overlook support and help given to dependents outside the household. For example, government statistics on low income define a family in terms of the assessment unit for supplementary benefit (now income support): i.e. a single person, or married couple with their dependent resident children (DHSS, 1988). This means that the economic needs of individuals living outside the unit, but economically supported by it, are not taken into account. The definition thus obscures transfers out of households. As a result, it is likely to underestimate the extent of financial hardship in households supporting relatives living elsewhere. With inter-household transfers being more common among black than white households, it is the incidence of poverty among black families that is most likely to be underestimated. In Brown's survey, 40 per cent of Afro-Caribbean households and 30 per cent of Asian households gave financial support to other households. Most of this (over 80 per cent) went to help relatives, with over half going to parents. Among white households, far fewer (5 per cent) gave financial support to other households; of those who did, the majority were giving money to children (Brown, 1984). Gender and class differences are also etched into these patterns. One study of older people suggests that men were more likely to give financial support and women to give goods. The level of kin-support was higher among middle-class households, where it typically took the form of money

(Qureshi and Simons, 1987). As these patterns suggest, kinship responsibilities for the care and support of relatives lies at the heart of many inter-household transfers, but this important economic dimension of informal care can be lost in our concept of 'household'.

Second, household-based measures can obscure not only inter-household but intra-household transfers of income and material resources. Where the unit is the household, the needs and resources of individuals are not considered separately: resources are assumed to be pooled and equitably distributed. However, studies of married and cohabiting couples suggest that, in the share-out of household resources, women can come off badly (Brannen and Wilson, 1987). While often responsible for the day-to-day health of the family, their access to material resources (like money and the 'family' car) can fail to reflect their responsibilities. Here, women – from different ethnic backgrounds and different class positions – can find themselves in a common economic position within the household. Two mothers, one white and one Afro-Caribbean, described in these terms their disadvantaged position within the average-income households in which they were caring for young children (Graham, 1987, p. 233):

> His hobby is fishing and do-it-yourself things and he'll just go out and buy the tools and I think, 'Oh that money, what I could have done with that money'. So I will budget and go around the markets and that, and find the best buys and he'll just go to the best shops because it's convenient.

> Ronald didn't like me spending money without his consent. If he wanted to go out and buy things, that was different. He was very keen on photography and he bought a lot of photographic equipment. What he wanted to buy was OK but the basics and things I needed for the children he thought were unreasonable.

While generally applied to households, the concepts of absolute and relative poverty can be usefully applied to individuals. Both concepts shed light on the economic position of carers within households. Absolute poverty is defined as an income below the levels needed to sustain health. As Seebohm Rowntree (1902) put it, poverty is an income 'below the minimum sums which families of different sizes could be maintained in a state of physical efficiency'. With an income insufficient for health, caring in poverty is likely to be a stressful as well as a contradictory experience.

The budgeting patterns that result show clearly the conflicts between health-keeping and housekeeping on a low income. Low-income households typically prioritize collective items essential for health (fuel, food), and try and restrict spending on non-essential items of individual expenditure (clothes, shoes, transport, leisure), as table 14.1 indicates. Within – or in conflict with – this system of priorities, financial commitments to outside agencies are met first. Rent, rates, fuel bills and debt and hire purchase payments thus have first call on household income.

Table 14.1 Weekly expenditure for two-adult, two-child households: average of all households and a household on supplementary benefit

	Average household		Supplementary benefit	
	£	%	£	%
Fuel	12	7	11	15
Food	45	24	31	41
Clothes/footware	17	9	4	5
Durable household goods	20	11	3	4
Transport	30	16	5	7
Services	25	13	5	7
Alcohol	9	5	2	3
Tobacco	5	3	5	9
Total	186		75	

Source: Bradshaw and Morgan (1987)

Despite the priority given to 'the bills', many households have difficulty meeting external commitments. One in five low-income households with children have arrears for either gas or electricity or both (Hutton, 1986). Fuel and other household debts are more common among households with children (Parker, 1988). In one recent study of sixty-four households with children living on benefit, 95 per cent were found to be in 'substantial debt'. The average household debt was over £400 (Bradshaw and Holmes, 1989).

This system of financial management has particular implications for those with responsibility for meeting health needs. Paying fixed costs first helps to secure some important health resources like housing and heating. But it means that spending on other resources directly related to health and child development – including food, clothes and shoes, public transport to social and health facilities, playgroup expenses, and toys – are squeezed. It is the food budget that is most clearly affected: it is the largest single item of weekly expenditure and, unlike most other items of collective health expenditure, it is not purchased through one lump-sum payment to an outside agency. It is also the largest item over which the mother is likely to exercise direct control. It is here, in the diet which she provides her family, that the struggle against poverty is most likely to be felt. A mother bringing up her children on supplementary benefit explained the implications for family feeding in these terms (Graham, 1987, p. 231):

> Food is the only place I find I can tighten up. So it's the food. ... You've got to balance nutrition with a large amount of food which will keep them not hungry. I'd like to be able to afford to give them more nuts and I'd like them to be able to eat fresh fruit whenever they wanted. But the good food has to be limited. Terrible, isn't it, when you think about it?

Relative poverty can further undermine the carer's work of protecting and promoting health. A relative definition highlights not only the physical effects of living below the subsistence level, but the psychological and social effects of having to live, not through choice, outside the day-to-day cultural and political life of the community. As Townsend (1979, p. 31) notes:

> Individuals, families and groups can be said to be in poverty when they lack the resources to... participate in the activities and have the living conditions and amenities which are customary, or at least widely approved, in the societies to which they belong. Their resources are so seriously below those commanded by the average individual or family that they are, in effect, excluded from ordinary living patterns, customs and activities.

As this definition suggests, a relative concept of poverty points, among other things, to the social isolation of the poor: to their enforced privacy and their restricted access to a world which, if available, could compensate for the material privations of the home. Poverty, in other words, is likely to intensify the isolation which often accompanies full-time caring. Strategies that could overcome or compensate for this isolation – a day trip, a holiday, day care or respite care, a car, a social life, leisure activities or simply going shopping – have to be jettisoned in the struggle to make ends meet. The nature and effect of such social exclusion is summarized by one mother as follows (Graham, 1986):

> We had a car but you can't afford it now. You can't afford a social life, not one where money is involved. I rarely meet people as I so rarely go out of the house. The older children go to school on their own, and with my husband around during the day, I don't have much opportunity to go out on my own. My husband does the big shop on the bus to the shopping centre. It's too expensive for us all to go in. So it's stressful in respect of the finances. You feel inadequate in that you can't provide for the children in the way you would like – food, clothing, most things. My finances isn't enough.

While not designed as an analysis of caring in poverty, Brown and Harris's (1978) study of depression highlights the vulnerability of women with young children caring in disadvantaged circumstances. The highest rates of clinical depression were found among working-class women, without paid employment, who were caring for three or more children under five and lacked a confiding relationship. One third of the women caring in these circumstances were identified as having the symptoms of clinical depression.

Conclusion

Already Britain's major health-care provider – the informal sector – is set for expansion. It lies at the heart of a pluralist philosophy which has informed British welfare policy over the last decade. As part of a pluralist system, unpaid, family-based care is seen as having a major role to play in tackling 'the crisis in care'.

While the place of the informal sector within the wider pluralist system has been a theme of recent policy documents, government enquiries have focused primarily on the formal sectors of welfare. As a result, there has been little policy debate about the informal sector itself. Research, however, has sought to establish the extent and experience of care within families. In seeking to chart the patterns of care, researchers have followed policy-makers in drawing a distinction between informal care and the routines by which families care for their able-bodied members. While this is clearly an important distinction, this chapter has been concerned to locate informal care within the wider routines of care within the informal sector. This is because it is the wider routines of care within households that provide both the resources and the context for informal care.

In seeking to locate informal care within the reproductive routines of households, the chapter has explored some of the contradictions raised by care in the informal sector. It has focused on the links between poverty and caring, looking at the lives of mothers for insights into the tensions experienced between house-keeping and health-keeping: between prudent budgeting and health promotion.

In exploring these contradictions, the chapter has drawn on a rich seam of research concerned with poverty within families. As the new pluralist policies take shape in the 1990s, poverty seems set to be an enduring feature of the lives of many of those involved in giving care within families (Berthoud, 1989; Glendinning, 1988). While wary of the over-worn concept of 'crisis', the evidence suggests that the informal sector will continue to face difficulties in meeting the health responsibilities prescribed for it.

ACKNOWLEDGEMENTS

I would like to thank two anonymous referees and those who took part in the Swedish–British Medical Sociology Workshop in Stockholm for their helpful comments on earlier drafts of this chapter.

REFERENCES

Allen, I., Wicks, M., Finch, J. and Leat, D. (1987), *Informal Care Tomorrow*, London: Policy Studies Institute.

Baldwin, S. (1985), *The Costs of Caring: Families with Disabled Children*, London: Routledge & Kegan Paul.

Baldwin, S., Parker, G. and Walker, R. (eds) (1988), *Social Security and Community Care*, Aldershot: Avebury.

Berthoud, R. (1989), *Credit, Debt and Poverty*, Social Security Advisory Committee, London: HMSO.

Bradshaw, J. and Holmes, H. (1989), *Living on the Edge: A Study of the Living Standards of Families on Benefit in Tyne and Wear*, London: Tyneside Child Poverty Action Group.

Bradshaw, J. and Morgan, J. (1987), *Budgeting on Benefit: The Consumption of Families on Social Security*, London: Family Policy Studies Centre.

Brannen, J. and Wilson, G. (eds) (1987), *Give and Take in Families: Studies in Resource Distribution*, London: Allen & Unwin.

Brown, C. (1984), *Black and White in Britain: The Third PSI Survey*, Aldershot: Gower.

Brown, G. and Harris, T. (1978), *The Social Origins of Depression*, London: Tavistock.

Caring for People: Community Care in the Next Decade and Beyond (1989) Cm 849, London: HMSO.

CSO (1989), *Social Trends 19*, Central Statistical Office, London: HMSO.

Dalley, G. (1988), *Ideologies of Caring: Re-thinking Community and Collectivism*, London: Macmillan.

DHSS (1981), *Growing Older*, Department of Health and Social Security, London: HMSO.

DHSS (1983), *Care in the Community*, Department of Health and Social Security, London: HMSO.

DHSS (1988), *Low Income Families: 1985*, London: Department of Health and Social Security.

Equal Opportunities Commission (1988), *Women and Men in Britain: A Research Profile*, Manchester: Equal Opportunities Commission.

Fenton, C. (1988), *Race, Health and Welfare: Afro-Caribbean and South Asian People in Central Bristol*, Bristol: University of Bristol.

Finch, J. and Groves, D. (eds) (1983), *A Labour of Love: Women, Work and Caring*, London: Routledge & Kegan Paul.

Glendinning, C. (1983), *Unshared Care*, London: Routledge & Kegan Paul.

Glendinning, C. (1988), 'Dependency and interdependency: the incomes of informal carers and the impact of social security', in S. Baldwin, G. Parker and R. Walker (eds), *Social Security and Community Care*, Aldershot: Avebury.

Graham, H. (1985), 'Providers, negotiators and mediators: women as the hidden carers', in E. Lewin and V. Olesen (eds), *Women, Health and Healing*, London: Tavistock.

Graham, H. (1986), *Caring for the Family*, Research Report no. 1, Milton Keynes: Open University Press.

Graham, H. (1987), 'Women's poverty and caring', in C. Glendinning and J. Millar (eds), *Women and Poverty in Britain*, Brighton: Wheatsheaf.

Green, H. (1988), *Informal Carers: General Household Survey 1985*, London: HMSO.

Griffiths Report (1988), *Community Care: Agenda for Action*, a Report to the Secretary of State for Social Services, London: HMSO.

Harris, R. (1988), *Beyond the Welfare State*, Occasional Paper 77, London: Institute of Economic Affairs.

Harris, R. and Seldon, A. (1987), *Welfare without the State*, London: Institute of Economic Affairs.

Hatch, S. and Mocroft, I. (1983), *Components of Welfare*, London: Bedford Square Press.

Hicks, C. (1988), *Who Cares: Looking After People at Home*, London: Virago Press.

Hutton, S. (1986), 'Low income families and fuel debt', in I. Ramsey (ed.), *Debtors and Creditors*, London: Professional Books.

Jallade, J. (ed.) (1989), *The Crisis of Redistribution in European Welfare States*, Stoke-on-Trent: Trentham Books.

Johnson, N. (1988), *The Welfare State in Transition: The Theory and Practice of Welfare Pluralism*, Brighton: Wheatsheaf.

Joshi, H. (1987), 'The cost of caring', in C. Glendinning and J. Millar (eds), *Women and Poverty in Britain*, Brighton: Wheatsheaf.

Jowell, R., Witherspoon, S. and Brook, L. (1988), *British Social Attitudes: The 5th Report*, Aldershot: Gower.

Land, H. (1978), 'Who cares for the family?', *Journal of Social Policy*, 7: 357–84.

Lewis, J. and Meredith, B. (1988), *Daughters Who Care: Daughters Caring for their Mothers at Home*, London: Routledge.

Mishra, R. (1984), *The Welfare State in Crisis*, Brighton: Wheatsheaf.

Offe, C. (1984), *Contradictions of the Welfare State*, London: Hutchinson.

OPCS (1984), *Census 1981: Key Statistics for Urban Needs*, Office of Population Censuses and Surveys, London: HMSO.

OPCS (1989), *General Household Survey 1986*, Office of Population Censuses and Surveys, London: HMSO.

Parker, G. (1985), *With Due Care and Attention: A Review of Research on Informal Care*, London: Family Policy Studies Centre.

Parker, G. (1988), 'Indebtedness', in R. Walker and G. Parker (eds), *Money Matters: Income, Wealth and Financial Welfare*, London: Sage.

Qureshi, H. and Simons, K. (1987), 'Resources within families: caring for older people', in J. Brannene and G. Wilson (eds), *Give and Take in Families: Studies in Resource Distribution*, London: Allen & Unwin.

Rowntree, B. S. (1902), *Poverty: A Study of Town Life*, London: Macmillan.

Seldon, A. (1981), *Wither the Welfare State*, London: Institute of Economic Affairs.

Social Services Committee (1985), *Community Care with Special Reference to Adult and Mentally Ill and Mentally Handicapped People, Second Report from the Social Services Committee Session 1984–5*, vol. 1, London: House of Commons.

Stacey, M. (1988), *The Sociology of Health and Healing*, London: George Allen & Unwin.

Townsend, P. (1979), *Poverty in the United Kingdom*, Harmondsworth: Penguin.

Ungerson, C. (1983), 'Why do women care?', in J. Finch and D. Groves (eds), *A Labour of Love: Women, Work and Caring*, London: Routledge & Kegan Paul.

Ungerson, C. (1987), *Policy is Personal: Sex, Gender and Informal Care*, London: Tavistock.

Waerness, K. (1984), 'Caring as women's work in the welfare state', in H. Holter (ed.), *Patriarchy in a Welfare State*, Oslo: Universitetsforlaget.

Wagner Report (1988), *Residential Care: A Positive Choice, Report of the Independent Review of Residential Care*, London: HMSO.

Walker, A. (1987), 'Enlarging the caring capacity of the community: informal support networks and the welfare state', *International Journal of Health Services*, 17: 369–86.

Warrier, S. (1988), 'Marriage, maternity and female economic activity: Gujurati mothers in Britain', in S. Westwood and P. Bhachu (eds), *Enterprising Women: Ethnicity, Economy and Gender Relations*, London: Routledge.

Webb, A. and Wistow, G. (1982), *Whither State Welfare? Policy and Implementation in the Personal Social Services*, London: Royal Institute of Public Administration.

Wenger, C. (1984), *The Supportive Network: Coping with Old Age*, London: George Allen & Unwin.

Westwood, S. and Bhachu, P. (eds) (1988), *Enterprising Women: Ethnicity, Economy and Gender Relations*, London: Routledge.

Wicks, M. (1987), 'Social change and the family's capacity to care', in I. Allen, M. Wicks, J. Finch and D. Leat (eds), *Informal Care Tomorrow*, London: Policy Studies Institute.

15

Obligations of Kinship in Contemporary Britain: Is There Normative Agreement?

Janet Finch and Jennifer Mason

Introduction

Since 'the family' emerged as an issue on the agenda of the main political parties in the mid 1970s, sociologists have recognized that there are many unexamined assumptions built into political debate concerning the nature of family relationships and the responsibilities associated with them (Finch and Groves, 1980; Allan, 1985; Gittins, 1985; Morgan, 1985). At the same time, sociological writing has always regarded a sense of 'obligatedness' as the cornerstone of kin relationships, even if its character has been subject to very little empirical investigation, at least in recent years (Wilson and Pahl, 1988). In this chapter, we use data from a recent study to consider how far some key assumptions about family responsibilities and obligations stand up to empirical scrutiny. Our focus is upon adult kin relationships, and the extent to which these provide a basis practical and material support of various kinds.

We believe that there are three key assumptions made in political debate, and embedded in social policies, concerning mutual assistance between adult kin. We shall spell them out briefly, indicating sources which support this view, including other work of our own where the political dimensions are examined in more detail (see especially Finch, 1989).

The key assumptions are first, that obligations and responsibilities between kin are both commonly and easily recognized and well understood at the normative level. In a given situation, most people will agree upon and recognize relatively easily what is 'the proper thing to do', even if some people will then try to avoid their responsibilities in practice. The norms of obligation are assumed to be fairly easily recognized because they constitute a 'natural' part of family life.

The idea that family support springs from moral impulses which are 'natural' represents a long-running theme in British social policy, which defined a role for the state in ensuring that the whole population – especially the working classes – were encouraged to recognize responsibilities to their kin. It has long been an imputed characteristic of the 'decent family' that such responsibilities are recognized without question.[1] However, most sociologists probably would want to question the idea that there is a normative consensus about these matters at the present time.

Our second key assumption is that obligations are stronger for 'close family' than they are for distant kin. Thus, it would be regarded as much more shocking for a parent to refuse help to an adult child than, say, for cousins to disregard each others' needs. The groups between whom the strongest obligations are presumed to exist are spouses, parents and children. These assumptions were built into the Poor Law in the concept of 'liable relatives', who could be obliged legally to offer each other financial support and – for a different sector of society – are present in inheritance laws, which give 'close' relatives stronger claims on an estate than more distant ones (Finch, 1989). Obligations between generations are presumed to operate in both directions. Not only should children support their parents, but parents should support their adult children. The latter assumption is evident in recent policies concerning the financial support of young adults, where parents increasingly are seen as having the main responsibility unless a young person can support her or himself through paid work (Harris, 1988).

The assumption that the strongest obligations are between parents and children is confirmed by the sociological literature on kinship (Morgan, 1975). In more recent literature on the care of elderly people, various writers have suggested that there is a 'hierarchy of obligations', which again gives priority to obligations between spouses, parents and children (Qureshi, 1986; Qureshi and Simons, 1987; Ungerson, 1987).

Third, there is a clear assumption in social policy that women's obligations to their kin are stronger than men's, especially in relation to the kind of assistance which entails practical, personal and domestic tasks. Many writers who have worked in the field of community care policies have documented this assumption, and there is no need to repeat the evidence here (for example, Finch and Groves, 1980; Walker, 1982; Henwood and Wicks, 1985; Dalley, 1988). This assumption again is also reflected in sociological literature, for example on the hierarchy of obligations, where daughters and even daughters-in-law emerge the designated carers ahead of sons. The image of family support as the domain of women comes through strongly in the earlier tradition of British kinship studies, expressed most graphically in Young and Willmott's description of the family as the 'women's trade union' (Young and Willmott, 1959).

The Family Obligations Survey

In this chapter we will use data from our study of Family Obligations to address these questions.[2] The study focuses upon obligations between adult relatives only (rather than responsibilities involving young children) and is not specifically concerned with spouses. We have concentrated upon responsibilities to support relatives in three key areas: personal care, financial support and accommodation.

The study of Family Obligations began in 1985 and the main phase of data collection was completed in late 1987. This chapter is based upon data from a large-scale survey which was undertaken in the first phase of the project. It was based on a random sample population, with an achieved sample size of 978 (representing a response rate of 72 per cent), conducted in the Greater Manchester area. The design of our empirical research was complex and reflected the overall conceptual and theoretical framework within which we were working.[3]

In this chapter we are using data only from the survey phase of the project, so we need to spell out the nature of the claims which can be made on the basis of these data alone. Its aim was to investigate whether it is possible to identify any level of agreement among a random sample of the population about appropriate obligations, duties and responsibilities between adult kin, in defined circumstances where people need some form of assistance. These are difficult kinds of issues to investigate empirically and conventional measures, such as attitude statements, are widely regarded as unsatisfactory. Indeed some readers may regard it as rather perverse that we chose to use the blunt instrument of a survey questionnaire to understand something as complex as the nature of obligation between kin. After all, it is well recognized that, whatever its other merits, the sample survey has been a very inadequate instrument in relation to the study of social meanings (Marsh, 1982). We want to emphasize that we did not attempt to answer all our questions about the nature of kin obligations through this means, but only a very particular set of questions about whether people recognize and agree upon normative responses to a defined set of circumstances. In attempting to document general levels of agreement in contemporary British society it was necessary for us to adopt a method which uses a representative sample and which enables this type of generalization to be made.

Our main strategy for asking questions was to present respondents with a series of hypothetical situations concerning third parties, and to ask them to decide what the fictitious people should do. In this sense we were inviting respondents to identify what would count as 'the proper thing to do'. This vignette technique enabled us to design questions which were situationally specific, yet where the judgements about what is proper need not be tied too closely to respondents' own circumstances. In this way the respondent is being invited to make normative statements about a set of social circumstances, rather than to express her or his views in a vacuum (Finch, 1987a). In adopting this method we were making no prior assumptions about how the answers to our questions might relate to our respondents' own actions, should they be faced with similar situations, nor about the normative dimension of relationships with their own kin. We certainly did not expect to be able to 'read off' actions from words, and of course there is justifiably an established critique of that kind of unsociological and crude reasoning (Condor, 1988; Deutscher, 1973; Finch,

1987b). Instead, a central purpose of the second stage of our research (not discussed in this chapter) was precisely to understand that relationship.

In approaching the survey this way we were reflecting our own theoretical stance on how norms, beliefs and values should be conceptualized and how they can be studied. We did not expect our survey respondents to present static 'underlying attitudes', even though that is often the basis of popular and policy assumptions about family responsibilities. Our perspective suggested that normative statements are more likely to be situationally specific than universal, that is, dependent on the given circumstances in which the judgement of appropriateness is to be made (Finch, 1987a, 1987b). So, for example, a judgement about whether or not parents should help their adult children might depend *inter alia* upon the relationship between the parties, the nature and degree of the assistance in question, notions of relative need and ability to help, the existence of other potential helpers, and so on. Questions asked in the form of vignettes enable respondents to specify a context within which normative judgements are to be made. The situations are not intended to match the complexities of real life, but do get closer to generating normative judgements of the kind made in 'real life' circumstances than do wholly decontextualized questions.

There remain some important issues about the status and meaning of the data generated on this kind of topic in a survey – questions which occur whether one uses the vignette technique or more conventional methods for generating so-called attitudinal data. In our view, the data generated in answers to survey questions should be considered as publicly expressed norms or judgements, which may well be pulled towards what the respondent feels is socially acceptable. In the case of our own work this is less problematic than in other studies, since we were precisely wishing to know what people regarded as socially acceptable actions. Whether and how individual experience influences these judgements is of course an empirical question and one which, we would argue, cannot be answered using survey methodology.[4] The mechanisms by which respondents arrived at their judgements are not accessible as part of the survey data but – in the context of this particular chapter – this is not a serious flaw, since our principal purpose is to document the outcome in terms of whether there is a normative consensus, however that outcome was arrived at. For the same reason, we are not giving here a full analysis of variations in the way our survey population answered the questions in terms of their own social characteristics (although we do mention some of these when they help in understanding the levels of agreement which we document).

Assessing Levels of Agreement

We are going to use some of our survey data to address the three broad assumptions in policy and in sociological wisdom about people's normative judgements concerning family obligations identified above, looking for points on which there is agreement or disagreement.

In using our data in this way, we are keenly aware of the need to think carefully about what we 'count' as a notable level of agreement on any issue. Clearly, we are unlikely to find a total consensus, but what level of agreement should we take as our baseline: over 90 per cent agreement? 75 per cent? 50 per cent? Whatever level we choose has to be related in some way to the number of choices offered in the question, since 75 per cent agreement clearly means something different when four options have been offered, by comparison with questions where there was a simple two-way choice. The problems raised here are sociological more than statistical, since they are matters of interpretation of data, and any across-the-board numerical measures of consensus will be arbitrary and inadequate for this reason. For example, our interpretation may ascribe different analytical 'weight' to response options within the same question, or we may wish to reorganize the data to understand divisions which do not directly coincide with the given options. Nevertheless, a consistent numerical measure is a useful starting point for sociological understanding. We have therefore calculated numerical indicators of normative consensus which we use throughout our discussion, as a way into more finely tuned sociological interpretations.

The logic that we have followed is to say that where our questions have offered two options, then for either option to accrue more than 50 per cent of responses would indicate a simple majority. If either option accrues half as many responses again (that is, 75 per cent for two-option questions), we will regard that as an initial indicator that we have a notable level of agreement. The corresponding figure for a three-option question is 50 per cent, for a four-option question it is 37.5 per cent, and so on.[5] We refer to this as our 'consensus baseline'. It is possible, of course, using the same logic, to come up with different figures. Instead of using 1.5 as the multiplier, we could argue that 1.75 would be a more appropriate figure. This produces a consensus baseline for two-, three- and four-option questions of 87.5 per cent, 57.75 per cent and 43.75 per cent. Using the logic of the null hypothesis, this would be a more rigorous test if we were assessing the hypothesis that there *is* agreement on a particular item. Similarly, if we were assessing the view that there *is not* agreement, we could use a multiplier of 1.25, producing consensus baseline figures of 62.5 per cent, 41.25 per cent and 31.25 per cent. For most of our discussion we use the multiplier of 1.5, but in places we also discuss the implications of using the more rigorous test. However, this exercise is only the starting-point for the interpretation of the sociological significance of particular choices, as our discussion will show.

Assumption 1: Family obligations are both commonly and easily recognized, and well understood at a normative level

In its crudest form, this assumption implies that, in a given set of circumstances, most people will be able to recognize relatively easily what constitutes 'the proper thing to do'. If this were the case, then we might expect high levels of agreement (or disagreement) in responses to questions throughout the Family

Obligations Survey. However, of a total of sixty-nine normative survey questions (including parts of questions), as many as 48 per cent show no consensus when measured in the pure percentage frequency terms described above. Even in the 52 per cent of questions which do show an initial baseline consensus, the emerging picture of obligations is not straightforward; for example, items where there *is* apparently quite a high level of numerical consensus do not always point in the same direction.[6]

Measured in this very crude way, therefore, responses to our survey questions indicated that there is nothing approaching normative consensus on many issues concerning obligations between adult kin. To elaborate this, in principle we could discuss all of our survey data. Clearly, that would be inappropriate in a chapter of this length. We shall concentrate here simply upon some examples which show the *range* of consensus and dissent in our data, and which indicate something of the complexity of the judgements which people make on these normative issues. The following two sections, whilst focused upon other specific assumptions, also serve to illustrate the lack of clear consensus on many issues.

In the survey we used fourteen questions in which we sketched out a situation where someone needed assistance, and then posed a choice of *whether* relatives should provide the assistance, or whether it should come from some other source (e.g. borrowing money from a bank, or the input of state support services for an infirm person). In response to these questions we have a variety of consensus and non-consensus levels, illustrating that people do not always unambiguously assign normative responsibility for meeting various needs to relatives. We will give some examples which demonstrate this variety, beginning with questions where there is some agreement that assistance *should* come from relatives.

If we take our standard consensus baseline (using a multiplier of 1.5) there is only one question where we have high levels of agreement that assistance should be provided by relatives, rather than coming from a specified alternative source. This is a question which read:

> Suppose that a young couple with a small child have returned from working abroad and can't afford to buy or rent anywhere to live until one of them gets a job. Should any of their relatives offer to have the family in their own home for the next few months?

A total of 86 per cent of our respondents said that they should (consensus baseline 75 per cent).

The fact that this is the *only* question – out of a possible fourteen in our survey – where assistance from relatives is clearly preferred to any other alternatives, gives a strong message about a lack of normative agreement over family obligations. If we apply the less rigorous test (using the 1.25 multiplier for our consensus baseline) we do not alter this picture very substantially. Just two more questions are identified as eliciting a substantial measure of agreement that relatives should provide help. One of them again concerns relatives providing a temporary home, this time for a couple with children who have been evicted for non-payment of rent, where 65 per cent said that relatives should offer (baseline 75 per cent or 62.5 per cent, depending on the multiplier). The other question concerns relatives' responsibility for helping an infirm elderly person, where 46 per cent said that they should pay for help in the elderly person's own home, rather than provide that help themselves or pay for residential care (baseline 50 per cent or 41.25 per cent).

The picture which emerges from these questions therefore scarcely represents a clear and straightforward normative agreement that adult relatives should be responsible for assisting each other. Equally, people do not indicate clearly that relatives should *not* be responsible for each other. Taking our standard consensus baseline, we have only three questions where there is a notable level of agreement that relatives should not take responsibility, but ten questions where there is a split response, with quite large proportions of our survey sample opting for each of two or three different answers. These ten questions concern a wide range of financial and practical assistance. We will give just two examples. The first concerns personal care, and the question read:

> A middle-aged couple have been injured in a car accident and need some simple nursing care at home until they are better. Who do you think they should seek help from first?

We gave four possible choices and the pattern of answers was: state-provided help 42 per cent; privately paid-for help 7 per cent; relatives 40 per cent; friends 6 per cent (baseline 37.5 per cent). It is certainly clear that our respondents favour help from the state or relatives rather than the other options, but they are split evenly over which one. Our second example of a split response concerns financial assistance. The question read:

> Suppose an elderly couple need money to redecorate their home. Do you think that relatives should offer to pay to have the work done?

A total of 55 per cent said that relatives should offer and 35 per cent said that they should not (baseline 75 per cent).

The very number of these questions on which there is a split – that is, there is no clear consensus in either direction – calls into question the idea that normative obligations are easily recognizable and commonly agreed upon. There are very few items on which there is a notable level of agreement if we use our standard multiplier of 1.5 for calculating the consensus baseline. If we use 1.25 as a multiplier, more items fall into the range which we are designating as a notable level of agreement, typically falling around the two-thirds level for a two-option question.

Respondents' Experience and Characteristics

Do the social characteristics and experiences of our respondents account for these variations in the pattern of answers, as has been suggested by other researchers who have used vignette-type questions (Thompson and West)? Our data suggest that the effect of these variables is very limited. In our survey we asked a limited number of questions about respondents' experiences of giving and receiving assistance within their own kin groups. We asked about assistance in the form of personal care, money and accommodation, the main areas explored in our survey. From these we constructed variables which represent reported experience of the various kinds. However, we believe that these have to be treated very cautiously, since the survey method can never elicit more than a superficial level of *reported* experiences, and it must always be questionable whether these reported experiences can be treated as comparable with each other. Furthermore the survey method cannot tell us about the way different kinds of experience, *inter alia*, are drawn upon by respondents in their normative reasoning.[7]

On the basis of these data it seems that people's answers to questions about personal care and accommodation are very little related in their own reported experience, certainly not in a consistent way. On questions about money, personal experience seems to be more relevant. As most of our 'split response' items do concern financial assistance, we shall say something about these variations. We asked our respondents whether they had ever given a gift or loan of money totalling £300 or more, to a relative. We also asked if they had ever received such a sum. This gave us a measure of reported experience of sharing quite *substantial* financial assistance within families, and the people who reported such experiences (especially those who had received large sums of money) were also likely to fall into our higher-income brackets, to be in paid work and to have post-school educational qualifications.

In general, the reported experience of both giving and receiving money within one's own family was correlated with answers which tended to favour financial assistance between relatives – though in some questions this tendency was very small. The clearest cases were three questions in which people who had themselves given money to a relative were more likely to favour one of our hypothetical characters giving money (significant at less than 1 per cent level in all three cases). These cases were: relatives should pay for the redecoration of an elderly couple's home; parents should pay off the debts run up by a student whilst at college; a young couple should try to borrow money for a house deposit from relatives rather than wait until they have saved it.

So it seems that, where sharing money on a fairly substantial scale has been part of the respondent's own experience, people are more likely to endorse this as an appropriate type of assistance for relatives to offer each other. Conversely, people who report little experience of such financial sharing are less likely to endorse it. So it does seem that experience bears some relationship to people's answers to some of these questions about money. Gender seems to be another social characteristic which has a bearing, though what we can say about it is very limited on the basis of these data. In general men seem more favourable to the idea of borrowing money than are women, but where the alternative is offered they tend to opt for loans from a bank rather than from relatives. Women were more likely to give answers which implied 'wait' or 'do without'.

If we assume that in general women have less secure access to financial resources than do men, this gendered pattern of answers may be a reflection of that particular aspect of the experience of gender, with women less likely to be in a position to imagine themselves taking on substantial loans.

Responses to Varying Circumstances

Whilst reported experience seems to account for the way people answer questions about money up to a point, it certainly does not straightforwardly explain the pattern of answers to our vignette questions. Neither our various measures of experience, nor other independent variables, show up a *consistent* pattern in our data. For every question where experience of assistance, or income, or gender seem to be related to the way questions are answered, there are at least as many where they are not. We would argue therefore that the observed variations are only marginally accounted for by the characteristics of our respondents, but much more so by the content of the questions themselves. We believe that *inter alia* people are basing their judgements on the circumstances being offered to them in the vignette question, and a full understanding about what family obligations look like at this normative level needs to take the strong relevance of circumstances on board. Of course this is not surprising. It is certainly consistent with some earlier work on British kinship, especially that of Firth and his colleagues (Firth, Hubert and Forge, 1969) which saw kin obligations as a set of general principles which need to be applied in a given situation, rather than detailed rules of conduct. However, it is in direct contradiction to the social policy assumption that people in general agree that relatives should support each other. Sometimes they quite clearly do not, even at this level of publicly expressed norms, and obligations are certainly not treated as unconditional across the board.

Our data can take us further than the simple observation that often there is no clear agreement about the proper thing to do. If we examine the variations in responses and contingent circumstances across questions, it is possible to start to say something about the factors upon which judgements are conditional.[8] Among the most obvious factors are norms about legitimate and non-legitimate need, and about deserving or non-deserving cases. Although we know that it has traditionally been regarded as appropriate for parents to give financial assistance to their children (Bell, 1968), our data suggest that legitimacy of need is a key factor in such situations. In one question, about a young couple wanting a family holiday, we attracted a consensus that they should 'do without the holiday' rather than approach relatives for a loan. This indicates that people see this as a luxury item, in comparison to financial 'needs' in the other questions which attract a higher proportion of answers indicating that relatives should help (although often still not a clear consensus). Similarly, a couple who want to borrow money from relatives to pay private school fees are not supported by the majority of our respondents, and neither is the student who has run up debts.

Another apparently relevant factor is the question of how limited – in time, effort and skill – is the task to be performed. We seem to be getting a message that the more limited the task, the more likely are people to allocate it to relatives. There is some support for this in our questions about personal care, although the pattern of responses there is quite complex (for a full discussion, see Finch and Mason, 1989). Conversely there is a high level of consensus in favour of relatives providing *short-term* accommodation to a couple returning from abroad, which may have been seen as fairly undemanding.

One way of interpreting these various 'contingent factors' is to make a distinction between substantive and procedural consensus. By substantive consensus, we mean fairly high levels of agreement about *what* a person should do in a given set of circumstances. Procedural consensus is agreement about *how to work out* the proper thing to do in specified circumstances, i.e. what factors people should take into account. This distinction between substance and pro cedures is different from the distinction between general guidelines and detailed prescriptions for action, both of which are (in our terms) about substance.[9]

We think our data suggest that there may often be a greater consensus over how to work out what to do, than over what constitutes the appropriate course of action. A number of the contingent factors which we have identified are actually concerned with procedural issues. They suggest that, when faced with a decision about whether to offer assistance to a relative, most people would agree that you should consider matters like: is this a deserving case? is it a request for a luxury or a necessity? how big a commitment would an offer of help entail?

We were first alerted to the importance of distinguishing between substance and procedures when looking at the patterns of responses to one particular question about the preferred type of help for an elderly dependent relative. Our sample is split between different substantive choices which we offered: pay for the relative to go into a nursing home, 16.5 per cent; pay for someone to help in the relative's home, 46 per cent; help the relative themselves, 29 per cent (.50 per cent baseline). However, when we asked respondents to give reasons for their choice, in an open-ended and post-coded question, many offered very *similar* reasons to support *different* options. For example, 60 per cent of the reasons given for choosing a nursing home indicated that the quality of care would be better; but 20 per cent of answers supporting the option of relatives providing care themselves also cited better quality of care. Another 32 per cent of reasons supporting the nursing-home choice indicated that an elderly person should not be a burden on relatives, as did 16 per cent of reasons for favouring paying for help in the elderly person's own home. It seems very clear in this question that there is more agreement about procedural than about substantive issues, that is, which factors should be taken into account in making a judgement rather than the judgement itself.

We recognize that much more could be said about the normative messages which emerge from our survey data, and we are developing some of these issues elsewhere (Finch and Mason, 1993). In this section we have simply been attempting to convey a sense of the variety and the complexity of people's judgements about 'the proper thing to do' for adult relatives. It is clear that most people do not give unconditional assent to the principle of kinship obligations. Although factors such as type of support, legitimacy of need and so on can be seen to be relevant, they are not necessarily definitive in producing a consensus. Such factors would seem to be taken into account, but not in an easy or straightforward way as the rhetoric of the naturalness of obligations might imply.

Assumption 2: Obligations are stronger for 'close family' than for more distant kin

This assumption implies, first, that people will recognize which kin constitute 'close family' and, second, that the strongest obligations will be accorded to close kin. Given the focus of the Family Obligations survey, we can say most about relationships between parents and children, the key relationship outside marriage within which strong obligations are presumed to exist. Some of our questions built in a specific genealogical relationship, but in others we were simply asking about 'relatives', including a number of questions where we outlined a situation, then asked in an open-ended way 'which relative should help?'. The answers to these questions were post-coded, and this meant that people were constructing their own normative frame of reference for deciding which relatives would be the most appropriate to offer assistance.[10]

Looking at parent–child obligations at the most general level to begin with, we had a series of attitude statements, one of which asked people to agree or disagree that 'Children have no obligation to look after their parents when they are old'. According to Assumptions 1 and 2 put together, we might expect a very high level of disagreement with this proposition, yet in fact our pattern of responses was ambiguous: 39 per cent agreed and 58 per cent disagreed. At the very least they raise some doubts about whether parent–child obligations should be seen as constituting a relatively unambiguous element in norms about family life.[11]

Moving on to our vignette-type questions, we had a number which concerned the care or support of middle-aged or elderly people specifically. Where respondents thought that assistance should be provided by relatives rather than in some other way, children were seen as the providers. For example, 77 per cent named children as the people who should be first to offer money for redecorating an elderly couple's home, and (on a different question) 78 per cent identified a child as the most appropriate relative to provide a home for an infirm elderly person.

The message about children's obligations for parents is very clear here (see also Finch and Mason, 1990a). What about the other way round? Are parents seen as having clear responsibilities to assist their adult children? In the question about a young couple needing a temporary home, where 86 per cent thought that relatives should offer (see above), 71 per cent named parents as the most appropriate people. So in all these questions, where we had left respondents to make their own choice of appropriate relatives, it is striking that preferences remain concentrated in the very narrow genealogical range concerning parents and children.[12] Categories such as siblings, grandparents, grandchildren, in-laws and secondary kin are much less significant, as existing evidence predicts they would be (Finch, 1989). On other questions, where we had specified or implied a parent–child relationship, there tended to be quite high levels of agreement that the parent or child should give assistance.[13]

However, although parent–child obligations do feature prominently in our data, it is clear that people do not treat them as unconditional. Other factors are also brought into people's judgements about whether such obligations should be acknowledged. This is apparent in two questions about parental responsibilities to young adult children, one concerning a nineteen-year-old woman with a baby and nowhere to live, the other about a twenty-three-year-old man who wants to remain at his parents' home although he has no job and cannot pay his way. In both these questions the option of parental help attracted large majorities (78 per cent and 79 per cent, respectively). By contrast, the student who had run up debts (see above) did not attract a majority supporting parental assistance. Indeed if we take the multiplier of 1.25 for our consensus baseline we have a notable measure of agreement that parents should *not* pay off a student's debt. It is interesting here that there is no evidence that people who might be more likely to identify with the student were more favourable to the debt being paid – neither respondents' own educational experience, nor their social class, nor their current income made any apparent difference to the way this question was answered. The pattern of answers to these questions about parents' responsibilities for young adults implies that parent–child obligations *are* strong but they are by no means expected to be unconditional.

This conclusion is also supported by questions about children's obligations to elderly parents. For example, some of the questions which we discussed in relation to Assumption 1 show an ambiguous pattern of responses on responsibilities towards middle-aged and elderly people, and also demonstrate that a variety of ways of giving assistance are seen as legitimate. In addition, our data suggest that most people regard it as quite proper for younger people to consider their own circumstances before making a commitment to give support to an elderly parent or other relative. In one question we offered the option of saying that an infirm elderly person should live with relatives only in certain circumstances, then asked respondents choosing that answer to specify what those circumstances should be. Most of these answers focus on the personal circumstances of the 'receiving' relative. The implied message is that children, as well as other relatives, should not have to accept an elderly parent into their home unless they really want it, or unless they have enough space, or unless it does not impose upon other aspects of their lives too much.

The message about filial obligations which emerges from the data which we have presented is quite complex. Most people *do* say that children have a strong responsibility to assist their parents and vice versa, but it also seems legitimate to work out what assistance will be offered in the light of other circumstances. This brings us back to substantive and procedural consensus. What do our data tell us about procedural issues between parents and children, that is, about how to work out what would be the proper thing to do? Is there consensus on these procedural issues? We are going to explore this by using data from one of our longer vignettes, where we tell a 'story' in several stages about John Highfield, who is in a situation where he needs to borrow some money to start a business. The vignette begins as follows:

> John Highfield is a married man in his early thirties. He and his wife have two young children. John is unemployed but has a chance to start his own business. He can get various grants to get him started, and the bank will lend most of the money he needs. But he still needs another fifteen hundred pounds.

Respondents were then asked to say whether John should ask his parents for money, if he thought they could afford to help. A total of 88 per cent said that he should, representing a high level of agreement (baseline 75 per cent). However, the later parts of the vignette tell us something about the procedural norms which should operate in this situation. Of those who think that John should ask his parents, almost all (98 per cent) say that the request should be for a loan (not a gift) of money, indicating clear rules about how such transactions should be negotiated. As the question proceeded we added more details indicating that John was reluctant to *ask* for money from his parents. This reticence seems to have been regarded as proper by the majority of our respondents, since 78 per cent (baseline 75 per cent) said that it was up to his parents to *offer* the money. We also wondered whether there might be circumstances in which it is 'proper' to *refuse* an offer, so we added a final piece of information that, although John's parents were prepared to offer him the money, it was probably going to cause them financial hardship. Our respondents were split here, with 48 per cent saying that John should accept the money none the less and 40 per cent saying that he should refuse.

What this vignette does particularly well is to spell out quite clearly the etiquette of asking and offering, accepting and refusing, in parent–child relationships. But ultimately there is a lack of consensus on the substantive issues, in this case whether or not the money should actually be provided under those circumstances. As with some other questions about money, there is some evidence of a relationship between people's answers and their own experience of financial transactions in their family: both people who had given a substantial sum of money to a relative, and those who had received such a sum, were more likely than other respondents to say that John should accept the loan (significant at 1 per cent and 2 per cent levels, respectively).

The emergent picture is then quite a complex one. Our data do suggest that obligations between 'close' kin are the strongest, but not in every situation and not unconditionally. Furthermore, although there is a consensus that obligations between parents and children do exist, there is not always consensus on how those obligations should be fulfilled. The John Highfield vignette indeed implies that for some people an expression of willingness to help should be reciprocated with a refusal to accept, and that is enough. Of course, considering the issue of parent–child relationships begs the question of which parents, and which children? Do people assign kin responsibilities along gender lines? We will now turn to consider that issue.

Assumption 3: Obligations of women are stronger than those of men, especially for practical support, personal care and domestic tasks

Do most people distinguish between the obligations of men and women to provide support? We are going to focus here on normative expectations about the gender of givers of support, although elsewhere we have developed other issues of gender in both giving and receiving assistance (Finch and Mason, 1987). Again, to start at the most general level, we asked for responses to an attitude statement as follows: 'Women rather than men should look after relatives who need care'. If the assumption is straightforwardly correct, then we should have a majority agreeing with this proposition. In fact we have a split response, with a majority of respondents (61 per cent) actually disagreeing with the proposition and a sizeable minority – 36 per cent – who agree.

What do our more situationally specific questions tell us? We will divide our discussion into questions about different types of support (personal care, financial, accommodation), as this highlights some contrasts in our data. We begin with financial assistance. The way we have formulated Assumption 3 – that women are the most appropriate people to provide personal care – leaves open the question of who should provide financial support. However, earlier work on kinship (notably Bell, 1968) suggests that money may be seen specifically as 'men's business' in the family, as elsewhere.

In our survey data there is no overarching numerical consensus about whether women or men should provide financial support, but there is a slight tendency for men to be named as favoured money providers. Our main evidence for this comes from a number of questions where we asked respondents to say 'which relative' should provide financial support. In fact, we posed this question at two levels, asking respondents first to say which relative should offer money then, if they named more than one, pressing them to cite their first preference. An example of one of these questions is:

> If an elderly person wants to go into a private nursing home to live, but can only afford to pay part of the price, do you think that relatives should offer to provide the rest of the money that is needed? Which relative, if any, should offer the money? (If more than one named) which relative should be the first to offer money?

In response to this question 57 per cent of first answers were 'children', meaning that people did not specify the gender of the child. More answers favoured son (7 per cent) than daughter (3 per cent), but the proportions are clearly small. But 16 per cent of responses said something like 'all equally', indicating that those people are unwilling to allocate responsibility to a particular relative, or gender. However, when respondents were pressed for their first preference, the pattern changed. This time only 17 per cent of people said 'children', while 40 per cent now said son, 9 per cent daughter and 29 per cent all equally. There is therefore an increase in those specifying 'son' and a decrease in those saying 'children'. A similar pattern occurs on other questions.

Thus, on their first answers, the majority of people seem to be seeking a kind of 'equal shares' solution, by specifying either ungendered children, or some kind of 'all equally' arrangement. When pressed, however, more people are willing to say that the son should offer the money. There remains, however, a 'core' of 46 per cent (17 per cent who still specify children, and 29 per cent who say all equally) who stick with an equality solution despite pressure to express a preference. It may be that this pattern occurs because the recipient of the money is to be an elderly person – perhaps some people are saying to us that there should be a 'sharing of the burden' element in the responsibility for elderly people specifically. Certainly a similar pattern was observed in another question, which asked whether relatives should offer to pay for an elderly couple to have some redecorating done in their home.[14]

As far as financial support is concerned then, it seems that men are marginally favoured as providers, and that this increases when people are pushed to choose their preferred relative. There are no obvious differences in respondents' answers according to their age, gender or social class, but there is a tendency for people in the highest of our three income bands to specify 'whole family' options rather than to say that a son specifically should pay (significant at less than 1 per cent level). Certainly, our data show that women are not favoured as the money providers – answers either specify men, or do not specify gender at all.

We will now turn to the questions about the provision of accommodation to relatives. These showed a similar pattern of 'equality' solutions being preferred by a substantial number of people in their first responses, but when pressed many made a gendered choice. However, this time the preferred providers tended to be women rather than men.

We shall illustrate this with reference to two questions which we have already discussed (see Assumption 1), one about a young family returning from living abroad, the other about a family who have been evicted for non-payment of rent. In both cases we asked initially whether relatives should offer a temporary home, then, if respondents said yes, followed up with our standard questions about which relatives. Many people (around 40 per cent on both questions) responded initially with the simple answer that 'parents' should provide temporary accommodation, but when they specified more precisely their choices focused upon women and upon the relatives of women – 'woman's parents' (around 15 per cent on both questions), 'mother' (around 10 per cent) and specifically 'woman's mother' (around 5 per cent). So it is apparent that, when pressed, there is a tendency to see female relatives as the appropriate people to provide accommodation, and this seems to apply equally to the male and female respondents in our sample. The same message comes through in a question which we asked about accommodation for a frail elderly person (see

Assumption 2), although this question is likely to conflate the issues of accommodation and personal care. In so far as providing accommodation can be taken to imply also giving domestic support (which it would be in this case), this can be taken as support for Assumption 3.

It is not the case, however, that the majority always saw the provision of accommodation as women's business, just as it was not the case that the majority always saw money as men's. The more striking point in sociological as well as statistical terms is the reverse: money was hardly ever specified as women's business, and accommodation hardly ever as men's.

We will now turn to questions about personal care. We have already seen that people do not allocate responsibility for personal care to relatives as readily as might have been expected. But is gender – i.e. the gender of the potential giver and receiver – a principle in their judgements? To summarize, the answer is that people show some tendency to allocate personal care responsibility to women, but again, there is still a consistent about this, and it is not an unambiguous pattern.

First, and very much in line with the pattern of answers identified in relation to finance and accommodation, many people seem to search initially for an 'equal shares' solution to personal care, saying something like 'all the family' should provide support, or using a term such as 'the children', which covers both women and men.

This is illustrated very clearly by one question where we asked whether a nephew and niece should be prepared to undertake shopping and a little domestic assistance for an elderly person who has no other relatives. We then asked whether this should be done by the nephew, the niece, or both equally. Answers to this question show a notable measure of agreement (84 per cent, baseline 50 per cent), that the niece and nephew should help out equally. However, where people were prepared to choose between the niece and the nephew (a minority of 15 per cent of our total sample), almost everyone chose the niece. Only one person chose the nephew, and ninety-seven people said it should be the niece. We found a rather similar pattern on one of our longer vignettes where we set up the question of whether either the husband or wife should give up their job to care for the husband's father. Although 64 per cent of respondents thought that neither should give up their job, where people were prepared to make a choice (22 per cent of our total sample), they almost always chose the wife (21 per cent), despite the fact that it was the husband's father.

These data suggest that most people do not automatically slot women into personal caring roles as the first normative option. They look for other alternatives (perhaps not involving relatives at all) or they begin with the principle that there should be equal sharing of the burden. But those people who *are* prepared to choose nearly always opt for women.

So do our data support the assumption that women's personal care and domestic obligations are stronger than men's? Certainly they show that the type of support needed has some impact on the identity of the relative most likely to be allocated the normative responsibility for providing it. Financial support is rather more likely to be seen as men's business, and the provision of both accommodation and personal care as women's, although in the case of personal care this is much more ambiguous than one might expect.

However, these gendered patterns usually only emerge or become clarified when people are pushed to make a choice of one relative. In questions about all three types of support, people's first response often seems to be an 'equal shares' solution, implicitly involving both women and men. This suggests that the identification of women as the most appropriate people to provide personal care is not so crude and immediate as is often supposed. The allocation of responsibilities along gender lines is by no means a matter of clear consensus in our data. What we do seem to have elicited is that normative expectations operate at two levels: at one level, concepts of equality and fairness can be openly discussed and applied, but on another level people recognize a set of principles which allows a gendered choice to be made.

Conclusion

In conclusion, it becomes clear that none of the three assumptions which we were testing is wholly accurate. This will not be startling to a sociological audience. Sociological common sense would predict that normative preferences are actually more complex than is suggested by the three assumptions with which we began. However, we see ourselves as having gone somewhat beyond common sense in demonstrating the points at which these assumptions more or less hold, and those where they do not. Our data also point fairly persistently to the importance of distinguishing between *procedural* and *substantive* consensus and to the significance of procedural issues (that is, questions about how people should work out 'the proper thing to do').

There are of course some fairly thorny issues of interpretation here. How, for example, should we interpret the apparently different levels of consensus? We began with fairly crude consensus levels but we obviously needed to move beyond these to understand the subtleties of gender preferences or parent–child obligations. This is significant in the face of policy (and sometimes sociological) assumptions that there does exist a consensus on these issues which can be apprehended fairly straightforwardly.

A related issue is how far we can relate our percentage levels to the existence of norms. Can we claim that what we have identified as a consensus is a *normative* consensus? Our survey questions were phrased in a normative way, but we cannot demonstrate conclusively that answers given were intended to be normative. People may answer in a number of ways which are not directly normative: for example in a predictive fashion, suggesting what people *would* do, rather than what people *should* do; or pragmatically, suggesting what it is realistically *possible* to do; or on the basis of experience, so that for some people the answer may be more like a *description* of what they did or do in that situation than a normative statement. More likely, people will answer in complex ways combining these and other elements.

These are issues which arise in all surveys which attempt to generate data on normative beliefs and values, whatever type of questions are asked, and we have already argued that it is only the *product* of normative reasoning (normative statements), not the *process*, which is susceptible to survey analysis. By specifying the context of moral judgements in the type of questions which we asked, we must have been locking on to some respondents' experience more directly than others. Some people may have been drawing substantially upon their own experience, and others reflecting to us a more abstract and generalized version of morality. However, experience itself cannot be easily or accurately 'measured' in a survey, and its relationship to normative judgements cannot be assumed to be straightforwardly causal. This means that any data we have on the relationship between reported experience and normative statements can only be indicative of themes and patterns worth pursuing with qualitative methods. Certainly we have some evidence, as we have indicated, of a relationship between reported relevant experience and answers to our questions, especially, it seems, questions about money.

Beyond issues of direct experience, there are important questions about the status of accounts which people give in a survey – or even in an in-depth study – and whether these are simply 'one kind of appearance rather than believed reality' (West, 1990). Some writers have reflected on this by using the distinction between public and private accounts of family life and the normative issues which surround them, arguing that these two types of account can be very different (see, for example, Cornwell, 1984; Finch, 1987a; Voysey, 1975). We find this distinction helpful up to a point but also potentially misleading, in that it implies that people have two fixed views of the world, one for public and the other for private consumption – rather like a very static concept of 'underlying attitudes', which sometimes get deployed to explain observed behaviour. The problem with both these conceptual formulations is that they presume that individuals carry round with them fixed views of the world, which are both clearly focused and also stable over time. The reality, we would argue, is much more fluid than that. For example, the significance of procedural rather than substantive consensus in our data suggests that people do not carry around with them stable sets of values and meanings, but construct them when they have to out of various materials available.

We would therefore be cautious about claiming that our data straightforwardly document the dimensions of the morality of kinship in Britain. Nevertheless, our data *can* indicate what level of agreement emerges when a large number of people is presented with a specified situation, and asked what is the proper thing to do. We can show what kind of morality people construct in those circumstances, presented with those situations. Almost certainly people arrive at such judgements in different ways, giving particular weight to different factors. But the question of how they *arrive* at their judgements (including the question of whether they utilize or construct 'general principles') is a separate issue, and almost certainly not amenable to analysis through the medium of a survey.

ACKNOWLEDGEMENTS

We would like to thank Graham Rodwell and Patrick West for their comments on an earlier draft of this chapter. This project was funded by ESRC 1985–9 under the title 'Family Obligations: Social Construction and Social Policy', award no. G00232197.

NOTES

1 For a discussion of the historical evidence on this issue see Finch (1989).
2 We continue to use the word 'family' because it is understandable in political discourse. Our work in fact is about kinship.
3 For discussion of this framework see Finch (1987a) and Finch and Mason (1990b, 1993).
4 There is evidence from Thompson and West (1984) to suggest a relationship between people's relevant personal experience (if they have any) and the way they frame their responses to vignette-type questions.
5 We have excluded the 'don't know' category from this calculation because this was not presented to respondents as a separate response option.
6 An additional piece of evidence, indicating that recognizing appropriate norms of kinship is not a straightforward matter, comes from the second stage of our study where we reused a few of the vignettes in qualitative interviews. We found that our interviewees saw the vignettes as raising the kind of dilemma which people do meet in real life, but seldom indicated that there is an obviously correct thing to do in any of the circumstances which we outlined.
7 This is one of the major foci in our qualitative study and we develop these issues further in Finch and Mason (1993).
8 We are not suggesting it is possible to 'control for' different circumstances in a precise statistical way in the analysis of our data, because of the perspective on norms which informed our research design. We have argued that norms are situated – that is, dependent on sets of circumstances – and have used the vignette technique accordingly. It would be contradictory to attempt to 'subtract' various of the circumstances in analysis if the crucial factor in people's judgements is the constellation or interaction of those circumstances. Nevertheless, a comparison across questions does help to indicate the ways in which different factors are taken into account in the making of judgements.
9 For a discussion of substantive and procedural consensus in a different context see Hyman (1978, pp. 16–36).
10 In these questions we always asked respondents to assume that the person concerned had a large family, who all lived nearby. Although it does not reflect the reality of many people's lives, this strategy was adopted as a way of trying to ensure that respondents thought as broadly as possible about who is the normatively appropriate person to offer help in given circumstances and were not constrained, for example, by thinking just of the people who would be available in their own kin group.

11 These attitude statements were taken directly from a survey of public attitudes to the care of dependent people, directed by Patrick West and conducted in Scotland in 1981. The aim was to build in an element of direct comparability. On the attitude statement quoted here, the Scottish results were quite similar to ours: 60 per cent said that children do have an obligation to care for elderly parents, and 39 per cent said that they do not. See West (1984, pp. 417–46).

12 Within the parent–child range, there does not seem to be any widespread inclination to distinguish in terms of birth order where children are seen as the providers of support. Although we never asked specifically about this, people had the opportunity to cite its relevance, yet only a tiny minority did so. There is a sense in the data of people wanting to follow an 'equal shares' principle, by choosing 'children' as an option rather than specifying which child, either by age or gender. This corresponds with a tendency to specify 'parents', rather than a particular parent by gender.

13 Our data also suggest that filial obligations are less likely to be conditional on the quality of the relationship than are obligations between more genealogically distant kin.

14 From the survey we cannot really know whether or not equality solutions are to do with the age of the recipient. For example, on the question about a young couple wanting a holiday, only 15 per cent of our sample said that relatives should lend them the money. This means that our data on 'which relative' and 'preferred relative' are only based on 15 per cent of our sample, and the patterns observed may not therefore be very reliable. In fact, the responses favoured parents (62 per cent on first answer, 50 per cent preferred relative), and apart from that were marginally more likely to favour father (13 per cent, and 11 per cent) than mother (2 per cent, 5 per cent). Interestingly though, the 'all equally' category is smaller here: 5 per cent first answer, 9 per cent preference. This therefore does not contradict the hypothesis that a 'sharing of the burden' is seen as appropriate for the support of elderly people.

REFERENCES

Allan, G. (1985), *Family Life*, Oxford: Blackwell Publishers.

Bell, C. (1968), *Middle Class Families*, London: Routledge & Kegan Paul.

Condor, S. (1988), 'Gender and individuality', in M. Billig (ed.), *Ideological Dilemmas*, London: Sage.

Cornwell, J. (1984), *Hard Earned Lives*, London: Tavistock.

Dalley, G. (1988), *Ideologies of Caring*, London: Macmillan.

Deutscher, I. (1973), *What We Say/What We Do: Sentiments and Acts*, Brighton: Scott Foresman.

Finch, J. (1987a), 'Family obligations and the life course', in A. Bryman, B. Bytheway, P. Allatt and T. Keil (eds), *Rethinking the Life Cycle*, London: Macmillan.

Finch, J. (1987b), 'The vignette technique in survey research', *Sociology*, 21: 105–14.

Finch, J. (1989), *Family Obligations and Social Change*, Cambridge: Polity Press.

Finch, J. and Groves, D. (1980), 'Community care and the family: a case for equal opportunities?', *Journal of Social Policy*, 9: 487–511.

Finch, J. and Mason, J. (1987), 'Gender and family obligations', paper given to Lancaster Women's Research Group, January.

Finch, J. and Mason, J. (1989), 'Relatives, friends, the market or the state: preferences for personal care', working paper, University of Lancaster.

Finch, J. and Mason, J. (1990a), 'Filial obligations and kin support for elderly people', *Ageing and Society*, 10: 151–75.

Finch, J. and Mason, J. (1990b), 'Decision-taking in the fieldwork process', in R. G. Burgess (ed.), *Studies in Qualitative Methodology*, London: Jai Press.

Finch, J. and Mason, J. (1993), *Negotiating Family Responsibilities*, London: Routledge.

Firth, R., Hubert, J. and Forge, A. (1969), *Families and Their Relatives*, London: Routledge & Kegan Paul.

Gittins, D. (1985), *The Family in Question*, London: Macmillan.

Harris, N. (1988), 'Social security and the transition to adulthood', *Journal of Social Policy*, 17: 501–23.

Henwood, M. and Wicks, M. (1985), 'Community care, family trends and social change', *Quarterly Journal of Social Affairs*, 1: 357–71.

Hyman, R. (1978), 'Pluralism, procedural consensus and collective bargaining', *British Journal of Industrial Relations*, 16: 16–40.

Marsh, C. (1982), *The Survey Method: The Contribution of Surveys to Sociological Explanation*, London: Allen and Unwin.

Morgan, D. H. J. (1975), *Social Theory and the Family*, London: Routledge & Kegan Paul.

Morgan, D. H. J. (1985), *The Family, Politics and Social Theory*, London: Routledge & Kegan Paul.

Qureshi, H. (1986), 'Responses to dependency: reciprocity, affect and power in family relationships', in C. Phillipson, M. Bernard and P. Strang (eds), *Dependency and Interdependency on Old Age*, London: Croom Helm.

Qureshi, H. and Simons, K. (1987), 'Resources within families: caring for elderly people', in J. Brannen and G. Wilson (eds), *Give and Take in Families*, London: Allen and Unwin.

Thompson, C. and West, P. (1984), 'The public appeal of sheltered housing', *Ageing and Society*, 4: 305–26.

Ungerson, C. (1987), *Policy is Personal*, London: Tavistock.

Voysey, M. (1975), *A Constant Burden: The Reconstitution of Family Life*, London: Routledge & Kegan Paul.

Walker, A. (ed.) (1982), *Community Care*, Oxford: Blackwell Publishers.

West, P. (1984), 'The family, the welfare state and community care: political rhetoric and public attitudes', *Journal of Social Policy*, 13: 417–46.

West, P. (1990), 'The status and validity of accounts obtained at interview: a contrast between two studies of families with a disabled child', *Social Science and Medicine*, 30: 1229–39.

Wilson, P. and Pahl, R. (1988), 'The changing sociological construct of the family', *Sociological Review*, 36: 233–72.

Young, M. and Willmott, P. (1959), *Family and Kinship in East London*, London: Routledge & Kegan Paul.

16

Gender Differences in Informal Caring

Sara Arber and Jay Ginn

Introduction

The adage that community care is a euphemism for family care and that family care means care by women (Walker, 1982; Finch and Groves, 1983) makes invisible the role of men in providing informal care. Men carers have hitherto been neglected by social scientists largely because the early studies of informal care were born out of a feminist concern with women's oppression in the family, first in terms of caring for their own children, and later caring for their elderly parents. Caring not only affected their own opportunities for paid employment and pursuing other desired goals, but had social and psychological costs (Braithwaite, 1990; Twigg, 1992).

Many of the early studies of caring focused on caring for mentally handicapped and physically disabled children (Wilkin, 1979; Glendinning, 1983; Baldwin, 1985). These studies found very little involvement of fathers or anyone else contributing to the support of mothers caring for a severely disabled child. In the early 1980s, work on informal caring emphasized the burdens faced by mid-life women in providing informal care for elderly people. Brody (1981) coined the term 'women in the middle' to characterize women in the USA who, after relinquishing the constant demands of child care, are called on to provide care for their ageing parents or parents-in-law. Thus women's opportunities are first constrained by caring for their own children and then by informal care for parents or parents-in-law.

A number of influential studies in Britain focused on women caring for their parents. Nissel and Bonnerjea (1982) interviewed married women caring for a parent in their home, and Lewis and Meredith (1988) interviewed single daughters caring for their mothers. In studies of caring for disabled children and for elderly parents there was little recognition of the role men played in providing informal care.

Finch and Groves (1983, p. 3) refer to 'the very small number of men who are front-line carers'. Caring was not only seen as the province of women, but as 'an activity which is culturally defined as being "natural" for women' (ibid.). Some writers have argued that it is a central part of women's feminine identity. This hinges on the duality within caring, that it encompasses both 'caring about' – that is, love or emotional concern for the care-recipient – and 'caring for', which is the practical labour of caring (Graham, 1983; Thomas, 1993). The assumption is that both women and men do the former but only women undertake the latter.

The following was written about care for frail elderly people and is equally applicable today:

> There is very little acknowledgement of the role of male carers or of the difficulties men carers face. Their caring is hidden from public view and has not been the subject of critical scrutiny by researchers, pressure groups or policymakers, mainly because of the assumption that the same unequal domestic division of labour is found in caring for infirm elderly as in caring for children and for the young mentally and physically handicapped. (Arber and Gilbert, 1989a, p. 80)

This chapter addresses the lack of attention given to men carers by examining the caring relationships in which men and women provide informal care, and gender differences in the nature of care provision.

The Neglect of Male Carers

The equation of caring with women's identity and the neglect of male carers made the finding that men comprised 40 per cent of carers (Green, 1988) particularly surprising. This nationally representative survey interviewed adults aged sixteen and over in 1985 as part of the annual General Household Survey (GHS). It found that equal proportions of men and women (4 per cent) were caring for someone in the same household, and more women than men (11 per cent compared with 8 per cent) were caring for someone in another household. Men were less likely to be main carers than women (6 per cent compared with 10 per cent) and less likely to care for twenty or more hours per week (3 per cent compared with 4 per cent).

Many early studies of carers comprised relatively small and specific samples, which neglected those family situations where men carers are more commonly found. The proportion of men who are carers differs markedly according to the relationship between the care-recipient and the carer. Arber and Gilbert (1989b) show that equal proportions of elderly men and women are caring for a disabled spouse and that about 40 per cent of elderly parents being cared for by an unmarried child at home are cared for by a son. These two caring relationships were of little concern to feminist writers, who were primarily concerned about married and single women caring for elderly parents.

Arber and Gilbert (1989a) argued that there are two ideal types of caring trajectories: one arises from 'lifelong' co-residence where the caring role is often taken on imperceptibly with a gradual change from a reciprocal relationship to one of dependency; in this case there is usually little conflict with other roles and obligations. The other trajectory involves some choice about taking on the caring role, either when an elderly person joins the carer's household or when care for someone in another household is undertaken. Where decisions about caring are made, the role of kinship obligations, which in our society are profoundly gendered, become paramount (Finch, 1989; Qureshi and Walker, 1989). In the first trajectory, caring is largely by default and men are nearly as likely as women to be carers. However, when decisions are made as to who should provide care, men who are married may have the option of having their wives fulfil their obligation to care for their parents. Married women are thus doubly disadvantaged, by being the first-line carers of their own disabled children, partners and parents and by being called upon to be carers for their husbands' parents.

Some research on men carers has emerged as a by-product of work on redundancy and retirement. Bytheway (1987) examined informal care in the families of fifty-nine redundant South Wales steel workers and found a high proportion providing care for their wives, elderly parents, handicapped adult children and others. Cliff (1993) found that a third of the men in his small-scale studies of early retirement had been involved in providing care, mainly for their wives. During their wives' illnesses, these men took over all the main house-work and personal care tasks, but

> they had all reverted to a more traditional masculine role after the illness was over. ... For these men, caring for the sick, along with taking the primary respon sibility for household and domestic tasks, was definitely regarded as 'female' work. In the absence of their own traditional masculine role as 'worker', however, it represented an arena that they were prepared to enter if necessary. (Ibid.: p. 134)

These men exemplify caring by default, taking on domestic and caring tasks when they could not avoid them, but only on a temporary basis until the conventional gender roles could be restored.

The suggestion that male caring is most likely following retirement is reinforced by Ungerson's (1987) in-depth study of nineteen carers of elderly people, which included four men above retirement age caring for their wives. Men used the language of love in explaining their reasons for caring, whereas women mainly used the language of duty. Ungerson (ibid.: p. 99) concludes that 'Men would be unlikely to care for someone whom they could not legitimately claim to love on an intimate basis'. Ungerson also suggests that there are gender differences in the nature of caring, with men adopting a more organized approach to the tasks of caring, often likening it to a job and making occupational references, while women emphasize the emotional side of their caring. Some women constructed their caring relationship as a maternal one. However, there was little difference in the actual tasks performed by men caring for their wives and wives for their husbands.

James (1992) conceptualizes caring in terms of three essential components: physical labour, such as practical help with shopping or cooking and help with personal care; emotional labour, relating to the ways in which carers reassure and provide psychosocial support to the care-recipient; and organizational or managerial labour, referring to the way carers often have to organize or manage the care-recipient's life in terms of making sure everything is done at the appropriate time and in a way which is acceptable to the person concerned. The latter two components are less visible than the first, but may be more important to the quality of life of the dependent person than simply the accomplishment of physical and personal care tasks. Where there is more than one carer, the primary carer is likely to be responsible for the management of care and the role of other carers is likely to be restricted to providing help with more practical tasks.

The role of men in informal care raises questions about their degree of involvement in the provision of personal care, that is, tasks concerned with personal hygiene, such as dressing, bathing and assisting with using the toilet. Provision of such care is likely to reflect the needs of the dependent person, with those who have higher levels of disability more likely to require personal care. Men may be less willing or able to give personal care for two reasons. First, giving personal care breaks norms about appropriate masculine behaviour, threatening their identity (Graham, 1983). Personal care is likely to be more emotionally demanding than other types of care provision. It may provoke anxiety for the care-giver, who may be uncomfortable about performing intimate tasks. Second, it may be unacceptable to the dependent person to have care provided by a man. There are often considerable tensions surrounding intimate care provision to other adults, since it demonstrates that the care-recipient is unable to perform basic human functions. The recipient may feel degraded by having personal care tasks performed for them, and see it as doubly disconcerting if the care is performed by a man.

Men providing personal care for women may violate a cultural taboo. Ungerson (1983) argued that there is a taboo in Western society against cross-sex personal care because of the incest taboo, but that 'cross-sex caring' is not problematic for marital partners (Ungerson, 1987). However, Parker (1993) shows that providing intimate personal care to a spouse may be acutely distressing for both partners and that it may be more difficult because it interferes with the couple's sexual relationship. The cross-sex taboo may be greater in relation to men caring for dependent women than women caring for dependent men: the latter can more readily be acted out in terms of a mothering relationship or a nursing role, although the mothering role itself will tend to infantilize the dependent person and may be experienced as objectionable by them (Hockey and James, 1993).

The issue of cross-sex caring is a particularly significant one with regard to informal care for frail elderly people. The demography of ageing means that the number of elderly women far exceeds elderly men, and elderly women are nearly twice as likely to be disabled as men in the same five-year age group (Arber and Ginn, 1991). Because women predominate among the elderly who need care, women may be more likely to be called on to provide that care to avoid any cross-sex taboos. Finch (1984) has argued that elderly women have the right to be cared for by other women, not by men, and that gender equality of caring may not be desired by elderly women.

Aims and Methods

This chapter aims to understand gender differences in informal caring and to examine whether the majority of men carers are providing care by default. Carers by default will include individuals caring for their spouse, where caring is expected as an integral part of the marital relationship, and unmarried children caring for their parents in the same home. We contrast gender differences in co-resident care with those in non-resident care, particularly focusing on the differing nature of obligations to care in these two settings. We argue that men's greater caring role in the former setting than the latter is because they are carers by default.

The chapter uses secondary analysis of the 1990–1 General Household Survey, which included a section on informal caring comparable to the questions asked in 1985 (Green, 1988). The GHS is a nationally representative sample of adults living in private households. It is a stratified two-stage sample selected from the Postcode Address File using 576 postcode sectors. Interviews were completed with over 17,000 adults over age sixteen living in nearly 10,000 households in Great Britain, with a response rate of 81 per cent (OPCS, 1992a, 1992b). The survey excludes informal care provided to people living in residential settings.

Over 2,700 people were identified as informal carers using two screening questions. The first screening question asked:

> Some people have extra family responsibilities because they look after someone who is sick, handicapped or elderly. ...Is there anyone living with you who is sick, handicapped or elderly whom you look after or give special help to ...?

The second screening question identified people with caring responsibilities outside the household:

> And how about people not living with you, do you provide some regular service or help for any sick, handicapped or elderly relative, friend or neighbour not living with you?

Any gender difference in the proportion of carers identified will depend partly on whether men and women interpreted these screening questions in different ways (Arber and Ginn, 1990; Twigg, 1992).

Gender differences in the nature of caring are assessed using three measures: first, the time devoted to caring each week; second, whether the carer is the sole or main carer; and third, whether the carer usually helps with personal care, such as bathing, cutting nails, using the toilet and feeding. We consider whether personal care is restricted to specific kin relationships between the carer and care-recipient, and assess whether personal care is less likely to be provided to care-recipients of the opposite sex, and if so, to what extent this cross-sex taboo holds only in certain kin relationships. Our analysis of the nature of caring is limited by the GHS questions, which do not address aspects of caring such as the provision of emotional support, reassurance, the need for a constant presence or degree of discretion in the timing of when care is provided (Arber and Ginn, 1990). These may vary between men and women carers.

Results

Characteristics of carers

The main distinction is whether care is provided for someone in the same household or for someone living in another household. These two settings differ markedly in the number of hours devoted to caring, the nature of tasks undertaken by the care-giver and the impact caring is likely to have on the care-giver's life (Arber and Ginn, 1990, 1991).

Men and women are equally likely to provide informal care for someone in the same household (3.8 per cent of men and 3.9 per cent of women – see table 16.1), but a higher proportion of women than men provide care for someone living in another household (13.3 per cent compared with 9.7 per cent). A small proportion of people (0.4 per cent) provide care for someone living in the same household and for someone living in another household. These 71 people are categorized as providing co-resident care in this chapter, resulting in 668 people providing co-resident care and 2,047 providing non-resident care. There are small diffrerences in base numbers between tables because of missing data on some questions.

For men, the likelihood of being a co-resident carer increases steadily with age, reaching 7 per cent for men over 75 (figure 16.1). For women, however, the

Table 16.1 Percentage of adults providing co-resident and non-resident care by marital status and gender

| Marital status | Co-resident* | | Non-resident | | Number of | |
	Men	Women	Men	Women	Men	Women
Married	4.0	4.5	13.3	15.5	5608	5828
Never married	3.5	3.7	6.2	7.5	1796	1615
Previously married	2.4	2.0	10.9	11.7	699	1989
All	3.8	3.9	9.7	13.3	8103	9432

*Includes 71 adults providing care to someone in their own household and someone living in another household.
Source: *General Household Survey, 1990/91*, authors' analysis.

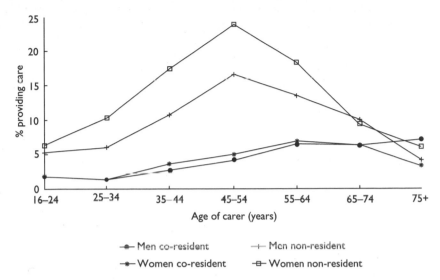

Figure 16.1   Percentage of adults providing co-resident care and non-resident care by age and gender.
Source: General Household Survey 1990/91.

peak age is 55–64, with 6.8 per cent of women in this age group providing co-resident care, falling to 3.3 per cent among women over age 75.

The similarity between the proportions of men and women providing co-resident care contrasts with the higher proportion of women than men who provide non-resident care (table 16.1). Women are about a third more likely than men to provide non-resident care in each age group under 65; but there is no gender difference among elderly people (figure 16.1). The peak age range is 45–54 for both men and women, reflecting the age at which their parents and parents-in-law are most likely to need care. The proportion providing non-resident care is low above retirement age, falling to around 5 per cent for men and women over age 75.

Despite the lower overall prevalence of caring among never-married than married people (table 16.1), the never married are particularly likely to be co-resident carers in mid-life: 22 per cent of single women aged 45–54 and 15 per cent of single men aged 55–64 (figure 16.2). Arber and Gilbert (1989a) showed that among unmarried people caring for a parent in the same household, three-quarters were living in their parents' household, that is, they were the child of the person identified as head of household. Thus it might be assumed that, although some may have moved in with their parents to care for them, the majority of single adult carers have never left the parental home and are caring by default for frail elderly parents.

Single women are more likely than single men to be co-resident carers in mid-life, between ages 35 and 54, but there is little gender difference above 55. For married people the likelihood of being a co-resident carer increases steadily with

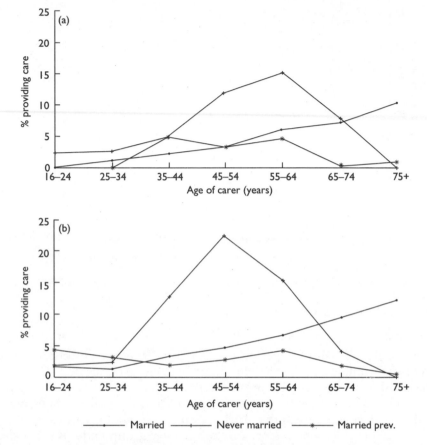

Figure 16.2 Percentage of (a) men and (b) women providing co-resident care by marital status, age and gender.

age; a somewhat higher proportion of married women than men are carers in each age group (figure 16.2). Previously married men and women are less likely to provide co-resident care than the never married or the married, especially above age 45.

Kin relationship to care-recipient

A total of 80 per cent of carers provide care to one person, 17 per cent to two people and 3 per cent to three or more people. To simplify the analysis, we restrict our attention to the relationship with the first-mentioned care-recipient.

Married men and women carers provide co-resident care for similar care-recipients, 20 per cent care for a disabled child and 55–57 per cent care for their spouse (table 16.2a). The only difference is that more married men report caring for a parent-in-law (11 per cent) than a parent (7 per cent), whereas more

Table 16.2 Relationship of care-recipient to carer by carer's marital status, gender and location of caring.

(a) Same household (co-resident carer)

| | Carer is | | | | | | | |
| Care-recipient | Married | | Previously married | | Single | | All* | |
	Men	Women	Men	Women	Men	Women	Men	Women
Spouse	57	55	–	–	–	–	42	40
Child	20	20	24	44	–	5	16	20
Parent	7	14	59	36	60	62	21	24
Parent-in-law	11	5	–	–	–	–	8	4
Other relative	4	4	18	13	33	32	10	10
Friend	1	1	–	8	8	2	3	2
Total	100%	100%	100%	100%	100%	100%	100%	100%
n =	223	285	17	39	63	60	304	364

(b) Different household (non-resident carer)

| | Carer is | | | | | | | |
| Care-recipient | Married | | Previously married | | Single | | All* | |
	Men	Women	Men	Women	Men	Women	Men	Women
Child	1	1	–	1	–	–	1	1
Parent	39	46	40	34	16	16	36	41
Parent-in-law	27	16	1	2	–	–	21	12
Other relative	14	15	15	22	56	45	20	19
Friend or neighbour	19	21	43	40	28	39	22	26
Total	100%	100%	100%	100%	100%	100%	100%	100%
n =	610	905	67	233	111	121	788	1259

* All – includes a small number of people caring for 'others'. Source: *General Household Survey 1990/91*, authors' analysis.

married women care for a parent (14 per cent) than a parent-in-law (5 per cent). This is mainly because inter-generational co-residence is more likely to be a married couple living with the wife's than the husband's parent(s) (Arber and Gilbert, 1989a). About 60 per cent of single men and women carers are caring for their elderly parents. Marital status, rather than gender, has a major effect on who is cared for co-residentially.

Married women are most likely to provide care to someone living in another household (15.5 per cent) and single men least likely to do so (6.2 per cent) (table 16.1). The kin relationship between non-resident carers and care-recipients is associated with marital status rather than gender (table 16.2b). A total of 62 per cent of married women and 66 per cent of married men carers provide care to a parent or parent-in-law. The main gender difference is that more single women than single men provide care for friends and neighbours. This category of caring relates to the choice of the care-giver rather than a kinship obligation.

In summary, there are substantial differences in the likelihood of being a co-resident carer by marital status and age, with single men and women in mid-life and married elderly people particularly likely to provide such care. This contrasts with care for someone in another household, which is most likely to be provided by married women. Thus for co-resident care there is no gender difference in the likelihood of caring, but for non-resident care, where a decision to care is made, the carer is more likely to be a woman. This supports the view that a higher proportion of men carers are doing so by default, while women carers are more likely to be doing so in response to kinship obligations.

The nature of caring

This section analyses gender differences in two aspects of caring. First, relating to the time spent providing care, and second, whether the carer has the sole or main responsibility for care provision. We consider how both the relationship between the carer and care-recipient and the gender of the carer influences the nature of care provision. Co-resident carers spend a great deal more time providing care each week than non-resident carers, women in each case providing more care than men.

Among co-resident carers, 60 per cent of women and nearly half of men care for over thirty-five hours each week, in other words the equivalent of a normal working week (figure 16.3a, last two columns). There is little difference between married men and women in the time spent caring for their spouse; a modest gender difference in time caring for a disabled child; and a very substantial gender difference in the time spent caring for a parent or parent-in-law, with married men spending much less time. It is primarily when their wives require care and they have no option, that married men fully take on the caring role. Men who are not married and who care for a parent in the same household devote substantially less time to caring than equivalent women.

Turning to non-resident care, the percentage of men and women carers with a heavy caring commitment is much lower; only 22 per cent of men carers and 34 per cent of women carers provide over ten hours of care each week (figure 16.3b, last two columns). There is a substantial difference in the time married men and women spend caring for a parent, but a negligible gender difference in time spent caring for a parent-in-law. Married men spend almost as much time supporting their parents-in-law as their own parents. It may be that a higher proportion of men's care is carried out jointly as a married couple, for example when they drive to visit the parents of their partner.

Men who are not married spend more time than married men caring for a parent living in another household; 40 per cent compared with 27 per cent care for ten hours or more per week. There are gender differences among those who are not married, with women spending more time providing care than men in each type of relationship. Overall, women carers spend more time providing care than men, and married men spend the least time, within each type of caring relationship.

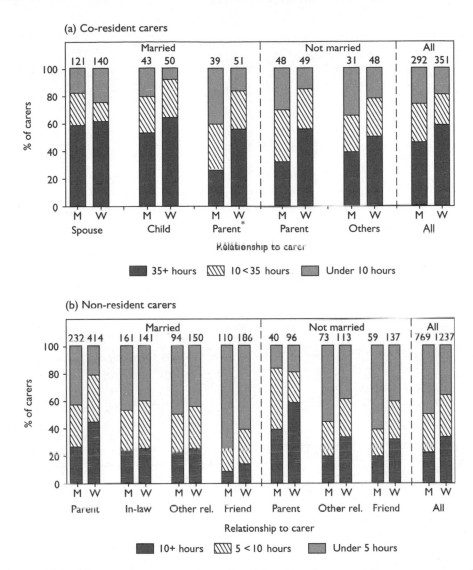

Figure 16.3 Time spent caring each week, relationship of care-recipient to carer, carer's marital status and gender.
* Includes parents-in-law, † includes some additional caring relationships, ‡ includes neighbours.
Source: General Household Survey 1990/91

Carers with sole or main responsibility provide a more demanding type of care than those who are subsidiary or joint carers. The former are more likely to be involved in the management and organization of caring and have a greater responsibility for the welfare of the dependent person. Being a sole or main carer is much more likely for co-resident than non-resident carers (figure 16.4). More women than men are co-resident sole or main carers: 86 per cent

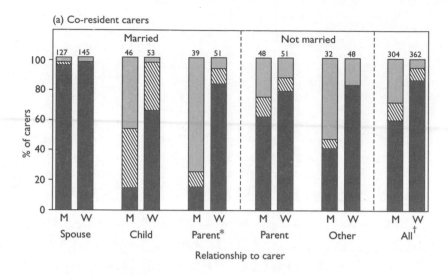

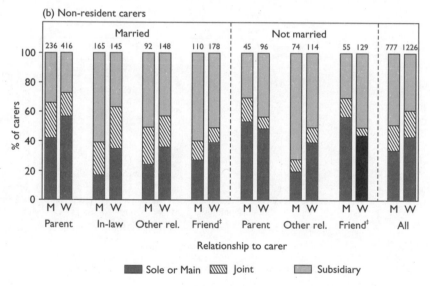

Figure 16.4 Type of carer by relationship of care-recipient to carer, carer's marital status and gender.
* Includes parents-in-law, † includes some additional caring relationship, ‡ includes neighbours.
Source: *General Household Survey 1990/91*

compared with 59 per cent. Fewer than half of women who care for someone in another household have sole or main responsibility for caring and this is the case for only a third of male carers.

Virtually all men and women caring for their spouse are the main or sole carer (figure 16.4a). The marital relationship is pre-eminent in determining that the spouse, of either gender, is the main carer (Arber and Ginn, 1992). Marriage for women seems to predefine them as the main carer of anyone requiring care within the household. In contrast to the lack of gender difference in caring for a spouse, there is a substantial gender difference in caring for a disabled child, parent or parent-in-law in the home. In these latter situations a married man's wife clearly takes over the responsibility for these caring roles, although where a disabled child needs care, a substantial proportion of husbands say they are joint carers. It is only when there is no option, for example if their wives require care, that married men fully take on the caring role.

Among men and women who are not married and who provide care, nearly two-thirds of men and four-fifths of women are the main carer for their parent in the household. The gender difference is much smaller than among married carers, probably because there is no alternative for men in this situation to taking on the main caring role.

Turning to non-resident care, married men are less likely than married women to be main carers for their parents 47 per cent compared with 57 per cent (figure 16.4b). Over a third of married women are main carers for their parents-in-law, compared with only 17 per cent of married men. Thus the marital relationship influences the likelihood of women and men being sole or main carers, with married men having a lesser involvement with each category of care-recipient than married women. Men who are not married are more likely than married men to be a main carer for a parent: 53 per cent compared with 42 per cent. The greater gender difference among those who are married than those who are not married in the likelihood of being a main carer reflects the marital division of caring labour.

Personal care provision

The majority of care-recipients, both in the same household and living elsewhere, are women (table 16.3). A total of 57 per cent of co-resident

Table 16.3 Percentage of care-recipients who are women by relationship of care-recipient to carer and location of care

Relationship of care-recipient to carer	Co-resident care		Non-resident care	
	% who are women	Number	% who are women	Number
Spouse	46	273	–	–
Child	36	123	71	24
Parent	82	151	68	797
Parent-in-law	87	38	69	315
Other relative	66	67	74	395
Friend or neighbour	47	15	75	502
All care-recipients[*]	57		71	
$n =$		667		2042

* All – includes a small number caring for people in other caring relationships. Source: *General Household Survey 1990/91*, authors' analysis.

care-recipients are women, and the gender differential is greater for non-resident care, where 71 per cent are women. In co-resident care the gender balance varies according to the relationship with the care-receiver. The majority of spouses and disabled children receiving care are male, whereas over 80 per cent of parents and parents-in-law receiving care in the same household are women. This contrasts with the gender balance among care-recipients in another household which varies little by the kin relationship. It largely reflects the high proportion of elderly women who live alone (Arber and Evandrou, 1993). The predominance of women among those who require care is a salient issue to the extent that cross-sex personal care may be culturally unacceptable, especially in certain caring relationships.

Despite the literature which suggests that men are unlikely to provide personal and intimate care, over 40 per cent of men caring for someone in the same household provide personal care, compared with two-thirds of women (see figure 16.5a). The gender difference is less among men and women caring for their spouse: 59 per cent of husbands provide personal care for their wives and 71 per cent of wives provide such care for their husbands. There is a relatively small gender difference in the proportions providing personal care to a disabled child, perhaps reflecting the lack of normative taboos about parents giving personal care, irrespective of the child's age or sex. Women are likely to provide personal care in all caring relationships, reflecting the greater acceptability of women performing such roles. The only exception is care of parents or parents-in-law: only 31 per cent of women carers provide personal care to their father or father-in-law, compared with 72 per cent to their mother or mother-in-law. The difference may be because of either the lower levels of need for personal care among co-resident fathers than mothers, or a cross-sex taboo. Men carers provide much less personal care than women carers to parents, but unlike women there is little difference according to whether the relationship is cross-sex or same-sex.

Personal care is provided much less often by non-resident than co-resident carers. However, the gender difference is greater, with over twice as many women as men providing personal care (figure 16.5b). Among those caring for parents or parents-in-law, cross-sex carers are less likely to provide personal care than same-sex carers. This suggests that gendered norms about the acceptability of personal care provision in another household militate against cross-sex caring of an intimate nature. It seems likely that married women are taking on some of the personal care role for their husbands' parents: over twice as many women carers provide personal care to their mothers-in-law (16 per cent) as men carers provide to their own mothers (7 per cent). A quarter of women caring for their mothers provide personal care. However, the same proportion of men and women caring for their fathers provide personal care: 15 per cent. Since the majority of frail elderly people living in the community are women, taboos against cross-sex caring put a substantially greater burden on women than men caring for parents and parents-in-law.

Few who care for friends, neighbours or other relatives provide personal care. It appears to be less acceptable within our society to provide such care, except

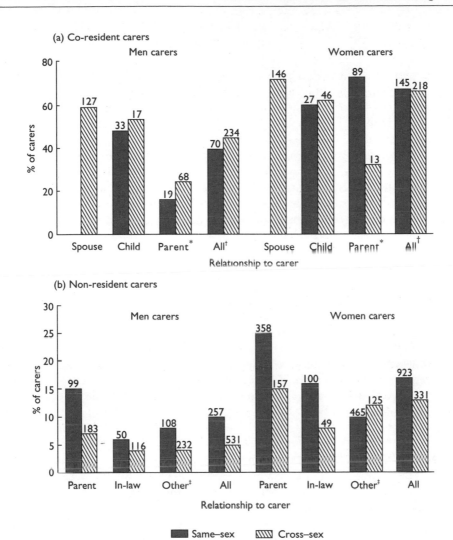

Figure 16.5 Percentage of carers usually giving personal care by relationship of care-recipient to carer, carer's gender and whether the relationship is same-sex or cross-sex. * Includes parents-in-law; † includes other relatives and friends; ‡ includes friends, neighbours and close relatives.

Source: *General Household Survey 1990/91*

as part of a close family relationship or from a professional care provider. Therefore, the state community care services are essential for the provision of personal care, especially if an individual's only source of informal care is from friends, neighbours or more distant relatives. State care plays a particularly important role where the care-giver is of a different gender to the care-recipient.

Conclusion

This chapter has shown that men's caring contribution is substantial, especially in later life when men often care for their marital partner, and among unmarried men caring for a parent within the same household.

However, men are less likely than women to provide care for someone in another household. Men carers also provide fewer hours of care each week and are less likely to be the main carer. The gender differences are most marked among married carers, except those caring for a marital partner, and least marked among unmarried carers. This suggests that married men can rely on their wives to a considerable extent to fulfil kinship obligations and perform caring roles, which they would otherwise have had to undertake personally. This marital division of caring labour primarily affects married women from mid-life onwards caring for elderly parents or parents-in-law. Women carers are more likely to provide personal care than men carers. The gender difference is least among those caring for their spouse or for a disabled child and greatest among those caring for a parent or parent-in-law.

There is some evidence of cross-sex taboos in giving personal care, primarily for care provided in another household. Within specific caring relationships, both men and women carers are more likely to provide same-sex personal care. Cross-sex personal care may be acceptable within the marital relationship and for parents caring for disabled children, but not in caring for parents, more distant relatives or friends. Since the majority of elderly people in need of care are women, cultural taboos against cross-sex personal care in the community may reinforce the pressure on mid-life women to care for mothers and mothers-in-law.

The policy of care in the community, with its aim of minimizing both National Health Service funded and Department of Social Security funded residential care, has increased the need for domiciliary services arranged by Social Services. Without a corresponding increase in the funds available to local authorities, rationing and the perceived fairness of needs assessment by care managers are likely to become major policy concerns. Care managers striving to allocate domiciliary services according to need face a particular dilemma where older women who are not married require personal care. Intimate care provision for someone living in another household is less culturally acceptable than within the same household, and is compounded by our finding of evidence of cross-sex taboos in providing personal care in another household. If care managers provide greater personal care support where there is a cross-sex informal caring relationship, this will inevitably advantage men carers, since nearly three-quarters of people receiving care from someone living in another household are women.

Such targeting would discriminate against both women and co-resident carers. The latter already provide long hours of care equivalent to full-time employment, often with adverse consequences for their health and financial well-being. If this kind of inequity is to be avoided and the positive benefits of community care – improving choice and independence for those needing care – are to be realized, additional resources must be channelled to local authorities to meet the full cost of transferring care to the community setting.

APPENDIX

	16–24	25–34	35–44	45–54	55–64	65–74	75+	All
Men	1172	1576	1464	1252	1132	991	516	8103
Women	1357	1691	1674	1359	1231	1179	941	9432

Base numbers for Figure 1

	16–24	25–34	35–44	45–54	55 64	65–74	75+	All
Men								
Married	173	1095	1216	1081	938	781	324	5608
Never married	994	429	145	83	66	51	28	1796
Previously married	5	52	103	88	128	159	164	699
Women								
Married	373	1268	1357	1097	878	629	226	5828
Never married	961	276	89	49	77	74	89	1615
Previously married	23	147	228	213	276	476	626	1989

Base numbers for Figure 2
Base numbers for figures 16.3–5 are included above each column in each figure. Source: *General Household Survey 1990–91*, authors' analysis.

ACKNOWLEDGEMENTS

For access to the General Household Survey data for 1990–1 we are indebted to the ESRC Data Archive, University of Essex, and to the University of Manchester Computer Centre. We are grateful to the Office of Population Censuses and Surveys for permission to use the GHS data.

REFERENCES

Arber, S. and Evandrou, M. (eds) (1993), *Ageing, Independence and the Life Course*, London: Jessica Kingsley.

Arber, S. and Gilbert, N. (1989a), 'Transitions in caring: gender, life course and care of the elderly', in B. Bytheway, T. Keil, P. Allatt and A. Bryman (eds), *Becoming and Being Old: Sociological Approaches to Later Life*, London: Sage.

Arber, S. and Gilbert, N. (1989b), 'Men: the forgotten carers', *Sociology*, 23:111–18.

Arber, S. and Ginn, J. (1990), 'The meaning of informal care: gender and the contribution of elderly people', *Ageing and Society*, 10: 429–54.

Arber, S. and Ginn, J. (1991), *Gender and Later Life: A Sociological Analysis of Resources and Constraints*, London: Sage.

Arber, S. and Ginn, J. (1992), '"In sickness and in health": care-giving, gender and the independence of elderly people', in C. Marsh and S. Arber (eds), *Families and Households: Divisions and Change*, London: Macmillan.

Baldwin, S. (1985), *The Costs of Caring*, London: Routledge & Kegan Paul.

Braithwaite, V. (1990), *Bound to Care*, Sydney: Allen & Unwin.

Brody, E. (1981), '"Women in the middle" and family help to older people', *The Gerontologist*, 21: 471–9.

Bytheway, B. (1987), 'Care in the families of redundant Welsh steelworkers', in S. di Gregorio (ed.), *Social Gerontology: New Directions*, London: Croom Helm.

Cliff, D. (1993), 'Health issues in male early retirement', in S. Platt, H. Thomas, S. Scott and G. Williams (eds), *Locating Health: Sociological and Historical Explanations*, Aldershot: Avebury.

Finch, J. (1984), 'Community care: developing non-sexist alternatives', *Critical Social Policy*, 9: 6–18.

Finch, J. (1989), *Family Obligations and Social Change*, Cambridge: Polity Press.

Finch, J. and Groves, D. (eds) (1983), *A Labour of Love: Women, Work and Caring*, London: Routledge & Kegan Paul.

Glendinning, C. (1983), *Unshared Care: Families with Disabled Children*, London: Routledge & Kegan Paul.

Graham, H. (1983), 'Caring: a labour of love', in J. Finch and D. Groves (eds), *A Labour of Love: Women, Work and Caring*, London: Routledge & Kegan Paul.

Green, H. (1988), *Informal Carers*, OPCS Series GHS, no. 15, supplement A, OPCS, London: HMSO.

Hockey, J. and James, A. (1993), *Growing Up and Growing Old: Ageing and Dependency in the Life Course*, London: Sage.

James, N. (1992), 'Care = organization + physical labour + emotional labour', *Sociology of Health and Illness*, 14: 488–509.

Lewis, J. and Meredith, B. (1988), *Daughters Who Care*, London: Routledge.

Nissel, M. and Bonnerjea, L. (1982), *Family Care of the Elderly: Who Pays?*, London: Policy Studies Institute.

OPCS (1992a), *General Household Survey: Carers in 1990*, OPCS Monitors, SS 92/2. London: HMSO.

OPCS (1992b), *General Household Survey: 1990 Report*, London: HMSO.

Parker, G. (1993), *With this Body: Caring and Disability in Marriage*, Milton Keynes: Open University Press.

Qureshi, H. and Walker, A. (1989), *The Caring Relationship*, London: Macmillan.

Thomas, C. (1993), 'Deconstructing concepts of care', *Sociology*, 27: 649–69.

Twigg, J. (1992), *Carers: Research and Practice*, London: HMSO.

Ungerson, C. (1983), 'Women and caring: skills, tasks and taboos', in E. Gamarnikow, D. Morgan, J. Purvis and D. Taylorson (eds), *The Public and the Private*, London: Heinemann.

Ungerson, C. (1987), *Policy is Personal: Sex, Gender and Informal Care*, London: Tavistock.

Walker, A. (1982), 'The meaning and social division of community care', in A. Walker (ed.), *Community Care: The Family, the State and Social Policy*, Oxford: Blackwell and Robertson.

Wilkin, D. (1979), *Caring for the Mentally Handicapped Child*, London: Croom Helm.

17

Living with Disability: The Experiences of Parents and Children

Sally Baldwin and Jane Carlisle

The literature on the everyday experience of living with a disabled child comes from parents themselves, from professionals and from academic researchers. It is striking in two respects – the similarities that emerge from a range of very different approaches; and the constancy of the picture over time. Studies carried out in the late 1970s (Wilkin, 1979, for example) are strikingly similar to contemporary accounts (see that of Gough, Li and Wroblewska (1993) and of Hubert (1991)). Studies of highly specific conditions such as cystic fibrosis (Burton, 1975), while idiosyncratic in some respects, demonstrate important commonalities with very different conditions such as deafness (Gregory, 1976), and with research on children with different conditions but similar impairments (Gough, Li and Wroblewska's (1993) survey of children with locomotor impairments). Surveys based on large and heterogeneous samples of disabled children (the OPCS surveys and Sloper and Turner's (1992) survey) find equally similar results. The literature is striking in two other respects. First, there seem to be no accounts from parents whose child has gone into residential care on a permanent basis. Second, very little of it is based on direct communication with the child. The child's own account of disability – what it means to need care, for example – is virtually absent. Notable exceptions are Donna Williams and Robert Hunter, who was disabled since birth and who wrote about his experiences and feelings in relation to being disabled when he reached the age of twenty-four (Hunter, 1992; Williams, 1992).

Parents: Learning About the Disability

Accounts of parents' experiences invariably encompass the highly stressful experience of discovering the child's disability – either at birth or subsequently. Many of these accounts find the process of confirming the disability badly handled by professionals. This is often because parents find it difficult to persuade health professionals to take seriously their suspicion that the child is disabled or ill. Harrowing accounts of this process can be found. Glendinning (1983), for example, tells of a mother whose fourth child's muscular dystrophy was undiagnosed for a significant period of time. His GP thought the mother was being 'neurotic' and 'over protective' because he was an only son. Gregory (1976) gives similar accounts of professional resistance to parents' observations in the case of deaf children. The OPCS survey of disability corroborates these smaller-scale studies. In most cases (66 per cent), parents were the ones who first suspected their child's disability. Some 43 per cent of parents were 'fairly' or 'very' dissatisfied with the process of discovery – increasing to more than half of the very severely disabled children's parents. The commonest reasons for dissatisfaction given were: the general lack of information or advice given at the time (48 per cent of the parents of most severely disabled children); lack of help or support given at the time (26 per cent); failure to take the child's problem seriously (24 per cent). The process of coming to terms with the disability, often over a long period of time, is described by Glendinning (1983), who also examines how this is affected both by factors intrinsic to the disability, and in parents' own lives and experience. It is very clear from this body of literature that both social and medical professionals and parents with similar experience can help significantly.

The Costs of Caring: Practical Problems

The burdens carried by parents – and particularly mothers – caring for a disabled child are well documented, particularly where a child is severely disabled (see, for example, Wilkin, 1979; Glendinning, 1983; 1986; Byrne and Cunningham, 1985, Gough, Li and Wroblewska, 1993; Hubert, 1991; Sloper and Turner, 1992.) Glendinning describes in detail the 'daily grind' that constitutes the experience of mothers and draws parallels between this and the repetitive, largely unrewarding nature of housework. Caring for children whose disabilities 'in many respects represent a prolonging of the dependencies of early childhood... gives rise to an essentially repetitive set of servicing functions which can be physically taxing, mentally exhausting and dispiritingly monotonous' (Glendinning, 1983, p. 41). It includes help with washing, bathing, feeding and dressing the child, carrying them up and down stairs, in and out of bed. It will often involve managing incontinence which, in older children or those who are doubly incontinent or have a colostomy, can be demanding and unpleasant. (Incontinence was the third most frequent disability in the 1985 OPCS survey and 70 per cent of the most severely disabled children were incontinent.) There is likely to be extra washing and housework. Alongside these routine tasks mothers have the demanding task of managing the amusement and supervision of children who are unable to go out to play – school holidays can be particularly difficult. Night-time disturbances are common (one Family Fund survey found that 75 per cent of children over four needed night-time attention, 29 per cent several times each night). There are difficulties in getting out and about with the child; many disabled children cannot walk independently. Parents are likely to find their own social lives restricted because of fatigue, difficulty in finding baby sitters or financial stress (60 per cent of the parents in Gough, Li and Wroblewska's Scottish study of children with loco-motor disabilities reported that their social life was restricted). Taking family holidays can be equally problematic because of difficulties in access, managing the child's treatment, behaviour problems and so on. The OPCS survey finds similar evidence of restrictions on parents' social lives, particularly among those whose child was very severely disabled. The restrictions were mainly caused by inability to get out but also by the disabled child's 'anti-social behaviour' (Meltzer, Smyth and Robus, 1989, p. 67).

It is common for parents to report problems with their physical health and to associate these with the disabled child's care. This has not been conclusively documented, though Philp and Duckworth (1982) report that many studies 'suggest a high prevalence or incidence of problems with health'. The OPCS survey found 13 per cent of parents reporting effects on their health, though only a minority of these parents identified effects on their *physical* health. The remainder pointed to effects on their psychological well-being. In both cases the effect rises with severity of disability.

Emotional Costs

The emotional stresses reported in the literature include many centring on the child and her condition – anxieties about illness, death, what will happen when she grows up. They centre, often, on milestones not reached and on transitional phases – starting school, adolescence or school-leaving age. They also extend to worries about effects on other children and on partners. The hard practical work and the isolation resulting from restrictions on social life and from restrictions on employment is clearly a potential source of emotional strain, particularly, perhaps, for single parents. The literature also cites the frustrations arising from aspirations unlikely to be fulfilled – returning to work when children are older, for example. Yet another possible source of strain is the difficulty parents report of battling with a range of 'helping' agencies of various sorts to obtain appropriate support. The evidence that parents of disabled children experience significant levels of stress is irrefutable, and docu-mented in a very large literature reviewed by Philp and Duckworth (1982), Parker (1990) and Beresford (1993). This literature, and that on the coping strategies families adopt, is discussed further below. It should be noted, however, that the OPCS survey data corroborate the findings of other studies on the relationship between a child's being disabled and poorer parental (espe-cially maternal) mental health. The effects are related to the severity of dis-ability and to the existence of support from a partner. Single parents consistently report higher levels of stress and anxiety (Meltzer, Smyth and Robus, 1989, p. 60).

Financial Consequences

It is, again, extremely well documented that disability in a child both creates a need for additional expenditure and, at the same time, reduces the income available to pay for this by restricting the labour-force participation of both mothers and fathers.

Employment

As Parker (1985) notes, most studies of childhood disability have documented some impact on, especially, mothers' employment opportunities. Burton's (1975) study of children with cystic fibrosis, Wilkin's (1979) of mentally hand icapped children, Bradshaw's (1980) study of Family Fund applicants and Cooke's (1982) study of disabled children in the 1970 birth cohort all found significantly lower numbers of mothers of disabled children in paid employment. Studies of childhood cancer (Bodkin, Pigott and Mann, 1982) and leukaemia (Pentol, 1983) also document effects on employment, especially when children are having treatment in hospital. The most extensive and methodologically rigorous study of the economic effects of a child's disability on parents' work and earnings (Baldwin, 1985) confirms these findings. This study, which replicated the Family Expenditure Survey for a large sample of families with disabled children, found that mothers with a disabled child were less likely to be in employment than mothers in a control group (33 per cent as against 59 per cent). When they were, they worked fewer hours and earned less. These differences increased as children grew up, indicating that – unlike the control – women with disabled children were less likely to rejoin the labour market as their children grew up. Gough, Li and Wroblewska's (1993) study finds similar effects, increasing with the severity of impairment. Restrictions on employment have effects that go beyond finance. A wide range of studies indicate that mothers with disabled children who want, but are unable, to work outside the home experience more stress than mothers who can work outside the home and want to (Burton, 1975; Wilkin, 1979; Bradshaw, 1980; Glendinning, 1983; Baldwin and Glendinning, 1983).

Fathers' employment and earnings are also affected, though the effects are less common and less marked than for mothers. Baldwin's (1985) study suggests that the effects may be different for men in manual and non-manual occupations. The largest differences in labour-market participation occurred among unskilled manual workers; their participation rates being 76.2 per cent and 90 per cent. Manual workers tended to take time off. Non-manual workers, on the other hand, found their employment and promotion opportunities restricted. These findings are echoed in other studies (Cooke, 1982; Bradshaw, Piachaud and Weale, 1981). Applications to the Family Fund confirm these trends. (In 1991 the labour-force participation of fathers was 61 per cent, as against 90 per cent for the general population.) Hirst's (1982, 1984) work confirms that effects on parents' employment continue into young adulthood.

The OPCS survey of disabled children also finds effects of this sort – though the fact that the survey spanned very slight to severe disabilities dampens the effect. A total of 9 per cent of mothers of disabled children worked full-time as against 15 per cent of all mothers; among mothers of older children the figures were 16 per cent and 26 per cent. Predictably, differences in part-time working were smaller.

Fathers' employment was also found to be affected: only 73 per cent of those with disabled children, as against 88 per cent of all fathers, were in full-time employment. The effect was greater among fathers of younger than of older children, the reverse of the picture for mothers. Only 66 per cent of men with disabled children aged 0–4 years were in full-time work, as against 85 per cent of all fathers with children of this age. As Parker (1985) notes, these differences may well be affected by class factors and fathers' ages.

Earnings

Both Baldwin's (1985) study and the OPCS survey (Smyth and Robus, 1989) demonstrate how these employment differences feed through into earnings and family incomes – even after benefits paid on account of disability are taken into account. In the OPCS survey, average gross earnings for people with children in the general population in the year the survey was carried out were 9 per cent higher for men and 7 per cent higher for women in part-time employment than among parents of disabled children. Using equivalent incomes, all types of family containing a disabled child were disadvantaged relative to similar families, with the exception of lone parents. (The lack of effect on lone parents is explained by the high proportion of lone parents in both groups who are dependent on benefit income.)

Baldwin's (1985) study provides detailed information on both women's and men's earnings losses. Among women the effects rose steeply with the age of the youngest child – a difference of £16.30 at 1978 prices. Differences in men's earnings were greatest among non-manual workers with older children (£41 a week).

Disability benefits for children are not designed to replace lost earnings. Even so, including them in family income evened out differences only for one group of families – manual workers with a child under five. Effects were clearest at later stages of the family life cycle. The disposable incomes of non-manual families with disabled children were £30 a week less than of similar families in the control when the youngest child in the family was over eleven. Among manual families, the difference was much smaller (£2.20). (Both sets of figures are at 1978 prices.) The introduction of Invalid Care Allowance will have made some difference. However, McLaughlin's (1991) evaluation of this benefit indicates that it does not remotely compensate for parental earnings loss.

Extra costs

From incomes that are lower, many families with a disabled child have to pay for special expenses. The detailed accounting of these extra costs is fraught with methodological problems (Baldwin, 1985; Smyth and Robus, 1989). Subjective estimates are flawed, comparative methods based on diaries perhaps equally so. Baldwin's (1985) study combined these methods. The 1985 OPCS study relied on subjective estimates. Both, however, find convincing evidence that a child's disability does create extra costs where money is available for these – often by diverting money from other members of the household.

Using the methods of the Family Expenditure Survey (expenditure diaries and information from parents), Baldwin found that families with disabled children incurred extra expense on items bought *regularly*, such as food, fuel, transport and children's clothing. The extra spent varied with family income, however, for families on average incomes nothing less than an extra £15 a week (at 1984 prices) would have been needed to cover these costs. In addition to these regular costs extra expense was needed at intervals for larger items such as house adaptations. Hospital out-patient and in-patient stays were a particularly worrying cause of extra expense – something which may become an issue if the NHS internal market means patients have to travel further to have treatment.

The OPCS survey also identified a number of items on which families reported spending more because of the disability – special equipment or adaptations to their home or to a car, for example. Average expenditure on such items in the year before the survey was £234. In addition to this, over two thirds of families had spent money on items or services required solely because of the child's disability – an average amount of £1.72 a week, though this varied substantially. Over a third of respondents said they spent an *additional* £1.13 a week on average on chemist's items because of the disability. On top of these 'special' expenditures, 70 per cent reported additional expenditure on 'ordinary' items such as clothing, fuel and food. This amounted to an average of £7.65 per week extra. *Total* extra expenditure averaged £6.54, but this varied with the severity of the child's disability. Families of the most severely disabled children (severity categories 9–10) were spending an average of £12.53 a week. As in Baldwin's study, the *extra* spent varied with available income; those on the highest incomes spending most. Families with the lowest incomes (under £80) and very severely disabled children (severity categories 9–10) were spending an average of £6.49 per week, less than half the amount (£15.47) spent by those families with the highest incomes whose children were similarly disabled (Smyth and Robus, 1989, p. 40). The poorest families were more likely to say they needed to spend more on their disabled child's needs but were unable to do so. Nearly half 'needed something for their child which they could not afford to buy' (ibid.).

A number of studies have reported indications of generally lower living standards and of financial stress among families with disabled children – from debts to severe financial crises. Gough, Li and Wroblewska's (1993) Scottish study, for example, found 63 per cent of families reporting a need for extra expenditure against a background of reduced parental employment and earnings. Over half of these families found the financial assistance they received to help with the child's special needs inadequate. The Family Fund, likewise, finds many instances of financial stress and needs families are unable to meet.

It is quite clear that some families suffer from financial difficulties they would not otherwise have encountered. However, some very severely disabled children are living in conditions of *extreme* hardship which are partly related to their condition – and which must reduce their quality of life.

Discussion

The OPCS survey confirms the finding of all other research on this topic – 'when additional expenditure due to disability has been met, families with a disabled child in general have resources lower than families with children in the general population' (Smyth and Robus, 1989, p. 48). This study also illustrates the indirect effect of severity of disability on family resources. Earnings are more heavily affected as severity increases, though the effect of disability benefits dampens this. On the other hand, the potential to spend on the greater needs the severely disabled child has is partly constrained by the income available.

The OPCS data illustrate the combined effects of income losses and extra costs on families' living standards. Just over a quarter of the families in the study said they were managing 'quite well'. Just over half were 'just getting by', while the remaining fifth were 'getting into difficulties'. However, 30 per cent of single parents, as against 17 per cent of married couples, were getting into difficulties. On a number of more objective measures of financial problems – borrowing, being unable to pay bills (for example, fuel), falling behind with payments – considerable numbers of respondents were clearly in trouble and single parents most so. The absence of control data make these findings difficult to assess, though they will clearly add to the pressures experienced by parents in managing a child's disability. Comparative data on living standards – that is, ownership of consumer durables – confirms that two-parent families with a disabled child have lower living standards than similar families in the general population. All single-parent families have lower living standards than all two-parent families and the difference between single parents with or without a disabled child is less clear. Overall, however, high proportions of both two- and one-parent families point to consumer durables they cannot afford and which would clearly make life easier for them – telephones, freezers, central heating, tumble dryers and so on. It is undoubtedly true that some families with a disabled child are simply not as comfortable as they would otherwise be. In other cases, however, very severely disabled children are clearly living in very poor conditions. This must increase the impact of the condition on their families' well-being. The living standards of single-parent families with a disabled child must be a particular cause of concern. The incidence of separation and divorce found in the OPCS surveys was higher than in the general population, that of never-married parenthood the same as the general population.

Effects on Marriage and the Marital Relationship

It is plausible that the emotional, practical and material consequences of caring for, particularly, a severely disabled child should place strains on a marriage, and it is often suggested that marriages are more likely to break down because of the stresses involved. Conversely, however, a significant minority of parents report that bringing up a child who is disabled has strengthened their relationship.

On the whole, the available research data supports the claim that significant disability in a child is associated with an increased risk of marital breakdown. Weale and Bradshaw's (1980) analysis of General Household Survey data, for example, concluded that a moderately to severely disabled child was more likely than a non-disabled child to find herself in a sole-parent family. Hirst (1991) found similar results. Results from other studies are contradictory, however. Cooke et al. (1986) found that the disabled children in their cohort of ten-year-olds were no more likely than the non-disabled children to be living with a sole parent. Likewise, studies of children with particular disabilities and illnesses report different, and contradictory, findings. Quine and Pahl's (1986) study of families whose child had severe learning difficulties found 'no indication that mothers were more likely to experience marital breakdown if they had a handicapped child' (p. 76). Tew et al. (1977), by contrast, found the rate of divorce between parents of children with spina bifida to be nine times the national average.

At a population level, however, the weight of the evidence is that the risk of marital breakdown is greater when a child is disabled and rises with the severity of disability. The difference is not dramatic. The OPCS surveys of disability, which provide the most recent and most reliable evidence, found 19 per cent of all parents of disabled children – as against 13 per cent of the general population – to be single parents. Among the least severely disabled children the percentage of single parents was closer to that of the general population – 15 per cent – while it rose to 20 per cent among the more severely disabled. More than half of the parents in this study reported that having a disabled child had *not* affected their marriage. Another 45 per cent said it *had*; this group was equally divided between those who felt it had placed strains on the marriage and those who thought it had made them closer. Parents of the most severely disabled children were, however, more likely to mention negative effects.

Surveys conducted at a single point in time cannot, of course, capture the full complexity of effects on a marriage. There is consistent evidence, for example, that mothers of disabled children are not only more likely to become single parents, but also less likely to remarry as quickly (Weale and Bradshaw, 1980; Hirst, 1991). This is particularly true of older mothers and those whose children are very severely disabled; single fathers with a disabled child appear to re-partner more quickly than mothers.

Clearly this is a complex topic which needs further research, both at a population level and via in-depth studies. At this point it is important to signal two, overridingly clear facts. First, many parents of disabled children will need practical and emotional support if their marriages are not to founder – mothers experience particularly high levels of stress (Quine and Pahl, 1986). Second, marriages do break down. A large number of parents are therefore caring for often quite severely disabled children on their own. The great majority are women. They are disadvantaged in material terms; and they carry heavy practical and emotional loads. Both they and their children require greater support than is currently available.

Stress, Adaptation and Coping: Parents

The evidence that parents – and particularly mothers – of significantly disabled children are likely to experience higher levels of stress than similar people in the general population is very clear. On a wide range of measures (for example, Malaise Inventory, General Health Questionnaire, Manifest Anxiety Scale, self-reported symptoms of anxiety and depression), their mental health is found to be poorer. This literature has been reviewed in depth in three key studies: Philp and Duckworth's (1982) review of the research on all types of childhood disability; Byrne and Cunningham's (1985) detailed review of the effects of a child's learning difficulty on families; and Parker's (1990) review of the research literature on informal care. All three studies conclude that while voluminous quantities of research confirm the presence of stress, research has so far failed to explain the factors causing some parents (particularly mothers) to experience high levels of stress while others are protected against it. Attempts to do this have focused mainly on four factors:

- structural and material aspects of parents' lives (socio-demographic factors, housing, transport, etc.);
- the nature of the disability and the kind and degree of care required;
- psychological and relational factors in parents;
- the helping networks available.

By and large, the search for predictive or causal factors which work at a general level to explain variations in stress has been inconclusive. Correlations do emerge in some studies, but are contradicted in others. Indeed, failure to find correlations by some researchers from the data they have collected has been followed by 'success' by subsequent researchers re-analysing the same data. Parker (1990), for example, found evidence of 'external' factors that predispose or prevent stress (employment, housing, beliefs about the contribution other family members make) from data which led Bradshaw and Lawton (1978) to conclude that stress was determined only by 'internal' factors such as the 'physiology' and 'personality' of the mother. From that analysis *they* had concluded that 'these factors were not affected in any specific way by the "external" social and physical conditions of the family and child' (Philp and Duckworth, 1982, p. 36).

It is clear from the research reviewed in these three studies that there are some factors which appear both to reduce parents' (mothers') experiences of stress and to help them to 'cope'. It seems a more profitable activity, as these authors suggest, to move away from research which attempts – and largely fails – to explore variations in stress via 'gross demographic and structural differences between families'. A more productive approach would 'emphasize the fact that many families *do* cope with and adapt to the stresses they experience and seek to discover how they do it' (Byrne and Cunningham, 1985, p. 84 – quoted in Parker, 1990, p. 89). Understanding parents' responses to a child's disablement is central to this.

Adaptation and Coping

A recurrent theme throughout the literature on disability is that professionals – including researchers – have difficulty in understanding the perspectives of parents. This is nowhere more clear than in early (1970–80) attempts to describe parents' responses and adaptations to disability in a child. There is a striking tendency in the literature to pathologize parents' responses. Most of what they do is regarded as wrong on one dimension or other. Concepts such as 'projection', 'rejection', 'denial' and 'over-protection' abound – sometimes linked to propositions about neglect and abuse. Another tendency of this literature is its inclination to polarization between studies which view birth or diagnosis of disability as an insurmountable – and damaging – disaster and those which describe a process of adaptation happening over time.

The exceptions are studies which focus on the 'meaning' parents construct for the child's disablement and the way this informs the variety of ways in which they adapt and cope (Voysey, 1975; Jaehnig, 1974). This – mainly sociological – research is characterized by a concern to understand how parents *make sense* of the child's disability. One of the important insights it delivers is the extent to which coping is linked to success in 'normalizing' the child's upbringing – finding a way of parenting which 'maintains habitual or expected child-rearing practices or customary goals' (Philp and Duckworth, 1982, p. 38). Another is the finding that the diagnosis of severe disability in a child need not be polarized as *either* tragedy or something adapted to. Grieving and adapting will coexist throughout the child's life. Moreover, as children grow into adolescence, new ways of coping may be required, particularly when a child is multiply disabled (Seed, 1989; Beresford, 1993).

Relatively few, especially early, studies in this field seem to understand the varied and contradictory demands placed on parents in dealing with something they could not have anticipated – demands in shaping a meaning both for the child's disability and for their role as parents; and practical demands in caring for the child lovingly and sensitively without spoiling her. Often the – predominantly psychoanalytic and psychologically based – research literature on adaptation starts from theoretical and pedagogic perspectives with a somewhat negative and judgemental focus, according to which most of what parents do is wrong in one way or another. On the whole, however, research has moved on – to greater understanding of parents' perspectives and problems and to a preoccupation with how they can be helped. Philp and Duckworth's (1982) conclusion, having reviewed the research on coping, was that, having moved away from a preoccupation with why some 'deviant' families did *not* adapt and cope, research was becoming less judgemental – focusing less on the 'faults' of some parents and more on ways they could be helped. From this perspective it has become clear that

> many families are not *really* coping, even though they are not breaking down. Rather, they experience and meet their problems to the best of their abilities, and often face secondary problems as a result. It is often the accumulation of these problems that disturbs relationships within the family and between the family and society. . . . In brief, therefore, research is now beginning to demonstrate that the real problem is not so much one of family pathology as one of how to give practical assistance to families while, at the same time, keeping in mind that the tasks they face are so difficult that only a few exceptional families can be expected to be fully equipped to undertake them without help from the outside. (Ibid.: p. 46)

In the decade since the publication of that review, this perspective has become much more firmly established and research work on coping has also taken a step forward. A recent review of the literature on the strategies families with a disabled child construct to cope with caring for a severely disabled child has been conducted by Beresford (1993) as part of a Joseph Rowntree Foundation funded project to investigate coping strategies. This research project, based in the Social Policy Research Unit, was part of the 'Management of Personal Welfare' initiative, which was jointly funded by the Joseph Rowntree Foundation and the Economic and Social Research Council.

Beresford's review is based on a theoretical framework which identifies coping processes which mediate the impact of stress on parental well-being. This, in turn, has implications for the well-being of the disabled child. The literature finds that an enormous number of factors impinge on the coping process and mediate it in two ways. First, they influence how an individual appraises events and circumstances and whether they are perceived as stressful. Second, they determine the coping strategies, or coping options, used to manage 'stressors'. Together these factors constitute coping resources, which are both *personal* and *social*. Individuals with few coping resources are regarded as vulnerable to experiencing greater stress, to be less able to manage the stress and, as a result, to adjustment difficulties.

Coping Resources

The following key points on coping resources and coping strategies emerge from Beresford's (1993) review of research:

- *Personal* coping resources are less well researched than social coping resources. There seem to be two reasons for this. First, some of them are very hard to 'measure'. Second, only the psychological literature has explored *intra-personal* factors; other disciplines have tended to focus on social or external factors.
- Research has shown that the following personal coping resources play a significant role in the ways parents adapt to stress: physical and mental health; life philosophies; ideological beliefs; beliefs about locus of control; previous coping experiences; personality characteristics; parenting skills.
- Further work is needed to explore other intra-personal factors which are important to how parents cope.
- *Social* coping resources are found in the individual's environment or social context. They include social support; money; utilitarian resources; housing; marital status.
- It is important to distinguish between *actual* social support and *perceived* social support. The latter is more predictive of how well a parent copes.
- There are numerous sources of social support, each providing different types of support.
- Personality factors may influence the availability of social support and the degree to which individuals choose to use social support to help them cope.
- Coping with the care of a disabled child usually occurs in the context of a family environment. Family-related factors such as adaptability, cohesion, integration and family expression have been shown to be important social coping resources for a parent caring for a disabled child.
- Research suggests that spouse support is one of the most important social coping resources, and includes the provision of practical and emotional support. However, while research suggests the presence of a spouse *per se* is an important coping resource, this may be a rather naive interpretation of data. Other factors associated with single parenthood (for example, financial and housing difficulties, social isolation) must be taken into account before the nature of the relationship between marital status and coping is fully understood.
- Support offered by the extended family tends to be predominantly practical, especially in providing child care. It should not be assumed that having an extended family necessarily implies a high level of support or reduces stress. The attitudes and responses of family members to the disabled child can be a source of stress.
- Support from formal agencies is usually specialized. It includes the provision of information and advice and a range of individual services.

- Respite or short-term care is an important coping resource. It should be remembered, however, that a number of factors mediate take-up of such services. These include the child's ability to cope with the care on offer and parents' beliefs about 'handing their child over'.
- Research suggests that those families who have been able to use respite care, especially family link-type schemes, benefit enormously from the chance to take a break from caring for their child. (The issue of respite/short-term care is discussed further below.) Another means of having a break from child care comes through employment, however. Mothers who are working because they want to (as opposed to financial reasons) find employment an important coping resource. The crucial factor is having the option to choose whether or not to work.
- Little research has explored the changing needs for support over a child's life. Existing research suggests that informal support wanes as the child grows older, often due to heavier physical demands, and parents become more reliant on formal services. Adolescence, the transition to adulthood and changed needs for support as between child and parent at this time needs further study.
- There has also been little research to evaluate the overall provision of services to families caring for a disabled child. That which has been done tends to be reports of isolated projects and initiatives. There is an increasing frequency of evaluative research on individual initiatives. This work needs to be reviewed and drawn together.
- The *economic* consequences of caring for a disabled child are well documented. Research shows that poor socio-economic circumstances increase vulnerability to stress, regardless of whether or not the individual is caring for a disabled child. Research needs to be more careful, however, about distinguishing between sources of stress in a family's life. In some cases the disability may be a minor problem relative to the family's living or financial circumstances.

Coping Strategies

- Coping strategies are those actions, behaviours and thoughts which are used to manage stress. The choice of strategy is mediated by the coping resources available.
- Coping strategies have two functions: to manage the source of stress and to manage distressing emotions caused by the stress. The former are known as problem-focused coping strategies, and the latter as emotion-focused coping strategies.
- No coping strategy can be regarded as intrinsically good or bad, adaptive or maladaptive. Account must be taken of the nature of stressor, possible coping options and the availability of coping resources. The long and short-term effects of choosing to cope in a certain way may differ.

- Relatively little research has focused on the coping strategies of parents caring for a disabled child. Most research has looked at how parents cope with the diagnosis or birth of a disabled child.
- Two streams of research can be identified. The first has merely described how parents cope, without attempting to explore outcome of different coping styles. Very recently some research has sought to identify the coping strategies which are more and less adaptive for parents caring for a disabled child.
- This work is very much in its embryonic stage, and has been hampered by methodological and definitional problems. However, there are some consistent findings. Use of *active* coping strategies such as planning, problem-solving and information-seeking have been found to be associated with greater levels of parental well-being. Cognitive coping strategies such as self-praise and 'positive restructuring' are also adaptive coping strategies. These are important because not all stresses faced by parents can be resolved, some just have to be lived with.
- Service providers should consider the ways they hinder or support these adaptive ways of coping.

Implications for Policy and Practice

This theoretical model advocates that the experience of stress is idiosyncratic and dependent on numerous personal and social factors. Professionals should not assume that all parents of disabled children experience the stressors. Parents will differ in the particular aspects of care they find difficult. This has clear implications for policy and practice.

- This model emphasizes the importance of both coping *resources* and coping *strategies* in the degree to which parents successfully adapt to caring for their disabled child. Services which aim to support and enhance both coping resources and strategies will be more effective than those which focus on only one.
- The model points to the importance of building on current strengths, resources and coping skills. This suggests an individualistic approach to intervention and service provision.
- The literature review also revealed a great range of coping resources and coping strategies used by parents. It is important that service providers respond appropriately. This will involve using expertise from many disciplines, and imagination in the types of resources provided.
- The transactional nature of the model implies that both the environment and the individual interact and affect each other over time. Consequently, the nature of the stressors and the individual's coping resources and coping options will vary. Service providers need to take account of this.
- A number of small pilot projects have used this model of stress and coping to inform intervention practices. Of note have been projects designed to

improve social support networks and social skills, parenting skills, use of information, coping skills training, problem-solving and self-maintenance techniques (for example, relaxation). Much of this work is found in the American literature, though there has been some in England. Very few of these projects have rigorously assessed the outcomes of the intervention, especially long-term outcomes.

Discussion

Existing research is beginning to point to factors influencing parents' coping strategies and to point up implications for professional practice. This approach seems likely to be of more practical use than studies of the way individual services affect stress, though these will have some value. More basic research on interventions designed to help parents develop better coping strategies is needed. It is also necessary to improve what we know about how the disabled child adapts to and copes with the experience of disability.

The Disabled Child's Experience

It was not possible in the short time available to carry out an exhaustive trawl of recent literature on children's experience of disability. Philp and Duckworth's (1982) review provides a valuable account of the literature up to that point, however. It is unlikely that major changes will have occurred since then. Two factors characterize this literature. First, as Philp and Duckworth point out, the bulk of research approaches the topic of how disability affects children socially or emotionally 'from one particular standpoint – exploring the child's adaptation to his *(sic)* experience'. This, mainly psychological, literature is about 'the interaction of social and psychological factors which interact with the child's impairments and disabilities to produce the residual limitations on the child's everyday life – his *(sic)* handicaps' (ibid.: p. 46). As such, it needs, somehow, to be integrated with the conceptualization developed in the *International Classification of Impairment, Disability and Handicap* so that the links between *intrinsic* and *extrinsic* factors shaping the experience of handicap can be more fully understood. The second point about this literature is that a relatively small number of studies draw *directly* on the child's view of disablement: her ideas about the kinds of life she wants to live and the support she needs; her views of how family members respond to her disability; her ideas about what makes life better or worse. Kennedy's (1989, 1992) work on self-esteem in disabled children and their vulnerability due to dependence is important in this area. We can, of course, theorize, but should acknowledge that our experience is too limited to be confident that we *know* what a disabled child thinks or feels. We found no studies focusing in detail on the disabled child's daily life and the way disability affects her.

The large literature on the psychological effects of disability cannot be summarized here. Broadly, however, it seems to assume that the majority of children born with impairments will have emotional problems in early childhood – partly as a consequence of maternal separation or ambivalence, difficulties in bonding or interaction with mothers, lack of parental confidence in handling the child and so on – and continuing psychological problems in childhood and adolescence. (Philp and Duckworth (1982, pp. 48–61) reference this literature fully.)

A major preoccupation concerns the child's subsequent problems in adapting to disability or chronic illness. Much of the literature relates to the experience of children with particular disorders. On the whole, this literature focuses much more on negative experiences than on what promotes positive adjustment. It makes sad reading by and large. Philp and Duckworth's (1982) review, for example, covers research on problems of adapting to disablement; emotional and behavioural problems in younger children; the special problems occurring in adolescence; stigma, social isolation; poor self-image; and reduced perceptions of control over one's life and environment. The overwhelming burden of this body of research is that disabled children do not, in general, adapt and cope well with the experience of disability. However, as noted later, some disabled children and young adults appear to adjust relatively well (Hirst and Baldwin, 1994). This is not easy to discern from the literature, which provides few examples of positive adjustments or coping strategies, or of attempts to explain what makes for better or worse adjustment.

Mattson (1972), for example, outlines three forms of *poor* adjustment: over-dependency, over-independency and isolation. Studies of children with asthma, myeloidplastic disorders, cystic fibrosis and so on, also report maladjustments of various sorts. A range of psychotherapeutic or psychoanalytic studies clearly view impairment as *inevitably* 'an emotionally as well as physically crippling event' (Philp and Duckworth, 1982, p. 48) as a result of deep-rooted abnormalities in mother–child relationships: first, between *mothers'* responses to the condition and the infant's early nurturing; second, between the *child's* response to aspects of the condition and self-disgust or self-blame. More practically, other researchers associate the emotional difficulties they find among disabled children with the restrictions the impairment places on their ability to move around independently, exploring their environment and learning by failure as other children do (ibid.: pp. 50–1). The many negative aspects of adjustment and development identified include underdeveloped social skills, lower self-confidence, greater self-deprecation, emotional and behavioural problems. It is striking that in general this – mainly psychological – literature does not address the degree to which these problems are shaped by environmental and social factors external to the child – rather than a direct product of the condition. To do so would suggest a very different policy response – towards structural change and change in professional and social attitudes and away from changing individual 'pathology'. The methodological problems occurring in many of these studies are, additionally, rarely recognized. One review of the literature, for example (on the effects of cystic fibrosis), 'points out that many studies have used projective tests which [the authors] consider to be of dubious value, and argues that the use of psychiatric interview requires independent validation if reasonable accuracy is to ensue'. It must nevertheless be acknowledged that the overwhelming direction of this research points to the presence of a raised degree of emotional disturbance among children with disabilities. As with the research on parental stress discussed above, however, the tremendous variation which is found is not well understood.

The Effect of Disability on the Child's Life and Activities

As noted above, accurate information on, especially younger, children's daily lives and the way disability affects them is relatively sparse. We lack children's accounts of pain, discomfort, dependence on others for feeding, bathing and toileting. We do not know how they feel about the way doctors, social workers, therapists and other children treat them. The OPCS survey did ask parents a few questions about the effect of the disability on the child. Table 17.1 shows the number reported as experiencing restrictions of different sorts, by degree of disability. As expected, restriction does increase with degree of disability; however, even moderately disabled children were said to experience significant restrictions.

Parents were questioned about the disabled child's friendships. Here the association between severity of a disability and restriction was more marked. Nearly a third of the most severely disabled children had no friends, as compared with only 1 per cent of the least severely disabled. The majority of disabled children (55 per cent) had 'lots' of friends and a substantial minority (27 per cent) two or three. There was evidence, however, of a lack of contact between disabled and non-disabled children: 11 per cent of parents reported that all their disabled child's friends were also disabled.

Table 17.1   Restrictions on child's school life by severity of child's disability: children living in private households

Restriction	Severity category					All disabled children
	1–2	3–4	5–6	7–8	9–10	
	Percentage reporting each restriction					
Absent for long-frequent periods	22	15	22	24	22	20
Disability restricts:						
Games and PE	30	26	31	32	48	33
Play and enjoyment	24	19	26	33	58	32
Going on outings	20	10	16	11	19	14
Taking part in some lessons	14	10	12	11	26	14
Other school activities	14	8	12	14	27	15

Percentages add to more than 100 because respondents could give more than one answer
Source: OPCS Disability Survey Report No. 6

Adolescence: Transition to Adulthood and Adult Services

Adolescence stands out in the literature as a time when disabled young adults are particularly likely to experience problems of different kinds. A large number of studies find indications of emotional disturbance and low self-esteem at this time. Philp and Duckworth (1982) review studies up to 1981. Significant later studies include those of Anderson and Clark (1982), Fish (1986), Harrison (1987), Thomas, Bax and Smyth (1987), Thompson et al. (1992) and Hirst and Baldwin (1994). In general, these studies – notably that of Anderson and Clark (1982) – find disabled adolescents to be unhappy, worried, isolated from their peers, lacking in self-esteem and a sense of personal control over their lives. They also point clearly to *objective* reasons for such feelings: lack of friends and sexual relationships; lack of information about their condition; restricted social lives; restricted access to and control of money, lack of and poor prospects for employment; uncertainties about the transition from familiar, and often good, child health, education and social services and so on. Hirst, in particular, has documented these disadvantages in a series of studies (Hirst, 1985a, 1985b, 1989, 1990, 1991; Hirst and Baldwin, 1994).

Many of these studies are methodologically flawed because restricted to particular conditions or lacking controls from the general population of young adults. Hirst's most recent piece of research (Hirst and Baldwin 1994) which meets both these conditions, demonstrates both the wide range of ways in which this age group are disadvantaged relative to their peers in the general population and their poorer state of mind. The young adults in Hirst's study (a follow-up from the 1985 OPCS Surveys of Disability), among other things,

- were less likely to have attained the goals of adult life;
- had lower self-esteem and less sense of personal control;
- felt restricted by their disability;
- had more restricted social lives, fewer friendships and sexual or 'romantic' relationships;
- were less likely to live independently;
- had generally lower incomes and less control over finance;
- were less likely to be in paid work;
- had less experience of going away or on holiday independently;
- were less likely to be treated as adult – i.e. have separate consultations – by health and social services professionals;
- had not maintained contact with the services they had access to as children – particularly physiotherapy;
- were much more likely to have no weekday placement or activity than their non-disabled peers.

Hirst's study is distinctive in including personal interviews with a sample of young adults with learning difficulties. The views and aspirations of this group are reported separately (Flynn and Hirst, 1992). This reveals a similar picture of segregation, isolation and disadvantage in reaching 'normal adult goals'. Young women with learning difficulties were particularly isolated from normal experiences of work and social participation. The authors conclude that the study sample as a whole was far from achieving an 'ordinary life'; the young people's psychological and emotional state reflected this. Research by Ward et al. (1991) generated information on the transition from school to adulthood of a sample (681) of young Scottish adults with special educational needs. This study found a similar picture of disadvantage in relation to employment and occupation.

How Disabled Children and Young Adults Adapt and Cope

Less research has been done on how children and young adults 'adapt to' or 'cope' with being disabled than on parents. We were unable to find work similar to that of Beresford (on parents) relating to children. The available information indicates, predictably, that the child's response is affected by: features of the condition, the strengths and resilience of family relationships, and parents' attitudes and adaptations – mothers' attitudes are reported to be of crucial importance for younger children and those suffering from chronic illness. Educational experiences also seem important; segregation and integration can offer different advantages in the shorter and longer term. Opportunities for independence and for friendships are also important. Improvements in morale and in coping are found to be related to having information about the condition, improvements in it, or – as in the case of epilepsy and diabetes – successful control.

> The concept of 'good adaptation' is not uncontested, however. What some researchers see as 'good' adaptation – accepting 'realistic limitations' and finding positive ways of compensating for the disability – others characterize as 'a means of ameliorating the guilt and anxiety caused by envy of others'. (Tinkelman et al., 1976; cited in Philp and Duckworth, 1982).

A large number of factors are suggested as influencing adaptation, however defined. As noted above, parental adaptation, mediating the child's attitude to herself and her disablement, is widely regarded as crucial. However, there is a real lack of information both on the range of factors involved and the relationship between them. There must be great differences in the strategies employed at different ages and probably differences between boys and girls. We know virtually nothing, too, about ethnic and cultural differences which seem likely to influence parent–child relationships and the formation of identity.

Siblings

Research reporting parents' anxieties frequently finds concern about the effect the child's disability has, or may have, on siblings. It also finds, though perhaps less often, assertions that the disabled child's condition has had no, or a positive, impact. In providing opportunities for understanding another child's difficulties and limitations, for example, it may be said that the non-disabled sibling has had the opportunity of becoming 'a better person'. This review has found very few studies which have talked directly to siblings (Macaskill, 1985, is an exception). We have to rely mainly on parents' views, with the limitations that imposes. Philp and Duckworth (in reviewing the research up to 1982) draw attention to the methodological flaws of research based on parents' views or – even more dangerously – on empathy by the researcher. 'As the empathizing observer and the child in his situation are really most unlikely to share the same value system as regards disablement, empathy is an unprofitable method of acquiring research evidence' (Philp and Duckworth, 1982, p. 63). Greater reliance is to be placed, therefore, on harder data relating to behaviour or signs of anti-social or maladjusted behaviour.

The literature indicates, unsurprisingly, that the majority of parents – of especially severely disabled children – feel that the child's disability has significantly affected other siblings. In a survey of 480 parents applying for help to the Family Fund, for example, only 28 per cent said that their other children's lives were unaffected (Glendinning, 1983). *Practical* effects were described mainly in terms of loss of parental time or restrictions on opportunities – either for activities of their own (peace to pursue hobbies, do homework or have friends round) or for family activities such as outings and holidays.

The consequences were not invariably regarded as damaging. Children were said to have become 'more mature', more independent and more understanding. Parents also reported making strenuous efforts to avoid spoiling the disabled child *and* attempting to compensate other children for things they had lost out on. On the whole, parents in this study seemed aware of possible difficulties and tried to moderate them. One thing they could not easily moderate, however, was the anxiety older siblings were thought to have – and sometimes expressed – about their longer-term responsibilities towards a disabled brother or sister. An earlier survey, by Butler et al. (1978), provides detailed evidence of the kinds of disturbance siblings can experience. These researchers found that 20 per cent were said to have problems with homework, 44 per cent with looking after possessions, 34 per cent in entertaining or playing with friends, 39 per cent were said to be jealous of the disabled child and 37 per cent to have other problems. In general, problems were most likely to arise when the disabled child had a mental impairment. Howlin (1988) has described how siblings may be affected by having an autistic brother or sister. The OPCS disability surveys (Meltzer, Smyth and Robus, 1989) support these findings. Some 37 per cent of parents with other children felt that the disabled child's condition had affected their other children. The greatest effect cited was on the time available for other children (28 per cent). Less than 10 per cent mentioned effects on other children's friendships, for example. Effects on siblings increased with the severity of the disabled child's condition: 56 per cent of parents of the most severely disabled children reported a range of effects on siblings. These parents were also much more likely to identify a variety of ways in which the behaviour of siblings was affected and their lives altered.

The important issue is whether, and if so how, such restrictions affect the emotional well-being of siblings, or their behaviour or school performance, for example. This is difficult to establish without control populations. We have not found recent research on this topic. Indeed, there seems to have been much less research on siblings over the last ten years than in the previous ten years or so.

Earlier research on how non-disabled siblings are affected tends – as with that on parents and the disabled child – to bifurcate between psychoanalytic studies which find pathology and sociological research which identifies more positive effects, both for non-disabled siblings and the family as a whole (Philp and Duckworth, 1982, p. 64). The direction of evidence on reported resentment and occasional hostility *between* siblings is clearer, with most studies finding half to two-thirds of parents reporting friction.

Evidence on the occurrence of emotional and behavioural *problems* manifested by siblings of disabled children is sparse and often methodologically dubious. Most of it comes from small studies of children with particular conditions, which do find evidence of some maladjustment. Available survey evidence suggests that *social* difficulties can also arise for a minority of children – arising both from what is termed 'courtesy stigma' and from the practical problems in socializing identified by Butler et al. (1978), Kew (1975), Glendinning (1983) and others.

It is difficult to be conclusive, on the basis of this evidence, about social and emotional effects on siblings. What *is* clear is that siblings can experience a range of difficulties which would benefit from acknowledgement, practical and emotional support. This might be tackled by focusing support directly on siblings or, alternatively, via parents.

Discussion

We do not know enough, from the child's point of view, about the experience of being disabled and dependent on others and what makes this better or worse. We should accept, on the basis of existing research, that many, many disabled children are very unhappy and have not found ways of coping with their disability and, probably more important, their handicap. We also know, from a number of studies, and particularly from Hirst's recent work (Hirst and Baldwin, 1994) that significant numbers of disabled children and young adults do attain normal goals, have a good image of themselves and a reasonable sense of personal control over their lives and optimism for the future. Or, perhaps more accurately, we know that they do not appear to differ significantly from non-disabled young adults of the same age in these respects. The research done so far suggests that both parental attitudes and behaviour and policy and practice in the fields of health and social care play a strong role in explaining differences in coping. Nevertheless, we do not really know what explains the difference between those who cope more or less well. The theoretical framework for testing these ideas is not well developed. There is a need for sound, methodologically rigorous work which draws directly on the views and experience of the children and young adults concerned. As with parents, it is the children's interpretations and experiences which need to be heard – and fed back into the development of policy and professional practice. In general, research so far has neglected both the child's perspective and the role of external determinants of well-being. This distorts discussion of interventions. Clearly, internal and external factors interact. We need to know much more about how they do and also about why some disabled children and young adults manage so much better – and worse – than others. This should be a high priority for research and for policy. Adolescence and the transition to adult life and services emerges very clearly as a difficult time for children and parents alike, and for children with very different disabilities and prospects. Again, this should be a focus of concern.

Research on siblings indicates that, as might be expected, living with a severely disabled brother or sister affects access to parental time, to space and possibly to friends. It is less clear whether this has negative effects on behaviour or attainment in the longer term, or on school performance, for example. If insufficient support is available to families, a ripple effect of deprivation may be felt by both siblings and parents. Again, however, the longer-term consequences of this are unknown.

REFERENCES

Anderson, E. M. and Clark, L. (1982), *Disability in Adolescence*, London: Methuen.

Baldwin, S. M. (1985), *The Costs of Caring: Families with Disabled Children*, London: Routledge & Kegan Paul.

Baldwin, S. M. and Glendinning, C. (1983), 'Employment, women and their disabled children', in J. Finch and D. Groves (eds), *A Labour of Love: Women, Work and Caring*, London: Routledge & Kegan Paul.

Beresford, B. (1993), *Exceptional Parents: Coping with the Care of a Severely Disabled Child*, Social Policy Research Unit, University of York.

Bodkin, C., Pigott, T. and Mann, J. (1982), 'Financial burdens of childhood cancer', *British Medical Journal*, 284: 1542–4.

Bradshaw, J. R. (1980), *The Family Fund: An Initiative in Social Policy*, London: Routledge & Kegan Paul.

Bradshaw, J. R. and Lawton, D. (1978), 'Tracing the causes of stress in families with handicapped children', *British Journal of Social Work*, 8: 181–92.

Bradshaw, J. R., Piachaud, D. and Weale, J. (1981), 'The income effect of a disabled child', *Journal of Epidemiology and Community Health*, 35: 123–7.

Burton, L. (1975), *The Family Life of Sick Children*, London: Routledge & Kegan Paul.

Butler, N., Gill, R., Pomeroy, D. and Fewtrell, J. (1978), *Handicapped Children – Their Homes and Lifestyles*, University of Bristol, Department of Child Health.

Byrne, E. and Cunningham, C. (1985), 'The effects of mentally handicapped children on families – a conceptual review', *Journal of Child Psychology and Psychiatry*, 26: 847–64.

Cooke, K. (1982), *1970 Birth Cohort – 10 Year Follow-up Study: Interim Report*, University of York, Department of Social Policy and Social Work.

Cooke, K., Bradshaw, J., Lawton, D. and Brewer, R. (1986), 'Child disablement, family dissolution and reconstitution', *Developmental Medicine and Child Neurology*, 28: 610–16.

Fish, J. (1986), *Young People with Handicaps: The Road to Adulthood*, Paris: OECD.

Flynn, M. and Hirst, M. A. (1992), *This Year, Next Year, Sometime? Learning Disability and Adulthood*, London/York: National Development Team/SPRU.

Glendinning, C. (1983), *Unshared Care: Parents and Their Disabled Children*, London: Routledge & Kegan Paul.

Glendinning, C. (1986), *A Single Door: Social Work with the Families of Disabled Children*, London: Allen & Unwin.

Gough, D., Li, L. and Wroblewska, A. (1993), *Services for Children with a Motor Impairment and Their Families in Scotland*, University of Glasgow, Public Health Research Unit.

Gregory, S. (1976), *The Deaf Child and His Family*, London: Allen & Unwin.

Harrison, J. (1987), *Severe Physical Disability: Responses to the Challenge of Care*, London: Cassell.

Hirst, M. (1982), *Young Adults with Disabilities and Their Families*, University of York, Social Policy Research Unit.

Hirst, M. (1984), *Moving On: Transfer from Child to Adult Services for Young People with Disabilities*, University of York, Social Policy Research Unit.

Hirst, M. (1985a), 'Young adults with disabilities: health, employment and financial costs for family carers', *Child: Care, Health and Development*, 11: 291–307.

Hirst, M. (1985b), 'Dependency and family care of young adults with disabilities', *Child: Care, Health and Development*, 11: 241–57.

Hirst, M. (1989), 'Patterns of impairment and disability related to social handicap in young people with cerebral palsy and spina bifida', *Journal of Biosocial Science*, 21: 1–12.

Hirst, M. (1990), *National Survey of Young People with Disabilities: Health and Social Services*, University of York, Social Policy Research Unit.

Hirst, M. (1991), 'Dissolution and reconstitution of families with a disabled young person', *Developmental Medicine and Child Neurology*, 33: 1073–9.

Hirst, M. and Baldwin, S. M. (1994), *Unequal Opportunities: Growing Up Disabled*, SPRU Papers, London: HMSO.

Howlin, P. (1988), 'Living with impairment: the effects on children of having an autistic sibling', *Child: Care, Health and Development*, 14: 395–408.

Hubert, J. (1991), *Home-Bound: Crisis in the Care of Young People with Severe Learning Difficulties: A Story of Twenty Families*, London: King's Fund Centre.

Hunter, R. (1992), *The Blood is Strong*, Perth: Muirfield Print.

Jaehnig, W. (1974), *Mentally Handicapped Children and Their Families: Problems for Social Policy*, unpublished Ph.D. thesis, University of Essex.

Kennedy, M. (1989), 'The abuse of deaf children', *Child Abuse Review*, 3: 3–7.

Kennedy, M. (1992), 'Not the only way to communicate: a challenge to voice in child protection work', *Child Abuse Review*, 1: 169–77.

Kew, S. (1975), *Handicap and Family Crisis*, London: Pitman.

Macaskill, C. (1985), 'The verdict of siblings', in *Against the Odds: Adopting Mentally Handicapped Children*, British Agencies for Adoption and Fostering.

McLaughlin, E. (1991), *Social Security and Community Care: The Case of the Invalid Care Allowance*, London: HMSO.

Mattson, A. (1972), 'The chronically ill child: a challenge to family adaptation', *Medical College of Virginia Quarterly*, 8: 171–5.

Meltzer, H., Smyth, M. and Robus, N. (1989), *Disabled Children: Services, Transport and Education*, report 6, London: HMSO.

Parker, G. (1985), *With Due Care and Attention*, 1st edn, London: Family Policy Studies Centre.

Parker, G. (1990), *With Due Care and Attention*, 2nd edn, London: Family Policy Studies Centre.

Pentol, A. (1983), 'Cost bearing burdens', *Health and Social Service Journal*, 8 September.

Philp, M. and Duckworth, D. (1982), *Children with Disabilities and Their Families: A Review of the Literature*, Windsor: NFER-Nelson.

Quine, L. and Pahl, J. (1986), 'Parents with severely mentally handicapped children: marriage and the stress of caring', in R. Chester and P. Divall (eds), *Mental Health, Illness and Handicap in Marriage*, Rugby: National Marriage Guidance Council.

Seed, P. (1989), *Day Services for People with Severe Handicaps*, London: Jessica Kingsley.

Sloper, P. and Turner, S. (1992), 'Service needs of families of children with severe physical disability', *Child: Care, Health and Development*, 18: 250–82.

Smyth, M. and Robus, N. (1989), *The Financial Circumstances of Families with Disabled Children Living in Private Households*, report 5, London: HMSO.

Tew, B., Lawrence, K., Payne, H. and Rawnsley, K. (1977), 'Marital stability following the birth of a child with spina bifida', *British Journal of Psychiatry*, 131: 79–82.

Thomas, A., Bax, M. and Smyth, D. (1987), *The Provision of Support Services for the Handicapped Young Adult*, Charing Cross and Westminster Medical School, Department of Child Health.

Thompson, G., Ward, K., Dyer, M. and Riddell, S. (1992), *Transition from School to Adulthood of Young People with Recorded Special Educational Needs* (Interlope no. 5), Scottish Office Education Department.

Tinkelman, D. G., Brice, J., Yoshida, G. N. and Sadler, J. E., Jr (1976), 'The impact of chronic asthma on the developing child: observations made in a group setting', *Annals of Allergy*, 37: 174–9.

Voysey, M. (1975), *A Constant Burden: The Reconstitutions of Family Life*, London: Routledge & Kegan Paul.

Ward, K., Riddell, S., Dyer, M. and Thompson, G. (1991), *The Transition to Adulthood of Young People with Special Educational Needs*, Universities of Edinburgh and Stirling, Departments of Education.

Weale, J. and Bradshaw, J. (1980), 'Prevalence and characteristics of disabled children: findings from the 1974 General Household Survey', *Journal of Epidemiology and Community Health*, 34: 11–8.

Wilkin, D. (1979), *Caring for the Mentally Handicapped Child*, London: Croom Helm.

Williams, D. (1992), *'Nobody, Nowhere' – The Remarkable Autobiography of an Autistic Girl*, London: Corgi Books.

Index